Play and Playscapes

Joe L. Frost

delmar publishers inc.®

NOTICE TO THE READER

Delmar Staff
  Administrative Editor: Jay Whitney
  Developmental Editor: Lisa Reale
  Project Editor: Carol Micheli
  Production Coordinator: Wendy Troeger
  Art Coordinator: John Lent
  Design Coordinator: Karen Kunz Kemp

For information, address Delmar Publishers Inc.
2 Computer Drive West, Box 15-015
Albany, New York 12212

Copyright © 1992
by Delmar Publishers Inc.

Printed in the United States of America
published simultaneously in Canada
by Nelson Canada,
a division of The Thomson Corporation

10 9 8 7 6 5 4 3 2

Library of Congress Cataloging-in-Publication Data

Frost, Joe L.
  Play and playscapes / Joe L. Frost.
    p. cm.
  Includes bibliographical references and index.
  ISBN 0-8273-4699-9
  1. Playgrounds—United States. 2. Playgrounds—United States—Safety measures. 3. Play—United States. 4. Child development—United States.
I. Title
GV423.F73 1992
796.06 '8' 0973—dc20

91-10701
CIP

Table of Contents

DEDICATION

To Hailey, a living expression of
the freedom, fun, and spontaneity of play.

Foreword

Brian Sutton-Smith
University of Pennsylvania

The known history of children's play is largely the history of our interference with it. Even the folklorists of the last century, who believed they were simply collecting the last survivals of an earlier form of adult play life, sought to teach some of what they collected for the benefit of the urban poor. Those interested in physical education, playgrounds, organized sports, youth camps, and recreation movements were even more directly interested in the organization of play for the improvement of child life. Until recently it has been possible to sit back and look at all of this with a confident sense, that despite all of this interference and whatever its benefits, children would nevertheless spend most of their time in their own play groups with their own traditional game curriculum through which they would discover the hard political reality of getting along with others.

The emergence of small families, of solitary play alongside the television set, and of prohibitions against playing in the dangerous streets have all made it less probable that children will learn to find their own way with the help of other children, which has been the royal road to social growth throughout most of human history. Until the last year or two, however, one could still argue confidently that even in these play limiting circumstances the children would still have opportunities for social play while at school during the recess and lunch periods. But now we have the growth of a movement to abolish recess. In some cases this is because in urban areas the playgrounds, covered with scattered glass and inhabited by drug related activity, are themselves dangerous places for children. In these neighborhoods the teachers may argue they can't let the children onto the playground in case they all go home. But even where this is not so, in play safe areas, superintendents increasingly contend that there is simply not enough school lesson time given current pressures for higher academic standards on the schools, so recess must go. Some teachers even argue that now that we have learned how to use play within the curriculum through sociodramatic and other techniques, there is simply no need for the relatively disorderly play that children conduct by themselves.

Yet despite differences of interpretation, everyone of the major original play theorists of this century, including Freud, Vygotsky, Huizinga, Erikson, Piaget, Berlyne, Bruner, Bateson, and Spariosu, has given the child's spontaneous solitary and social play a primary role in child development. No one has defended the older puritanic view that play is useless or harmful to growth. On the contrary, we know now that the best predictor of adult mental maladjustment, of adult homicide, and suicide is an aberrant play life during childhood. Recent surveys show, however, that although most teachers fortunately still believe that play is for children on their own rather than for teachers to control, very few have ever had any academic training in the nature of play or in the writings of the above theorists.

Given the recent growing antagonism to children's own play, the time has clearly come when those who educate children need to have more specific knowledge of its nature. They need to be able to defend children's play time against the aggressive encroachments of a public ever ambitious to have their children learn orthodox curricula at an ever earlier age. Given that for the first seven or so years of life children play together more naturally than they converse together, it is not too much to see children's rights to free play as the equivalent of adult's rights to free speech. Children's play in these terms should be envisaged as a first amendment right.

Given that what teachers need to know in particular is what to do about the playgrounds under their own control, the present book is most timely. It surveys our current knowledge of children's play and relates it directly to the playscapes in which children find themselves and it informs us on the ways in which teachers can be useful to children in their acquiring of social play competence. It is of course an interference, but now we have a situation where we have to interfere in order to protect children against those who would interfere to reduce children's rights to play. We must interfere to ensure the places and the times where they can get on with the central substance of their own social and motivational lives. It is their right to play and our duty to preserve it for them.

Preface

During the 1980s and early 1990s, the national emphasis on children's play and play environments gained a degree of momentum not seen since the early 1900s, when the Playground Association of America spearheaded the growth of playgrounds in the United States from 35 American cities with organized playgrounds in 1905 to 336 cities in 1909.

The 1990s is a time of unprecedented interest in play and the redevelopment of play environments. The primary reasons for this are:

- The growing emphasis on play research among professionals in the behavioral sciences at universities and the resulting increase in both professional and popular publications on play and play environments.
- A renewal of interest in play by professional organizations, notably the American and International Associations for the Child's Right to Play; the National Association for the Education of Young Children; the Association for the study of Play; the American Alliance for Health, Physical Education, Recreation and Dance; and the Association for Childhood Education International.
- Increasing awareness among parents and professionals of the deleterious effects of pressuring children through overemphasis of "academics" at the expense of play.
- The negative influence of television on children's health, fitness, moral development, and school achievement and the emerging realization that play is an essential counteracting influence.
- The emergence of a "suing society" wherein many parents are suing cities, private and public schools, child care centers, and play equipment designers, manufacturers and installers for injuries sustained by their children on playgrounds.
- The growing awareness of parents and professionals that most American playgrounds are in a state of gross disrepair, featuring antiquated, poorly designed, improperly maintained equipment.
- The accelerating research into safety and play value by a growing number of play equipment designers and manufacturers and their involvement in developing national safety guidelines/standards for play equipment and playground surfacing.

In Chapter 1 the nature of play, its importance, and its nurture are explored. Chapter 1 is both historical and theoretical, tracing the evolution of play theory and proposing an integrated theory of play. It draws from five interrelated perspectives: characteristics of play, motives for play, play behaviors, developmental correlates of play, and content of play. Each of these perspectives is linked to implications for practitioners. Perhaps the central conclusion emerging from Chapter 1 is that play is a natural phenomenon, not to be forced but allowed and enhanced by the adults in the child's world—parents, caretakers, and teachers.

Chapter 2, Child Development and Play, reinforces this central conclusion by reviewing research and theory on cultural, social, cognitive, language, and motor development as they relate to and are influenced by play. Play is an indispensable element in child development and its enhancement is deeply influenced by the nature of play environments. They must be developmentally relevant; that is, they must provide for the various play behaviors of children according to their developmental status or needs. Further they must do this in ways that allow freedom and spontaneity, and that stimulate the senses and challenge the child—socially, cognitively and physically.

Misunderstandings of the phenomenon of play abound, even among professionals. In Chapter 3, several of the most important issues are explored: gender differences in play, play versus work, and the roles of television, war toys, and aggression in children's play.

Chapter 4, continues the focus on understanding play with an examination of children's play behaviors and the inclusion of instruments and procedures for studying children's play and outdoor play environments. The first four chapters are addressed essentially to *understanding* play; the remaining chapters are oriented to bridging play theory/research and the creation and use of play environments. Outdoor environments are stressed but direct implications can be drawn for indoor environments.

The historical evolution of American playgrounds is traced in Chapter 5, beginning with the "outdoor gymnasia" of the early 1800s and progressing through various stages of design and energy to the 1990s. Chapter 6 extends the description of contemporary play environments with an extensive description of fundamentals for playground development, culminating with a visionary glimpse of the "magical playscapes" of the future. In Chapter 7, the work of selected designers/builders/manufacturers of play equipment and playgrounds is featured. Photographic vignettes illustrate the status and trends of thought among some of the most innovative playground specialists.

The discussion of child development and play, understanding play and play value of playscapes must be tempered with awareness and understanding of playground safety. Chapter 8 traces the history of playground safety in America, revealing unconscionable neglect and extreme hazards in existing playgrounds. Chapter 9 builds upon the research documenting these conditions. The nationwide efforts to improve playground conditions are illuminated and current and proposed safety guidelines/standards are examined. Lest the reader misinterpret the intent and result of safety standards on creativity and challenge in play environments, the author invites a comparison of the results of playground design and community participation of designers/builders/manufacturers featured in this book with typical public school, public park, or private school playgrounds. The more innovative, contemporary playscapes are light years apart from the monolithic, antiquated, hazardous, sterile, uninspired places that America calls its playgrounds. We *can* have it both ways—play environments can be both challenging and inviting and reasonably safe.

In Chapters 10, 11, and 12, special types of playgrounds are featured: infant–toddler play environments, adventure playgrounds, and playgrounds for *all* children, including those with mental, behavioral, or physical disabilities. In response to the kind, skillful reviewers of the original manuscript, I did not order these or other chapters by level of importance but merely by personal logic and sense of order. I am committed to the concept of integrating *all* children into the "least restrictive setting" in play environments as well as classrooms and other public places.

In the final chapter, the history of play leadership is traced, principles of play leadership are elaborated, and research on adult intervention in children's play is examined. A fundamental principle relevant to this chapter is that play, in order to be play, is spontaneous and free. Adults must weigh carefully the consequences of their involvement in children's play lest in their charitable motives they destroy the very phenomenon they seek to enhance.

I am indebted to many people who contributed directly or indirectly to the ideas expressed in this book. Although the list will inadvertently omit some who made substantial contributions, I express my appreciation to the following friends and professional associates.

Barry Klein, Sheila Campbell, Betty Wagner, Erik Strickland, Jim Dempsey, Libby Vernon, Michael Henniger, Norman Stuemke, Jackie Myers, Paul Hogan, Marion Monroe, Michael Bell, Lily Chiang, Suzanne Winter, Marcy Guddemi, Gwen Myers, Judi Blalock, James Jolley, William Weisz, Linda Jones, Cynthia Wade, Robin Moore, Brian Sutton-Smith, Donna Thompson, Larry Bruya, Jay Beckwith, Jim Tuomey, Christopher Clews, Gary Moore, Peter Heseltine, Roger Hart, Kim Blakely, Britt Alexius, James Talbot, Louis Bowers, Susan Goltsman, Harris Forusz, Elizabeth Hrncir, Tom Jambor, Steve King, Barbara Sampson, Steve Silvern, Helge Stapel, Marshal Wortham, Sue Wortham, Tex Schofield, Ramon Garza, B.J. Knori, Kevin Haines, Ross Gordon, Larry Michalk, Steen Esbensen, Robert Barron, Nita and Tommy Drescher, Terry and William Battles, Betty Frost, Ron Jackson, Dorothy Stuemke, Robert Walker, Frances Heyck, Debra Johnson, Carolyn and Don Arick, Isabel Keesee, Mary Ruth Moore, and Carol Riddell. A special thanks to Nancy Treffler-Hammonds, Selina Jasso, and Alita Zaepfel for their assistance in preparing the manuscript.

I also wish to express my appreciation to the following schools/agencies that served as research or playground development sites or contributed invaluable materials and/or ideas for this book.

Redeemer Lutheran School, Austin, Texas
St. Louis Catholic School, Austin, Texas
St. Stephen's Episcopal School, Wimberly, Texas
St. Martin's Lutheran School, Austin, Texas
Stepping Stones School, Austin, Texas
The Austin, Texas, Parks and Recreation Department
DeKalb County Schools, Atlanta, Georgia

Graham Schools, Graham, Texas
Cuero Schools, Cuero, Texas
Grapevine-Colleyville Schools, Grapevine, Texas
New Braunfels Schools, New Braunfels, Texas
Austin Community College Nursery School, Austin, Texas
University of Texas Nursery School, Austin, Texas
U.S. Army Child Care Center, Fort Huachuca, Arizona
Holland Hall School, Tulsa, Oklahoma
Hermann Hospital, Houston, Texas
Trinity Day School, Tulsa, Oklahoma
Waco Parks and Recreation Dept., Waco, Texas
Manor Schools, Manor, Texas
Hyde Park Baptist School, Austin, Texas
Riverbend Baptist School, Austin, Texas
Circle C Development Corp., Austin, Texas
Internal Revenue Service Child Care Center, Austin, Texas
U.S. Air Force Child Care Centers
Plaza of the Americas Child Care Center, Dallas, Texas
Evansville Day School, Evansville, Indiana
St. Luke's Methodist School, Houston, Texas
Good Shepherd Episcopal School, Austin, Texas
Temple Beth Israel School, Austin, Texas
Scottish Rite Hospital for Crippled Children, Dallas, Texas

Finally, a special note of caution. This book was developed primarily as a reference textbook for college and university classes. The material on playground safety and design is representative of the *present* array of information, but it is not intended, nor should it be considered a complete or current reference or standard. Playground guidelines/standards vary across agencies and are periodically revised.

If involved in playground development or operation, the reader should consult the *current*, applicable guidelines, regulations, laws, and standards. These may include the U.S. Consumer Product Safety Commission Guidelines for Public Playground Equipment (a new edition is scheduled for publication in late 1991), and the American Society for Testing and Materials Standards for Playground Equipment and for Playground Surfacing (expected in 1992).

In addition to national guidelines/standards, playgrounds may be regulated by State Education Agencies (public schools), State Departments of Human Services (child care centers), and/or State laws (California law addresses public playground safety). Local ordinances may also apply.

Playground specialists and reputable manufacturers should be consulted in the design and development of playgrounds. Regular training on maintenance and supervision should be conducted for all staff.

Joe L. Frost
University of Texas at Austin
May 31, 1991

"Apples on a stick,
Just make me sick.
Makes my tummy go two forty-six.
Not because I'm thirty.
Not because I'm dirty.
Not because I'm clean.
Not because I kissed my boy-friend
  on the mezzanine . . ."[1]

1

Why Children Play

This modern-day version of word games, rhythmic chanting is peculiar only because its words are contemporary. Such games and rhymes of children are as old as civilization but they are modified by children to fit the world they know. Across cultures and eras, healthy children play and, although the positive developmental consequences of their play are well documented, the motives for their play are argumentative. The intent of this chapter is to review the present state of knowledge about *why* children play and to draw implications for play settings.

Archaeological excavations of ancient Egypt, China, and Peru reveal toys, tops, rattles, dolls, and other playthings made of pottery and metal as well as drawings by adults depicting various play scenes. Anthropological studies of primitive people reveal the existence of play among all cultures and identify several characteristic types: dancing and rhythmic movement, mimicking and acting, singing, conversing and story telling, arts and crafts, and games and contests (Mitchell 1937).

Throughout history children have played their way into adulthood, yet, until recently, few adults have regarded children's play as serious or considered play to be important in child development. Plato and Aristotle attached practical significance to play, considering it valuable in learning such subjects as arithmetic

---

[1]Composed and recited by Hailey Drescher and Peggy Davis pictured in the above photo.

FIGURE 1.1 Across cultures and eras, healthy children play.

and construction skills. Plato's view that children should play out roles expected of adults was a precursor of the *preparation for life theory* expounded by Groos (1898) in the late nineteenth century.

Early educators such as John Amos Comenius (1592–1670), Jean-Jacques Rousseau (1712–1778), Johann Pestalozzi (1782–1827), and Friedrich Froebel (1782–1852) rebelled against the harsh discipline and rote memorization that characterized the education of children during their lifetimes and stressed the importance of play both as a natural occupation of childhood and as a vehicle for learning.

Froebel, the originator of the kindergarten, best articulated the contribution of play to the development of the child. Writing in 1826, he made the following statement about play:

> Play is the purest, most spiritual activity of man at this stage, and at the same time, typical of human life as a whole—of the inner hidden natural life in man and all things. It gives, therefore, joy, freedom, contentment, inner and outer rest, peace with the world. (Harris 1906:55)

Although the importance of play has long been appreciated, theorists present contrasting definitions of play and disagree about the biological and psychological motivation and utility of play. At first it would seem that play would readily lend itself to definition. Unlike abstract constructs such as intelligence, self-concept, and motivation, play can readily be observed and measured. However, after examining various definitions of play it appears that there is little general agreement.

The definitions represent a variety of theoretical positions ranging from Schiller's and Spencer's view of play as expenditure of excess energy, to Groos's theory of play as instinctive practice for later life, to Gulick's theory of play as recapitulation to earlier stages of man, to Piaget's views of play as a vehicle for cognitive development.

It is important to study the early theories because they serve as the foundation for contemporary theories. In this chapter we will examine both classical and contemporary theories of play. An integrated theory of play will serve as a basis for conclusions and implications in play and playground practice.

EARLY THEORIES OF PLAY

Roots of theory can be traced to Aristotle and Plato, but the first serious efforts at theory building were not seen until the last half of the nineteenth century. As early as the seventeenth century a simple-minded explanation of play was that it was useful as recuperation from work. This same notion was elaborated by Schiller and Lazarus in the nineteenth century (Millar 1968).

The Surplus Energy Theory

The first serious theory of play, the *surplus energy theory*, originated with Schiller (1954) in 1800 (Groos 1898), was formalized by Spencer (1896), and was reiterated by Tolman (1932). Schiller believed that play was the aimless expenditure of exuberant energy. Spencer explained that the organism expends energy either in goal-directed activity (which is work) or nongoal-directed activity (which is play). When the child has more energy than needed for work, play occurs. It is to the credit of both Schiller and Spencer that they recognized the relationship between play and the arts; they viewed play not only as the expression of exuberant energy but also as the origin of art.

When asked to explain the motivating factor behind children's play, a common response among educators is "Children need to run off excess energy . . . ." Without realizing the origin of their view, many people promote the surplus energy theory.

A shortcoming of the surplus energy explanation of play is that children frequently play even when in a state of near exhaustion. The notion of surplus energy is based upon circular reasoning (Beach 1945). When a cat chases, catches, and devours a mouse, energy is expended, but no one suggests that this is surplus energy. When the same cat chases, catches, and chews on a ball, energy is also expended, but this is said to be surplus energy. Because ball chasing serves no practical end, it must be play, but mouse catching is not play. The decision about whether the expended energy is surplus depends upon whether the behavior is considered serious or playful. Therefore, to explain play as the release of surplus energy is to do no more than complete the circle. For an excellent critical analysis of this and other early theories of play, see Rubin (1982).

The Recapitulation Theory

The speculative writings of Spencer had only limited impact compared with the systematic observations in Charles Darwin's *The Origin of the Species* (1859). The *recapitulation theory* originated in Darwin's view that humans evolved from lower species. This theory holds that the child at play mirrors the behavioral evolution of the species and that play rehearses the activities of the race during forgotten ages (Gulick 1898). G. Stanley Hall's (1906) interest in both evolution and child psychology led him to formalize the recapitulation theory. Children are a link in the evolutionary chain from animals to humans and reenact through play the interests and occupations of prehistoric people and their remote animal ancestors. Water play proved primeval origins in the sea; climbing trees showed vestiges of ape-like ancestors; gang play echoed primitive tribal life.

The recapitulation theory breaks down under modern scrutiny. Piloting space ships and firing laser guns can hardly be considered rehearsal of ancient experiences. There is not tidy linear progression in play that links it to primitive eras, but the theory was a natural outgrowth of the intense interest in human origins. Compared with the present time, society at the turn of the century was very simple. Radio, television, airplanes, automobiles, electricity, and other miraculous devices were not available to lend perspective to the play and playthings of children. Fortunately, theory does not have to be correct in order to be useful. As Millar (1968) aptly points out, Hall's theorizing about play had the excellent effect of stimulating interest in children's behavior.

The Instinct–Practice Theory of Play

The instinct–practice theory was elaborated by Groos in *The Play of Animals* (1898) and in *The Play of Man* (1901). The concept of play as preparation for adult life was a derivative of earlier instinct theories, which held that play is caused by instinctive need (McDougall 1923). Like most of his scholarly counterparts of the period, Groos was heavily influenced by the work of Darwin. Animals inherit instinctive behaviors, but practice is needed to perfect them. Kittens chasing yarn balls become adept at catching mice. Infants learn to control their bodies through crawling, reaching, grasping, and moving.

The child's models are the behaviors of his parents and the occupations of others. In imitating adults, the child tests various possibilities, and this influences his later choice of a life's calling. It is to his credit that Groos (1901) extended his point of view beyond the mere mechanical, preparatory for life activities to approach a contemporary view of play:

> I would remark that imitation is almost never merely that; it is creation as well, production as well as reproduction. Close on the heels of imitation comes imagination. (p. 290)

The impact of early experiences on later life is now well documented. The opportunity or lack of opportunity to play during childhood certainly has consequences for later life. However, Groos proposed that the infant plays in order to train for specific skills. A more accurate view is that play leads to mastery of self and environment from a general development aspect, that is, personality and intelligence as opposed to specific skills. Children at play are not concerned with any possible future benefits of their play.

The Relaxation Theory

In contrast to the surplus energy theory of play, Patrick (1916) argued that play serves a person's need for relaxation as a relief from mental fatigue. Patrick maintained that work in a modern society calls for abstract reasoning, high concentration, and fine-motor activity. These work demands are comparatively recent in human history and are more likely to cause nervous disorders than the work demands of older or less advanced societies. In those societies, according to Patrick, people made greater use of their large muscles in activities such as running, jumping, and throwing, the same activities that modern humans use for recreation and relaxation.

Patrick's theory certainly has both appeal and application to today's high-stress society; however, it does not adequately explain the play of children. If play is motivated by the need to recuperate from work, then why does the child play? Patrick argued that "He plays because he is a child and to the child's natural and active life we give the name 'play' to distinguish it from the life of conscious self-direction, of strain, and effort and inhibition which evolution has imposed on the adult human being" (Patrick 1916:79–80).

Patrick's theory was primarily relevant for adults. He believed that the child's play life is natural and free as contrasted with the strain and inhibitions of adult activities. The relaxation theory is not necessarily inconsistent with the surplus energy theory, for excess muscular energy can be used up while the brain is being rested.

CONTEMPORARY THEORIES OF PLAY

Contemporary psychology is dominated by three main theories, psychoanalytical, Piagetian, and behaviorism. The psychoanalytic theories of Freud and Erikson are primarily concerned with the dynamics of personality development. From this theoretical base, play may be viewed as a class of affective behavior. The cognitive-developmental theory of Jean Piaget is concerned with the process and content of intellectual development. Therefore, from a Piagetian position, play may be viewed as cognitive behavior. The section to follow will treat these two main theories. Views on social play will be abstracted from a number of sources. The stimulus-response (S-R) theories of Hull, Thorndike, and Skinner address the contingency relationships between the organism and environment. From an S-R position, play is not viewed as a special class of behavior, but simply part of the response repertoire of the organism and will not be treated in this discussion.

The Psychoanalytical Theory

The *psychoanalytical theory* of play has roots in the earlier *cathartic theory*, which proposed that play was an activity for the pursuing of unpleasant or painful feelings and emotions. The interest of psychoanalysts in children's play originated with Freud in the early 1900s and was elaborated by Robert Wälder (1933) and Erik Erikson (1950).

In his classic article, Wälder (1933:209) discussed the limitations of the theory. He maintained that play has multiple functions and cannot be explained by a single interpretation.

Freud (1959) maintained that play is motivated chiefly by what he called the pleasure principle. Pleasure is achieved, according to Freud, through wish fulfillment in play. For example, the child who plays at being an astronaut, race car driver, nurse, or mother is expressing a desire to be one. In playing, the child is able to bend reality in order to gain gratification.

Freud (1959) also explained play as the projection of wishes and the reenactment of unpleasant experiences in order to master them. The assumption that play revealed the inner life and motivation of the child led to the development of projective techniques, such as interpreting ink blots and making up stories from pictures. Freud's influence on play extended to various types of therapy for disturbed children using spontaneous play. In general, Freud believed that children link imagined objects and situations to the tangible and visible things of the real world. Desiring to be grown up and in control, the child converts passive roles into active ones, frequently imitating adult roles where a greater degree of control is exhibited.

Wälder argued that Freud's original concept of cathartic play, that is, play that reduces anxiety, does not explain the repetition of the play activity associated with an unpleasant experience. In explaining this phenomenon Wälder refers to the concept of "repetition compulsion." When a child has an unpleasant experience, it may be too difficult for him to assimilate it all at once. The child recreates the experience over and over again in play, thus gradually diminishing the intensity of the experience.

Brown, Curry, and Titlnich (1971) give a graphic example of repetition compulsion in their description of how a group of preschoolers dealt with a traumatic experience. A group of children in an early childhood center were playing outside while a workman climbed up a ladder to make some repairs on the building. Unfortunately, the workman fell from the ladder and was seriously injured. The children watched as the teachers administered emergency first aid and saw an ambulance take him to the hospital. The teachers observed that for several weeks after this incident the children enacted through play the events that they had observed. One child playing the part of the workman would climb up on a stack of large building blocks and pretend to fall to the ground. Other children playing the part of the teachers would administer first aid while other children would pretend to be ambulance attendants. Immediately after the incident, the role play took place frequently during the day. After several days had passed the frequency diminished; after several weeks had passed the role play rarely occurred and then only in a very abbreviated manner. Thus, through playing out unpleasant experiences, their effect on the child is diminished and he comes to terms with them. The need for play is reduced as the child grows older and greater control is achieved.

Freud also dealt with the question of reality in children's play and adult fantasy which he saw as similar processes. He compared the child at play to the creative writer in that the child creates his or her own imaginary world. Although the child engages in fantasy, he or she takes the play very seriously and expends large amounts of energy on it. Freud maintained that "The opposite of play is not what is serious but what is real" (1959:143). He viewed a child's fantasy as being centered around real objects while adult fantasy is covert and separate from reality. In summing up this distinction Wälder stated that "Fantasy woven about a real object is however nothing other than play" (Wälder 1933:223).

Erik Erikson added new dimensions to Freud's work by describing play as developmental progression in which the child adds new and more complex understandings about the world at each stage. We now see for the first time a theory of play that begins to tap play's broad dimensions and potential influences. Erikson's initial stage, autocosmic play, begins at birth. Play is centered on the infant's body and consists of "the exploration by repetition of sensual perceptions of kinesthetic sensations, vocalizations, etc." (Erikson 1950:220). Later in this stage the object of the child's play turns to other properties and things. The next stage of play, the microsphere, is a manageable world of toys and objects, a place for the child to visit when his or her ego needs an overhaul. If the child is unable to master this stage he or she may regress to the autocosmic stage, characterized by daydreaming, thumb sucking, or masturbating. The third stage, the macrosphere, occurs at nursery school age when the child shares play with others. Earlier stages are integrated into this one, so macrosphere play contains elements of the earlier stages. Major tasks of this stage are learning to participate in social play and learning when to engage in solitary play. Solitary play "retains an indispensable harbor for the overhauling of shattered emotions after periods of rough going in the social seas" (Erikson 1950:194).

From a scientific perspective, the chief fault of the psychoanalytic theory—a serious one—is that it is primarily a subjective interpretation of play motives. Erikson's most important contribution to the understanding of play is not in his subjective explanation of motives for play but in his recognition of the uniqueness of play and in his descriptions of play as a developmental phenomenon contributing to mastery of the environment. Erikson (1950) stated:

> What is infantile play, then? . . . It is not the equivalent of adult play, it is not recreation. The playing adult slips sideward into another reality; the playing child advances forward to new stages of mastery. I propose the theory that the child's play is the infantile form of the human ability to deal with experience by creating model situations and to master reality by experiment and planning. (pp. 194–195)

Erikson concludes that play has a unique and personal meaning for each child, and that the meaning can only be determined by careful observation of its form and content and of the verbalizations and feelings that are associated with it.

As the reader shall see in Chapter 13, The Role of Adults in Children's Play, this conclusion has deep significance for adults. They are no longer viewed as passive observers of children's play but assume functions to enhance children's development through play. These include observation for diagnostic purposes, involvement to enhance play and provision of appropriate materials for play.

Piaget's Cognitive-Developmental Theory

Freud's notion that play is motivated chiefly by the pleasure principle and Erikson's view that the child achieves mastery through play are also basic elements in Piaget's *cognitive-developmental theory*. Piaget (1962) attributed the initial appearance of play to the pleasure derived from the infant's mastery of his own behavior. Play has a dual role in Piaget's theory. It serves as a vehicle for knowing and as an indicator of the child's cognitive development. In order to understand the significance of Piaget's views of play, they must be linked to his overall theory of intellectual development.

Piaget offers the most comprehensive theoretical framework available for understanding the intellectual development of the child. His theory of development is based primarily on a biological model of environment–organism interchange. Play has a dual role in Piaget's theory. It serves both as a vehicle for knowing about the world and as a by-product or indicator of the child's level of cognitive development. To fully comprehend Piaget's theory of play, it is important to understand the relationship between play and the larger theory. While the scope of this text does not allow for a detailed description of the theory, a few comments on the basic components of Piagetian theory are in order.[2]

Piaget's rich description of intellectual development may be divided into two components: stage-independent theory and stage-dependent theory. Stage-dependent theory is concerned with the process by which the child comes to know the world, and the general principles by which the individual changes his or her intellectual state during the course of development. The stage-dependent portion of Piagetian theory is concerned with the progression of intelligent behavior from birth through adolescence. Piaget divides this time span into three major periods with various subperiods, stages, and substages within these. Table 1.1 provides an outline of progression of cognitive development.

Piaget views intelligence as the organization of adaptive behavior. Adaptation is said to occur whenever a given organism–environment interchange has the effect of modifying the organism in such a way that further interchanges, favorable to its preservation, are enhanced (Flavell 1963:45). The process of

TABLE 1.1   PERIODS OF INTELLECTUAL DEVELOPMENT

	Approximate Age Range
Sensorimotor period—six stages	
1. Exercising the readymade sensorimotor schemata	0–1 month
2. Primary circular reaction	1–4 months
3. Secondary circular reactions	4–8 months
4. Coordination of secondary schemata	8–12 months
5. Tertiary circular reactions	12–18 months
6. Invention of new means through mental combinations	18–24 months
Concrete operations period	
Preoperational subperiod	2–7 years
Concrete operations subperiod	7–11 years
Formal operations period	11–15 years

[2]For a comprehensive description and analysis of Piaget's work see Flavell, J.H., *The Developmental Psychology of Jean Piaget*, Princeton, N.J.: Van Nostrand-Reinhold, 1963.

adaptation occurs through the mutually reciprocal processes of assimilation and accommodation. Flavell draws analogies between assimilation and accommodation and the ingestion and digestion of food.

> First the organism must and will transform the substance it takes in order to incorporate their food values into its system. An initial transformation occurs when the substance is ingested by chewing. Thus, hard and sharply contoured objects become pulpy and formless. Still more drastic changes occur as the substance is slowly digested, and eventually it will lose its original identity entirely by becoming part of the structure of the organism. (p. 45)

Cognitive assimilation is then "the action of the organism on surrounding objects, insofar as the action depends on previous behavior involving the same or similar objects" (Piaget 1962:7). However, quite often a new piece of information cannot be accommodated by the already existing mental structure. The organism then faces the alternative of either rejecting this new material or modifying its own structure to accommodate the material. In this way the environment acts upon the organism. For example, suppose a young child has learned the word "dog" and to identify a certain class of animals as dogs. Now suppose that on a visit to a farm she sees a large, four-legged animal with a tail and says "Look Mommy a dog!" Her mother then explains that the animal is not a dog but a horse, a separate class of animal with distinct characteristics. At this point the child either rejects the new information and continues to call it a dog or creates a new schema for horse; in other words her mental structure has changed in order to accommodate the new information.

Along with the processes of assimilation and accommodation, Piaget assigns four general factors to mental development: maturation, experience, social transmission, and equilibration. Piaget calls equilibration the fundamental factor of development because it balances and regulates the other three. The continous process of assimilation creates a state of disequilibrium. It is this state of imbalance that provides the primary motivation for learning.

Piaget (1962) devoted a separate book to the development and nature of play titled *Play, Dreams, and Imitation in Childhood*. Given Piaget's notion of adaptation in which the equilibrium of assimilation and accommodation is part of every act of intelligent behavior, there are two important kinds of behaviors that do not manifest this delicate balance. The first is behavior that includes all the various forms of play, dreams, and make-believe. The second is imitation that includes all copying or imitative behavior.

Play may be viewed as the assimilation of environmental stimuli with little regard to the limitations imposed by accommodations.

> In play the primary object is to mold reality to the whim of the cognizer, in other words, to assimilate reality to various schemas with little concern for precise accommodation to that reality. Thus, as Piaget puts it, in play there is the "primacy of assimilation over accommodation." In imitation, on the other hand, it is accommodation which reigns supreme. All energy is focused on taking exact account of the structural niceties of the reality one is imitating and in precisely dovetailing one's schematic repertoire to these details. In other words, as in play the primary concern is to adapt reality to the self (assimilation), in imitation the paramount object is to adapt the self to reality (accommodation) (Flavell 1963:65–66).

Like Freud, Piaget attributes the initial appearance of play to the pleasure derived from the infant's mastery of his own behavior. As Piaget states, "Play . . . proceeds by relaxation of the effort at adaptation and by maintenance or exercise of activities for the mere pleasure of mastering them and acquiring thereby a feeling of virtuosity of power" (1952:89).

Since Piaget offers the most comprehensive theory available for understanding the intellectual development of children, his integration of play into that framework enhances its applicability for research and practice. Indeed, his theory of play, among those discussed in this book, stands alone in this respect. Thus far it is the only one subjected to extensive empirical testing.

LIMITATIONS OF PLAY THEORY

The limitations of play theory are numerous, confounded by the absence of a clear definition. First, the theories deal only with specific elements or a limited sampling of the broad concerns of play. For example, Piaget's developmental play theory, though broader than most, is encapsulated in his massive theory of cognitive development. Consequently, in order to understand the broad dimensions of play, one must study a monumental array of information.

Second, several theories (e.g., surplus energy, relaxation) involve single or limited variables and, from a scientific perspective, hardly qualify as theory at all. In practice, they have done a great deal of harm. Many practitioners at the present time still consider play a waste of time or an avenue to let off steam, and they construct play environments that are poorly suited to children's cognitive, social, affective, and psychomotor needs.

Third, the theories tend to be tied to the academic roles of their developers. Explanations of play are available from the disciplines of psychology, sociology, anthropology, child development, physical education, art, and education. Specialization has the advantage of isolation of specific variables for study, but such isolation does not necessarily lead to study of integrative elements.

Hoppes (1984) illustrates these concerns.

> Physical education addresses play when it becomes sport and has physical ramifications. Sociology deals with play when it is an expression of social structure and values. Education takes up the topic when play has a bearing on learning and teaching. And anthropology speaks of play when it is a key to the understanding of the development of humankind. Yet each discipline also accepts, in practice, the multi-faceted nature of the phenomenon of play and the inadequacy of a mono-disciplinal explanation of it. Because of the limitations caused by the rigidity of the classification system of academia, play has been relegated to the periphery of these disciplines' attention. While these four disciplines profess an interest in play, none takes the responsibility of embracing this subject as a specialty. (pp. 3–4)

The result, Hoppes aptly points out, is that a crazy quilt of theories and research has sprung up over the years, and the study of play continues to suffer from a reliance upon antiquated theory, a puritanical bias against play, a quest for seriousness by academicians, and a prevailing view that play is trivial and inconsequential.

Problems in Defining Play

Acknowledging the seriousness of these concerns, a central restriction on efforts to understand play is failure to agree on what play is. A few sample definitions illustrate this point.

Schiller	(1954)	The aimless expenditure of exuberant energy.
Froebel	(1887)	The natural unfolding of the germinal seeds of childhood.
Groos	(1901)	Instinctive practice, without serious intent, of activities that will later be essential to life.
Dewey	(1916)	Activities not consciously performed for the sake of any result beyond themselves.
Gulick	(1898)	What we do because we want to do it.
Patrick	(1916)	Those human activities which are free and spontaneous and which are pursued for their sake alone (Sapora & Mitchell, 1948, p.114).

In his classic book *Homo Ludens* (1950), written in 1938, Huizinga said that play is not subject to exact definition logically, biologically, or aesthetically, and Ellis (1973) stated that pure play is only theoretically possible. Hence, we have to restrict ourselves to describing the main characteristics of play.

Huizinga (1950) characterized play in broad terms as necessary for culture, voluntary, irrational, limited in time and space, bound by rules, and free of imposed tasks.

> Play is a voluntary activity or occupation executed within certain fixed limits of time and place, according to rules freely accepted but absolutely binding, having its aim in itself and accompanied by a feeling of tension, joy and the consciousness that it is "different" from ordinary life. (p. 28)

Huizinga avoided psychological interpretation of play and restricted his inquiry to its creative qualities and its special manifestations, using anthropological terms and explanations.

Piaget (1962), on the other hand, dealt in psychological interpretations. Although he avoided a precise definition, he linked play to his overall cognitive theory, pointing out that "play constitutes the extreme pole of assimilation to the ego, while at the same time it has something of the creative imagination which will be the motor of all future thought and even of reason" (p. 162).

As this is written, scholars continue their inquiries into the meanings of play. In the *Handbook of Child Psychology*, Rubin, Fein, and Vandenberg (1983) used about 450 citations published between 1970 and 1982, with over 50% more recent than 1975. Over 700 articles on play were published between 1880 and 1980, growing from a dozen or so articles a decade before 1930 and accelerating to over 200 during the 1970s (Sutton-Smith 1985).

Sutton-Smith (1985) added new dimensions to the study of play. He proposed that there are two kinds of play—the rational and the irrational. Rational play is studied in the psychology of play and in the playground movement. The contexts for the study and pursuit of rational play are nursery schools, laboratories, and supervised playgrounds. Typically, investigators of rational play explore play and problem solving, play and creativity, play and cognitive development, and play materials and equipment. He argues that "One will get a very limited view of what children's play is about from such studies."

Irrational play, on the other hand, is more characteristic of the play research in folklore and in anthropology. Sutton-Smith implies that play scholars should follow the lead of early psycholoanalytical approaches that dealt with the "disturbed and the deviant . . . and with regressive and animalistic play." His irrational play subjects would include "violent sports, libidinous foreplay, addictive gambling and war games," hardly the subject matter of nursery schools yet obviously relevant objects of study if we are to understand the complex dynamics of the subject. Sutton-Smith does not suggest that irrational play be our sole object of study: "Little league baseball, Barbie doll play, playing house, playing with toy trucks and mobiles hanging over a crib are all a part of the necessary subject-matter we must tackle if we are to deal with play." Play and game concepts are rapidly becoming the source of metaphors for life activities by scientists, politicians, and others and increasingly replacing traditional political and evolutionary concepts for describing human affairs. In these terms, "games are neither inherently rational or irrational. They can be both . . . It is high time to pay it [play] a more cosmic kind of respect."

Contemporary theorists recognize that play is a complex class of behaviors, yet their creative energies have been directed to explaining play essentially within the framework of respective disciplines or interests. Researchers have followed their lead, collecting and analyzing data on explicit categories of play or on patterns of play behavior and effects of play, relevant to specific disciplines rather

FIGURE 1.2 *Play is a source of pleasure; free of imposed tasks or rules; spontaneous and voluntary.*

than across disciplines. As a result, explanations and mountains of data are available, but critical analysis that would explain interrelationships across academic disciplines and corresponding dimensions of play needs to be conducted.

TOWARD AN INTEGRATED THEORY OF PLAY*

Among major disciplines, the need for an integrated theory of play is perhaps greatest in education and child development, for these disciplines are deeply concerned with the practical consequences of theory. Those dealing with children need access to theory and research from both the social and the behavioral sciences, and they need theory to explain and to evaluate their child care or educational practices.

In order to be useful, theory must (a) explain the dimensions of its concern, (b) explain the data or experiences upon which it is based, (c) have predictive power, and (d) guide future research and practice. The older classical theories fail on all four counts. Narrow in perspective and shallow in conceptualization, they reflect the influence of eras when children were viewed as little adults and childhood was not yet discovered. Based upon little systematic observation and no scientific data, the recapitulation, the surplus energy, the instinct-practice, and the relaxation theories are all ways of saying that play, like childhood, is unimportant.

An integrative theory of play changes the pattern of theory building *within* disciplines to theory building *across* disciplines. Such an explanation must, of course, meet common criteria for theory. It lends depth and breadth to understanding play and provides practitioners with a comprehensive, utilitarian, and unified view of the phenomenon. Consequently, educators and child developmentalists can extract meaningful implications and interrelationships for practice in family, school, and community contexts. An integrative explanation of play does not mitigate against continued theory building within disciplines or research on isolated dimensions of play; rather, it uses such data for its explanation and is refined from continuing contributions. Further, dimensions of an integrated theory will serve as the conceptual base for this book, providing essential elements for decisions about enhancing play and play environments.

It is proposed that play be explained from five interrelated perspectives: characteristics, motives, behaviors, developmental correlates and content. We shall examine each of these in turn.

Characteristics of Play

Play can be explained by its characteristics. There are two common ways of doing this. The first is to narrow the domain of play to specific features borrowed from various theoretical perspectives. Examples of this approach are found in the work of Piaget (1962:147, 150); Garvey (1977); Rubin et al. (1983); and Almy (1984). An assumption of those using this approach is that play is a special activity with distinctive, though not exclusive, characteristics that set it apart from other activities.

---

*Adapted from Frost, J.L. (1984). "Toward an Integrated Theory of Play." *In The Young Child and Music.* By permission of Music Educators National Conference.

- Play is a source of pleasure, evidenced by expressions of joy and excitement by the participants (Froebel 1887; Groos 1901; Valentine 1942; Huizinga 1950; Garvey 1977).
- Play is carried on for its own sake with emphasis on the play itself rather than its outcome (Froebel 1887; Groos 1901; Patrick 1916; Valentine 1942; Huizinga 1950; Piaget 1962; Bruner 1972).
- Play is free of imposed rules or tasks (Huizinga 1950, Bateson 1955; Piaget 1962; Schwartzman 1978).
- Play is intrinsically motivated (Huizinga 1950; Berlyne 1960; Bruner 1972; Garvey 1977; Schwartzman 1978).
- Play is spontaneous and voluntary (Patrick 1916; Huizinga 1950; Piaget 1962; Garvey 1977).
- Play requires active involvement of the individual player (Piaget 1962; Klinger 1971; Garvey 1977).

In addition to these general characteristics of play there are special characteristics, specific to types and stages of play, that contribute to our understanding of play.

- In symbolic or dramatic play characteristic of early childhood, play is a simulative, nonliteral, symbolic behavior that bridges the imaginary and real worlds and is characterized by an "as if" consciousness (Isaacs 1933; Sutton-Smith 1967; Reynolds 1976: Fein 1981).
- In organized play or games with rules, characteristic of early and middle childhood, play is bound by rules (K. Buhler 1937; Huizinga 1950; Piaget 1962).

A major fault of this process is that behaviors other than play contain elements of these characteristics. For example, such behaviors as exploration and imitation may be pleasurable, intrinsically motivated, spontaneous, and require active involvement.

Finally, the identification of characteristics is beset with contradiction. As Duncan (1988) expressed it:

> Groos (1898) argued that play is instinctual, Eifermann (1971) argued that play is learned. Ellis (1973) described play as arousal-seeking, Patrick (1916) described play as relaxation. Berlyne (1960) claimed that play serves no function, Welker (1961) claimed that play serves a biological function. Pieper (1952) argued that play—or leisure *par excellence*—is a mental and spiritual attitude; Gadamer (1975) argued that play has its own essence . . . .(p. 29)

Despite these limitations the identification of characteristics may be useful in explaining play, particularly when play is viewed as a disposition or tendency determined by a certain orientation of the activity. This can be illustrated by comparing play with behavior that is not play. Among the primary human behaviors, work comes closest to representing the antithesis of play. Although pure play and pure work may be theoretically possible, in practice play may contain elements of work and vice versa. Both Huizinga (1950) and Ellis (1973) identified the need to contrast play and nonplay and play and work, but neither proposed a scheme for doing it.

The activities of children can be classified as more playful or less playful, depending upon such factors as degree and nature of adult involvement, the behavior of the child, source of the activity, and nature of materials used. An outdoor construction activity, wherein children are instructed by the teacher on the use of tools and the building of a rabbit hutch according to scale drawing, would likely be less playful than a free choice construction activity, wherein children make their own choices from a wide array of materials, procedures, and outcomes.

Implications for Practice

Contrasting play and behaviors that are not play allows the practitioner to assess the nature of children's activities in school, home, or neighborhood playground/ classroom contexts. Consequently, decisions about scope and sequence in curricula and developmentally appropriate activities can be made and a desired balance between play (active, spontaneous, serious, etc.) set play apart from other activities. The enhancement of these qualities requires special attention by adults who must provide time, space, materials, and appropriate intervention —all aimed toward ensuring that play is developmentally appropriate and safe.

The skillful adult observes play events and asks such questions as: Is the activity pleasurable? Is it free of imposed rules? Does the activity emphasize the play itself rather than its outcomes? Is it spontaneous? Is everyone involved? A yes response to such questions, constructed from knowledge of characteristics of "pure play," helps to determine whether the environment is properly equipped and arranged; whether adult intervention is needed; whether individual and group play needs are being met.

Motives for Play

Play can be explained by its *motives*. The earliest definitions and theories of play addressed the issue of why children play. Froebel (1887) believed that the aims of early play in children changed as they advanced in age, from the seeking of activity as such to representation as such. Through play, children are filled with joy, and their physical, intellectual, and moral powers are fed. In the psychoanalytical tradition, Isaacs (1933) observed the motives of possession, power, rivalry, recognition, sexual impulses, and guilt in children's play. The early energy, the recapitulation, and the instinct-practice theories all implied a corresponding motive. The aims, respectively, were to rid oneself of excess energy, to recapitulate the history of the race, or to practice skills needed in later life.

Several of the more recent views of motive have roots in Pavlov's (1927) *orienting reflex* notions. The orienting reflex triggers an automatic response to changes in the environment. Appropriate receptor organs orient to and investigate the source of the change. *Drive* theorists believe that learning results from the association of stimuli with responses that reduce basic drives such as hunger, thirst, and sex. According to Berlyne (1960, 1969) and Hebb (1948) the organism seeks an optimum level of arousal. A low level of environmental stimulation results in boredom, and an excessive level of stimulation results in uncertainty and diverse exploration. In play situations when arousal reaches an optimum level, neither too high nor too low, play stops.

Berlyne (1969) also helped to place the concepts of internal and external motivation in perspective. Early studies of animals revealed that they often played just for the fun of it, even when basic drives such as hunger had been met. Berlyne proposed that intrinsically motivated behavior serves tissue needs. Play decreases arousal by increasing stimulation. From these perspectives, stimulus seeking is intrinsically motivated behavior aimed toward elevating arousal of the individual to an optimal level. Work, the corollary of play, is goal oriented, extrinsically motivated behavior aimed toward reducing arousal. Rather than attempting to force play to becoming a conceptual opposite of work, Ellis (1973) suggests facing the problem.

> A behavior may have many motives that are not mutually exclusive and an adequate explanation must recognize this . . . . It seems that pure play can occur only when all extrinsic consequences are eliminated and the behavior is driven on solely by intrinsic motivation. Pure play is probably only theoretically possible. (p. 110)

The formulations of Bateson (1955, 1956) give insight into how play aids cognitive development. Play and fantasy allow children to learn the process of framing and reframing roles and, to a lesser extent, to learn the specific roles they play. The play itself, then, is a more important factor than the roles being played out. Bateson's work has influenced other contemporary play researchers.

Bruner (1972) and Bruner et al. (1976) contend that children can "safely" engage in play and, being freed of the constraints of concern, can explore, discover, and practice new behaviors. In playing out behaviors, novel combinations are created; through attention to means over ends, new strategies, applicable to novel situations, are developed. The views of Sutton-Smith (1967, 1977) about the importance of play in development parallel those of Bruner. He notes that play provides *adaptive potentiation*. Through play, children develop cognitive prototypes and associations that can be used in novel situations. In direct response to the question of motive ("Why do children play?"), these contemporary views focus on play as an avenue for adaptive struggles or, if you will, play as a medium for cognitive and social development.

Implications for Practice

In sum, popular motives for play include *power motives* (rivalry, recognition, and possession), *therapeutic motives* (pleasure, relaxation, and arousal), and *acculturation motives* (mastery, self identification, and adaptation).

The knowledgeable adult understands that these motives are linked to play behaviors (e.g., practice play, dramatic play, organized games) which are discussed in Chapter 4. If, for example, children are to achieve the power motive of recognition by peers, they must have opportunities to engage in games of skill and/or exercise (practice) play activities for developing motor skills. Similarly, the adaptation motive of mastery is facilitated by providing time, space, materials and adult support for construction (building) play and for make-believe (dramatic) play. Clearly, the less orderly forms of play are also relevant-rough and tumble and traditional games of rivalry.

Play Behaviors

Play can be explained by the play behaviors of children as they engage in play. These behaviors are frequently connected to areas of development presumed to be influenced by the play in question and are classified by some authorities across developmental periods. To exemplify, Piaget's (1962) explanation of play behaviors relates play and cognitive development and Parten's (1932) description of social play relates play and social development. Both Piaget's cognitive play behaviors (e.g., functional, symbolic, games with rules) and Parten's social play behaviors (e.g., solitary, parallel, cooperative) are discussed extensively in Chapter 4.

Both Piaget's and Parten's play categories have been used extensively by researchers and modified over time. These investigators include Shure (1963); Smilansky (1968); Seagoe (1970); Barnes (1971); Iwanaga (1973); Garvey (1974); Moore, Evertson, & Brophy (1974); Rubin, Maioni, & Hornung (1976); Tizard, Philps, & Plewis (1976); Rubin, Watson & Jambour (1978); Campbell & Frost (1978); Strickland (1979); Frost & Klein (1983); Henniger (1985); Myers (1985); Winter (1985); Pellegrini and Perlmutter (1987); Keesee (1990); Hutt (in press).

Implications for Practice
Studies of play behaviors allow clearer understandings of how children play and result in implications for play leaders.

First, the nature of children's play across age and developmental levels is illuminated, particularly with respect to the types of cognitive and social play engaged in by infants, toddlers, preschoolers, and primary age children in various types of play environments. Such insight is valuable in the assessment and design of both indoor and outdoor environments, including material and equipment choices and in playground zoning choices appropriate to developmental levels of children.

Second, the nature and extent of sex differences during play, in varying contexts and across developmental levels, is better understood. Although sex differences in play are obvious, we are only beginning to understand their antecedents or, perhaps more importantly, to understand the dynamics of intervention. Should practitioners attempt to modify play environments and, consequently, change sex role behaviors? If so, in what ways? And for what specific changes?

Third, these studies are contributing to the development of methods and instruments for assessing play behaviors and play environments. These methods and instruments identify physical environments that support or enhance particular forms of play, and they allow comparisons of play behaviors across levels of development.

Developmental Correlates of Play

Play can be explained by its developmental correlates, including cognitive, social, cultural, psychomotor, emotional, artistic, and educational, as studied, respectively, by the disciplines of psychology, sociology, anthropology, physical education, psychiatry, art, and education.

Over the years, a body of research has accumulated within each of these disciplines and occasionally across disciplines, confirming and explaining the dynamic relationships between play and development. The developmental correlates of play include:

- From a therapeutic perspective, play is a means for overcoming fears, anxieties, and tensions (Klein 1932; Isaacs 1933; Axline 1947; Erikson 1950)
- Play serves as a useful mirror of the development of symbolic representation (Rubin 1982; Rubin & Pepler 1980). In play, newly developed schemas (mental

structures or abilities) are consolidated and strengthened (Fein 1979; Saltz 1980), and play directly influences cognitive and social development (Saltz & Brodie 1982)

- Play provides *adaptive potentiation*. Through play, children develop cognitive prototypes (Sutton-Smith 1967, 1977).
- Through play, novel combinations are created and new strategies, applicable to novel situations, are developed (Bruner 1972; Bruner, Jolly, & Sylva 1976).
- Through play, the child assimilates objects to actions and these become mental schemas. These schemas are the functional equivalents of concepts and of the logical relationships of later development (Piaget 1962).
- Play leads to discovery, verbal judgment, and reasoning. It is significant for manipulative skills, imaginative art, discovery, reasoning, and thought (Isaacs 1933).
- Play is necessary for culture. It actually becomes culture. Culture arises in the form of play. Civilization arises and unfolds in and as play (Huizinga 1950).
- Play with objects results in divergent production or more uses for objects (Sutton-Smith 1968; Goodnow 1969; Dansky 1980b) and improves problem solving (Sylva 1977; Smith & Dutton 1979).
- Divergent play experiences result in improvement in creative thinking (Pepler & Ross 1981; Pepler 1982).
- Pretend play experiences result in improved problem solving (Sutton-Smith 1968; Dansky & Silverman 1973; Dansky 1980b).
- Play training for children enhances imaginative play (Smilansky 1968; Feitelson & Ross 1973; Smith & Syddall 1978), creativity (Feitelson & Ross 1973;

FIGURE 1.3 Play leads to discovery, verbal judgment, and reasoning.

Dansky 1980a), language development (Vygotsky 1967; Lovinger 1974; Saltz, Dixon, & Johnson 1977), and group cooperation (Rosen 1974; Smith & Syddall 1978).

- Motor abilities are formed during play (Staniford 1979; Bennett 1980; Seefeldt 1984; Gallahue 1987).
- Play training for teachers enhances their interaction with children during play (Busse, Ree, & Gutride 1970; Singer & Singer 1974; Wade 1985).
- From educational/developmental perspectives, play is readiness. That is, play is a means for mastery of the environment and leads to readiness for further mastery.

Implications for Practice

At present the American public is being influenced by national task force reports on education, popular media, and legislators to place greater emphasis upon academics in education and to reduce "frills" in school programs. Play has traditionally been regarded as a frill, trivial and inconsequential. The scientific evidence, however, presents a profoundly different conclusion.

Play is an indispensable element in child development. It is the child's natural process of learning and development and, consequently, a critical ingredient in the educative process. Wise teachers, playleaders, and parents ensure that an array of play opportunities is available from infancy and continues throughout the life span. Both formal and informal play environments are developed indoors and outdoors to serve the developmental play needs of children.

Despite the rapidly expanding evidence that play influences or is associated with development, the precise nature of these correspondences is yet to be identified. The evidence does indeed point to hypotheses that are useful both for future research and, in the absence of conflicting data, for present practice. There is no body of research or modern theory suggesting that play is not valuable or of no consequence. Investigators of play would likely agree that play is valuable in child development and that the research of the coming decade will further illuminate this fact.

Content of Play

Play can be explained by its *content*. The content of play can be classified into two major categories: concrete materials or equipment, and symbolic representations or imaginary symbols. Equipment includes large, manufactured, fixed structures such as swings, seesaws, merry-go-rounds, climbers, and superstructures or combinations of such equipment. Electronic equipment includes videogames, television, electronic and mechanical vehicles, and computers. Play materials include manufactured, theme-specific materials such as dolls and guns and theme-non-specific materials such as building blocks and Tinkertoys. Natural materials include trees, rocks, plants, and fluid materials such as water and sand. Materials are used in both indoor and outdoor contexts. The larger, fixed equipment is usually installed only in outdoor playgrounds. If the function of play is no more than acting out our animal origins, letting off excess energy, or practicing adult type skills of bygone times, the most primitive types of playgrounds would serve very well. Consider those conceived in this country during the early 1900s. They were arenas of steel and concrete, featuring swings, slides, jungle gyms, seesaws, and merry-go-rounds, arranged in rows and suitable for

FIGURE 1.4 Play is an indispensable element in child development.

only one form of play-exercise or practice. Such playgrounds remain the predominant pattern to this day—throwbacks to primitive, outmoded theory and hazardous and ill suited to the developmental needs of children.

In contrast, modern creative or adventure playgrounds accommodate the various types of play. Functional play is enhanced by provision of exercise equipment. Dramatic play and symbolic representation are encouraged by a wide range of loose parts or portable materials to be used in combination with large structures, such as play houses, superstructures, and stripped Volkswagens. Construction play uses tools, pieces of lumber, and building blocks. Organized games, such as football and soccer, are played on separate flat, grassy areas, and games such as hopscotch and basketball are played on special hard surfaces. The same playground contains storage facilities for art, music, gardening, building, and other creative materials. Social processes are also enhanced. Solitary play occurs in out of the way, partially private areas; associative play and cooperative play in wheel vehicle play, sand and water play, play houses, and in organized games.

CONCLUSION

While theorists have long recognized the importance of play in contributing to the development of the child, they have also presented contrasting definitions of play and have disagreed about why children play. The motivation to play has been attributed t o the need to "run off" excess energy, the need to relax and seek relief from tension, recapitulation to earlier stages of evolution, and the necessity of practicing skills that will be used in adulthood. While there may be some common-sense wisdom contained in these theories, they are for the most part archaic and insufficient in explaining play.

The psychoanalytic theories of Freud and Erikson have contributed significantly to the understanding of play. From their perspectives, play contributes to the development of a healthy personality. Through play children gain pleasure by fulfilling their wishes; play has a therapeutic value in that it helps children to overcome and eventually master fears and unpleasant experiences. Through play children develop mastery of their physical and social environment.

Piaget has linked the development of play to cognitive development. Like Freud, Piaget attributes the initial appearance of play to the pleasure derived from the infants' mastery of their own behavior. Play is both a vehicle and a by-product of cognitive development in that through play children produce interesting effects in the environment and discover cause and effect relationships resulting from their own behavior. Children then use play to perfect the behavior and to cause the interesting effect to reoccur at will.

Play is a multifaceted phenomenon and, as such, is the subject of inquiry in many disciplines including psychology, anthropology, sociology, child development, physical education, and education. None of these disciplines has explored the qualities of play in sufficient depth or exactness to develop a complete explanation of play. Each, however, has made substantial contributions toward this end, and the rapidly accumulating body of information gives a substantial basis for proposing an integrated theory of play.

There are numerous advantages of such a theory. An integrated theory of play provides a comprehensive description of the qualities of play, points out interrelationships between those qualities, opens up creative possibilities for the design of play environments, and serves as a sounding board or test for selecting play materials and for designing indoor and outdoor play environments.

Certain dimensions of play are commonly examined across disciplines and each gives a partial explanation of play. These dimensions include characteristics of play, motives of play, play behaviors, developmental correlates of play, and play content. Examination of these interrelated dimensions may lend depth and breadth to understanding play and may result in a comprehensive, utilitarian, and unified view of the phenomenon, useful in the development of developmentally appropriate play environments.

After having reviewed major theories of play spanning the last 3,000 years, from Plato to Piaget, it is still not possible to arrive at a simple, clear, scientific definition of play. Erikson advises that play has a very personal meaning for each individual. Perhaps the best thing that we as adults can do to discover this meaning is to go out and play; to reflect upon our own childhood play; to once again look at play through the eyes of the child.

REFERENCES

Axline, V. (1947). *Play Therapy*. Boston: Houghton Mifflin.

Barnes, K. (1971). Preschool play norms: A replication. *Developmental Psychology*, 51: 99–103.

Bateson, G. (1955, 1956). The message "This is play." In *Group Processes*. ed. B. Schaffner. New York: Josiah Macy.

Beach, F.A. (1945). Current concepts of play in animals. *American Naturalist*, 79: 523–541.

Bennett, C. (1980). Planning for activity during the important preschool years. *Journal of Physical Education, Recreation and Dance*. September: 30–34.

Berlyne, D.E. (1960). *Conflict, Arousal and Curiosity*. New York: McGraw-Hill.

————. (1969). Laughter, humor and play. In *The Handbook of Social Psychology*, (vol. 3), eds. G. Lindzey & E. Aronson Reading, MA: Addison-Wesley.

Brown, N., Curry, N.E., & Titlnich, E.T. (1971). How groups of children deal with stress through play. In , *Play: The Child's Drive Toward Self-Realization*, eds. N.E. Curry & S. Arnaud, Washington, D.C.: National Association for the Education of Young Children.

Bruner, J.S. (1972). The nature and uses of immaturity. *American Psychologist*, 27: 687–708.

Bruner, J.S., Jolly, A., & Sylva, K. eds. (1976). *Play: Its Role in Development and Evolution*. New York: Penguin.

Buhler, K. (1937). *The Mental Development of the Child*. London: Routledge & Kegan Paul.

Busse, T., Ree, M., & Gutride, M. (1970). Environmentally enriched classrooms and the play behavior of Negro preschool children. *Urban Education*, 5: 128–140.

Campbell, S.D., & Frost, J.L. (1978, August). *The Effects of Playground Type on the Cognitive and Social Play Behaviors of Grade Two Children*. Paper presented at the Seventh World Congress of the International Playground Association, Ottawa, Ontario, Canada.

Dansky, J.L. (1980a). Cognitive consequences of sociodramatic play and exploratory training for economically disadvantaged preschoolers. *Journal of Child Psychology and Psychiatry*, 20: 47–58.

————. (1980b). Make believe: A mediator of the relationship between free play and associative fluency. *Child Development* 51: 576–579.

Dansky, J.L., & Silverman, I.W. (1973). Effects of play on associative fluency in preschool-aged children. *Developmental Psychology* 9: 38–43.

Darwin, C. (1859). *The origin of the species*. London: John Murray.

Dewey, J. (1916). *Democracy and Education*. New York: The Free Press.

Eifermann, E. (1971). Social play in childhood. In *Child's Play*, R. Herron & B. Sutton-Smith. New York: John Wiley. (A more detailed description appears in Rivka R. Eifermann, School Children's Games, U.S. Office of Education, Bureau of Research. June, 1968, Mimeographed Report.)

Ellis, M.J. (1973). *Why People Play*. Englewood Cliffs, NJ: Prentice-Hall.

Erikson, E.H. (1950). *Childhood and Society*. New York: Norton.

Fein, G. (1979). Play in the acquisition of symbols. In , *Current Topics in Early Childhood Education*, ed. L. Katz. Norwood, NJ: Ablex.

————. (1981). Pretend play in childhood: An integrative review. *Child Development*, 52: 1095–1118.

Feitelson, W., & Ross, G.S. (1973). The neglected factor—play. *Human Development*, 16: 202–223.

Freud, W. (1959). Beyond the pleasure principle. In ed., *The Standard Edition of the Complete Psychological Works of Sigmund Freud*. J. Strachey London: The Institute of Psychoanalysis. (Original work published 1922).

Froebel, F. (1887). *The Education of Man*, (trans.) W.N. Hailmann New York: D. Appleton.

Frost, J.L., & Klein, B. (1983). *Children's Play and Playgrounds*. Austin, TX: Playgrounds International (P.O. 33363). Reprinted from Allyn & Bacon 1979.

Gallahue, D. (1987). *Developmental Physical Education for Today's Elementary School Children*. New York: Macmillan.

Garvey, C. (1974). Some properties of social play. *Merrill-Palmer Quarterly* 20: 163–180.

————. (1977). *Play*. Cambridge, MA: Harvard University Press.

Goodnow, J.J. (1969). Effects of handling, illustrated by use of objects. *Child Development* 40: 201–212.

Groos, K. (1898). *The Play of Animals*. New York: D. Appleton.

————. (1901). *The Play of Man*. New York: D. Appleton.

Gulick, L. (1898). Some physical aspects of physical exercise. *Popular Science Monthly* 58: 793–805.

Hall, S.G. (1906). *Youth*. New York: D. Appleton.

Harris, W.T., ed. (1906). The mottoes and commentaries of Friedrich Froebel's *Mother Play*. New York: D. Appleton.

Hebb, D.O. (1948). *The organization of Behavior*. New York: Wiley.

Henniger, M.L. (1985). Preschool children's play behaviors in an indoor and outdoor environment. In eds., *When Children Play*. J.L. Frost & S. Sunderlin Wheaton, MD: Association for Childhood Education International.

Hoppes, S.M. (1984). *An Interdisciplinary Study of the Phenomenon of Play*. Unpublished doctoral dissertation, The University of Texas at Austin.

Huizinga, J. (1950). *Homo Iudens: A Study of the Play Element in Culture*. London: Routledge & Kegan Paul.

Hutt, C. (in press). Towards a taxonomy and conceptual model of play. In eds., *Developmental Processes in Early Childhood*, S.J. Hutt, D.A. Rogers, & C. Hutt. London: Routledge & Kegan Paul.

Isaacs, S. (1933). *Social Development in Young Children: A Study of Beginnings*. London: Routledge & Kegan Paul.

Iwanaga, M. (1973). Development of interpersonal play structure in three, four, and five year-old children. *Journal of Research and Development in Education*, 6(3): 71–82.

Keesee, B. (1990). *Comparison of Traditional and Developmentally Appropriate Play Environments for Toddlers*. Unpublished doctoral dissertation, The University of Texas at Austin.

Klein, M. (1932). *The Psychoanalysis of Children*. London: Hogarth.

Klinger, E. (1971). *Structure and Functions of Fantasy*. New York: Wiley.

Lovinger, S.L. (1974). Sociodramatic play and language development in preschool disadvantaged children. *Psychology in the Schools* 11: 313–320.

Millar, S. (1968). *The Psychology of Play*. Baltimore: Penguin Books.

Mitchell, E.D. (1937). *The Theory of Play*. Baltimore: Penguin Books.

Moore, N., Evertson, C. M., & Brophy, J. E. (1974). Solitary play: Some functional reconsiderations. *Developmental Psychology* 10: 830–834.

Myers, J. (1985). Perceived and actual playground equipment choices of children. In eds., *When Children Play*, J. Frost & S. Sunderlin, Washington, DC: Association for Childhood Education International.

Parten, M. (1932). Social participation among preschool children. *Journal of Abnormal and Social Psychology* 27: 243–369.

Patrick, G.T.W. (1916). *The Psychology of Relations*. New York: Houghton-Mifflin.

Pavlov, I.P. (1927). *Conditioned Reflexes*. Oxford: Clarendon Press.

Pelligrini, A.D., & Perlmutter, J.C. (1987). A re-examination of the Smilansky-Parten matrix of play behavior. *Journal of Research in Childhood Education* 2: 89–96.

Pepler, D.J. (1982). Play and divergent thinking. In *The Play of Children: Research and Theory.* eds., D.J. Pepler & K.H. Rubin Basel. Switzerland: Karger AG.

Pepler, D.J., & Ross, H.S. (1981). The effects of play on convergent and divergent problem solving. *Child Development* 52: 1202–1210.

Piaget, J. (1962). *Play, Dreams and Imitation in Childhood.* New York: W.W. Norton.

Reynolds, P. (1976). Play language and human evolution. In *Play: Its Role in Development and Evolution*, eds. J.S. Bruner, A. Jolly, & K. Sylva. New York: Penguin.

Rosen, C.E. (1974). The effects of sociodramatic play on problem solving among culturally disadvantaged children. *Child Development.* 45: 920–927.

Rubin, D.H. (1982). Early play theories revisited: Contributions to contemporary research and theory. In *The Play of Children: Current Theory and Research,* eds., D.J. Pepler & K.H. Rubin New York: S. Karger.

Rubin, K.H., Fein, G., & Vandeberg, B. (1983). Play. In *Handbook of Child Psychology: Social Development.* ed., E.M. Hetherington. New York: Wiley.

Rubin, K., Maioni, T., & Hornung, M. (1976. Free play behaviors in middle- and lower-class preschoolers: Parten and Piaget revisited, Child Development. 47: 414–419.

Rubin, K.H., & Pepler, D.J. (1980). The relationship of child's play to social-cognitive development. In *Friendship and Childhood Relationships*, eds. H.C. Foot, A.J. Chapman, & J.R. Smith. London: Wiley.

Rubin, K.H., Watson, K.S., & Jambour, T.W. (1978). Free play behaviors in preschool and kindergarten children. *Child Development* 49: 534–546.

Saltz, E. (1980). *Pretend Play: A Complex of Variables Influencing Development.* Paper presented at the Annual Meeting of the American Psychological Association.

Saltz, E., & Brodie, J. (1982). Pretend-play training in childhood: A review and critique. In *The Play of Children: Current Theory and Practice,* eds. D.J. Pepler & K.H. Rubin. New York: S. Karger.

Saltz, E., Dixon, D., & Johnson, J. (1977). Training disadvantaged preschoolers on various fantasy activities: Effects on cognitive functioning and impulse control. *Child Development*, 48: 367–368.

Schiller, F. (1954). *On the Aesthetic Education of Man.* New Haven: Yale University Press.

Schwartzman, H.B. (1978). *Transformations: The Anthropology of Children's Play.* New York: Plenum.

Seagoe, M.Y. (1970). An instrument for the analysis of children's play in an index of degree of socialization. *Journal of School Psychology* 8(2): 139–144.

Seefeldt, V. (1984). Physical fitness in preschool and elementary school-aged children. *Journal of Physical Education, Recreation and Dance* November/December: 33–40.

Shure, B. (1963). Psychology ecology of a nursery school. *Child Development* 34: 979–992.

Singer, J., & Singer, D. (1974). *Fostering Imaginative Play in Preschool Children: Effects of Television Viewing and Direct Adult Modeling.* Paper presented at the annual meeting of the American Psychological Association, New Orleans. (ERIC Document Reproduction Service No. 089 873)

Smilansky, S. (1968). *The Effects of Socio-Dramatic Play on Disadvantaged Preschool Children.* New York: John Wiley.

Smith, P.K., & Dutton, S. (1979). Play and training in direct and innovative problem solving. *Child Development* 50: 830–836.

Smith, P.K., & Syddall, S. (1978). Play and non-play tutoring in preschool children: Is it play or tutoring which matters? *British Journal of Educational Psychology* 48: 315–325.

Spencer, H. (1896). *Principles of Psychology.* (3rd ed., vol. 2, p. 2). New York: Appleton.

Staniford, D.J. (1979). Natural movement for children. *Journal of Physical Education, Recreation and Dance* 50: 14–17.

Sutton-Smith, B. (1967). The role of play in cognitive development. *Young Children* 22: 361–370.

————. (1968). Novel responses to toys. *Merrill-Palmer Quarterly* 14: 151–158.

————. (1977). Play as adaptive potentiation. In *Studies in the Anthropology of Play.* ed. P. Stevens. Cornwall, NY: Leisure Press.

————. (1985). Play research. State of the art. In *When Children Play.* eds. J. Frost & S. Sunderlin. Washington, D.C.: Association for Childhood Education International.

Sylva, K. (1977). Play and learning. In *Biology of Play*, eds. B. Tizard & D. Harvey. London: Heineman.

Tizard, B., Philps, J. & Plewis, I. (1976). Play in preschool centers–I: Play measures and their relation to age, sex and I.Q. *Journal of Psychology and Psychiatry* 17: 265–274.

Tolman, E.C. (1932). *Purposive Behavior in Animals and Man.* New York: Century. (Republished: New York: Meredith, 1967.)

Valentine, C.W. (1942). *The Psychology of Early Childhood.* Cleveland: Sherwood.

Vygotsky, L.S. (1967). Play and its role in the mental development of the child. *Soviet Psychology* 12: 62–76.

Wade, C. (1985). Effects of teacher training on teachers and children in playground settings. In *When Children Play*, eds. J. Frost & S. Sunderlin. Washington, DC: Association for Childhood Education International.

Wälder, R. (1933). The psychoanalytical theory of play. *Psychoanalytic Quarterly* 2: 208–224.

Winter, S.M. (1985). Toddler play behaviors and equipment choices in an outdoor playground. In *When Children Play*, eds. J.L. Frost & S. Sunderlin Wheaton, MD: Association for Childhood Education International.

"The country that once proudly proclaimed the pursuit of happiness as a decent and legitimate goal now feel apologetic if its children have fun."[1]

2

Child Development and Play

Traditionally, there has been little appreciation in American culture for the importance of play and its contribution to child development. This has been due in part to the puritan work ethic which views with suspicion anything that is fun or not related to work. In addition, assembly-line technology has dominated the American educational system and play has been relegated the role of the ten-minute coffee break, whereby little "workers" are allowed a few minutes to run off excess energy so that they can better concentrate and produce more work (see the excess energy theory of play in Chapter 1).

Against this backdrop of historical disregard for play, Sara Arnaud (1974) declares, "Nourishers of curious minds, take heed. The case for play has gained new respectability." She points to the fact that play is now deemed worthy of serious scientific study. Just as the 1960s saw the "rediscovery" of early childhood education (Frost 1968), in which there was a proliferation of studies and experiments concerned with providing optimal learning conditions for young children, so in the 1970s and 1980s we have seen a rediscovery of children's play in which there have been a large number of investigations (Sutton-Smith 1985) into the nature and function of play. Arnaud (1974:73) attributes this shift in attitude toward play to several independent factors.

---

[1]James L. Hymes (undated, p. 1). *Why play is important*. Unpublished manuscript.

1. The work of ethologists such as Goodall-van Lawick's study of chimpanzees, DeVor's study of baboons, Harlow's work with rhesus monkeys, and other studies with a variety of mammals has shown that many species engage in playful activities. In general, it has been found that the more intelligent the animal, the greater the quantity and variety of play behavior. Through play, animals develop skills needed for survival and become socialized into the group.

2. Piaget's rich description of the scope and sequence of intellectual development and his study of play have shown that intellectual competence is achieved through intense interaction (play) with the environment.

3. Dissatisfaction with traditional early childhood programs and a movement toward programs that emphasize problem-solving skills and learner autonomy.

4. Movement away from a work ethic to a leisure ethic in which individuals devote increasingly greater time, energy, and money to leisure activities in the form of recreation, sports, travel, and the arts.

During the 1980s and early 1990s the national emphasis on children's play and play environments gained a degree of momentum not seen since the early 1900s when the Playground Association of America spearheaded the growth of playgrounds in the United States from 35 American cities with organized playgrounds in 1905 to 336 cities in 1909.

The 1990s is a time of unprecedented interest in play and the redevelopment of play environments. The primary reasons for this are:

1. The growing emphasis on play research among professionals in the behavioral sciences at universities and the resulting increase in both professional and popular publications on play and play environments.

2. A renewal of interest in play in professional organizations, notably the American and International Associations for the Child's Right to Play; the National Association for the Education of Young Children; the Anthropological Association for Play; the American Alliance for Health, Physical Education, Recreation and Dance; and the Association for Childhood Education International.

3. Increasing awareness among parents and professionals of the deleterious effects of pressuring children through overemphasis of "academics" at the expense of play.

4. The negative influence of television on children's health, fitness, moral development, and school achievement and the emerging realization that play is an essential counteracting influence.

5. The emergence of a "suing society" wherein thousands of parents are suing cities, private and public schools, child care centers, and play equipment designers, manufacturers and installers for injuries sustained by children on playgrounds.

6. The growing awareness of parents and professionals that most American playgrounds are in a state of gross disrepair, featuring antiquated, poorly designed, improperly maintained equipment.

7. The accelerating research into safety and play value by a growing number of play equipment designers and manufacturers and their involvement in developing national safety guidelines/standards for play equipment and playground surfacing.

With the rediscovery of play has come a wealth of investigations into the relationship between play and other areas of human development as well as the relationship between play and play materials. The central purpose of this chapter then is to describe these relationships and to draw implications for children's play.

CULTURE, SOCIAL CLASS, AND PLAY

As with cognitive development, the development of play follows a universal, invariant sequence. The content of a child's play and the rate with which she moves through the developmental sequence of play is in part a function of the specific culture in which she lives. One method of making cross-cultural and intercultural comparisons is to study the games children play. Roberts, Arth, and Bush (1959) distinguished between games and amusements. A game is characterized by organization, competition, two or more sides, criteria for determining a winner, and agreed upon rules, whereas noncompetitive activities are described as amusements. Games may be grouped into three classes on the basis of outcome attributes: 1) games of physical skill, in which the outcome is determined by the player's motor activities; 2) games of strategy, in which the outcome is determined by rational choices among possible courses of action; and 3) games of chance, in which the outcome is determined by guesses or by some uncontrolled artifact such as dice or a wheel. In addition, games are also models of various cultural activities and therefore exercises in cultural mastery. For example, games of skill are related to mastery of the environment, games of strategy are related to mastery of the social system, and games of chance are related to mastery of the supernatural. There is a relationship between the complexity of cultures and the complexity of games: "simple" societies do not have a need for games of strategy, but in complex societies all types of games are present. Thus, while games are universal there is a great deal of variation in the type and number of games from one culture to another.

Stress Reduction Through Games

Roberts and Sutton-Smith (1962) developed and tested what they called the conflict-enculturation theory of games. They hypothesized that the child-rearing practices of various cultures would reflect the essential characteristics of a culture, and that these patterns in themselves would create stresses. Children would then compensate for this stress by playing games that relieve it (stress-reduction model). In addition, the playing of these games would aid in the enculturation of the child.

The results of this study showed a definite association between style of child-rearing and the predominance of a particular type of game found in a given society. Tribes possessing games of strategy were found to be more likely to have high ratings on child-training procedures that involved rewards for children for being obedient, punishment for being disobedient, anxiety about nonperformance of obedience, and high frequency of obedient behaviors. Roberts and Sutton-Smith argue that conflicts over obedience are manifested in games that provide the players opportunity to control others. Games of strategy provide opportunities to force obedience on others and thereby allow the players to reduce their aggressive and hostile feelings induced by strict child-rearing practices.

Games of chance predominated in societies in which children were reared for responsibility or that stressed strict routines that allowed little scope for individuality or creative problem solving. Life in general was marked by drudgery and children were required not to reason but to do as they were told. As a result, children saw their lives as being dominated by fate or luck.

Games of physical skill were found in societies stressing achievement and performance. The games are often used by tribal societies as training procedures for hunting. In societies that consistently pressure children to perform better, anxiety concerning performance and failure develop. Anxiety over achievement may then be lessened through play where the sanctions for failure are not as great. In summary, each type of game in unique fashion contributes information as to the relative values and nature of different types of chance, skill, and strategy in assuaging conflict and in learning how to handle social competition. Between the ages of 7 and 12 the child learns, in simple direct form, how to take a chance, how to show skill, and how to deceive. Increasingly, in complex games, he learns the reversibility of these styles—when to rely on one type of success gambit rather than another, how to combine them, etc. What he learns from the games are the cognitive operations involved in competitive success (Roberts & Sutton-Smith 1962:183).

The stress-reduction model of play has also been seen in psychoanalytic theories of play. When children are disturbed by a particular incident they recreate the experience over and over again in play, gradually diminishing the intensity of the experience (a common play theme in Northern Ireland is sniper and bomber). When this stress-reduction model is applied to American culture some very disturbing trends arise. In observing the play of young children, it is obvious that many of the themes enacted in their play are taken from the popular media (television, movies, comic books). One set of play themes involves violent acts with weapons. Here the dichotomy between fantasy and reality is not clear. A child may watch a television fantasy depicting violent acts and death followed by a news story involving the same elements. Fact and fantasy become blurred and the child may come to believe (and rightly so) that he lives in a dangerous world (the legal defense of a 15-year-old accused of murdering an elderly woman was based on the fact that he was addicted to violent television dramas). A visit to any toy store will also reflect these same themes. The shelves are lined with a variety of realistic-looking weapons and artifacts of war.

Another commonly observed play theme involves taking the role of one of a variety of super heroes (G.I. Joe, Batman, She Ra). The play theme involves the acquisition of god-like qualities and conflict between good and evil. Typically, this play is stereotyped and nonelaborated (jumping, running, wrestling). De-Mille (1967) speaks to play themes derived from the popular media:

> Television and comic book fantasy can hardly be expected to cultivate the imagination, because it is already completely formed, on the screen or on the page. Nothing is left for the child to do but absorb it. The experience of the child is passive. It is not his imagination that is being exercised but that of some middle-aged writer. (p. 18)

Cultural, Ethnic, and Social Class Differences in Play

While the stress-reduction approach presents a plausible explanation concerning the functional relationship between culture and games, play may also have different adaptive roles in different cultures. One of the classical theories of play examined earlier was the instinct-practice theory of Karl Groos (1898) in which play was viewed as a vehicle for perfecting instincts and skills needed in later life. In Western societies little direct correspondence can be seen between the play behavior of young children and skills needed in adulthood. This is due in part to the advanced technological nature of Western civilization and a dichotomy between work and play. In nontechnological societies, however, there seems to be a greater correspondence between children's play and adult role behavior. Leacock (1971) points out in her description of play in African villages that "playing house" is a rehearsal for adult roles by children around the world. In Western societies this activity plays primarily a socialization function; however, in African societies it entails technical as well as social practice. In playing house children learn and perfect skills that will be needed in adult life. Boys and girls build small thatch houses and make and use a variety of tools, utensils, and weapons. Unlike in Western culture there is a smooth natural transition from play to work. She presents the following description of tribal life in Uganda. A boy tagging after his father watches him milk the cows or thatch the house, whittle a hoe handle or roast a bit of meat on a stick. Playing with a small gourd, a child learns to balance it on his head, and is applauded when he goes to the watering-place with other children and brings back a little water in it. As he learns, he carries an increasing load, and gradually the play activity turns into a general contribution to the household water supply.

Turnbull (1961) also points to this phenomenon in his description of the play of Pygmy children. Like children everywhere, Pygmy children love to imitate their adult idols ... at an early age boys and girls are "playing house" or "playing hunting" and one day they find the games they have been playing are not games any longer, but the real thing for they have become adults (p. 129).

The work of anthropologists and others studying play in various cultures of the world reveals a rich variety of play forms contributing to societal rules, roles, and values (Schwartzman, 1976a, 1976b, 1978). The issue of cross-cultural differences in play is closely related to social class differences in play. It should be acknowledged that cultural status and social class are "umbrella variables" and not sufficient as explanatory variables in themselves (Johnson, Christie, & Yawkey 1987). We shall see that specific environmental factors such as availability of play materials, adult modeling and support, and familiarity with play materials may be more important in explaining cultural or social class differences in play than is the umbrella variable of class membership.

Cultural or ethnic class differences in the play of young children have been documented by Feitelson (1977), Seagoe (1971), Murphy (1972), Udwin and Shmulker (1981), and Smilansky (1968). Perhaps the most frequently cited research on the play of lower socio-economic status (SES) children is that of Smilansky who compared the play of lower and middle SES 3- to 6-year-old Israeli children. Her finding that the lower SES children engaged in less sociodramatic play than the middle SES children was supported by studies of children in the United States (Rosen 1974; Griffing 1980; Fein and Stork 1981), and in Great Britain (Smith & Dodsworth 1978). Smilansky's conclusions were challenged in other studies (Eifermann 1971; Golumb 1979). Eifermann concluded that Smilansky's lower SES subjects lagged behind middle SES children, but this reflected a developmental lag rather than a lack of ability.

There are several explanations as to why SES differences occur in play. The studies of different SES groups are typically conducted in group settings rather than in more familiar home and neighborhood settings (Schwartzman 1979). The children may be encountering the classroom play materials for the first time —materials that are foreign to their usual play activities. Consequently, delays and anxiety in use of materials may result (Rubin, Fein, & Vandenberg 1983). The novel materials coupled with exposure to unfamiliar authority figures may result in inhibitions and anxiety on the part of the children (Schwartzman 1979). It is also important to note that children's play differs across environments (indoors vs. outdoors) and classroom contexts (Tizard et al. 1976; Huston-Stein

FIGURE 2.1 Cultural and social class play differences may result from economic conditions of growing up.

et al. 1977; Henniger 1985). The influence of family variables can also confound SES play differences. Griffing (1980) reported that in a study in which children were asked to role play "mommies and daddies," 83 per cent of the lower SES children came from single parent families.

In a broader world context, cultural and social class play differences may result from economic conditions of growing up in a Third World country. A critical factor in determining whether young children will participate in pretend play is whether they work and are considered to be economic assets (Sutton-Smith 1977).

The prevailing attitude in Colonial America, that children "should be seen and not heard" and that children should be discouraged or prevented from playing, still prevails in some societies (Feitelson 1977). Studies in Israel and South Africa reported social class differences but not cultural differences in imaginative play of lower SES children (Udwin and Shmulker 1981). The apparent deficits were attributed to the failure of lower SES parents to assist children in integrating diverse stimuli from everyday life. Sutton-Smith and Heath (1981) describe cultural style differences that may account for differences in imaginative play. The stories of working-class Afro-American children tended to be taken from real-life experiences and were relatively personal (oral style); the stories of middle-class tended to be fantasy-like stories in the third person (literate style). Earlier, Sutton-Smith (1972) hypothesized that imaginative play differences between Western and traditional societies may be related to differences in game cultures. *Ascriptive* culture children use realistic toy representations that are imitative but not transformational. Their models tend to be their elders. In contrast, *achievement* culture children use make-believe transformations that are flexible and diversified, drawing from a range of models.

Whatever the cultural, ethnic, or socioeconomic background, children play. The failure of observers to see play may result from their contrived settings and cultural attitudes, or the limited or different backgrounds of children. It appears that play can be temporarily blocked by required work roles or even by trauma or illness, but, overall, play across cultures is a matter of differences rather than substance.

SOCIAL DEVELOPMENT AND PLAY

Social development does not stand alone in the developmental processes of childhood but is linked to emotional development, cultural development, social class, and cognition. Another section of this chapter discussed cognitive development but other factors are explored here. The first and central issue, definition of social competence, is followed by a range of topics centering around the contributions of play to social development.

The literature is characterized by a lack of consensus on a definition of social competence and, for that matter, a lack of agreement about the influence of social class on play and socio-cultural development. Eisenberg and Harris (1984) reviewed the various definitions of social competence offered by researchers.

Zigler and Trickett (1978) linked their definitions to successfully meeting the expectations of society and to an individual's level of self-actualizations. Their key variables were cognitive abilities, motivational and emotional variables, achievement, and physical well-being. Social competence is also viewed as interpersonal problem solving (Shure 1981) or skill in interpersonal problem solving, such as mutually satisfying interactions between a child and/or adults (O'Malley 1977). Others (Putallaz & Gottman 1982; Waters & Sroufe 1983) link social competence to adaptation or adequate functioning and to the quality of peer relations. In sum, the competent individual is one who functions effectively in society, deals with issues appropriate to one's age or developmental group, and gains peer acceptance through quality social interaction.

Central issues in this context are how children develop social competence and what the role of play is in social development? Although a number of researchers (Shure 1981; Ford 1982; Ladd & Mize 1983) have identified developmental contributors to social competence, the five aspects identified by Eisenberg and Harris (1984) are a good representation of the various views. They are: perspective taking, conceptions of friendship, interpersonal strategies, problem solving, moral judgement, and communication skills (Eisenberg & Harris 1984:269). Although children's cognitive, verbal, and behavioral competencies change with age, neither the quality of social behavior or the number of social contacts is stable across age (Hops 1983). An apparent deficit at one age may be considered average behavior at another.

It is clear that many factors contribute to social competence, but the play of young children is a central process of social-emotional development (Eriksen 1956; Freud 1971) and opportunity for social play with peers is an essential contributor to healthy development (Hartup 1976).

Mother–Infant Play Interactions

As early as infancy, examination of play reveals the existence of turn-alternation, reciprocity and following rudimentary rules in infants' social interactions with mothers (Ross & Kay 1980). By the end of their first year, infants play games with parents, other adults, and peers (Bruner 1975, 1977; Ross, Goldman, & Hay 1979). These games give new meaning to infant competence and illustrate that infants advance well beyond Piaget's functional play schemes as they develop social and cognitive competence. The familiar games of pat-a-cake, peek-a-boo, and tack and tear down involve roles for the players, rules for the game (e.g., taking turns), interchange between the players, and repetition. Ross and Kay (1980) include nonliterality in their explanation of infant games. During play in general, the infant explores boundaries between the real and the make-believe. The interactions of mothers are also seen as nonliteral, for in the first few months they accept minimal participation from their infants and continue to enact the same repetitious games, content to engage, arouse, and amuse their babies (Ratner and Bruner 1978; Gustafson, Green, & West 1979).

The relatively passive game activity of infants rapidly shifts to more active roles so that by one year of age, they begin to initiate games. Mothers engage in infant-initiated exchanges and by their second birthday, infants (now toddlers) are the chief initiators of interchanges (Hay 1979; Ross & Kay 1980) and mothers continue to encourage their infants' creative contributions. Needless to say, such supportive actions by adults are essential to healthy development. Herein, questions must be raised about the common notion (based on Piaget's descriptions of games-with-rules) that children do not engage in organized games until the onset of the concrete operations stage (about age seven). The origins of games-with-rules are clearly seen in infancy as are the origins of other "cognitive categories" of play—symbolic play and constructive activity.

Infant Games With Peers

Peer games before 12 months are rarely studied, but Maudry and Nekula (1939) devised an experiment wherein one or more objects were placed between infants (6 to 25 months old) for brief periods. A game was defined as two or more similar actions with the same object. The two categories were *socially blind games*, where children played with the same object without attention to one another, and *personal games*, where friendly actions were directed to one another or where mutual influence was solicited. All of the games before 8 months were socially blind; 33 per cent of those played between 9 and 13 months were personal games; between 19 and 25 months, 77 per cent were personal games. Such a shift from socially blind to personal games was also observed by Mueller and Lucas (1975).

During the second year of life peer games are much more frequent and they involve acquainted as well as unacquainted children (Mueller & Brenner 1977; Goldman & Ross 1978). There is also a progression from imitative games to

FIGURE 2.2 Fathers, and grandfathers too, engage in play with their infants.

complementary and reciprocal games. Structured peer games are seen as emerging from socially-blind activities involving toys (Mueller & Lucas 1975).

The early development of infant games seems to depend upon a mother (adult) who initiates, models, organizes, or structures and repeats games for the infant. The importance of adult involvement is illustrated by the existence of mother–infant games by 6 months of age, while peer games are much less common before 12 months (Ross & Kay 1980). Greater abilities are required for two infants to play games with one another. These skills are learned through mother–infant play and employed in later peer play.

Early infant games are essential for social development for games and social interchanges that require cooperation between players. The rules that govern later social interchange are learned in early games.

Fathers, too, engage in play with their infants, but they are more likely to engage them in physical play and to hold them during play than mothers (Lamb 1976). These differences continue into preschool age, when mothers are more likely to initiate fantasy (adult pretending with child), joint positive play (interactive, exchange of toys), and domestic fantasy (playing house, making phone calls, etc.) and fathers more likely to initiate rough and vigorous play, usually in the absence of objects (Roopnaire & Mounts 1985). Children are more likely to cooperate following the initiations of play by mothers than fathers. Both mothers and fathers initiate sex-stereotypic play activities according to societal conventions.

Social Development of Preschoolers

The play of preschoolers becomes more social as they grow older (Pellegrini 1982) and social skills are influenced by engaging in dramatic play (Smilanski 1968; Rubin & Maroni 1975; Garvey 1977). Participation in fantasy play requires a high level of both social and cognitive abilities, including sharing and cooperation, appreciation of behavioral role reciprocity and self regulation of affect. During fantasy play children provide one another with positive feedback and support as they develop social skills. The familiarity of the playmates influences social interactions. Social play is more frequent and the cognitive level of play is higher with a familiar peer (Doyle, Connolly, & Rivest 1980). Connolly and Doyle (1984) found that the amount and complexity of fantasy play predicted social skills, popularity, affective role taking, and positive social activity. Consequently, social fantasy play appears to facilitate the emergence of new social skills and to result in their consolidation and refinement.

In sum, young children who engage frequently in social fantasy play are more socially competent than those who play less frequently. Given these findings, the teacher of preschoolers can be encouraged to provide appropriate indoor and outdoor spaces and materials for children's fantasy play.

Social Development and Play Materials

A growing strand of research establishes a link between availability of toys and children's social-cognitive development (Wacks 1978; Barnard, Bee, & Hammond 1984; Siegel 1984; Bradley 1985). The prevailing findings that toys are important in children's development also have theoretical ties. Vygotsky (1978) held that intellectual development was determined by the child's degree of development and by his mastery of tools (p. 21), that in the second year of life, speech joins eye and hand in the solution of practical problems. Mueller's (1979) observational studies of toddlers revealed that emerging social structure,

> relies on the toddlers attachment to toys and skill with toys. From the start, toddlers find themselves coming together because they share skills for things like opening the jack-in-the-box or sliding down the slide. (p. 174)

He went on to propose a cross-systems model of early social development. Both cognitive structures and social structures are operative in social development and structured social interactions result in cognitive growth. As children change (grow), new forms of social structure are created, which foster further cognitive growth. Thus, reciprocal interaction exists between cognitive and social development and play materials are important in mediating social-cognitive interactions and result in complexity and growth. The teacher or adult, then, can be confident in providing a range of play materials and toys for young children. These should be appropriate for the age-developmental levels of children and should include materials that are flexible, open-ended, or theme non-specific as well as theme-specific materials (e.g., role play materials). Materials such as building blocks (various types) and water and sand meet the role play requirement.

The creative potential of blocks is so varied that they have been described as the most important material for preschool or kindergarten classrooms (Starks

FIGURE 2.3 Raw materials such as water and sand and loose parts such as blocks and wheel toys are essential for flexible, open-ended, creative play.

1960; Benish 1978). They are available in most early childhood classrooms and they are one of children's most popular materials (Hartley, Frank, & Goldenson 1952; Clark, Ulyon, & Richards 1957). Block play is but one example of the contexts in which young children engage in and refine their social skills. Both boys and girls engage extensively in social play—group, solitary, and parallel—with blocks (Rogers 1985). This play provides young children with extensive experiences that extend social development. Theme specific and non-theme specific materials should be available both indoors and outdoors.

The frequency and nature of children's outdoor social play is linked to the range of materials available. Comparisons of children's play behaviors and equipment/materials choices on different types of playgrounds reveal that both boys and girls engage in more cooperative and socio-dramatic play in environments containing a rich array of fluid materials (sand, water, etc.), portable materials (blocks, containers, etc.), and vehicles (tricycles, wagons, etc.) than in those featuring large fixed equipment (e.g., climbers, slides, etc.) (Frost & Strickland 1978; Campbell & Frost 1985). Further, young children (ages 4 to 8) prefer such materials over static equipment (large, fixed, play structures).

COGNITIVE DEVELOPMENT AND PLAY

The values of play for promoting cognitive development are overshadowed by an educational climate committed to keeping children on task, a system that stresses academic achievement. The influential report, *A Nation at Risk* (Goldberg & Harvey 1983), calls for increased time on task, adherence to traditional methods and educational basics, and a longer school day. Children's natural modes of learning—exploration and practice through play—are still underutilized in preschools and almost totally ignored in public schools. Perhaps the primary reason for this state of affairs is the universal pattern of preparing teachers to teach the three R's while neglecting to assist them in understanding and promoting social competency and creative problem solving.

A growing number of studies are supporting the thesis that play influences cognitive development. These studies include three types: 1) the effects of training on certain forms of play (chapter 12); 2) the relationships of play to different areas of cognitive functioning; and 3) the relationships of play with materials.

Play and Problem Solving

The research on play and problem solving dates back to early studies of primate play. A number of studies focused on the tool-using abilities of chimpanzees to secure food placed out of reach (Jackson 1942; Birch 1945; Schiller 1957). When chimpanzees are allowed to play with sticks they learn to use the sticks in solving problems. Even in native habitats, young chimpanzees that play with sticks learn to use them to secure termites (Van Lawick-Goodall 1976).

Similar studies with preschool children (Sylva, Bruner, & Genova 1976; Sylva 1977) revealed that those who engaged in free play with sticks learned to clamp sticks together to rake a prize toward them more readily than a control group and as well as a group who actually observed the solution. The children in the free play group were more goal directed, more persistent, and more motivated than those in the other groups.

FIGURE 2.4 Play in general and pretend play in particular promote problem solving.

This study, with modifications to improve methodology, was repeated by Smith and Dutton (1979). One group was trained (helped) to assemble the sticks and clamps; one group used the materials in free play; the third group (control) was not exposed to the sticks and clamps. Despite the fact that the distance between the child and the prize was varied, free play group did as well as the trained group in joining two sticks to reach the prize and better than the trained group in using three sticks. On both tasks the two groups performed better than the control groups. It was concluded that free play is superior to training in flexible, innovative problem solving.

These studies were extended by Vandenberg (1981), who examined the effects of play on problem solving with children 4 to 10 years of age. One task required children to connect two long sticks to reach a lure; the other required the children to tie two pipe cleaners together to dislodge a sponge stuck in a tube. The play group performed better than a control group on the stick task, but not the pipe cleaner task. Older children performed better than younger children and the play was most beneficial for the 6- and 7-year-olds. It was concluded that the relationship between play and problem solving through tool use is complex and mediated by factors such as age, characteristics of the task, and previous experience with tools.

These studies provide tentative support for the thesis that play is beneficial in convergent problem solving. To conclude a direct cause–effect relationship would be premature. A second series of studies, directed to *divergent* problem solving, lend additional support to the contention that play contributes to problem solving.

In studies of problem solving by preschool children (Pepler 1979; Pepler & Ross 1981), addressed to a variety of problems, the subjects were exposed to two play conditions. In the convergent condition (one and only one solution) they played with puzzle pieces and their associated form boards; in the divergent condition (multiple solutions) they played only with the puzzle pieces. Children in the convergent condition spent two-thirds of their time assembling the puzzles, but children in the divergent play condition investigated the properties of the materials, used them for constructive play, and engaged in symbolic play with them. Although the convergent play led to more proficient puzzle completion, the learning from convergent play did not transfer to convergent tasks with different form boards. The divergent play led to superior performance on divergent, creative tasks, and greater problem solving flexibility. In addition, the greater the degree of symbolic play engaged in by the divergent play group, the more successful their problem solving ability. In sum, children's problem solving is enhanced by opportunities to engage in divergent play involving materials with open-ended or creative applications, and by symbolic or pretend play which promotes a wide range of meaningful associations. (For additional information related to play and cognitive development, see Sutton-Smith, 1967; Rubin, Fein, & Vandenberg 1983; Christie & Johnson 1983).

The value of symbolic play to problem solving has also emerged in other studies. Make-believe is an important element in establishing a playful set and pretend players are more likely to use objects creatively (Dansky 1980). "Collectively, these findings are consistent with Piaget's contention that symbolic play can be a source of creative imagination" (p. 59). Over two decades ago Sutton-Smith (1968) identified play with objects as an important variable in divergent object use and as a basis for problem solving. Play in general, and pretend play in particular, promotes problem solving.

The writer would be remiss to omit the criticisms of research methodology for a number of studies of play and problem solving. Simon and Smith (1985) concluded that, "a major research effort should be directed at discovering whether children develop any significant part of their intellectual skills through play experience" (p. 276).

In sum, the evidence is particularly compelling that play facilitates associative fluency (ability to achieve flexible, innovative solutions). Play not only establishes a "set" or attitude toward immediate play materials (Sutton Smith 1977; Dansky 1980) but this set transfers to subsequent encounters with problem solving materials and contributes to problem solving (Dansky & Silverman 1973, 1975; Pepler & Ross 1981). There is an empirical relationship between unstructured play and subsequently enhanced associative fluency.

Play and Creativity

Creativity may be defined as ideational fluency, flexibility, and originality (Wallach & Kogan 1965) and is closely linked to associative fluency, discussed above. Playfulness is a unitary trait characterized by spontaneity, manifest joy, and sense of humor (Lieberman 1965, 1977). Vandenberg (1980) and Krasnor and Pepler (1980) summarized the common elements found in most definitions of play: intrinsically motivated, spontaneous, self-generated, pleasurable, nonserious, flexible, and non-literal. The reader should note the similarities between playful behavior and creative behavior.

A growing body of evidence indicates a link between play and creativity. Lieberman's (1965) research supports the possibility of a link between play, creativity, and intelligence. Children who play (players) are better able to suggest alternate uses for objects than are non-players (Dansky 1980). Divergent thinking is linked with inventive, imaginary play (Hutt & Bhavnani 1976) and creativity in general is linked to playfulness (Lieberman 1965, 1977; Durrett & Huffman 1968). As we found in the examination of play and problem solving, several investigators conclude that players in group studies produce more nonstandard responses with objects and that play leads to a "generalizable set for the production of novel responses to objects (associative fluency) (Sutton-Smith 1968; Dansky & Silverman 1973, 1975; Dansky 1980).

Play Materials and Creativity

Children who play with unstructured or minimally structured (divergent) play materials perform better on measures of creativity than those who play with convergent materials (Pepler 1979; Pepler & Ross 1981) and they engage in a wider variety of fantasy play (Pulaski 1973). Children's activities with structured (convergent) materials are limited and unlikely to foster creativity (Goldman & Chaillé 1981).

Both indoor and outdoor environments are targets for providing a rich array of flexible materials for children's play. Creativity is not for the gifted few but for everyone who is allowed to play around with all the things that satisfy one's curiosity and give us pleasure. In a widely quoted and intriguingly titled article "How Not to Cheat Children: The Theory of Loose Parts," Nicholson (1971) said,

> . . . all children love to interact with variables, such as materials and shapes; smells and other physical phenomena, such as electricity, magnetism and gravity; media such as gases and fluids; sounds, music, and motion; chemical interactions, cooking and fire; and other people, and animals, plants, words, concepts and ideas. With all these things all children love to play, experiment, discover and invent, and have fun. (p. 30)

The common element in all these things is variables, or as Nicholson puts it, "loose parts." "In any environment, both the degree of inventiveness and creativity, and the possibility of discovery, are directly proportional to the number and kind of variables in it."

LANGUAGE DEVELOPMENT AND PLAY

Language has an important role during play but, conversely, play has an important role in the development of language. As the child explores or plays with objects, discovering meanings and relationships, language is attached and intelligent behavior is enhanced.

Language serves several functions during play (Smilansky 1968): it appears as an imitation of adult speech, it is used for make-believe (let's pretend); and it serves for the management of play in the form of explanations, commands, and discussion. In addition, speech allows children to amplify the meaning of what they visualize; it sustains their imaginative role; it enables them to hear themselves from the "outside"; it allows them to sense the inner conversation taking place between themselves and the person (within them) who is taking the role; and it adds new words to their vocabulary.

The research on language development and play is extensive. Most studies addressing the relationship between language and play have found a positive relationship (Goodson & Greenfield 1975; Mueller & Brenner 1977; Fein 1979; McCune-Nicolich 1981; Schirmer 1989). Levy (1984) conducted an extensive review of research on the role of play in language and cognitive development and drew several major conclusions:

1. Play stimulates innovation in language (Garvey 1977; Bruner 1983b).
2. Play introduces and clarifies new words and concepts (Chukovsky, 1968; Smilansky, 1968).
3. Play motivates language use and practice (Vygotsky 1962; Smilansky 1968; Garvey and Hogan 1973, 1977; Bruner 1983).
4. Play develops meta-linguistic awareness (Cazden 1976).
5. Play encourages verbal thinking (Vygotsky 1962).

Levy further concluded that using language to facilitate play, playing with language, and egocentric speech in play contribute to children's play and cognitive development (1984:59).

Only with humans does one find the games of childhood such as peek-a-boo and patty-cake that serve as preparation for technical-social life we call human culture (Bruner 1983). Such games offer a number of distinctive contributions to the development of language. They are the child's first systematic interactive language with an adult; they are an opportunity to get things done through words; they allow various means of reaching a *goal*; they require interchangeable turn-taking roles; and they distribute attention over an ordered sequence of events (Bruner 1983:46–47).

Early mother–infant interaction plays an important role in early language development. Mothers contribute by initiating and continuing interaction with their children. They use exaggerated voices, repeat utterances, and in other ways stimulate their infants to engage in paralinguistic dialogues.

By his second birthday the child dramatizes or pretends favorite roles (Waite-Stupainsky 1989). They have moved beyond the side-by-side play (parallel) with peers and the patty-cake games with adults to entering into and participating in role play with other children. Through role play they learn to take turns, follow themes, and share materials. Pretend play appears to aid growth and learning of both oral and (later) written expression (Yawkey 1983). The crucial elements in role play for language growth are make-believe with objects, role play involving situations and actions, and interaction and verbal communication.

By the age of three play with peers has become an important factor in language development. Play is a vehicle for language practice and language growth. Children imitate others but they also create their own words and phrases, sometimes engaging in nonsense dialogues which appear to have meaning for them. Teachers and other adults continue to promote language development by encouraging or providing games, puppets, songs, play materials, and stories. Language flourishes in the play of children and through the efforts of adults.

These early play activities are essential to later thinking, reading, and writing. They form what may be considered "readiness" for the more complex tasks of school. Although play continues to contribute to the child's social, emotional, intellectual, and linguistic life, it gradually reduces verbal interaction, reflection, manipulative devices (computers, television), and print.

Play with Language

A little-recognized but valuable activity is children's play with language itself. Garvey (1977) documented the progression of this activity beginning in infancy. During the babbling stage of 6 to 10 months, the infant produces a great variety of random sounds. By one year of age the child engages in long episodes of melodic vocal modulation of single vowels. As the child begins to talk, episodes of verbal play can be identified. The adult models early vocal play by tongue clicking, tummy tickling, and mock threats previewed by oooh sounds, all accompanied by signs of pleasure.

During the toddler period (two to three) children learn sounds that allow them to identify events and actions of self, others, and objects such as the telephone, dog, and automobile horn. Through speech children can now use these sounds to accompany their physical movements. Playing with sounds appears to be private activity or at least requires considerable familiarity with the play partner. This type of playful language exploration, repetitive and predictably structured, is a form of practice play.

Anthony experimented with nonsense syllables and words:

Let Bobo bink.
Bink ben bink.
Blue rink.

He substituted words:

What color mop.
What color glass.

He built up and broke down sentences:

Stop it.
Stop the ball,
   and Anthony jump out again.
Anthony jump. (Garvey 1977:65)

From about age three and a half virtually all types of language structures are used in social play. The analytical language, usually private, is replaced by language more like normal conversation in play with peers. This social play with language takes three forms: spontaneous rhyming and word play, fantasy and nonsense, and play with conversation.

Speech enters into all aspects of play as a vehicle for mere pleasure and as a means of managing complex activities of make-believe. For the most part early language play is spontaneously generated rather than quoted, having little ap-

FIGURE 2.5 *Speech enters into all aspects of play as a vehicle for more pleasure and as a means of managing complex activities of make-believe.*

parent relationship with home or nursery school experiences. But as children enter the stage of dramatic or make-believe play, familiar props and adult-type language enter play activities with increasing frequency. This seems to result from opportunities to interact with others rather than from explicit adult instructions. Piaget appeared to understand this principle for when asked to state the educational implications of his theory of cognitive development, he replied that there were only two: first, provide the child with a wealth of unstructured materials and ample opportunity to play with them; and, second, ask a lot of good questions.

Does Adult Intervention Make a Difference?

Given the important relationships between language and play, the natural inclination is to explore ways to enhance them. Does direct intervention by adults make a difference?

The answer to this question appears to be Yes. Smilansky (1968) divided disadvantaged children into three treatment groups. In group A the children were provided with a rich variety of experiences and field trips followed by discussions. In group B the children were systematically "taught" how to engage in and sustain sociodramatic play. Group C received a combination of treatment A and B.

Improvement in verbal communication, although slight, was noted in groups B and C. After the nine-week period of intervention, the children in group B engaged in lively, verbal negotiations, although the quality of discussion was far from adequate to satisfy the demands of the play situation. The children in group C showed even more marked improvement.

In a study by Lovinger (1974), a speech specialist interacted with 4- and 5-year-old children during free play for 1 hour per day for 25 weeks. The specialist used three levels of intervention: (a) following, adding to, and enriching the natural play of the children; (b) using experiences the children had to play out, such as a visit to the zoo; and (c) creating a play situation and encouraging the children to become involved. This daily hour of intervention was not a training program per se, and the children were not required or encouraged to imitate, but rather were encouraged to respond to the speech specialist's play and verbalizations in any way they desired.

The play intervention was effective in increasing the verbal expression and play complexity for the experimental group while no changes were found for the control group. The development of sociodramatic play in disadvantaged preschool children resulted in increased language use and increased their ability to deal with a psycholinguistic task (the verbal expression scale of the Illinois Test of Psycholinguistic Abilities). Thus, a functional relationship was established between play and language.

The wise adult is aware of the language activites of children, understands the nature and stage of their verbalizations, and realizes that language development is essentially a spontaneous process of trial and error as opposed to a process of imposed rules. The adult role is to provide a wide range of unstructured play materials and to serve mediating, motivating roles. There is time for individual privacy, time for social play, and time for interacting with adults. Some adult verbalizations help to extend play while others have a negative influence. Some motivate play not yet thought of by the child. A steady stream of adult talk is usually less helpful than a well-placed question or remark modulated in stress and rhythm to the circumstance of the moment. The facilitative, not the directive, adult is needed in children's play environments.

MOTOR DEVELOPMENT AND PLAY

The carefully conceptualized motor development program encompasses three major concerns; physical fitness, perceptual-motor development, and movement skills. Physical fitness refers to the functional capacities of the body (heart and lung or cardiovascular endurance, muscular strength, and flexibility). Perceptual-motor development refers to the child's ability to perceive and interpret sensory data and respond through movement. This includes time, space, direction, and visual and auditory awareness. Movement skills refer to basic locomotor skills, manipulative skills, and balance skills (Poest et al. 1990).

Physical Fitness

The physical fitness of American children is declining rapidly. While adults are devoting increasing time and energy to health and fitness, children are engaged in television viewing, other sedentary activities, and eating junk food. Consequently, children are fatter and less fit than their 1960's counterparts (Jambor & Hancock 1988). A study by Deitz and Gortmaker (1985) shows that watching television makes kids fat. Television contributes to obesity by promoting extended resting and metabolic rates, by reducing energy-extensive activities, and by promoting consumption of calorie dense or junk food through advertisements.

Sedentary lifestyles and junk food, coupled with increased emphasis upon academics and reduced physical education, play, and work, have resulted in a nation of flabby, short-winded kids with elevated cholesterol and blood-pressure levels and declining strength and heart-lung endurance (Winston 1984). These compelling conclusions are supported by studies by the American Academy of Pediatrics, the President's Council on Physical Fitness and Sports, the U.S. Department of Health and Human Services, and research by the American Alliance for Health, Physical Education, Recreation and Dance (Ross & Gilbert 1985; Javernick 1988; Dennison et al. 1988). Samples of the statistics show:

- Forty percent of 6- through 12-year-old boys cannot do more than 1 pull-up.
- Seventy percent of 6- through 17-year-old girls cannot do more than 1 pull-up.
- About 50 percent of American children aren't getting sufficient exercise to develop healthy heart and lungs.
- Forty percent of 5- to 8-year-old children have at least 1 of 3 risk factors for heart disease—high cholesterol, elevated blood pressure, or physical inactivity.
- About 50 percent of 6- to 16-year-old girls and 30 percent of 6- to 12-year-old boys cannot run a mile in less than 10 minutes.

In addition to extensive TV viewing and abuse of junk food, several other factors appear to be contributing to this state of affairs. The absence of adults during the daytime due to divorce, both parents working outside the home, etc., and associated fear of violence reduce the availability of support, encouragement, and availability of outdoor physical activity and nourishing food. Education reforms typically emphasize "academics" and "extended school hours" over play, play equipment, and physical education. National surveys of public school, public park, and preschool playgrounds (Bruya & Langendorfer 1988; Thompson & Bowers 1989; Wortham & Frost 1990) revealed that American playgrounds are hazardous and poorly equipped for the developmental needs of children. Among these three contexts for playgrounds—public schools, public parks, and preschools—the public schools rank a poor last in safety and equipment provisions. Further, public schools in eight states have no state-established requirements for physical education and only one state requires students in all grades to take physical education every day.

Clearly, there is no simple solution to these problems. Parents and schools have shifted the responsibility for children's physical exercise to other agencies. The typical school age child spends 80 percent of his/her exercise time in community centers, churches, and other group sponsored contexts (Ross & Gilbert 1985). We must continue to encourage participation in these settings while increasing involvement in home and school related contexts. Perhaps the most under-valued, yet potentially effective, physical exercise settings are the playground, public school, public park, preschool, and back yard.

Perceptual-Motor Development

Perceptual-motor is an apt term. The hyphen signifies the mutual dependency between perceptual information and voluntary motor activity. Perceptual abilities are learned and depend upon movement as a medium for this learning. Conversely, movement involves a perceptual awareness of sensory stimulation. If both abilities are to develop in a normal fashion, there must be a reciprocal interaction of perceptual information and motor or movement data.

Unfortunately the decline in children's perceptual-motor development has paralleled the decline in their general fitness levels. These perceptual-motor skill declines are particularly in the areas of visual, auditory, and time awareness (Weikart 1987). Fewer than half of first grade children and fewer than one-fourth of fourth to sixth grade children can pat or walk to the beat of a musical selection, mimic movements presented in sequence, or execute movements to verbal instructions.

The human body is wonderfully equipped with perceptual nodalities for transmitting information to the brain for organization and response. These nodalities are auditory (hearing), visual (seeing), tactile (touching), kinesthetic (feeling), gustatory (tasting), and olfactory (smelling). They are developed naturally or informally as children play, they are the subject of formal training as in physical education programs, and they are approached by special remedial and readiness programs.

Scientific studies of developmental patterns frequently result in the construction of tests to measure, and to formally intervene in, the activities of children. The application of tests and formal programs of instruction, thought useful for certain purposes, frequently interfere with normal development. This is nowhere more obvious than in perceptual-motor development.

Perceptual-Motor Training Programs

Over the years a number of perceptual-motor training programs have been developed. Three of the best known are those of Doman-Delacato (Delacato 1966), Frostig (1969), and Kephart (Chaney & Kephart 1968). Numerous publications by these people are available. The great majority of studies do not reveal special advantages of these over regular programs.

The American Academy of Neurology (18 = 967) issued a joint executive board statement discussing the lack of controlled studies of the Doman-Delacato method and cases in which the method did not help the patient. Freeman (1967) listed nine objections to the method. A pediatrician, Ottinger (1964), considered Delacato's data to be fallacious, the rationale poor, and the conclusions untenable.

Klesius (1970) reviewed 28 research studies on the effectiveness of perceptual-motor programs on reading achievement.

1. In general, perceptual-motor programs employing a wide variety of experiences appear to show promise with underachieving intermediate grade children and preschool children.
2. The effectiveness of Delacato- and Frostig-type programs is doubtful.
3. The inclusion of individualized perceptual-motor programs for kindergarten and primary grade children in physical education classes is developmentally appropriate.

Shick and Plack (1976) reviewed 16 studies concerned with Kephart's perceptual-motor training program to conclude that

The Purdue Perceptual-Motor Survey may screen perceptual deficiencies at a gross level but it is not a useful predictive tool. They also conclude that the only evidence that supports the contention that Kephart's training program enhances academic achievement exists in the form of case studies and these must be interpreted cautiously. Further, studies that use an experimental design do not support the claim.

Finally, extensive analysis of these and other programs (Nakken & den Ouden 1985) for children with severe motor or multiple disabilities led to the following conclusion: "We found almost no theoretical or experimental evidence in support of the use of these programs for brain-damaged children" (p. 49). The investigators believed that most of the formal psychomotor programs do not train functions specifically and do not take into account children's lack of experiences with interaction and communication. They suggested that training should be specific to diagnosis of individual needs, be planned individually for children, be conducted by the child's teacher, and be conducted in close communication with parents.

Movement Skills

There are certain fundamental movement skills that must be developed during the preschool years and further refined during the elementary school period. These are not dependent solely upon maturation but must be improved through regular instruction and practice (Seefeldt 1984). It is also clear that frequent opportunities to engage in free play are critical in enhancing movement skills. Both formal and informal programs take certain movement skills into account.

> *Gross motor activities:* throwing, catching, kicking, jumping, swinging
> *Fine motor activities:* cutting, lacing, hammering, buttoning, pouring
> *Body awareness activities:* naming, pointing, identifying, moving, and performing tasks using body parts
> *Spatial awareness activities:* moving, exploring, locating, comparing, and identifying using walking, running, catching, rolling, tunnels, mazes
> *Directional awareness activities:* moving, stationing, pointing, identifying, and imitating using body, objects, and apparatus
> *Balance activities:* walking, bounding, and clapping using balance beams and boards, trampoline, and spring boards
> *Integration activities:* hitting moving ball, tracking moving objects, matching visual and motor responses, and responding to auditory signals
> *Expressive activities:* art, music, dance, and dramatic play

The Playground and Motor Development

The research on effects of play and playgrounds on children's motor development is limited but the results are positive. Gabbard (1979) tested the effects of specific play apparatus experience on upper body muscular endurance of four- to six-year-olds. The results indicated that well equipped play environments, providing "upper body" movement variety, contributed to increased muscular endurance performance. Myers (1985) compared the motor behaviors of kindergarten children who participated in two different motor activity environments, a physical education class and a well-developed playground during free play. The children engaged in significantly more motor behaviors in free play than in structured physical education activities. In physical education, more time was spent in getting out supplies, waiting in line, and listening to instructions than was observed in free play. In free play, the students judged above average in motor skills were the more physically active ones. It appears that children with poorly developed skills need more encouragement and direction by adults. The most effective physical education or regular classroom teacher may well be the one who complements directed activity and free play activity. Abundant equipment to promote various motor functions is essential for both playgrounds and physical education settings.

Particularly for children with limited motor abilities, combinations of free play and directed motor activity should be employed. Kindergarten children receiving direct instruction in motor skills for 10 weeks scored significantly higher on a post-test than did controls (Matronia 1982). Developmental play programs improve the motor performance of mildly handicapped children (Roswal et. al. 1984; Jones 1987). The comprehensive developmental program should include the major components of motor fitness-coordination, speed, power, agility, and balance (Gallahue 1982) and may include locomotor skills (walking, running, hopping), stability movement activities (bending, stretching, balancing), gross motor activities (throwing, catching, propelling), and fine motor activities (lego play, block construction, threading, sand play).

Motor development is enhanced in both directed or physical education in free or spontaneous play. Directed activity has the advantage of concentration on specific motor/fitness needs while free play has the potential of developing not only motor skills, but also prelinguistic and linguistic skills, and creative cognitive and social abilities.

Enhancing Motor Development

Which direction should be pursued in nurturing motor development in children. The authors believe (based on case studies and direct observation) that specific programs such as those of Frostig and Kephart are useful in providing guidelines for understanding the nature of perceptual-motor development and for selective application with handicapped and low-functioning children. But even these children have potential rarely tapped on the sterile playgrounds of America. The exciting adventure playgrounds for handicapped children in London (Chapter 10) illustrate this contrast.

All too frequently, remedial and physical education personnel disregard the value of free play in perceptual-motor development. We are especially concerned that children in the early childhood (preconceptual) period have opportunities to develop naturally through play, without the ever-present test-perform-test cycle imposed by the adult whose primary concern is motor development for participation in sports. Motor skills are developed naturally during free play on the new creative playgrounds now appearing in greater frequency. Simultaneously, related skills are developing. Our greatest challenges are (1) to make exciting, challenging play environments available to all children both at schools and in close proximity to their homes, and (2) to provide facilitative adult leaders who understand that perceptual-motor development is but one among many important developmental tasks of children.

FIGURE 2.6 *Play enhances motor development*

CONCLUSION

The purpose of this chapter has been to examine the relationships between play and other aspects of human development and to make suggestions about the role of adults in children's play. Human development refers to the process of acquiring competence in dealing with the physical and social world. From the moment of birth, when children are thrust into an alien universe, they become explorers, attempting to discover through play, the rules by which the universe operates. Powerful forces interact to shape their development through the medium of play. Chief among these seems to be culture, supported, of course, by biology.

Culture governs the content of children's play and controls the rate at which they move through the developmental sequence of play. The playing of games aids in the enculturation of children, teaching them to cope with stress and preparing them, particularly in primitive cultures, for adult work roles. In modern societies, technology has complicated adult roles and heavily influenced the play of children.

Play is the chief vehicle for the development of imagination and intelligence, language, social skills, and perceptual-motor abilities in infants and young children. Development occurs naturally when healthy children are allowed freedom to explore rich environments. Adults can also influence development by becoming involved in children's play. This results in increased verbal fluency, verbal expression, imaginativeness, positive affect, concentration, and better performance on intellectual tasks.

Materials (toys, nontoy objects, and playground equipment) are critical variables in children's play. The primary way in which the child learns rules is through operations on objects. From Piaget's rich description of intellectual development, based on a model organism—environmental interchange—we know that when a child acts on an object in the environment, both the object and the child are changed, not in a physical sense, but in a mental sense. That is, play with objects follows a developmental progression and results in the development of intelligent behavior. Three factors, novelty, complexity, and realism, influence children's interest in play objects. Adult models, peer models, and television influence play themes.

Language and play go hand-in-hand. Play promotes imitation of adult speech while speech serves for the management of play in the form of explanations, commands, and discussions. Through play, both vocabulary and thought are extended and enriched. The involvement of adults in nonthreatening, facilitative ways increases the range and quality of language during play. In sum, children learn to master their environment through the wedding of play and language.

Motor development encompasses physical fitness, perceptual-motor development, and movement skills. Both formal and informal procedures are employed in fostering motor development. These include specific readiness and remedial programs, planned physical education programs, and supervised and/or free play on playgrounds. The appropriateness of specific programs is a subject of considerable professional controversy, and there is need for improvement in physical education programs, and the physical state of playgrounds.

The chief focus of this book, outdoor play environments, has been subjected to only limited research. However, the principles about play and development explored in Chapters 1 and 2 are directly relevant to the construction and use of playgrounds. Playgrounds should be developmentally relevant (accommodate various types of play) to the play needs of children. Complexity and variety of equipment influences play types, equipment choices, social behavior, and verbal interaction. The evidence for rebuilding the traditional American playground continues to accumulate. Just how to do this is the subject matter for much of this book.

REFERENCES

Arnaud, S.H. (1974). Some functions of play in the educative process. *Childhood Education* 51:72–78.

Barnaud, K., Bee, H., & Hammond, M. (1984). Home environment and cognitive development in a healthy low-risk sample: The Seattle study. Pp. 118–150 in *Home Environment and Early Cognitive Development*, ed. Gottfried. New York: Academic Press.

Benish, J. (1978). *Blocks: Essential Equipment for Young Children*. Charleston, W.V.: West Virginia State Department of Education. (ERIC Document Service No. 165-901).

Birch, H.G. (1945). The relation of previous experience to insightful problem solving. *Journal of Comparative Psychology* 38:267–283.

Bradley, R.H. (1985). Social-cognitive development and toys. *Topics in Early Childhood Special Education* 5:11–30.

Bruner, J.S. (1975). The ontogenesis of speech acts. *Journal of Child Language* 2:1–19.

—————. (1977). Early social interaction and language acquisition. In *Studies in Mother-Infant Interaction*, ed. H.R. Schaffer. London: Academic Press.

—————. (1983a). *Child's Talk: Learning to Use Language*. New York: W.W. Norton.

—————. (1983b). Play, thought, and language. *Peabody Journal of Education* 60:6–69.

Bruya, L.D., & Langendorfer, S.J. (1988). *Where our Children Play: Elementary School Playground Equipment*. Reston, Virginia: American Association for Leisure and Recreation.

Campbell, S.D., & Frost, J.L. (1985). The effects of playground type on the cognitive and social play behaviors of grade two children. In *When Children Play*, eds. J.L.

Frost & S. Sunderlin. Wheaton, M.D.: Association for Childhood Education International.

Cazden, C. (1976). Play and language and metalinguistic awareness. In *Play: Its Development and Evolution*, eds. J. Bruner, A. Jolly, & K. Sylva. New York: Basic Books.

Chaney, C.M. & Kephart, N.C. (1968). *Motoric Aids to Perceptual Training*. Columbus, OH: Charles E. Merrill.

Christie, J.F., & Johnson, E.P. (1983). The role of play in social-intellectual development. *Review of Educational Research* 53:93–115.

Chukovsky, K. (1971). *From Two to Five*. Los Angeles: University of California Press.

Clark, A.H., Ulyon, S.M., & Richards, M.P.M. (1969). Free play in nursery children. *Journal of Child Psychology and Psychiatry* 10:205–216.

Connolly, J.A., & Doyle, A.B. (1984). Relation of social fantasy play to social competence in preschoolers. *Developmental Psychology* 20:797–806.

Corrigan, R. (1982). The control of animate and inanimate components in pretend play and language. *Child Development* 53:1343–1353.

Dansky, J.L. (1980). Make believe: A mediator of the relationship between free play and associative fluency. *Child Development* 51:576–579.

Dansky, J.L., & Silverman, I.W. (1973). Effects of play on associative fluency in preschool-aged children. *Developmental Psychology* 9:38–43.

——————. (1975). Play: A general facilitator of associative fluency. *Developmental Psychology* 11:104.

Deitz, W.H., & Gortmaker, S.L. (1985). Do we fatten our children at the television set? Obesity and television viewing in children and adolescents. *Pediatrics* 75:807–812.

Delacato, C.H. (1966). *Neurological Organization and Reading*. Springfield, IL: Charles C. Thomas.

Dennison, B., et. al. (1988). Childhood physical fitness tests: Predictor of adult physical activity levels? *Pediatrics* 82:3.

DeMille, R. (1967). *Put your Mother on the Ceiling: Children's Imagination Games*. New York: Walker.

Doyle, A.B., Connolly, J., & Rivest, L.P. (1980). The effect of playmate familiarity on the socialization of young children. *Child Development* 51:217–223.

Eifermann, R.R. (1971). Social play in childhood. In *Child's Play*, eds. R. Herron & B. Sutton-Smith. New York: John Wiley.

Eisenberg, N., & Harris, J.D. (1984). Social competence: A developmental perspective. *School Psychology Review* 13:267–277.

Eriksen, E. (1956). *Childhood and Society*. New York: Norton.

Fein, G.G. (1979). Play in the acquisition of symbols. In *Current Topics in Early Childhood Education*, ed. L. Katz. Norwood, NJ: Ablex.

Fein, G., & Stork, L. (1981). Sociodramatic play: Social class effects in integrated preschool classrooms. *Journal of Applied Developmental Psychology* 2:267–279.

Feitelson, D. (1977). Cross-cultural studies of representational play. Pp. 6–14 in eds. B. Tizard & D. Harvey. Philadelphia: Lippincott.

Ford, M.E. (1982). Social cognition and social competence in adolescence. *Developmental Psychology* 18:323–340.

Freeman, R.D. (1967). Controversy over "patterning" as a treatment for brain damage in children. *American Medical Association Journal*, 202, 358–385.

Freud, A. (1971). *Normality and Pathology in Childhood: Assessments of Development*. New York: International Universities Press.

Frost, J.L. (1968). *Early Childhood Education Rediscovered*. New York: Holt, Rinehart and Winston.

Frost, J.L., & Strickland, E. (1978). Equipment choices of young children during free play. *Lutheran Education* 114:34–46.

Frostig, R.D. (1967). *Move—Grow—Learn*. Chicago: Follett.

Gabbard, C. (1979). Playground apparatus experience and muscular endurance among children 4-6. (ERIC Document Reproduction Service, SP 022 020; ED 228 190)

Gallahue, D. (1982). *Developmental Movement Experiences for Children*. New York: John Wiley.

Garvey, C. (1977). *Play*. Cambridge, MA: Harvard University Press.

Garvey, C., & Hogan, R. (1973). Social speech and social interaction: Egocentricism; revisited. *Child Development* 44:565–568.

Goldberg, M., & Harvey, J. (1983). A nation at risk: The report of the national commission on excellence in education. *Phi Delta Kappan* 65:14–18.

Goldman, B.D., & Ross, H.D.(1978). Social skills in action: An analysis of early peer games. In *Studies in Social and Cognitive Development*, vol. 1, eds. J. Glick and K.A. Clarke-Stewart.

Goldman, J., and Chaillé, C. (1981). Object use in the preschool: An underdeveloped resource. Paper presented at the Biennial meeting of the Society for Research in Child Development, Boston.

Golumb, C. (1979). Pretense play- a cognitive perspective. In *Symbolic Functioning in Childhood*, eds. N. Smith & M. Franklin. New York: Wiley.

Goodson, B., & Greenfield, P. (1975). The search for structural principles in children's play. *Child Development* 39:734–746.

Griffing, P. (1980). The relationship between socioeconomic status and sociodramatic play among black kindergarten children. *Genetic Psychological Monographs* 101:3–34.

Groos, K. (1898). *The Play of Animals*. New York: D. Appleton.

Gustafson, G.E., Green, J.A., & West, M.J. (1980). The infants' changing role in mother-infant games: The growth of social skills. *Infant Behavior and Development* 2:301–308.

Hartley, R.E., Frank, K.L., & Goldenson, R.M. (1952). *Understanding Children's Play*. New York: Columbia University Press.

Hartup, W.W. (1976). Peer interaction and the behavioral development of the individual child. In *Psychopathology and Child Development*, eds. E. Schlopfer & R. Reichler. New York: Plenum.

Hay, D.F. (1979). Cooperative interactions and sharing between very young children and their parents. *Developmental Psychology*, 5, 647–653.

Henniger, M.L. (1985). Preschool children's play behaviors in an indoor and outdoor environment. In *When Children Play*, eds. J.L. Frost and S. Sunderlin. Wheaton, MD: Association for Childhood Education International.

Hops, H. (1983). Children's social competence and skill: Current research practices and future directions. *Behavior Therapy* 14:3–18.

Huston-Stein, A., Friedrich-Cofer, L., & Susman, E.J. (1977). The relation of classroom structure to social behavior, imaginative play, and self-regulation of economically disadvantaged children. *Child Development* 48:908–916.

Hutt, C., & Bhavnani, R. (1976). Predictions from play. In *Play*, eds. J.S. Bruner, A. Jolly, & K. Sylva. New York: Penguin.

Jackson, T.A. (1942). Use of sticks as a tool for young chimpanzees. *Journal of Comparative Psychology* 34:223–235.

Jambor, T., & Hancock, K. (1988). The potential of the physical education teacher as play leader. Paper presented at the American Association for the Child's Right to Play Conference, Washington, D.C.

Javernick, E. (1988). Johnny's not jumping: can we help obese children? *Young Children* 43:18–23.

Johnson, J.E., Christie, J.F., & Yawkey, T.D. (1987). *Play and Early Childhood Development.* Glenview, Illinois.

Jones, C. (1987). Using the soft-play room as an educational environment for the young child and those with special educational needs. *British Journal of Physical Education* 18:227–229.

Klesius, S.E. (1970). Perceptual-motor development and reading. (E.R.I.C. ED 040 823, Microfiche)

Krasnor, L., & Pepler, D. (1980). The study of children's play: Some suggested future directions. *New Directions for Child Development* 9:85–94.

Ladd, G., & Mize, J. (1983). A cognitive-learning model of social-skill training. *Psychological Review* 90:127–157.

Lamb, M.E. (1976). *The Role of the Father in Child Development.* New York: Wiley.

Leacock, E. (1971). At play in African villages. *Natural History,* special supplement on play, 60–65.

Levy, A.K. (1984). The language of play: The role of play in language development. *Early Child Development and Care* 17:49–62.

Lieberman, J.N. (1965). Playfulness and divergent thinking: An investigation of their relationship at the kindergarten level. *Journal of Genetic Psychology* 107:219–224.

————. (1977). *Playfulness: Its Relationship to Imagination and Creativity.* New York: Academic Press.

Lovinger, S.L. (1974). Sociodramatic play and language development in preschool disadvantaged children. *Psychology in the Schools,* 11, 313–320.

Matronia, C.A. (1982). Relationship of direct instruction and practice to development of motor skills. (ERIC Document Retrieval Service, ED 239774)

Maudry, M., & Nekula, M. (1939). Social relations between children of the same age during the first two years of life. *Journal of Genetic Psychology* 54:193–215.

McCune-Nicolich, L. (1981). Toward symbolic functioning: Structure of early pretend games and potential parallels with language. *Child Development* 52:785–797.

Mueller, E. (1979). Toddlers + toys = an autonomous social system. In *The Child and its Family,* eds. M. Lewis & L. Rosenblum. New York: Plenum.

Mueller, E., & Brenner, J. (1977). The origins of social skills and interaction among playgroup toddlers. *Child Development* 48:854–861.

Mueller, E., & Lucas, J. (1975). A developmental analysis of peer interactions among toddlers. In *Friendship and Peer Relations,* eds. M. Lewis & L.A. Rosenblum. New York: Wiley.

Murphy, L.B. (1972). Infant's play and cognitive development. In *Play and Development,* ed. M.W. Piers. New York: W.W. Norton.

Myers, G.D. (1985). Motor behavior of kindergartners during physical education and free play. In *When Children Play,* eds. J.L. Frost & S. Sunderlin. Wheaton, MD: Association for Childhood Education International.

Nakken, Hanand den Ouden, & Wouter, J. (1985). Research on a psychomotor program with severe motor or multiple disabilities. *International Journal of Rehabilitation Research* 8:47–60.

Nicholson, S. (1971). How not to cheat children: The theory of loose parts. *Landscape Architecture* 62:30–34.

O'Malley, J.M. (1977). Research perspective on social competence. *Merrill-Palmer Quarterly* 23:29–44.

Ottinger, L. (1964). The theory from the standpoint of pediatrics. In Claremont Reading Conference 28th Yearbook, 28, 123–136.

Pellagrini, A.D. (1982). Development of preschoolers social-cognitive play behaviors. *Perceptual and Motor Skills,* 55, 1109–1110.

Pepler, D.J. (1979). *Effects of Convergent and Divergent Play Experience on Preschooler's Problem-Solving Behaviors.* Unpublished doctoral dissertation, University of Waterloo.

Pepler, D.J., & Ross, H.S. (1981). The effects of play on convergent and divergent problem solving. *Child Development* 52:1202–1210.

Poest, C.A., Williams, J.R. Witt, D.D., & Atwood, M.E. (1990). Challenge me to move: Large muscle development in young children. *Young Children* 45:4–10.

Pulaski, M.A. (1973). Toys and imaginative play. In *The Child's World of Make-believe,* ed. J.L. Singer. New York: Academic Press.

Putallaz, M. & Gottman, J.M. (1982). Pp. 1–33 in *Improving Children's Competence,* eds. P. Karoly and J.J. Steffen. Lexington, KY: Lexington Books.

Ratner, N., & Bruner, J.S. (1978). Games, social exchange, and the acquisition of language. *Journal of Child Language* 5:391–401.

Roberts, J.M., Arth, M.J., & Bush, R.R. (1959). Games in culture. *American Anthropologist* 61:597–605.

Roberts, J.M., & Sutton-Smith, B. (1962). Child training and game involvement. *Ethnology* 1:166–185.

Rogers, D.L. (1985). Relations between block play and the social development of young children. *Early Child Development and Care* 20:245–261.

Roopnaire, J.L., & Mounts, N.S. (1985). Mother-child and father-child play. *Early Child Development and Care* 20:157–169.

Rosen, C.E. (1974). The effects of sociodramatic play on problem solving among culturally disadvantaged children. *Child Development* 45:920–927.

Ross, H.S., & Kay, D.A. (1980). *New Directions For Child Development* 9:17–31.

Ross, H.S., Goldman, B.D., & Hay, D.F. (1979). Features and functions of infant games. In *Play and Learning,* ed. B. Sutton-Smith. New York: Gardner Press.

Ross, J., & Gilbert, G. (1985). The national children and youth fitness study: A summary of the findings. *Journal of Health, Physical Education, Recreation and Dance* 56:45–60.

Rubin, K.H., Fein, G.G., & Vanderberg, B. (1983). Play. In *Handbook of Child Psychology*: vol. IV, ed. P.M. Mussen. New York: John Wiley.

Rubin, K.H., & Marioni, L. (1975). Play preference and its relationship to egocentrism, popularity and classification skills in preschoolers. *Merrill-Palmer Quarterly* 21:171–179.

Schiller, P.H., (1957). Innate motor action as a basic of learning. In *Instinctive Behavior*, ed. C.H. Schiller. New York: International University Press.

Schirmer, B.R. (1989). Relationship between imaginative play and language development in hearing-impaired children. *American Annals of the Deaf* 134:219–222.

Schwartzman, H.B. (1976a). The anthropological study of children's play. *Annual Review of Anthropology* 5:289–328.

————. (1976b). Children's play: A sideways glance at make believe. In *The Anthropological Study of Play: Problems and Prospects*, eds. D.F. Lancy & B.A. Lindall. Cornwall, New York: Leisure Press.

————. (1978). *Transformations: The Anthropology of Children's Play*. New York: Plenum.

————. (1979). The sociocultural context of play. In *Play and Learning*, ed. B. Sutton-Smith. New York: Gardner Press.

Seagoe, M.V. (1971). A comparison of childrens play in six modern cultures. *Journal of School Psychology* 9:61–72.

Seefeldt, V. (1984). Physical fitness in preschool and elementary school-aged children. *Journal of Physical Education, Recreation, and Dance* 55:33–40.

Shick, J. & Plack, J.J. (1967). Kephart's perceptual-motor training program. *Journal of Physical Education and Recreation*, 47, 58–59.

Shure, M.B. (1981). Social competence as problem solving skill. Pp. 158–185 in *Social Competence*, eds. J.D. Wine & M.D. Smye. New York: Guilford Press.

Siegel, L. (1984). Home environment influences on cognitive development in pre-term and full-term children during the first 5 years. Pp. 197–234 in *Home Environment and Early Cognitive Development*, ed. A. Gottfried. New York: Academic Press.

Simon, T., & Smith, P.K. (1985). Play and problem solving: A paradigm questioned. *Merrill-Palmer Quarterly* 31:265–277.

Smilansky, S. (1968). *The Effects of Sociodramatic Play on Disadvantaged Preschool Children*. New York: John Wiley.

Smith, P.K. & Dodsworth, D. (1978). Social class difference in the fantasy play of preschool children. *Journal of Genetic Psychology*, 133, 183–190.

Smith, P.K., & Dutton, S. (1979). Play and training in direct and innovative problem solving. *Child Development* 50:830–836.

Starks, E.B. (1960). *Block-building*. Washington, D.C.: National Education Association. (ERIC Document Service No. 020-011)

Sutton-Smith, B. (1967). The role of play in cognitive development. *Young Children.* 22:361–370.

————. (1968). Novel responses to toys. *Merrill-Palmer Quarterly* 14:151–158.

————. (1972). *The Folkgames of Children*. Austin: The University of Texas Press.

————. (1977). Towards an anthropology of play. In *Studies in the Anthropology of Play*, ed. P. Stevens. West Point, New York: Leisure Press.

————. (1985). Play research: State of the art. In *When Children Play*, eds. J. Frost & S. Sunderlin. Washington, D.C.: Association for Childhood Education International.

Sutton-Smith, B., & Heath, S.B. (1981). Paradigms of pretense. *Quarterly Newsletter of the Laboratory of Comparative Human Cognition* 3:41–45.

Sylva, K. (1977). Play and learning. In *Biology of Play*, eds. B. Tizard & D. Harvey. London: Heineman.

Sylva, K., Bruner, J., & Genova, P. (1976). The role of play in the problem-solving of children 3–5 years old. In *Play-Its Role in Development and Evolution*, eds. J. Bruner, A. Jolly, & K. Sylva. New York: Penguin.

Thompson, D., & Bowers, L. (1989). *Where our Children Play: Public Park Playground Equipment*. Reston, Virginia: American Association for Leisure and Recreation.

Tizard, B., Philps, J., & Plewis, I. (1976). Play in preschool centers-II. Effects on play of the child's social class and of the educational orientation of the center. *Journal of Child Psychology and Psychiatry* 17:265–274.

Turnbill, C. (1961). *The Forest People*. New York: Simon & Schuster.

Udwin, O., & Shmulker, D. (1981). The influence of sociocultural economic, and home background factors on children's ability to engage in imaginative play. *Developmental Psychology* 17:66–72.

Vandenberg, B. (1980). Play, problem-solving and creativity. *New Directions for Child Development* 9:49–68.

————. (1981). The role of play in the development of insightful tool-using strategies. *Merrill-Palmer Quarterly* 27:97–109.

Van Lawick-Goodall, J. (1976). Early tool using in wild chimpanzees. In *Play—Its Role in Development and Evolution*, eds. J. Bruner, A. Jolly, & K. Sylva. New York: Basic Books.

Vygotsky, K. (1962). *Thought and Language*, trans. E. Hanfman & G. Valar. Cambridge: M.I.T. Press (original work published in 1934).

————. (1978). *Mind in Society*. Cambridge, MA.: Harvard University Press.

Wacks, T. (1978). The relationship of infants physical environment to their performance at 2½ years. *International Journal of Behavioral Development* 1:51–65.

Waite-Stupiansky, S. (1989). Sociodramatic play and language development. *Scholastic Pre-K Today* 32–34.

Wallach, M.A., & Kogan, N. (1965). *Modes of Thinking in Young Children: A Study of the Creativity-Intelligence Distinction*. New York: Holt, Rinehart, and Winston.

Waters, E. & Sroufe, L.A. (1983), Social competence as a developmental construct. *Developmental Psychology*, 3, 79–97.

Weikart, P.S. (1987). *Round the circle: Key experiences in movement for children ages three to five*. Ypsilanti, ML: High Scope Press.

Winston, P. (1984). Despite fitness boom, the young remain unfit. *Education Week* (Oct. 31, 1984):9.

Wortham, S.C., & Frost, J.L. (1990). *Playgrounds for Young Children: American Survey and Perspectives*. Reston, Virginia: American Alliance for Health, Physical Education, Recreation, and Dance.

Yawkey, T.D. (1983). Pretend play and language growth in young children.

Zigler, E., & Trickett, P.K. (1978). IQ, social competence and evaluation of early childhood intervention programs. *American Psychologist* 9:789–798.

"... the otherness or 'as ifness' of play and games can be the fantasy of Alice in Wonderland or the demoniacal possession of professional football ... a contest, a representation or a transformation ... the ultimate reality or the ultimate unreality."[1]

3

Contemporary Issues in Play

As interest in play grows and research accumulates, new issues are raised and new evidence, sometimes conflicting, emerges. Essentially, this entire book is about issues and evidence (with a sprinkling of author opinion) but certain issues are particularly relevant or volatile and deserve highlighting here:

- **Gender Differences.** Do boys and girls play differently? Do some play environments favor one gender over the other? Are gender differences cultural or biological?
- **Work vs. Play.** Is the old axiom, "The child's play is the child's work," accurate? How do play and work differ? Should play be distinguished from activities that are non-play?
- **Television, War Toys, and Aggression in Play.** What are the effects of television on play and development? Should television be monitored by adults? Are war toys and war cartoons harmful? Is rough-and-tumble a legitimate form of play? Does rough-and-rumble differ from violent play?

---

[1]Brian Sutton-Smith (1985). Play research: State of the art. P. 16 in *When Children Play*, eds. J.L. Frost & S. Sunderlin. Wheaton, MD: Association for Childhood Education International.

GENDER DIFFERENCES IN PLAY

Gender or sex differences in children's play is a common topic of interest to both researchers and practitioners. Although it is commonly acknowledged that differences are observed very early in life, the sources of these differences are matters of conjecture and disagreement. One of the common ways of exploring the issue is through toy and game preferences.

Sex differences in toy preference appear as early as 13–14 months (Jacklin, Maccoby, & Dick, 1975). Goldberg and Lewis (1969) found striking sex differences in 13-month-old infants toward their mothers and in their play. Girls were found to be more dependent, showed less exploratory behavior, and their play reflected a quieter style. Boys were independent, showed more exploratory behavior, played with toys requiring gross motor activity, were more vigorous, and tended to run and bang in their play. Fein et. al. (1975) found that the toy preferences of 20-month-old children during free play and toy ownership match adult stereotypes. In relation to toy ownership, girls were less likely to have boy toys and boys were less likely to have girl toys. Rosenberg and Sutton-Smith (1960) conducted a large-scale survey of the play activities of boys and girls. The results showed that, while the play activities conformed to sex role stereotypes, girls now evidence greater interest in male activities than in the past.

By age 18 to 24 months many children exhibit sex-typed behavior, both at home and in group child care settings (Huston 1983; Perry, White, & Perry 1984; O'Brien & Huston 1985a). Parents select toys and play activities for their children and, in so doing, promote gender stereotypes (O'Brien & Huston 1985a; Eisenberg et al. 1985).

As children play with sex-typed toys, differences in behaviors are observed. Blocks elicit high levels of aggression (Gump 1975); play with dolls elicits social proximity, nurturance, and role play (Liss 1983); masculine toys such as action dolls and trucks elicit motor activity (O'Brien & Huston 1985b; Liss 1983).

Caldera, Huston, and O'Brien (1989) examined the social interaction and play patterns of parents and toddlers (18–23 months) with feminine, masculine, and neutral toys. The feminine toys were dolls and a kitchen set. The masculine toys were trucks, a car, and blocks. The neutral toys were puzzles and shape sorters. Fathers with sons were most excited when opening a box of masculine toys and least excited when opening a box of feminine toys. Mothers with daughters were most excited when opening a box of feminine toys and least excited when opening a box of neutral toys.

The toddlers active involvement differed according to the category of toys played with. Boys were more actively involved than girls with masculine toys and girls were more actively involved than boys with feminine toys. Similarly, boys rejected feminine toys more than girls, and girls rejected masculine toys more than boys. Parents responded more positively to, and were more involved with, same-sex than cross-sex toys. They did not overtly promote or discourage play with either type of toys, yet subtly modeled by their interest and involvement. Some parents exhibited difficulty with the instructions when they required play with cross-sex toys. When one father and daughter opened a box of trucks the father said, "Oh, they must have boys in this study," closed the box, and returned to playing with dolls (Caldera, Huston & O'Brien 1989:75).

The major finding of this study was that sex-stereotyped toys had clear effects on parent–child interaction, irrespective of the gender of the parent or child. Masculine toys were associated with low levels of teaching and questions, low levels of proximity between parents and children, and high levels of correction. Play with feminine toys was associated with more verbal interactions (comments and questions) and close physical proximity. Neutral toys, commonly viewed as relevant to cognitive development, elicited more positive and informative verbal behavior from the parents than did either the masculine or feminine toys.

The evidence strongly supports the view that sex differences in behavior result, in part, from toy differences. Parents help to socialize children's sex-typed play through involvement (modeling, questioning, interacting).

Sex differences in toy selection persist into preschool. Three-to five-year-old boys prefer blocks, tools, manipulatives, and transportation toys, while girls prefer art activities, kitchen utensils, dolls, and dressing up. Boys play is more active and aggressive and girls is more nurturant (Fagot 1977; Liss 1981). The make-believe play of girls features domestic themes while boys are involved in adventure and fantasy themes (Singer 1973; Fein 1981). There are indications that fathers helping at home and reduction of sex stereotyping in preschools may be modifying sex-typed play. Beeson and Williams (1985) found that play choices of preschool boys had expanded to include house play, even though male-oriented play activities (art activities) continued to be same-sex oriented.

Gender Differences in Playgrounds

Only a limited number of studies of sex differences have been conducted in outdoor play environments. In a study prepared for *Ms.* magazine, Lever (1977) observed 181, 10- and 11-year-old boys and girls for nearly a year. The girls tended to play indoors, limiting their body movement, their vocal expression, and their play areas. Boys on the other hand preferred outdoor play, especially team sports and fantasy games such as "war." They played in larger, more mixed age groups and learned to resolve disputes more quickly. Lever believes that play for the fifth-grade boy provides a direct rehearsal for competitive work situations and survival in the adult world.

Significant sex differences are also found among younger children on playgrounds. In a study of second-graders boys engaged in richer forms of play—dramatic and games with rules—more frequently than girls (Campbell & Frost 1985). The girls played at the lower levels—parallel and functional—more frequently than the boys. Similarly, Henniger's (1985) study of nursery school children revealed differences between boy and girl play. In the indoor environment there were significantly greater amounts of dramatic play for girls and constructive play for boys. The outdoor environment was observed to be an important stimulus for the dramatic play of boys.

Tizard, Philps, and Plewis (1976) studied preschool children (ages 3–4) during free play on playgrounds at child care centers. Sex differences were most pronounced in the choice of play materials. Girls spent considerably more time than boys playing with fixed physical equipment such as climbing frames and swings, while boys played more often than girls with wheeled vehicles, and construction materials such as tires, crates and ladders. Boys played less often than girls with domestic equipment. At age three, the girls engaged in less symbolic play, less complex games, and a "lower level" of social play (solitary, parallel), but by age four most of these differences had disappeared or been reversed. The only differences remaining were the choices of play materials and the symbolic play themes (domestic for girls; driving vehicles, fighting, and killing for boys). Boys were more likely to engage in pretend fighting and in real fighting than girls.

The value of outdoor play at preschool centers was brought into question by Tizard, Philps, and Plewis. Having found that much of the play was sporadic and at a "rather low level," they suggested that the reluctance of the staff to become involved in play might well detract from the child's initiating and sustaining complex play themes, games, or construction and reduce their opportunities to learn from adults. Further, the "decidedly female orientation" of pre-school centers (predominantly female staff and preponderance of female sex-typed materials) may foster an early mismatch between the interests of boys and teachers.

It appears that outdoor play environments may be more favorable for boys than indoor environments. Several studies conclude that boys engage in more dramatic/fantasy play outdoors than girls (Sanders & Harper 1976; Frost & Strickland 1985; Campbell & Frost 1985). This suggests that open spaces and large apparatus for motor activity may be consonant with the play interests of boys and the masculine sex-role expectations of adults.

Gender Differences: Cultural or Biological?

Conclusions drawn from studies by Erikson (1951), Honzik (1951), and Lewis (1972) question whether sex-stereotyped play behavior is determined exclusively by social learning.

When preadolescents were asked to create an exciting motion picture scene using blocks, dolls, animals, and other toys, Erikson reported significant sex-related differences in the scenes produced. Girls tended to create indoor scenes, with significantly greater use of family dolls, furniture, and domestic animals, while boys characteristically created outdoor scenes, with significantly greater use of blocks, vehicles, and uniformed male dolls. In addition to these differences in choice of play materials, boys and girls could also be distinguished by the spatial configurations they constructed and by the themes related to these configurations. For example, girls showed an interest in open, inner space, as portrayed by scenes representing interiors of homes without walls, and in the entrance into that space such as ornamental gateways. Boys, on the other hand, were concerned with construction activity as represented by tall towers, turrets, and buildings. Girls also showed some anxiety about having the inner space intruded upon by animals, men, or boys, while boys indicated some anxiety about the collapse of erected structures or falling from heights.

While some of these differences may reflect learned, sex-stereotyped behaviors, other aspects of the findings are less easily explained by social-learning theory. For example, it is not clear why the concern for gateways and entrances should more likely be part of a girl's learning history than a boy's. Nor is it evident from the child's learning history why girls should be more concerned about intruders, or boys about buildings collapsing, especially since the likelihood of either event having actually occurred in the child's life was exceedingly low.

Erikson rejected the notion that sex-related differences in fantasy play are entirely a function of cultural conditioning. He concluded that the results of his dramatic production procedure reflected basic psychological differences that, in turn, reflect the differences in the anatomy and functioning of the two sexes.

While Erikson's study was primarily concerned with sex differences in spatial arrangements of the blocks and toys, Honzik (1951) was concerned with sex differences in the occurrence of various play materials used in the children's constructions. Using the same procedure and materials as Erikson, as well as a similar population, Honzik reported that boys used more blocks, vehicles, and persons in uniform at all ages, while girls used more play furniture and persons in ordinary dress. In addition, the boys' constructions suggested a greater output of energy and more varied use of materials. The girls, on the other hand, portrayed more passive, peaceful indoor scenes using the furniture and family figures.

In studies at the infant laboratory of the Educational Testing Service in Princeton, New Jersey, Lewis (1972) discovered sex differences in the play behavior of one-year-old infants. The girls were more likely to touch, stay closer, and vocalize to their mothers than infant boys. Boys explored their environment more than girls. Girls preferred animal toys more than boys, while boys played more with non-toy objects than did girls. The style of play also differed. Boys used more gross motor activity and girls used more fine motor activity. Lewis believes that these early differences may be due to three factors. One possible explanation is biological. Male primates, even rats, show more exploratory behavior than females. Second, parents teach their children sex role behaviors by reward and punishment. Third, children appear to learn rules which guide their sex role behavior.

Clearly, there is no definitive answer to the question of relative contributions of biology and culture to gender differences, Bettelheim (1988) argued that the belief that boys are innately more competitive than girls is largely a stereotype. Both are active and competitive but in different ways . . . "the basic difference is inborn and instinctive" (p. 46).

An extensive review of research on gender differences in *Newsweek* (Shapiro 1990) traced gender differences from before birth through childhood. Clearly, biology is not out of the picture. There are demonstrable differences between males and females in sex hormones, cardiovascular function, immune systems, brain functions, sensitivity to stimuli, bone growth, and fat storage. Yet, despite these biological differences, children are programmed from before birth (e.g., room arrangement, colors, clothes, toys) and at every successive stage to assume gender-specific roles. Differences such as boy's higher activity level are observable in infants but the typical observer needs clues such as haircuts, names, and clothing to tell the difference. By the age of four or five, children embrace their respective roles with determination. Boys for example, work out their power needs with guns and girls with "put-downs and social cruelty." Gender differences exist in academics; math and science for example. Girls do better in reading and boys in math, but such differences are clouded by questionable research methodology. The efforts of toy stores, child care workers and some parents to stimulate cross-gender play by providing "open-gender" toys and/or encouragement have met with mixed results. Limited involvement in cross-gender play in one context may be overshadowed by influences of television, toys, advertisement, games, and both peers and adults in other contexts.

The Role of Adults in Boy/Girl Play

Although we cannot determine the precise proportion, sex differences in the play behavior of children may, for the most part, be attributed to social learning. From birth, parents selectively reinforce sex-stereotyped behaviors based on cultural norms. This results in subtle differences in behavior during the first year of life. Psychosexual theories offer interesting but unsubstantiated explanations for sex differences in behavior. Recently, due primarily to popular media and professional literature concerning sexism in education and in child-rearing practices, the respective roles of boys and girls have been under intense scrutiny by professionals. Those concerned with the issue of sexist practices in education point to the fact that, from preschool through secondary schools, girls are directed toward traditional feminine occupations (teaching, nursing, secretarial, homemaking, and so on) and are discouraged from preparing for traditional male occupations (law, medicine, science, engineering, and business). With

FIGURE 3.1 *Adults influence children's sex-typed play through modeling, questioning, and interacting.*

regard to child-rearing practices, boys are taught at an early age that men must be strong, and not to show openly their emotions or affection. It is acceptable for boys to engage in rough-and-tumble play, but girls are expected to play quietly.

Many well-meaning adults mistakenly believe that it is their duty to actively teach appropriate sex role behavior and to quash what they believe to be inappropriate sex-related behavior. For example, young boys must not be allowed to spend too much time playing with dolls or allowed to dress up in women's clothing for fear that they will become sissies or worse. By age four, children spend a great deal of time imitating and acting out the adult behaviors that they observe. At this stage of development children may observe and act out the behaviors of both sexes. It is through the vehicle of sociodramatic play that children learn and practice sex-related roles of the specific culture in which they live. Adults must be sensitive to this need and provide opportunities for play that include a wide variety of behaviors and roles. It is also important that they provide play materials and encourage games representing minority cultures and seek to preserve the cultural identify of minority children.

PLAY AND WORK

Play in seventeenth and eighteenth century America was suppressed by both religious belief and legislation. By the end of the eighteenth century, play was gradually acquiring the approval of adults and higher socio-economic classes were engaging regularly in play. Child labor persisted in America into the twentieth century and lower socio-economic class children engaged in work to help support their families. During the twentieth century play and games became institutionalized and were formally confirmed in the 1930 White House Conference on Child Health and Protection which stated, "with the young child, his work is his play and his play is his work" (Ritchie & Koller 1964:206).

The writers of the Charter may have unwittingly confessed educator's distinction between play and work, for since its writing they have held firmly to the misguided tenet, *"Play is the child's work."* The consequences of this notion have fueled such false beliefs as "all children do in preschools is play," and that preschool teachers are merely baby sitters. It is high time to distinguish and contrast play and work and acknowledge that both are valuable, appropriate activities for young children.

The following will summarize and contrast the views of prominent professionals regarding play versus work.

John Dewey

Dewey (1966) sets his play/work distinction in an education/development context. When children have opportunities for physical activity which employs natural impulses or native tendencies, going to school is joyful and learning is easier. Native tendencies to explore, construct, and manipulate tools and materials, through play or work (the "active occupations"), engage the whole child, reduce the artificial gap between school and home life, and accomplish social and intellectual ends. Both play and work are employed by children in learning how to do things and an educational result is a by-product of play and work in most out-of-school activities. But these out-of-school activities are *incidental* and the resulting educational growth is more or less accidental.

Dewey acknowledges that his active occupations include both play and work. Both involve the entertainment of ends and the use of materials designed to affect the desired ends. The difference between them is time-span or directness of connection between means and ends. In play the activity is the end; in work the end is central and may be ulterior.

> When fairly remote results of a definite character are foreseen and enlist persistent effort for their accomplishment, play passes into work. Work is psychologically simply an activity which consciously includes regard for consequences as a part of itself. (1966:204, 206)

Subordinating activity to an ulterior material result, or carrying out activities under external pressure result in drudgery. In drudgery, there is no significance attached to the doing by the doer and the action is not intrinsically satisfying. Work regards consequences as a part of itself, while the ends of play are directing ideas which "give point to the successive acts" (Dewey 1966:203). In the practical sense there are no exclusive periods of play activity and work activity. Educationally or psychologically, mere amusement or aimlessness is not the defining characteristic of play and drudgery is not considered to be the desirable equivalent of work. Indeed, Dewey's play/work distinction is one of emphasis:

> Work which remains permeated with the play attitude is art—in quality if not in conventional designation. (1966:206).

FIGURE 3.2 *Since the 1930 White House Conference on Child Health and Protection, educators have held firmly to the misguided tenet, "Play is the child's work." Even children know the difference between play and work.*

Jean Piaget

Piaget (1962) examined the main criteria used for distinguishing play or ludic activities from non-play (non-ludic) activities, namely:

- Play is an end in itself but work (and other non-ludic activity) involves an aim not contained in the activity.
- Play is spontaneous but work is compulsive.
- Play is pleasurable but work is directed toward a useful result regardless of its pleasurable character.
- Play is devoid of organized structure but work is ordered.
- Play is free of conflicts but work ("serious activity") must grapple with conflicts.
- The act of play itself adds incentives not contained in the original action. Pleasure is gained through unrestricted combinations and play emerges (e.g., cleaning the table is not a game but may become so as the child introduces elements of make-believe).

In sum, Piaget concluded that these criteria do not distinguish clearly between play and non-play, but rather the distinction is one of degree "... the tonality of an activity is ludic in proportion as it has a certain orientation" (1962:150).

Piaget proceeds to tie the play/work distinction to his overall scheme of cognitive development "... if adapted activity and thought constitute an equilibrium between assimilation and accommodation, play begins as soon as there is predominance of assimilation." It follows, theoretically, that "pure play" would represent "pure assimilation," yet assimilation and accommodation always operate together. Consequently, play is bound up with thought as a whole and begins with the first disassociation between assimilation and accommodation. Let us explain further. Play, in the Piagetian scheme, is assimilation which is the incorporation of the environment (materials, mental images) to match existing concepts. When a child molds dirt and water into a pie or role plays a fictitious character, assimilation or play is taking place. When the child imitates an adult in copying a letter of the alphabet or in cleaning a paint brush, work or accommodation is taking place. Accommodation is the changing or modification of one's concepts or behaviors (schema) to meet the demands of the environment.

Johan Huizinga

Huizinga (1950) reflects that play is the direct opposite of seriousness, yet upon closer examination he contends that the contrast between play and seriousness is "... neither conclusive nor fixed. ... Some play can be very serious indeed" (p. 5). Play is not subject to exact definition either logically, biologically or aesthetically, so we must confine ourselves to identifying and describing the main characteristics of play. Play is a *voluntary activity*, never a task, done at leisure during "free time." Play is not "ordinary" or "real life" but "only pretending free time." It is a disinterested activity. That is, it is satisfying in itself and stands outside the immediate satisfaction of wants and appetites. Play *serves culture*, indeed it actually becomes culture. It is played out within *limits of time and space*; it begins and at a certain moment it is over, playing itself to an end.

All play *exists within a playground* identified or marked off materially (toys, etc.) or ideally (symbolic play) and all *play has its rules.*

Despite its resistance to exact definition, Huizinga believes that play is absolutely independent from other forms related to its truth and falsehood, good and evil, grace and beauty. He distinguishes play from non-play activities such as work when he states, "It (play) is never imposed by physical necessity or moral duty . . . it is free, is in fact freedom. ". . . It is not real life but only pretending (1950:6)."

L.S. Vygotsky

Similar to the deliberations and conclusions of Huizinga and Piaget, Vygotsky (1978) contends that common definitions of play are inaccurate. For example, pleasure is an insufficient definition, for many activities (e.g., sucking a pacifier) give the child a much keener sense of pleasure than play, and some games (those that can be won or lost) may lead to displeasure. Further, he believes that it is incorrect to view play as activity without purpose. In organized games and sports, the object of winning is recognized in advance.

Vygotsky distinguishes play as a leading factor in development. Play fulfills children's needs which change across periods or stages of development. With maturity, needs of the toddler replace those of the infant and, consequently, the nature of the play changes and matures. Imaginary situations are created to allow gratification of needs or tendencies that could not otherwise be gratified. The child does not necessarily understand the motives giving rise to such play. In this respect, play differs from work and other activities (1978:93).

Vygotsky traces the course of development through play into the school-age years. With maturity, play becomes a more limited form of activity, emphasizing athletics, which fills the needs of the school child. This change in play represents a growing emphasis on reality, and more complex forms of thought which are characteristic of advanced stages of development (e.g., Piaget's formal operations). It may be extrapolated that this shift or growth pattern follows a developmental trend from play to work.

Mihaly Csikszentmihalyi

Csikszentmihalyi (1975, 1990) too, takes the view that play and work are not necessarily opposites. Acknowledging that man at play is at the peak of his freedom and dignity, he set out to determine what makes play such a "liberating and rewarding activity." Perhaps, he reflected, if such experimental qualities could be better understood and applied to other human activities such as work, the quality of life could be improved. In his search for knowledge, he observed that artists were frequently "fanatically devoted to their work." Nothing else seemed to matter until they finished the painting, then all interest in it was abandoned.

From such observations and from the study of works of other scholars, Csikszentmihalyi identified three central sources or clues for resolving the riddle of why certain activities are enjoyable and others are not. First is intrinsic motivation, essential for play but, he believed, applicable to work and other non-play activities. Second (borrowing from figures such as Abraham Maslow and Marghanita Laski) are the concepts of peak experiences and self-actualization. Third, the phenomenon of play itself might give the unifying concept for resolving the issue of why some experiences are pleasurable and others are not. Play, he concluded, provides both peak experiences and intrinsic motivation (1975:xiii).

Csikszentmihalyi concluded that the deeply entrenched dichotomy between play and work is artificial, that the essential difference is not between play and work but between the "flow experiences" which are typical of play but *may* also be present in work and other non-play activities. The characteristics of flow are: (1) the merging of action and awareness. The person is aware of his actions but not of the awareness itself. (2) A centering of attention on a limited field or subject; a narrowing of consciousness to the immediate activity (as in a play theme). (3) A loss of ego and self-consciousness; integrating one's actions with those of others (as in games). (4) Being in control of one's actions and environment; being able to cope. (5) The existence of coherent, noncontradictory commands for action and unambiguous feedback for one's actions (as in play where the activity itself is the motive).

Csikszentmihalyi is not alone in emphasizing the experiential (feeling state) distinction over the structural one. Huizinga (1950), Callois (1961), and others held that a "spirit of play" prevails during play. Csikszentmihalyi set about to study the spirit or experience of play while others explored its structural dimensions.

In sum, the significance of Csikszentmihalyi's work in the context of this chapter is the elimination of a hard and fast distinction between play and work and the promise of extending the spiritual, joyful, flow qualities of play to work. Such extension is perhaps easier and more likely in simpler societies where the environment is more varied and less structured. The adventure playgrounds (Chapter 11) of Scandinavian and England are promising efforts to re-create simple yet complex environments and compensate for sterile, structured, hazardous urban environments. Csikszentmihalyi proposes (1975:201) that we should try to make the total environment one that is geared to growth—to the flow experience of play.

Conclusion: Is Play Work?

The five scholars represented here were in agreement that play and work are distinct but related activities. For Dewey, the difference is one of time-span or directness of connection between means and end. In play, the activity is the end; in work, the end is central and may be ulterior. For Piaget, the difference is one of degree—the relative emphasis upon assimilation (play) versus accommodation (work). Huizinga held that the contrast is neither conclusive or fixed. Some play is very serious. In Vygotsky's view play changes as children develop, becoming more serious and representing a growing emphasis on reality—that is, a shift from play to work. Csikszentmihalyi takes the view that play and work are not necessarily opposites, that the dichotomy between them is artificial.

There is general agreement that play is a special activity, possessing certain attributes or encompassing certain experiences that set it apart from other activities normally classified as non-play or work. Although play—in order to be play—must be true to these attributes or experiences, they *may* also be present in work. Whereas play must be pleasant, intrinsically motivated, etc., no such

TABLE 3.1   PLAY-WORK RELATIONSHIPS

	Qualities Essential for Play ⟵⟶	Qualities of Work
Dewey	Activity as end	End is central
	Employs native tendencies	Results are foreseen
	Incidental	Planned
Piaget	Assimilation	Accommodation
	End in itself	External ends
	Spontaneous	Compulsive
	Pleasurable	Utilitarian
	Free of organized structure	Ordered
	Free of conflicts	Conflicts
Huizinga	Voluntary activity	Planned task
	Pretense	Real life
	Free (freedom)	Imposed by physical necessity
Vygotsky	Imaginary need fulfillment	Emphasis on reality
	Play changes and natures	Developmental trend from play to work
Czikszentmihalyi	Intrinsic motivation	Applicable to work but rarely achieved in work
	Peak experience	
	Flow experiences	
	Spirit of play	

requirement is assessed for work—which may be pleasant or unpleasant, intrinsically or extrinsically motivated, etc. A fundamental conclusion of this analysis is that work, like play, can have playful qualities, ostensibly within the control of individuals, and that activities may have qualities of both play and work. Consider the work/play activities of the preschool, where children are free to make choices within limits but adults also assume guidance/teaching functions. Art, music, and gardening are common examples. Following Csikszentmihalyi, the *quality* of the experience sets it apart as play or non-play.

Wise adults can indeed ensure that playful qualities permeate the work experience. This is not to say that all activities should be playful nor that play should be the sole occupation of young children. Rather, children learn from both play and work and both are appropriate activities for home and school contexts. Just as this book is very specific about how children learn and develop through play, work also embodies an unlimited array of opportunities for learning and development. The task of the adult is to first come to terms with the fact that play is play and work is work, but they are complementary and integrative processes in learning and development. Then the adult is in a better position to enhance children's free, spontaneous play and also to temper the rigid structure of the typical curriculum with ludic qualities—freedom, spontaneity, and pleasure.

TELEVISION, WAR TOYS, AND AGGRESSION IN PLAY

In modern, industrialized societies, toys and television must be examined together, for since the advent of television there has been increasing linkage between the two. Many cartoons for children are essentially full-length advertisements for toys; in reality, toys in action. In popular programs—She-Ra, He-Man, Transformers, Rambo, G.I. Joe—life-like characters play out roles that children can emulate by purchasing the facsimile dolls and their clothing, weapons, and other related play objects. Some (e.g., Nintendo) have become so sophisticated that there is no distinction between the toy and the TV action. Children can now participate via television in the game, competing with a machine in a range of competitive games, including those featuring mass destruction. Between the ages of 6 and 18, American children view over 15,000 hours of television compared to 13,000 spent in school and they are exposed to 350,000 commercials and 18,000 murders (*U.S. News and World Report* 1985). In a sobering, incisive review, *Forbes* magazine (Newcomb 1990) portrays kids as runaway consumers of trivia. Parents' spending on kids' toys and related paraphernalia is growing at a record pace. Total spending on and by kids (ages 4–12) grew 25 percent in 1989 to $60 billion and is expected to reach $75 billion in 1990. The largest portion of kids' recreation dollars is spent on videogames—over $10 billion in 1989. Nintendo alone accounted for $1.8 billion of this—a thirtyfold increase since 1985. Even traditional toy sales are booming. Barbie doll sales are clipping along at $600 million in annual world-wide sales and new offerings include Barbie mansions that cost up to $400.00, fashion dresses with $120.00 price tags, and elaborate Barbie swimming pools. Kids are also influencing the movie market. Five of the eight box office hits (over $1 million each) in 1989 were oriented to kids: Batman, Indiana Jones and the Last Crusade, Honey, I Shrunk the Kids, Ghostbusters II, and Back to the Future II. Eight of the 10 bestselling videocassetes of all time especially appealed to children. In 1990, children were lining up to see the movie Ninja Turtles and to buy Ninja Turtle breakfast food, dishes, T-shirts, and toys. The prime time television smash, *The Simpsons*, a bug-eyed, irreverent, marginally literate family, threatens to spawn yet another wave of mind-boggling hyper-mania. The one ray of hope identified by Newcomb was the increasing sale of children's books, expected to exceed $1 billion in 1990.

The irony of this picture is that two extreme groups of children exist side by side in the United States and across developed versus underdeveloped countries. One, an overindulged, overweight, brain-dead group who live to consume; the other, a poverty ridden, neglected group whose chief motivation is day-to-day survival. Parents of the 1980's, the decade now widely recognized as the decade of greed in the United States, have been remarkably successful in cloning themselves.

Effects of Television

Research on the effects of television on children is painting an increasingly gloomy picture. Television heroes are replacing parents and public leaders as role models (*U.S. News and World Report* 1985). Watching television contributes to obesity in children, elevated cholesterol and blood pressure levels and reduced fitness (Winston 1984; Dietz and Gortmaker 1985). A California study (*Austin*

TABLE 3.2 COPING WITH TV (ADULTS)

Select Your Cable System Wisely
Select a TV Set that Cancels out Unwanted Channels
Review Schedules with Children
Place Limits on Extent of Viewing
Limit Your Own Viewing
Help Children Select Programs—Watch with Them
Discuss Programs with Children
Let Children Know What Your Values Are
Be Sure Your Viewing of TV Reflects These Values
Establish Priorities—Family Activities, Homework, TV
Substitute Family Time for TV—Talk, Church Events, Homework, Libraries, Art Activities,
    Nature Activities, Visiting Friends and Relatives, Working Together on Household   Jobs,
Playing Games, Free Play, Picnics, Gardening, Building Projects, etc.
Prohibit Viewing of Adult-type Programs (Violence, Sex). Restrict Viewing of the Most
    Violent Children's Programs (Discuss Alternatives, Reason, Evaluate with Children).

American Statesman 1980) of 500,000 school-age children concluded that the more students watch television the worse they do in school. Television, toys, and travel form a barrage of information that results in sketchy and incomplete knowledge, lacking in substance and integration (Zimiles 1982). Teachers may deal with a more knowledgeable student but they are dealing with a more confused person, one who is accustomed to being confused and sees little need to sort out his experiences.

Children are too exhausted from late night television viewing to engage in meaningful school work (Larrick 1979). The early years of childhood are violated by flooding the mind with sounds and images (Pearce 1985). When adults read to children they are required to *create* their own images. Trelease (1989) contrasts the relative effects of reading and television on literacy in children. An essential conclusion is that television detracts from the acquisition of literacy.

Equally compelling is the conclusion by Postman (1981) that television is robbing children of their childhood. With every existing taboo brought out of the closet for children to see, differences between what adults and children know and do are obliterated.

For over 30 years (Steinfield 1973), studies have shown that watching television violence leads to aggressive behavior in children, and the effects are long term. In 1972, the Surgeon General's Scientific Advisory Committee on Television and Social Behavior, having reviewed hundreds of scientific investigations, concluded, "We have impressive evidence that watching television violence causes a significant increase in aggressive behavior" (Steinfield 1973). During the 1980s the American Psychiatric Association, National Parent-Teachers Association, U.S. Surgeon General, and the National Institute of Mental Health all concluded that viewing television violence increases violence and aggression in children and adults. The National Coalition on Television Violence (1985) identified over 850 studies and reports of 120,000 people of all ages' showing the harm of television violence. These studies were conducted in twenty nations (United

States, Canada, Puerto Rico, Brazil, Japan, Taiwan, Australia, England, Scotland, France, Belgium, Germany, Finland, Poland, Sweden, Ireland, Denmark, Italy, Holland, and South Africa). Additional reports are available from Russia, Spain, New Zealand, Venezuela, Egypt, and Hong Kong, but formal studies have not been conducted.

> This research shows that the most common effects are: increases in anger and irritability, loss of temper, increased verbal aggression, increased fear and anxiety, and a desensitization toward violence. Increases in fighting, distrust and dishonesty, decreases in sharing and cooperation, increases in depression, willingness to rape, and actual criminal behavior.... (National Coalition on Television Violence [N.C.T.V.] 1983)

Cartoons and War Toys

Multi-million dollar budgets are supporting a growing number of war cartoons. The research shows relationships between viewing violent cartoons and violent behavior in children. Out of 31 studies from 6 countries (United States, England, Canada, Netherlands, Australia, and Lebanon) reported by the N.C.T.V. (1985), 28 found harmful effects.

A sampling of the research shows that viewing cartoon violence: increases aggression in children (Siegel 1956; Lovaas 1961; Mussen & Rutherford 1961; Bandura, Ross, & Ross 1963; Steur, Applefield, & Smith 1971; Ellis & Sekrya 1972; Ross 1972; Stein, Friedrich, & Vondracek 1972; Stoessel 1972; Hapkiewicz & Stone 1974; Wiegman 1975; Belson 1978; Day & Ghandour 1984; Singer, Singer, & Rapaczynski 1984), increases verbal hostility (Berkowitz 1970), reduces sharing behavior (Hapkiewicz & Stone 1974), increases emotionality (Osborn & Endsley 1971), increases anger and intensity of violent responses (Baron 1978), decreases enthusiasm for school (Zuckerman, Singer, & Singer 1980), produces anxiety (Koelle 1981), causes violence on the playground (Singer & Singer 1981), maintains long-term aggression (Huston-Stein et al. 1981), produces false understandings of social realities (Hawkins & Pingree 1981), reduces charitable behavior toward others (Teachman & Orme 1981), increases anxiety (Bjorkquist 1983), and increases negative play interactions and reduces imaginative play (Kolpadoff 1983).

The International Coalition Against Violent Entertainment (I.C.A.V.E. 1985) reports that war cartoon programming in the United States increased from 1½ hours per week in 1982 to 27 hours per week in 1985. War cartoons average 41 acts of violence an hour, with an attempted murder every 2 minutes. In 1985, the average U.S. and Canadian child saw 800 TV advertisements promoting war toys and 250 episodes of war cartoons designed to sell war toys. This is equivalent to 22 days of classroom instruction. The sale of war toys in the U.S. increased by 600 percent between 1982 and 1985.

A number of studies document harmful effects of playing with war toys. Playing with aggressive toys increases aggressive behavior of children (Feshbach 1956; Mallick & McCandless 1966; Mendoza 1972; Turner & Goldsmith 1976; Slife 1982). Such play may desensitize children to the dangers of violence and provides them with opportunities to rehearse, learn, and legitimize violent behavior. We are teaching violence to the next generation of children, not only in the United

States but around the world and the primary motive is corporate profit. The toy industry estimated that sales of war toys would reach $1.3 billion in 1985 alone, making up 7 of the top 10 selling toy lines in America. Each of these seven are promoted by war cartoons. Broadcasters are given war cartoons free by toy companies who build in national advertisements (N.C.T.V. 1986). War cartoons are used to advertise breakfast cereal and other food for children, much having questionable nutritional value.

There are several levels of cartoon violence. Those giving most concern are filled with intense militaristic combat, portraying opponents as evil and the appropriate solution as force or death (e.g., Transformers, G.I. Joe). The most violent cartoon in 1985, Dungeons and Dragons, was linked to over 40 real-life homicides and suicides. The Bugs Bunny and Roadrunner cartoons represent a second-level slapstick comedy, representing violence as a laughing matter. Such cartoons, though harmful, are considered less harmful than war cartoons. A third level of violent cartoons mixes pro-social material with a limited amount of violence. At the fourth and more desirable levels are cartoons with a great deal of pro-social material. The small amount of violence present is depicted as harmful and foolish and unsuccessful in resolving conflicts.

Parents and teachers are faced with a seemingly unresolvable dilemma in the face of such concern about children's television viewing. Peer pressure, universal availability of television sets, and the attraction of violent themes conspire to form an almost irresistible attraction. Few adults will prohibit television viewing in the home, for television has become a major source of information and enjoyment. The reasonable solution is ensuring balance in viewing, substitution of other meaningful activities for television, and on-going guidance by adults. Children should be assisted in making responsible choices and the amount of time spent in viewing should be balanced with other activities. (See Table 2). In early 1990, the American Pediatric Association recommended that children's television viewing be limited to 10 hours per week. This seems to be a reasonable goal, one that can be meaningful indeed if adults assume a responsible role in planning and evaluating with children and in providing alternate, developmentally relevant activities.

Perspectives on War Toys and War Play

During the late 1980s and early 1990s a new generation of war cartoons were introduced (Rambo, Karate Kommando, etc.), an extensive array of interactive war games (e.g., Nintendo) entered the market, and corresponding war toys flooded the toy stores of America. The widespread availability of war toys and the media emphasis on potential harmful effects led adults to take a range of positions and actions. Some chose to prohibit war toys. The Swedish government banned their manufacture and Malta banned their sale. The options exercised by parents and teachers ranged from banning war toys and war play altogether to facilitating war play.

A thoughtful, practical approach to war toys and war play was written by Carlsson-Paige and Levin (1987). Recognizing that play, including war play, is a primary vehicle for children in working out developmental issues (controlling impulses, discriminating fantasy and reality, etc.) and in early political learning (conflict, interdependence among people, etc.), they propose that adults facilitate war play. In so doing, they can influence the quality of children's play—helping to foster development—and can influence such political concepts of friends and enemies, good and bad, war and peace.

The approach to facilitating war play in classrooms taken by Carlsson-Paige and Levin (1987) promotes the entire classroom (or playground) as a context for reflecting nonauthoritarian and nonmilitaristic values—a place where adults listen to and respond to children's thoughts, feelings, and needs, and a place where conflicts are resolved peacefully (p. 53). Their guidelines for working with war play include:

- Helping children develop the quality of war play and the political understandings within their play.
- Helping children work with war play issues outside of play.
- Helping children establish limits for keeping war play safe.
- Helping children to make decisions about the type of war play and the type of weapons used (making weapons from open-ended materials).
- Helping children to expand gender roles in play.
- Studying children's play and assisting staff and parents in understanding and facilitating war play.

In their insightful book, *How to Play with Your Children (and When Not To)*, Sutton-Smith and Sutton-Smith (1974) contend that children must deal with warlike influences. They must experience fantasied courage and adequacy in their play so ". . . . you should not ban war play altogether and you should instead insist that children play in a make believe way" (p. 128). Pretend weapons and weapons created by the children themselves are clearly superior to realistic weapons for much of the value of play is in the *transformation* rather than the imitation. Piaget emphasizes the importance of the child's actions upon objects and symbols, which is assimilation, or play versus imitation, which is accommodation, or reacting to outside stimuli (demands, models).

The adult must also take into account the differences between real aggression and playful aggression (rough and tumble). After reviewing eight studies on war toys, Sutton-Smith (1988) concluded that all were unreliable yet he identified some common conclusions. The "greatest sin" in these studies was their "failure to distinguish between real aggression and playful aggression" (p. 64). Children themselves know the difference but adults frequently fail to distinguish between the two, and, consequently, forbid both forms of aggression. However, rough-and-tumble play has developmental value (Pellegrini & Perlmutter 1986), and it leads to games with rules rather than violent behavior in popular children. Rough-and-tumble play leads to aggression among rejected children who may have limited opportunities for modeling different social problem-solving strategies during play (Pelligrini in press).

Rough-and-tumble is engaged in by boys more than girls and boys play more aggressively. It becomes rougher and more varied with age (Smith & Boulton 1987) but no intent to hurt or injure is implicit in such play. As children approach puberty, rough-and-tumble begins to merge with true aggression but, in the main it occurs in a friendly, nonaggressive context. Indeed, sociometric studies show that rough-and-tumble partners like each other at all ages better than chance would predict, so the play appears to perform an affiliative function (Humphreys & Smith 1987).

FIGURE 3.3 *Toys should be simple in design so that the quality of imaginativeness comes from the child, not the toy.*

Aggressive activity of both types—rough-and-tumble and true aggression—are inappropriate in classrooms when space is limited and safety would be threatened. However, chase and other games involving rough-and-tumble can be played out in playgrounds which are designed for very active movement and large motor activity. The teachers role, similar to that in war play, is to facilitate peaceful, non-violent, active play involving toys and/or peers.

Making Decisions about Toys

What are the criteria for a good toy? Do the criteria change with the age of the child? Novelty is a critical element in the child's attraction to the length of time spent playing with a particular toy. However, the interaction between novelty and complexity inhibits sustained creative play. The amount of time children direct toward a particular play object is a function of the degree of novelty or number of novel elements contained in the object (Hutt 1966). When children are first presented with a novel toy, they explore the object in an attempt to determine what the object does. Once the various qualities of an object have been thoroughly explored and tested, children begin to play with the object. Once the novelty of the object begins to fade, the amount of time spent with the object also decreases. Complex toys that are very detailed in design are initially novel; however, the novelty soon wears off and the toy is disregarded.

The vast majority of toys purchased for children are of little or no value. Toys should be simple in design so that the quality of imaginativeness comes from the child, not the toy. Toys should be selected that will help establish an atmosphere conducive to dramatic play both in the school and at home. Many of these can be leftover items such as cooking utensils, empty containers, and articles of clothing. Toys that have multiple functions, such as building blocks,

TABLE 3.3   CHILDREN'S NEW TV PROGRAMS RATED* (1991 SEASON)

Ages 2–5	Ages 6–11
Best	*Best*
Tiny Toon Adventures (Syndication)	Maniac Mansion
Tale Spin (Syndication)	Big Brother Jake
Storybook Musicals	Captain Planet and the Planeteers
Jim Henson's Mother Goose Stories	(Syndication)
	Wake, Rattle, and Roll (Syndication)
Worst	*Worst*
Teenage Mutant Ninja Turtles (Syndication)	The New Kids on the Block
GI Joe (Syndication)	Uncle Buck
The New Adventures of He-Man	Guys Next Door
(Syndication)	
Honor Roll (2–5)	**Honor Roll (6–11)**
Sesame Street (PBS)	Reading Rainbow (PBS)
Mister Rogers Neighborhood (PBS)	Wonderworks Family Movie (PBS)
Storybook Classics (Showtime)	Square One TV (PBS)
Welcome to Pooh Corner (The Disney	3-2-1 Contact (PBS)
Channel)	Mr. Wizard's World (Nickelodeon)
Jim Henson's Muppet Babies (CBS,	
Syndication)	

*Rated by a panel of experts, *TV Guide*, March 2–8, 1991. 39,6–12.

are generally superior to those with more limited function, such as puzzles. Once the child can solve a puzzle it loses much of its value.

It is part of American folk wisdom that when you buy children an expensive toy, they soon tire of playing with it and discard it in favor of the box it came packed in. Why does this scenario typically occur? As the level of object complexity increases, the time spent playing with it decreases. A complex, highly detailed toy co-ops a child's ability to play creatively and imaginatively with the toy because it can only be used for what it was designed. The box in which it came, however, is a unstructured object that can be used as a space station, a hangar, a fort, an aircraft carrier, another spaceship, and so on. The best toys and play materials are those that are relatively simple in complexity and design, thus allowing children to supply the element of novelty with their imagination rather than having it imposed by the structure of the toy. This is true except for very young children who find it difficult to transform more than one object at a time, and who need realistic supports for their sociodramatic play.

CONCLUSION

A number of issues related to play and play environments are sufficiently meaningful and volatile to deserve special attention: (1) gender differences in play,

(2) work-play differences or play versus non-play, and (3) television, war toys, and aggression in play.

Gender differences are observable in infants and they continue through each successive developmental stage, becoming pronounced and readily observable by age four or five. The sources of gender differences are subjects of speculation and research. Most researchers acknowledge that biology plays a role but social/cultural influences are powerful contributors. Parents and teachers influence sex-role behaviors by toy selections, language distinctions, rewards and punishment, and performance expectations and should provide opportunities for boys and girls to play out a wide variety of roles.

In 1930, the White House Conference on Child Health and Protection formally stated, "With the young child, his work is his play and his play is his work." This misconception continues to hold favor among many adults, including child care professionals. The consequences include the assumption that all children do in preschools is play and that teachers are merely baby sitters. Distinctions between play are identified and explained by a large number of prominent scholars including John Dewey, Jean Piaget, Johan Huizinga, L.S. Vygotsky, and Mihaly Csikszentmihalyi. Although differing in specifics, they agree that play and work are distinct but related activities. Play is a special activity, having certain attributes and encompassing certain experiences that set it apart, both conceptually and practically, from activities normally classified as non-play or work. Work like play can have playful qualities and the common activities of preschools and primary schools may have qualities of both work and play, or work/play. Such factors as means/ends distinctions, seriousness of the activity, reality versus symbolic distinctions, source of motivation, and quality of experience set play apart from non-play. Since children learn from both play and work, beginning at an early age, *both* are developmentally appropriate activities for preschools and primary schools.

Television, war toys, and aggression in play are inextricably interrelated. Many war cartoons are full-length advertisements for war toys and junk food. Extensive television viewing is influencing aggression, health, school achievement, and symbolic functioning of children. Their play is increasingly dominated by television super-heroes and associated toys, clothes, and play themes.

There are several levels of cartoon violence ranging from the most objectionable level—intense militaristic combat—to slapstick comedy, pro-social/anti-social mixes, and the more acceptable level—pro-social cartoons. Parents and teachers should assist children in making responsible choices of television programs, in limiting television viewing, and in selecting valuable activities to substitute for television.

Several nations are considering bans on war toys. The central issue is one of balance. Many children in industrialized countries, especially the United States, are spending inordinate amounts of time watching violent cartoons, playing violent video games, and playing out war themes with war toys. Rather than assume the position that war play should be banned, parents and teachers can help children realize a thoughtful, acceptable balance in their play by encouraging them to make their own toys, encouraging make-believe play rather than merely imitative activities, encouraging other non-aggressive play through stories and books, and by making interesting non-war toys and equipment

TABLE 3.4   TOY SELECTION

- Selected multi-purpose toys (A Gun Can be Used for One Purpose Only)
- Select materials that allow children to make their own toys (tools, blocks, erector sets).
- Combine toys with natural materials (sand, water, etc.) and in natural settings (backyards, etc.).
- Select toys that expand discovery—seeds, soil, magnifying glass, etc.
- Select safe toys. Look for sharp edges, parts that can break off, parts that can cause choking, parts that can puncture or cut.
- Select toys that are durable—expect heavy use, abuse.
- Consider ages of children—select toys that can be used in different ways at different levels of development.
- Balance your selection—promote physical, intellectual-emotional, language, creative development.
- Match toys to developing interests (music, pets, board games).
- Avoid bombarding children with too many toys.
- Avoid toys that encourage voilent fantasy or games that encourage physical risk.
- Discuss toy selection with children.
- Limit the number and variety of "bought" toys, especially theme-specific toys. Encourage children to make or adapt toys.
- Consider involving children in donating toys to charitable organizations as they are outgrown and more appropriate ones are purchased.
- Ensure that toys reflect ethnic/cultural balance.

available. The adult can reasonably restrict these specific war toys while allowing war play, and in so doing, can assist children in developing political understandings and developmental issues. Finally, adults should distinguish between nonviolent aggression (rough-and-tumble) and real aggression and provide time and space for children to develop physical skills and social/cognitive learning through rough-and-tumble play.

REFERENCES

Austin American Statesman. 1980. Survey shows viewing tube graded an F. (November 8, 1980).

Bandura, A., Ross, D., & Ross, S.A. (1963). Imitation of film-mediated aggressive models. *Journal of Abnormal and Social Psychology* 66:3–11.

Baron, R.A. (1978). The influence of hostile and nonhostile humor upon physical aggression. *Peers Social Psychology Bulletin* 4:77–81.

Beeson, B.P., & Williams, R.A. (1985). Differences in the play of young children. In *When Children Play*, eds. J.L. Frost and S. Sunderlin. Wheaton, MD: Association for Childhood Education International.

Belson, W.A. (1978). *Television violence and the adolescent boy (England)*. Hampshire, England: Saxon House.

Berkowitz, L. (1970). Aggressive humor as a stimulus to aggressive responses. *Journal of Personality and Social Psychology* 16:710–717.

Bettelheim, B. (1988). Boys and girls at play. *Scholastic Pre-*

kindergarten Today ——:45–46.

Bjorkquist, K. (1983). Children's psychological, verbal, and nonverbal reactions to different types of film violence (Finland). *Aggressive Behavior* 9:115–116.

Caldera, Y.M., Huston, A.C., & O'Brien, M. (1989). Social interaction and play patterns of parents and toddlers with feminine, masculine, and neutral toys. *Child Development* 60:70–76.

Callois, R. (1961). *Man, Play, and Games.* New York: Free Press.

Campbell, S.D., & Frost, J.L. (1985). The effects of playground type on the cognitive and social play of grade two children. In *When Children Play*, eds. J.L. Frost, and S. Sunderlin. Wheaton, MD: Association for Childhood Education International .

Carlsson-Paige, N., & Levin, D.E. (1987). *The War Play Dilemma: Balancing Needs and Values in the Early Childhood Classroom.* New York: Teachers College Press.

Csikszentmihalyi, M. (1975). *Beyond Boredom and Anxiety: The Experience of Play in Work and Games*. San Fransisco: Jossey-Bass.

Csikszentmihalyi, M. (1990). *Flow: The Psychology of Optimal Experience*. New York: Harper & Row.

Day, R., & Ghandour, M. (1984). The effect of television mediated aggression and real-life aggression on the behavior of Lebanese children. *Journal of Experimental Child Psychology* 38:718.

Deitz, W.H., Gortmaker, S.L. (1985). Do we fatten our children at the television set? Obesity and television viewing in children and adolescent. *Pediatrics* 75: 807–812.

Dewey, J. (1966). *Democracy and Education*. New York: The Free Press. (Originally published 1916.)

Eisenberg, N., Wolchik, S.A., Hernandez, R., & Pasternack, J.L. (1985). Parental socialization of young children's play: a short-term longitudinal study. *Child Development* 56:1506–1513.

Ellis, G.T., & Sekrya, F. (1972). The effect of aggressive cartoons on the behavior of first grade children. *Journal of Psychology* 81:37–43.

Erikson, E.H. (1951). Sex differences in play configurations of preadolescents. *American Journal of Orthopsychiatry* 21:667–692.

Fagot, B.I. (1977). Consequences of moderate cross-gender behavior in preschool children. *Child Development* 48:902–907.

Fein, G. (1981). Pretend play in childhood: An integrative review. *Child Development* 52:1095–1118.

Fein, G., Johnson, D., Kosson, N., Stork, L., & Wasserman, L. (1975). Sex stereotype and preferences in the toy choices of 20-month-old boys and girls. *Developmental Psychology* 11:527–528.

Feshbach, S. (1956). The catharsis hypothesis and some consequences of interaction with aggressive and neutral play objects. *Journal of Personality* 24:449–462.

Frost, J.L., & Strickland, E. (1985). Equipment choices of young children during free play. In *When Children Play*, eds. J.L. Frost and S. Sunderlin. Wheaton, MD: Association for Childhood Education International.

Goldberg, S., & Lewis, M. (1969). Play behavior in the year-old infant: Early sex differences. *Child Development* 40:21–31.

Gump, P. (1975). Ecological psychology and children. Pp. 75–126 in *Review of Child Development Research*, vol. 5, eds. E.M. Hetherington. Chicago University of Chicago Press.

Hapkiewicz, W.G., & Stone, R.D. (1974). The effect of aggressive cartoons in children's interpersonal play. *Child Development* 42:1583–1585.

Hawkins, R.P., & Pingree, S. (1981). Uniform messages and habitual viewing: Unnecessary assumptions in social reality effects (Australia). *Human Communications Research* 7:291–301.

Henniger, M.L. (1985). Preschool children's play behaviors in an indoor and outdoor environment. In *When Children Play*, eds. J.L. Frost and S. Sunderlin. Wheaton, MD: Association for Childhood Education International.

Honzik, M.P. (1951). Sex differences in the occurrence of materials in the play construction of preadolescents. *Child Development* 22:15–35.

Huizinga, J. (1950). *Homo ludens*. Boston: The Beacon Press. (Originally published 1939.)

Humphreys, A.P., & Smith, P.K. (1987). Rough and tumble, friendship, and dominance in school children: Evidence for continuity and change with age. *Child Development* 58:201–212.

Huston, A.C. (1983). Sex typing. Pp. 387–468 in *Handbook of Child Psychology: vol. 4. Socialization, Personality, and Social Development*, 4th ed., ed. E.M. Hetherington. New York: Wiley.

Huston-Stein, A., Fox, S., Greer, D., Watkins, B.A., & Whitaker, J. (1981). The effects of TV action and violence on children's social behavior. *Journal of Genetic Psychology* 138:183–191.

Hutt, G. (1966). Exploration and play in children. *Synopsis of the Zoological Society of London* 18:61–81.

International Coalition Against Violent Entertainment. (1985). Press Release, November 27. P.O. Box 2157, Champaign, IL 61820, U.S.A. Tel: (217) 384-1920.

Jacklin, C.N., Maccoby, E.E., & Dick, A.E. (1975). Barrier behavior and toy preference: Sex differences (and their absence) in the year-old child. *Child Development* 44:196–200.

Koellei, B.S. (1981). Primary children's stories as a function of exposure to violence and cruelty in the folk fairy tale. University of Pennsylvania. *Dissertation Abstracts International* 42:1203-B.

Kolpadoff, M.H. (1983). The relationship between aggressive behavior and imaginative play skills in preschoolers. *Dissertation Abstracts International* 44:1241-B.

Larrick, Nancy (1979). TV and Kids: What teachers are complaining about. *Learning* October:44–46.

Lever, J. (1977). Little girl's play patterns may hinder career. Austin Texas: The *Austin American-Statesman*, March 3.

Lewis, M. (1972). Sex differences in play behavior of the very young. *Journal of Health, Physical Education, and Recreation* 43:38–39.

Liss, M.B. (1981). Patterns of toy play: An analysis of sex differences. *Sex Roles* 7:1143–1150.

Liss, M.B. (1983). Learning gender related skills through play. Pp. 147-166 in *Social and Cognitive Skills: Sex Roles and Children's Play*, ed. M.B. Liss. New York: Academic Press.

Lovaas, O.I. (1961). Effect of exposure to symbolic aggression on aggressive behavior. *Child Development* 32:37–44.

Mallick, S.K., & McCandless, B.R. (1966). A study of catharsis of aggression. *Journal of Personality and Social Psychology* 4:591–596.

Mendoza, A. (1972). The effects of exposure to toys conducive to violence. Doctoral dissertation, University of Miami.

Mussen, P., & Rutherford, E. (1961). Effects of aggressive cartoons on children's aggressive play. *Journal of Abnormal and Social Psychology* 62:461–464.

National Coalition on Television Violence. (1983). "TV/Film Violence Bibliography" 1933–83. *N.C.T.V. News* 4 (May).

National Coalition on Television Violence.(1985). *N.C.T.V. News* 6 (May-June).

National Coalition on Television Violence.(1986). *N.C.T.V. News* 17 (Jan.-Mar.).

Newcomb, P. (1990). Hey dude, let's consume. *Forbes* 145:126–131.

O'Brien, M., & Huston, A.C. (1985a). Development of sex-typed play behaviors in toddlers. *Developmental Psychology* 21:866–871.

O'Brien, M., & Huston, A.C. (1985b). Activity level and sex stereotyped toy choice in toddler boys and girls. *Journal of Genetic Psychology* 146:527–534.

Osborn, D.K., & Endsley, R.C. (1971). Emotional reactions of young children to TV violence. *Child Development* 42:321–331.

Pearce, Joseph C. (1985). The art of mothering. *Mothering* Spring: 17–24.

Pellegrini, A.D. (In press). Elementary children's rough-and-tumble play and social competence. *Developmental Psychology*.

Pellegrini, A.D., & Perlmutter, J. (1986). The developmental and social significance of children's rough-and-tumble play. American Educational Research Association. (April). San Francisco.

Perry, D.G., White, A.J., & Perry, L.C. (1984). Does early sex typing result from children's attempts to match their behavior to sex role stereotypes? *Child Development* 55:2114–2121.

Piaget, J. (1962). *Play, Dreams, and Imitation in Childhood.* New York: W.W. Norton.

Postman, Neil. (1981). TV's disastrous impact on children. *U.S. News and World Report* January 19:43–45.

Ritchie, O.W., and Koller, M.R. (1964). *Sociology of Childhood.* New York: Appleton Century-Crafts.

Rosenberg, B.G., & Sutton-Smith, B. (1960). A revised conception of masculine-feminine differences in play activities. *The Journal of Genetic Psychology* 96:165–170.

Ross, L.B. (1972). The effect of aggressive cartoons on the group play of children. Doctoral Dissertation, Miami University, *Dissertation Abstracts International* 33:1–8.

Sanders, K.M., & Harper, L.V. (1976). *Child Development* 47:1182–1185.

Shapiro, L. (1990). Guns and dolls. *Newsweek* 65:56–65.

Siegel, A.E. (1956). Film-mediated fantasy aggression and strength of aggressive drive. *Child Development* 27:365–378.

Singer, J.L. (ed.) (1973). *The Child's World of Make Believe: Experimental Studies of Imaginative Play.* New York: Academic Press.

Singer, J.L., & Singer, D.G. (1981). *Television, Imagination and Aggression: A Study of Preschoolers.* Hillsdale, N.J. Eribaum.

Singer, J.L., Singer, D.G., & Rapaczynski, W.S. (1984). Family patterns and TV viewing as predictors of children's beliefs and aggression. *Journal of Communication* 34:73–89.

Slife, B.D.(1982). *Journal of Personality and Social Psychology* 43:861–868.

Smith, P.K., & Boulton, M. (1987). How rough is rough-and-tumble? *SET Research Information for Teachers* 1, item 11.

Stein, A.H., Friedrich, L.K., & Vondracek. (1972). Television content and young children's behavior. In *Television and Social Behavior*, vol. 2, eds. J.P. Murray, E.P. Rubenstin & G.A. Comstock. Washington, D.C. U.S. Government Printing Office.

Steinfeld, Jesse L. (1973). TV violence is harmful. *Readers Digest*, April. *U.S.A. Today* (May 15, 1985), 9-A.

Steur, F.B., Applefield, J.M., & Smith, R. (1971). Televised aggression and the interpersonal aggression of preschool children. *Journal of Experimental Child Psychology* 11:442–447.

Stoessel, R.E. (1972). The effects of televised aggression cartoons on children's behavior. *Dissertation Abstracts International* 33:942–2B.

Sutton-Smith, B. (1988). War toys and childhood aggression. *Play and culture* 1:57–69.

Sutton-Smith, B., & Sutton-Smith, S.(1974). *How to Play with Your Children (and When Not To).* New York: Hawthorn Books.

Teachman, G., and Orme, M. (1981). Effects of aggression and prosocial film material on altruistic behavior of children (Canada). *Psychology Reports* 418:699–702.

Tizard, B., Philps, J., & Plewis, I. (1976). Play in pre-school centers I. Play measures and their relation to age, sex and I.Q. *Journal of Child Psychology and Psychiatry* 17:251–264.

Trelease, J. (1989). *The New Read-aloud Handbook.* New York: Penguin Books.

Turner, C.W., & Goldsmith, D. (1976). Effects of toy guns and airplanes on children's antisocial free play behavior. *Journal of Experimental Child Psychology* 21:303–315.

U.S. News and World Report. (1985). What entertainers are doing to your kids, October 28:46–49.

Vygotsky, L.S. (1978). *Mind in Society: The Development of Higher Psychological Processes.* Cambridge, MA: Harvard University Press.

Wiegman, O. (1975). Research study of the effect of puppet film violence on young children. In *Aggression in Global Perspective*, ed. A.P. Goldstein. New York: Pergamon Press.

Winston, P. (1984). Despite fitness boom, the young remain unfit. *Education Week* 9 (October 31).

Zimiles, H. (1982). The changing American child: The perspective of educators. A Report to the National Commission on Excellence in Education, October.

Zuckerman, D.M., Singer, D.G., & Singer, J.L. (1980). Television viewing, children's reading and related classroom behavior. *Journal of Communication* 30: 66–174.

"...the realization of the pedagogical opportunities offered through the promotion of sociodramatic play depends on changing attitudes at the teacher training level. Advocates of structured curricula tend to overlook the learning potential of sociodramatic play and regard it as just 'play for the sake of relaxation'."[1]

4

Studying Play and Play Environments

Adults, including teachers, are generally poor observers of children's play. They have very little idea of what children actually do during play time, (Sluckin 1981). In the absence of play training in their professional preparatory programs, teachers may subscribe to the traditional myth that play is wasteful and unproductive. Professional programs in child development typically include extensive guided opportunities for prospective teachers and child care professionals to observe children at play. Programs in colleges of education and other disciplines address this need in limited fashion or disregard the topic altogether. Consequently, the perceptions of children and their teachers about children's play activities and play preferences may be quite different. Interacting with children's play requires that teachers be able to take the perspective of the child (Rivkin 1986). Myers (1985) found that primary school teachers' perceptions of their pupils' play choices were not significantly related to their actual play choices. The teachers (female) were more accurate in identifying boys' play choices than girls' choices, and their perceptions of children's favorite play materials were only half as broad as the children's choices (Myers 1981). Myers noted that:

[1]Smilansky, S. & Shefatya, L. (1990). *Facilitating Play: A Medium for Promoting Cognitive. Socio-emotional and Academic Achievement in Young Children.* Gaithersburg, M.D.: Psychosocial and Educational Publications. p. 232.

> ...teachers appear to be poor sources of information about children's play in-
> terests.... depriving them of a highly complex play environment.... they could talk
> with their children and observe them closely during play noting what the children
> tell them and what they see children doing. (pp. 174–175)

The failure of teacher education institutions to provide play training for prospective teachers seems to affect their attitudes about play materials and equipment, the relevance of play, and the role of the teacher in play. Smilansky and Shefatya (1990) surveyed 60 kindergarten and preschool teachers in the United States and 60 from Israel. Although all their classrooms were equipped for sociodramatic play, such was not part of the conscious curriculum. The teachers did not promote sociodramatic play every day or even every week and did not encourage such play. They were not taught the importance of sociodramatic play, nor how to promote children's play. None of the teachers knew how to assess play and were unaware of any play assessment tools.

Some basic information is needed for observing, analyzing, and understanding the play of children. Over several decades researchers identified a set of play categories or behaviors corresponding to the cognitive and social development of children. These will be reviewed in some detail and followed by observation and assessment methods for studying children's play and play environments.

COGNITIVE PLAY

Piaget built upon the work of Charlotte Buhler (1935), who developed an inventory of children's play during the first year of life, and Karl Buhler (1937), who first described the developmental progression of games (Table 4.1).

He described three stages of games that roughly approximate the stages of intellectual development. These stages are practice games or functional play which predominate during the sensorimotor period (0–2 years) just described, symbolic games which emerge during the pre-operational subperiod (2–7 years), and games with rules which emerge during the concrete operations subperiod and continue through the formal operations period (11–15 years).

Functional Play

The first play of children consists of simple, repetitive actions. This play, which is called functional or exercise play, occurs during the early sensorimotor period of development in which infants exercise their ready-made or "wired-in" repertoire of behaviors. These behaviors soon give way to newly acquired motor responses. For example, children discover that they can strike a suspended toy and cause it to move back and forth. At first children stare intently at the toy and strike it again and again until this new action is mastered. Play begins when children engage in the activity for functional pleasure (Buhler 1937). Children no longer stare intently, but now laugh and smile at the results of their actions. Functional play may also include vocalizations. Valentine (1942) observed that at four months infants practice "singing" or babbling for pleasure, "starting on a high note and running down a kind of scale." Functional play does not involve symbolism or any specific play technique, but consists in repeating an action

TABLE 4.1 CATEGORIES OF COGNITIVE PLAY

Piaget's Periods of Cognitive Development	K. Buhler (1937)	Piaget (1962)		Smilansky (1968)
Sensorimotor period (0–24 months)	Functional games	Practice games		Functional games
Preoperational period (2–7 years)	Construction games	Symbolic games	Construction Play	Construction play
	Make-believe games			Dramatic play
Concrete operations period (7–11 years)	Collective games	Games with rules		Games with rules
Formal operations period (11–15 years)				

for the pleasure of it (Piaget 1962). As children repeat their actions, they eventually try new combinations that are in some ways similar to previously learned ones. For example, children first learn that they can make a sound by shaking a rattle. They next learn that they can make a different sound by striking the rattle against the side of the crib or playpen. Thus, through functional play, children learn their physical capabilities and cause and effect relationships by acting on their environment. Functional play is not limited to the first two years of life but is to be found throughout childhood whenever a new skill is acquired. Functional play is accompanied by the pleasure of being the cause of an event and a feeling of power that comes with the mastery of a new action.

For practical purposes we reemphasize that functional or exercise play does not disappear with the onset of other forms of play. Rather, exercise play becomes more complex, involves new play materials or equipment, and is frequently integrated with dramatic and construction play. In the outdoor play environment, exercise play for children in the early childhood age range (about 2–8), or Piaget's preoperational period, is typically accommodated by seesaws, merry-go-rounds, slides, and teeter-totters. In fact, public school playgrounds are traditionally equipped as though this were the only form of play. Understanding the nature of play helps the adults responsible for children's play to supplement this traditional equipment and promote construction and dramatic play as well as exercise play.

Construction Play

Piaget, in contrast to Buhler and Smilansky, does not view construction play as a distinct stage of play as he does with functional and symbolic play and games with rules. He maintains that construction play transcends the other three categories of play and occupies a position between play and work. While the three stages of games (practice, symbolic, and games with rules) correspond to the three forms of intelligence (sensorimotor, representational, and reflective), construction games are not a distinct stage like the others but rather "occupy at the second and particularly at the third level, a position half-way between play and intelligent work or between play and imitation" (Piaget 1962:113).

On the other hand Smilansky views construction play as a distinct stage that emerges around 22–24 months of age. At this stage children begin to use various play materials and functional or goal-less play gives way to purposeful play that results in a "creation." Children are now able to sustain their play and to attend for longer periods of time. "Development from functional play to constructive play is progression from manipulations of form to formation" (Smilansky 1968:6).

Two- and three-year-olds build upon functional play, replacing random movements with purposeful movements, language, imitation, and dramatics. Later, they will include others in their activity, giving rise to sociodramatic play. Play equipment should adjust to more than one child and more than one developmental level. Equipment such as building blocks, paints, play, carpentry tools and wood, materials for collage and construction, scissors and paste, and sand and water allow for multiple usage, and satisfy children's urge to create and to have an impact on their environment.

That Piaget does not assign construction activity the status of a play stage in no way diminishes the need to provide an environment for its enhancement. Perhaps nowhere is this done as well as on the adventure playgrounds of certain European countries such as England and those in Scandinavia. Construction areas form a major area of these environments. Scrap lumber, tools, and full-time play leaders are available. Purposeful activities such as building housing for farm animals and play structures for exercise and dramatic play are regular "construction play" activities for children. Americans and people of many other countries are now redeveloping many of their playgrounds to promote such valuable activities.

Symbolic Play

By the end of the second year children begin to make use of words and images in guiding their behavior, and it is at this point that functional or practice games develop into symbolic behavior or games of make-believe. However, some of the elements of symbolic play are present at an earlier age. Valentine (1942) reported that "real play with an imaginary object" appears at about one year, and that direct imitation becomes increasingly apparent in the play of children at the beginning of their second year. In describing the behavior of his daughter, Piaget (1962) reported the following:

> At 1;6 she pretended to eat and drink without having anything in her hand. At 1;7 she pretended to drink out of a box and then held it to the mouths of all who were present. These last symbols had been prepared for during the preceding month or two by a progressive ritualization, the principal stages of which consisted in playing at drinking out of empty glasses and then repeating the action making noises with lips and throat (1962:97).

Symbolic play, frequently called dramatic play, involves representation of an absent object. In the example cited, drinking from an empty box and imagining it as a cup filled with liquid is symbolically representing the cup by the box. The child is satisfied with the pretense because the link between the signifier and signified is entirely subjective.

Piaget asks the question, why does play become symbolic instead of continuing merely as a sensorimotor exercise of mental development? The answer to this question lies in the fact that two-year-olds live in a world dominated by elders whose interests and rules remain external to them, and in a physical world that they understand only slightly and which does not satisfy their intellectual and affective needs. They are unable to accommodate themselves to the environment that is reality; they must assimilate reality or, in other words, create their own reality. They construct a system of symbols for self-expression including both language and actions from information transmitted to them by adults and peers. Through language and their actions, children resolve, through symbolic play, the conflicts they meet. They also explore and resolve role conflicts and unsatisfied needs, leading to increased mastery of their environment and extension of self. For example, a two-year-old asks his mother for a cookie. His mother replies, "I'm sorry but you can't have a cookie now. We are going to eat supper in a few minutes." The child then brings his hands to his mouth and chews and smacks his lips as if he were eating a cookie. Thus, through imagination, he has resolved a conflict.

Sociodramatic Play

The most highly developed form of symbolic play is sociodramatic play. In dramatic play children pretend or take on the role of someone else, imitating actions and speech they have encountered in some situation. When the imitation is carried out with another role player, the play becomes sociodramatic. Sociodramatic play contains two elements. The first and central element is the imitative one in which children imitate real-life people and situations that they have experienced firsthand. This is the reality element. However, because of children's inability to imitate exactly what they observe, the element of nonreality or make-believe enters into their play. Make-believe aids in imitation and gives children satisfaction by enabling them to enter the world of adults (Smilansky 1968:7).

In her classic study, the *Effects of Sociodramatic Play on Disadvantaged Preschool Children*, Smilansky (1968) spelled out the following six criteria for well-developed sociodramatic play (see Smilansky 1990 for elaboration):

1. *Imitative role play*. The child undertakes a make-believe role and expresses it in imitative action and/or verbalization. Example: "I am the daddy, you will be the mommy, and the doll is our baby."
2. *Make-believe in regard to objects*. Movements or verbal descriptions are substituted for real objects. Example: "I am drinking from the bottle," when the child is drinking from his fist.
3. *Make-believe in regard to actions and situations*. Verbal descriptions are substituted for actions and situations. Example: "Let's pretend I already returned from work, I cooked the food, and now I am setting the table," when only the last activity is actually imitated.
4. *Persistence*. The child persists in a play episode for at least ten minutes.
5. *Interaction*. There are at least two players interacting in the framework of the play episode.
6. *Verbal communication*. There is some verbal interaction related to the play episode.

The first four criteria apply to dramatic play in general, the last two to the sociodramatic play only. If a child playing by himself makes a declaration such as, "I am Batman," only dramatic play has occurred. On the other hand, if he makes the same declaration to another child who takes on or is assigned an imaginary role, then a sociodramatic play episode has begun.

Sociodramatic play contributes to the development of creativity, intellectual growth, and social skills (Smilansky 1968, 1990). Through participation in socio-dramatic play the child learns to synthesize scattered experiences and create new ones; to identify and enact central characteristics of a given role and to concentrate around a given theme; to control herself and to discipline her own actions in relation to a context; learns flexibility in responding to other role players; facilitates the transition from an egocentric being to a social being; and facilitates more abstract thought and the ability to generalize behavior to different situations.

It would be difficult to overemphasize the role of symbolic or dramatic play in social and intellectual development. It is a major avenue for integrating cultural and social mores of the adult world while developing language and concepts of time, space, number, and so on. Many preschool indoor environments contain dramatic play spaces and rich arrays of supporting materials and equipment; for example, the house play center is a common fixture. But outdoor play environments, particularly public school and city park playgrounds, are frequently barren of needed props for dramatic play—play houses, water and sand areas, wheeled vehicle areas, dress-up clothes, containers, tools, and so forth. The consumer of play theory is likely to be a proponent of dramatic play for children.

Games with Rules

As children move from the preoperational subperiod of development (2–7 years) to the concrete operations subperiod (7–11 years), they become more and more social beings through the vehicle of sociodramatic play. Prior to this time, children's perceptions of their environment are limited to "before the eye reality" from their egocentric perspective only. Now children are able to learn and imitate the roles of others. At about five or six years of age (earlier than Piaget suggests), children's play takes on a new dimension in that it is bound by rules. The following example illustrates this transition: Given a handful of marbles, the 15-month-old would play with them by himself by rolling them on the floor or putting them in a cup and shaking them (functional play); the three-year-old might line them up in various patterns or use them to decorate a mud pie (construction play); the four-year-old might declare "Let's pretend that these marbles are diamonds and that we have to protect them from robbers!" (sociodramatic play). The six-year-old, however, would play a game of marbles. His actions and the actions of his playmates would be regulated by a commonly agreed upon set of rules: the marbles must all be placed in a ring; each player must attempt to knock his opponent's marbles out of the ring; the players will lag to see who goes first; no substitutions may be made; and so on. Any change in the rules must be agreed upon by the other players. Any violation of the rules will be met with protests and perhaps aggression on the part of the other players.

In sociodramatic play, rules are also present, but they are imposed by standards of life. Dentists examine teeth; mechanics fix cars. Games with rules tend to emphasize one skill at a time; they are competitive rather than cooperative; and they demand a minimum of verbalization. Smilansky (1968, 1990) believes that games with rules are valuable in teaching specific skills or content, but that socio-dramatic play is more relevant for overall social and intellectual development.

In explaining the relatively late appearance of games with rules and their persistence through adolescence and into adulthood, Piaget states that the explanation is simple: "they are the ludic activity of the socialized being. Just as the symbol replaces mere practice as soon as thought makes its appearance, so the rule replaces the symbol and integrates practice as soon as certain social relationships are formed, and the question is to discover these relationships" (1962:142).

Games with rules represent a high form of play development. Hence children have to accept prearranged rules and adjust to them. More important, they learn to control their behavior within limits. This appears to be assisted by the American emphasis on competitive sports, beginning at an early age. Little league baseball and football, coupled with college and professional sports on television, stimulate children to participate in highly organized competitive games with rules at an early age. This stringent, probably unhealthy, emphasis can be tempered by the provision of age-appropriate games areas and equipment on playgrounds, supervised by adults who value spontaneous games with minimal adult or peer pressure.

TABLE 4.2 CATEGORIES OF COGNITIVE PLAY FOR TODDLERS*

Repetition	The child performs repetitive motor actions. These actions may be an effort to sustain an activity which provides vestibular stimulation.
Combination	The child performs repetitive motor movements in an identifiable pattern. This category also refers to vestibular stimulation activities in which the child is actively engaged (e.g., pumping legs to swing). The child may also place two or more objects into spatial relationships. The child may choose to place himself into a spatial relationship with other objects.
Constructive	The child engages in goal-oriented play in which he/she tests hypotheses or creates end products.
Conversion	The child uses a concrete object to symbolize an absent object. The child may use gestures to indicate that an object is being symbolized rather than a concrete object.
Animation	The child pretends that an inanimate object is alive (growls for a toy lion) or operational (moves a toy truck).
Role-play	The child portrays the role of a real or imaginary character.
Spontaneous Games	The child engages in playful interactions with another peer. These interactions are governed by mutually understood rules which arise spontaneously and are temporary in nature. The children alternate turns in performing actions and may reverse roles during the game.

*adapted from Winter (1985)

Toddler Play

Researchers have found that the play categories of Buhler, Piaget, and Smilansky are too advanced for assessing the play of toddlers and do not discriminate special play activities within broad categories. Winter (1985) found that toddlers did not engage in Piaget's category, "games with rules," but did engage in game-type interactions involving spontaneous, temporary rules. Winter's system (see Table 4.2) allows for a more accurate and precise description of toddler play than do previous systems. (See Wagner & Frost 1986, for an instrument to assess developmental levels of infants and toddlers using play behaviors as a base).

SOCIAL PLAY

Many years ago Bailey (1933) and Isaacs (1933) noted that the three-year-old hunts out live contact with other children in order to play with them, and during

Developmentally appropriate playgrounds provide for all types of children's play. *

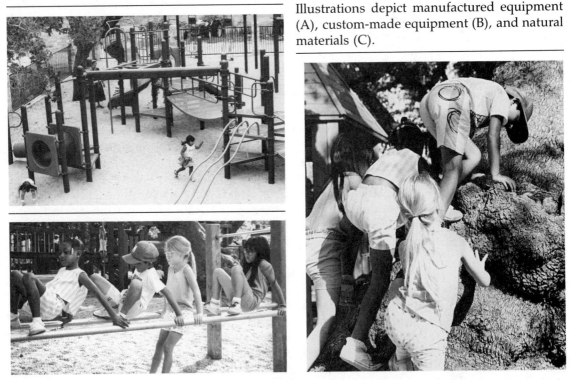

Illustrations depict manufactured equipment (A), custom-made equipment (B), and natural materials (C).

FIGURE 4.1 Exercise/motor play (group)

*The photos in this chapter are by courtesy of parents at St. Stephens Episcopal School, Wimberly, Texas (Joe Frost, design consultant) and St. Martins Lutheran School, Austin, Texas (Britt Alexius, Designer/Builder).

the three- to four-year-old period the child reaches the height of concentration with other children. This sociability appeared to result from and depend on the child's experience in kindergarten.

Categories of Social Play. In her classic study, Parten (1932) discovered that social participation among preschoolers increased with the child's age. Parten defined six social play categories: unoccupied behavior, solitary play, onlooker behavior, parallel play, associative play, and cooperative play. Her category system is still being used and refined by researchers and students of play.

- **Unoccupied Behavior.** The child is not playing but occupies him- or herself with watching anything that happens to be of momentary interest. When there is nothing exciting taking place, he plays with his own body, gets on and off chairs, just stands around, follows the teacher, or sits in one spot glancing around the room (playground).
- **Onlooker Behavior.** The child spends most of his time watching the other children play. He often talks to the children being observed, asks questions or gives suggestions, but does not overtly enter into the play. This type differs from unoccupied in that the onlooker is definitely observing particular groups of children rather than anything that happens to be exciting. The child stands or sits within speaking distance from other children.
- **Solitary Play.** The child plays alone and independently with toys that are different from those used by the children within speaking distance and makes no effort to get close to other children. He pursues his own activity without reference to what others are doing.

FIGURE 4.2 Solitary play (exercise)

FIGURE 4.3 *Parallel play*

- **Parallel Play**. The child plays independently, but the activity chosen naturally brings him among other children. He plays with toys that are like those the children around him are using but he plays with the toys as he sees fit, and does not try to influence or modify the activity of the children near him. He plays beside rather than with the other children.
- **Associative Play**. The children plays with other children. The communication concerns the common activity; there is borrowing and loaning of play materials; following one another with trains or wagons; mild attempts to control which children may or may not play in the group. All the members engage in similar activity, there is no division of labor, and no organization of the activity around materials, goal, or product. The children do not subordinate their individual interests to that of the group.

    In onlooker behavior children spend most of their time watching other children play. They sit close enough to hear and see what is going on in the group.
- **Cooperative Play**. The child plays in a group that is organized for the purpose of making some material product, striving to attain some competitive goal, dramatizing situations of adult and group life, or playing formal games.

FIGURE 4.4 *Group/dramatic play (cooperative, sociodramatic)*

FIGURE 4.5 *Group/dramatic play (cooperative, sociodramatic)*

From two to two and one-half years of age preschoolers engaged primarily in solitary play; from two and one-half to three and one-half, parallel play; from three and one-half to four and one-half, associative play; and from four and one-half on, cooperative play (Parten 1932). In a replication of Parten's study, Barnes (1971) found that three- and four-year-olds displayed significantly more unoccupied, solitary, and onlooker activity and significantly less associative and cooperative play than Parten found in her original sample. He suggested that caution should be exercised in using Parten's data for the purpose of establishing play norms. Today's preschoolers are less skilled in associative and cooperative activities than were their contemporaries of the late 1920s. In a study comparing the free play behaviors of middle- and lower-class preschoolers, Rubin, Maioni, and Hornung (1976) reported that middle-class children engaged in significantly less parallel and functional play, and significantly more associative, cooperative, and constructive play than did their lower-class age mates. The middle-class preschoolers engaged in associative and cooperative play approximately 40 percent of the time, a figure directly corroborating Parten's study. On the other hand, the lower-class preschoolers engaged in the two highest levels of social play 27 percent of the time, thereby supporting Barnes's study (Rubin, Maioni, & Hornung 1976:418).

In light of recent research (Rubin 1982), the role of solitary play in development should be reconsidered. Beginning with Parten (1932), psychologists and early educators maintained that solitary behavior is the least mature of all play forms. Moore, Evertson, and Brophy (1974) studied the solitary play behavior of 116 white, middle-class kindergarten children. Their findings did not support the traditional image of solitary play as indicative of poor or immature social adjustment. To the contrary, solitary involved active, goal-directed activities such as blocks, arts and crafts, large muscle play, puzzles, workbooks, and reading (most of these activities are not usually defined as play). They concluded that solitary play appears to be independent, task-oriented behavior that is functional to school situations and indicative of maturity rather than immaturity (p. 834).

Seagoe (1970) developed an instrument called the Play Report to analyze children's play as an index of degree of socialization. The Play Report, based upon Sullivan's (1953) concept of emotional-social development, is a structured interview in which the child responds to a set of five questions with two responses required for each item: "What do you spend most of your time playing at school?", "What do you spend most of your time playing at home?", "What do you spend most of your time playing at other places?", "What do you like to play most?", "What do you like to play least?"

A scoring guide was developed paralleling the theoretical framework. It requires categorizing each response and giving it a numerical weight in terms of the social context indicated. The categories are:

1. *Informal-Individual* play that is self-directed and not imitative of adults nor formally patterned.
2. *Adult-Oriented* play that is adult-directed and formally patterned though not imitative of adult life.

FIGURE 4.6 Construction play

3. *Informal-Social* play that is self-directed, imitative of adult life but not formally patterned.
4. *Individual-Competitive* play that is formally patterned toward individual victory.
5. *Cooperative-Competitive* play that is formally patterned toward team victory.

The Play Report was standardized on a population of 1,245 suburban, middle-class children aged 5 to 11 years. Seagoe analyzed the data in terms of sex and age differences. She found that boys engage in play requiring more complex interpersonal interaction earlier and emphasize it more at all ages. Girls play with friends as much as boys do, but their play is more often of an informal-individual or a competitive nature. Boys also appear to anticipate and welcome more socially complex forms of play. The school leads the home in encouraging play socialization. It achieves less socialization with girls, however, than with boys. This may be due to the impact of team sports on boys.

Iwanaga (1973) developed a scheme for classifying the structure of play from a cognitive role-taking perspective. Play structure refers to the way in which children structure their interactions with peers while playing together. She maintains that, while the content of play behavior may vary from one setting to another, the interpersonal play structure tends to remain constant.

- **Independent Structure.** Play activity that involves only a single child, no peer interaction.
- **Parallel Structure.** Involves undifferentiated roles assigned to self and others; two or more children structure a situation in which they are engaged in the same activity; they play independently but maintain awareness of and contact with each other by pointing out to each other what they are doing. An

example would be several children building independent block structures and one another's attention to their constructions, "Look what I built!"

- **Complementary Structure**. Two or more children are engaged in the same activity, but take different roles. For example, children playing hospital where one child is the doctor, another a nurse, and a third the patient.

- **Integrative Structure**. Here the child's awareness of the presence of companions, seen in parallel and complementary structures, grows more intense in that there is an increased checking out of how the play companion is behaving through visual, verbal, and physical contacts; the child seems more aware of the shifts in peers' behaviors. This increased awareness is accompanied by greater adjustment of the child's own behavior in response to shifts and adjustments made by companions.

Iwanaga (1973) used her taxonomy of interpersonal play structure to observe the play of 30 three-, four-, and five-year-old children from an all Chinese nursery school in Chicago. She found that the types of interpersonal play structure engaged in increased with age. The three-year-olds engaged in two types—independent and parallel; the four-year-olds in three types—independent, parallel, and complementary; and the five-year-olds engaged in the first three types plus integrative play structure.

Howes (1980) and Winter (1985) developed and implemented research instruments (Table 4.3) for observing and assessing the cognitive and social play behaviors of toddlers. Howes studied friendship patterns between children. Winter's findings related to social play agreed with earlier conclusions of Parten (1932). Although toddlers engaged in each of the social play categories, the majority of those play behaviors were concentrated at the lower end of the scale. More than half of the social play was categorized in the proximal category and the lowest percentage was categorized in the most complex form—interactive.

As the reader has seen, social play can be categorized in a number of ways. Table 4.3 compares the categories of Parten, Erikson, Seagoe, Iwanaga, Howes, and Winter. There is general agreement that children develop from playing alone, or egocentrically, to playing cooperatively with others. However, as children develop social awareness they do not outgrow their need for solitary activity. Rather, they appear to engage in increasingly reflective activity or merely seek private places for quiet and relaxation.

Pellegrini and Perlmutter (1987) re-examined the Smilansky–Parten matrix of play behavior utilizing factor-analysis. The results indicated that the social-cognitive aspects of play could be reduced to dramatic-constructive play, solitary behavior, and functional-constructive play. The student of play should be cautious, however, for these three factors only accounted for 47 percent of the variance in children's *classroom* free play, leaving 53 percent unaccounted for. Pellegrini and Perlmutter suggest that observers begin their research with an ethological orientation (Blurton-Jones 1972), inventorying play behaviors in molecular categories (e.g., chase) then moving to molar categories (e.g., dramatic play). This should allow researchers to account for the majority of children's play behaviors.

In the chapters to follow the author will explore ways to construct equipment and arrange play environments that take into account the social play needs of young children. For example, cooperative play is stimulated by substituting a

TABLE 4.3 CATEGORIES OF SOCIAL PLAY

Parten (1932)	Eriksen (1950)	Seagoe (1970)	Iwanaga (1973)	Howes (1980)	Winter (1985)
Developmental stages	Categories refer to broad stages of development	Play Report: based on structured interviews with child	Categories pertain to how an individual child structures the play situation in regard to other children	Categories show increasing complexity	Categories relevant to toddlers of interaction
Solitary Play plays alone and independently; different activity; no reference to others	**Autocosmic** world of self; explores own body and body of mother; repetition of activity	**Informal-Individual** self-directed; not imitative of adults; not formally patterned	**Independent** no involvement of peers in play	**Parallel** engaged in similar activities; no attention to one another	**Independent** plays alone at a distance from others or facing away from others
Parallel Play play independently but near or amongst others; similar toys or activities; beside but not with	**Microcosmic** world of small, manageable toys and objects; solitary play; pleasure derived from mastery of toys	**Adult-Oriented** adult-directed; formally patterned; not imitative of adult life	**Parallel** play with peers; undifferentiated roles; roles enacted independently; close physical proximity; awareness of activity of others	**Mutual Regard** similar activities; eye contact and awareness of each other; no verbalization or other social bids	**Proximal** plays near others; plays in his own way; does not communicate with others
Associative Play plays with others; conversation is about common activity, but does not subordinate own interests to group	**Macrocosmic** world shared with others	**Informal-Social** self-directed; imitative of adult life; not formally patterned	**Complementary** differentiated roles, enacted independently; some cooperation but each child engaged in a different activity; little adjustment to others' behavior	**Simple Social** similar activities; social bids such as talking, smiling, offering toys	**Relational** plays as he sees fit without involving others; communicates with others; uses verbal or nonverbal modes
Cooperative activity-organized; differentiation of roles; complementary actions		**Individual-Competitive** formally patterned; directed toward individual victory	**Integrative** roles enacted interactively; intense awareness of others; adjustment of behavior to shifts in others; complementary roles	**Complementary** collaborating in the same activity; mutual awareness but no social bids	**Interactive** plays with one or more peers in a common activity; conversation relevant to the activity
		Cooperative-Competitive formally patterned toward team victory		**Complementary Reciprocal** collaborating in the same activity; social bids	

FIGURE 4.7 *Organized games (games with rules)*

horizontal tire swing that seats three people for the traditional one-seat swing. Complex climbing/sliding structures that accommodate several children at once replace the narrow ladder/slides that force one-at-a-time play. Loose parts are provided in abundance to support cooperative constructions. Open, grassy spaces and appropriate props are available for games with rules that involve many children. Cooperative/dramatic play is enhanced by indoor/outdoor integration of play equipment and themes. In addition, out of the way, cozy places are provided for quiet, reflective activity.

STUDYING PLAY

The play leader or teacher uses observation not only to determine children's current status in play but also as an aid in planning for future play. As the adult determines that the setting or materials are inappropriate, corrective steps are taken. Observation also allows identification or diagnosis of specific needs. Children who do not play, play only in brief erratic patterns, exhibit behavior problems, or have motor difficulties during play become the objects of reflection and possible intervention by adults.

In order to make decisions about children's play—how to best provide materials and whether and in what ways to become involved—the adult should first become an observer, a student, of their play. Observation of play should become a regular, habitual part of the day for adults who have responsibility for children. This can take several forms, ranging from the use of checklists to anecdotal accounts to informal, casual observations. In observing play and in analyzing the results it is helpful to address certain questions:

1. Is the play setting right for the child? Is space (indoor or outdoor) arranged to allow a free flow of movement from one play area, or zone, to the other? What seems to attract the child and lead to play? Is the play area too open (too large

or too few play choices) or too closed (too small or too many play choices)? Is the play area too crowed? Is sufficient time allowed for children's play?

2. Are the play materials (small, portable) and equipment (large, fixed) appropriate? Are they designed for the age groups involved? Are they sufficiently varied to accommodate a wide range of play activity and play types (e.g., dramatic, constructive)? As an aid in observing details of outdoor play settings and play materials and equipment the reader may use the Playground Rating System on pp. 107.

3. In what types of social play does the child engage? Does the child play alone or with others? Does the child play with a wide range of playmates? What are the signs of social development (e.g., taking turns, sharing materials, verbal interaction)? Does the child take proper care of materials, put them away after use? Signs of development include ability and willingness to share materials, engaging in highly developed socio-dramatic play, taking turns, and taking responsibility for action.

4. In what types of cognitive play (dramatic, constructive, organized games) does the child engage? Does the child initiate and carry-on a pretend sequence with other children? Are pretend activities varied-object transformations, role assumptions, verbally complex? Are signs of growth evident as the child participates in different types of play? Does the child willingly take on new types of play? Does the child persist in play? Does the play become more elaborate with age?

5. What is the symbolic content of the play? What themes do children play out—domestic roles, community helper roles, super-hero roles? Are violence or family conflict reflected in children's role play? Adult's gain insight into the complexity and level of children's thinking through observing role play, and they may identify areas of conflict or concern on the part of the child. Further, observation assists the adult in assessing cognitive style characteristics as related to play behavior (Saracho 1987).

6. What are the nature and range of interactions with peers and adults? Does the child get along with peers? Does he cooperate, share, ask questions, volunteer information, dominate? To what extent does the child depend on the teacher for instructions, modeling, involvement in play reinforcement, or support? Is rapport established between adult and child? As children develop they increasingly initiate exchanges with others. Interaction becomes more specific, better planned, and more complex. Gestures and physical communication between children is gradually replaced by verbal interaction. The child becomes less dependent upon adults and is able to resolve problems without teacher intervention.

7. Does the child persist in play? Is the child's attention fleeting and characterized by brief, shallow, play episodes or does the child persist in play roles over a period of time? Persistence at play demonstrates ability to concentrate on a task, a quality that is vital to success in school (Yawkey 1990). The role play involvement of preschool children is generally brief, but fours and fives should be able to persist in a role for at least five minutes, and fives to eights should be able to persist in a role for at least ten minutes (Smilansky 1968).

Using these questions as a guide, the student of play, child caretaker, playleader, or teacher may periodically observe individual children. Coupled

TABLE 4.4   ANECDOTAL ACCOUNT OF PLAY

Name of Child: _____   Date: _____

In order to maintain and sharpen skills, the teacher or caretaker should periodically assess the play environment (indoors and outdoors) and observe children at play. A simple, anecdotal account of observations oriented to specific, relevant questions will guide this activity.

Instructions: Select a child during free play (indoors or outdoors). Observe for 30 minutes while recording anecdotes for each category. Review the questions above before beginning.

1. Is the play setting appropriate?
2. Are the play materials and equipment appropriate?
3. Describe the child's social play.
4. Describe the child's cognitive play.
5. Identify the symbolic content of the play.
6. Describe the child's interactions with peers and adults.
7. Does the child persist in play?

with the information gained from using the Frost-Wortham Developmental Checklist which follows, a detailed account of the play behavior and status of each child in a group or class will be available. This information will be invaluable for assessing progress, diagnosing needs, reporting to parents, making program decisions, and understanding the nature of children and play.

OBSERVING PRESCHOOL CHILDREN

The Frost-Wortham Checklist[2]

The student of play can improve skills in observing play through guided observations in preschools or with preschool age children in any context (home, public parks, etc.). The Frost-Wortham checklist is an aid to observing and understanding the play behaviors and abilities of three- to five-year-old children. It is *not a test* but merely a useful guide to learn about play and individual children. As the adult observes and interacts mental notes can be taken about each child's play behavior and recorded at the end of each session. Regular recording of observations will result in a running account of each child's progress in selected aspects of dramatic play, social play, and motor development.

The Play Observation Form

The Parten social categories or types of play and the Piaget cognitive categories are the most widely used for introducing students to first-hand observation of play and by researchers who attempt to categorize play. The Play Observation Form (Table 4.6) uses these categories and is adapted from several sources: Sponseller and Jaworski (1979); Rubin, Watson, and Jambor (1978); Johnson, Christie, and Yawkey (1987); and Bergen (1987). The student may use this instru-

[2]© 1980, 1990, by Joe L. Frost and Sue C. Wortham

ment to gain experience in observing children at play and to learn to correctly identify and classify the types of play.

Procedure

The children or subjects to be observed may be selected in several ways, depending on the needs of the observer. If the purpose is to better understand how play develops across age or developmental levels, the observer may select a toddler (18 to 36 months) and a 4- to 5-year-old and observe them alternately. If the intent is to understand differences in the play of males and females, the observer would obviously select a boy and a girl. If the observer, perhaps a teacher or caretaker, wishes to understand the play behaviors of a given group or class of children the procedure may follow a random order for observing the children. Each child may be observed for the selected time period (15 to 30 seconds). Then a brief description of the play behavior is written for coding later. The observer moves on to the next child, and repeats the process until all tthe children are observed. The entire process may be repeated as frequently as desired.

After each child has been observed a number of times (at least 20 to 25), the child's patterns of play will become evident and the observer will be able to develop (write) a summary of the child's play behaviors.

The steps for observation are outlined below using examples from observations.

Step 1 is collecting the anecdotal data or recording the actual play behavior of the child or children. This should be done in 1,2,3 order for each observation made. For example,

1. Billy, Mary, and Juanita are making pies in the sand area. They are sharing information and materials. (group-dramatic)
2. Tom and Jimmy are alternately wrestling and chasing each other. They are laughing and talking. (rough-and-tumble)
3. Sue is alone on a swing, pumping vigorously back and forth. (solitary-functional)
4. Juan is selecting and removing plastic containers from the storage facility. (transitional)
5. Eddie pulled Angie's hair violently when she tried to take over the steering wheel he was playing with. (aggression)
6. Lillie is standing at the texture wall, carefully stroking the textured materials and rubbing them against her face. (exploratory)
7. John is playing tag with several boys and girls. (group-organized games)

Step 2 is marking or coding the anecdotal information on the Play Observation Form (Table 4.6). For example, anecdote 1 would be coded as follows in the space provided in the Play Observation Form. All anecdotes should be recorded, using a separate form for each child.

Step 3 is writing a summary of the observations for each child. Pertinent questions should guide the summary: What types of play were engaged in predominantly? How extensive were the non-play and aggression behaviors? Were the social and cognitive levels of play appropriate for the child's age? Was the child a leader or a follower? Did the child initiate play episodes? Did the child engage in a wide variety of play activities? Was the child dependent upon

TABLE 4.5 FROST-WORTHAM DEVELOPMENTAL CHECKLIST

Motor Development: Preschool (Fine Movement)

Level III (approx. age 3)	Introduced	Progress	Mastery
1. Places small pegs in pegboards	⎯⎯	⎯⎯	⎯⎯
2. Holds a paintbrush or pencil with the whole hand	⎯⎯	⎯⎯	⎯⎯
3. Eats with a spoon	⎯⎯	⎯⎯	⎯⎯
4. Buttons large buttons on his or her own clothes	⎯⎯	⎯⎯	⎯⎯
5. Puts on coat unassisted	⎯⎯	⎯⎯	⎯⎯
6. Strings bead with ease	⎯⎯	⎯⎯	⎯⎯
7. Hammers a pound toy with accuracy	⎯⎯	⎯⎯	⎯⎯
8. Works a three- or four-piece puzzle	⎯⎯	⎯⎯	⎯⎯

Level IV (approx. age 4)			
1. Pounds and rolls clay	⎯⎯	⎯⎯	⎯⎯
2. Puts together a five-piece puzzle	⎯⎯	⎯⎯	⎯⎯
3. Forms a pegboard design	⎯⎯	⎯⎯	⎯⎯
4. Cuts with scissors haltingly and pastes	⎯⎯	⎯⎯	⎯⎯
5. Eats with a fork correctly	⎯⎯	⎯⎯	⎯⎯
6. Holds a cup with one hand	⎯⎯	⎯⎯	⎯⎯
7. Puts a coat on a hanger or hook	⎯⎯	⎯⎯	⎯⎯
8. Manipulates large crayons and brushes	⎯⎯	⎯⎯	⎯⎯
9. Buttons buttons and zips zippers haltingly	⎯⎯	⎯⎯	⎯⎯

Level V (approx. age 5)			
1. Cuts and pastes creative designs	⎯⎯	⎯⎯	⎯⎯
2. Forms a variety of pegboard designs	⎯⎯	⎯⎯	⎯⎯
3. Buttons buttons, zips zippers, and ties shoes	⎯⎯	⎯⎯	⎯⎯
4. Creates recognizable objects with clay	⎯⎯	⎯⎯	⎯⎯
5. Uses the toilets independently	⎯⎯	⎯⎯	⎯⎯
6. Eats independently with a knife and fork	⎯⎯	⎯⎯	⎯⎯
7. Dresses and undresses independently	⎯⎯	⎯⎯	⎯⎯
8. Holds and manipulates pencils, crayons, and brushes of various sizes	⎯⎯	⎯⎯	⎯⎯
9. Combs and brushes hair	⎯⎯	⎯⎯	⎯⎯
10. Works a twelve-piece puzzle	⎯⎯	⎯⎯	⎯⎯

TABLE 4.5   FROST-WORTHAM DEVELOPMENTAL CHECKLIST (cont.)

Social Play and Socializing: Preschool

Level III (approx. age 3)	Introduced	Progress	Mastery
1. Engages in independent play	____	____	____
2. Engages in parallel play	____	____	____
3. Plays briefly with peers	____	____	____
4. Recognizes the needs of others	____	____	____
5. Shows sympathy for others	____	____	____
6. Attends to an activity for ten to fifteen minutes	____	____	____
7. Sings simple songs	____	____	____

Level IV (approx. age 4)			
1. Leaves the mother readily	____	____	____
2. Converses with other children	____	____	____
3. Converses with adults	____	____	____
4. Plays with peers	____	____	____
5. Cooperates in classroom routines	____	____	____
6. Takes turns and shares	____	____	____
7. Replaces materials after use	____	____	____
8. Takes care of personal belongings	____	____	____
9. Respects the property of others	____	____	____
10. Attends to an activity for fifteen to twenty minutes	____	____	____
11. Engages in group activites	____	____	____
12. Sings with a group	____	____	____
13. Is sensitive to praise and criticism	____	____	____

Level V (approx. age 5)			
1. Completes most self-initiated projects	____	____	____
2. Works and plays with limited supervision	____	____	____
3. Engages in cooperative play	____	____	____
4. Listens while peers speak	____	____	____
5. Follows multiple and delayed directions	____	____	____
6. Carries out special responsibilities (for example, feeding animals)	____	____	____
7. Listens and follows the suggestions of adults	____	____	____
8. Enjoys talking with adults	____	____	____
9. Can sustain an attention span for a variety of duties	____	____	____
10. Evaluates his or her work and suggests improvements	____	____	____

TABLE 4.5   FROST-WORTHAM DEVELOPMENTAL CHECKLIST (cont.)

Motor Development: Preschool (Gross Movement)

Level III (approx. age 3)	Introduced	Progress	Mastery
1. Catches a ball with both hands against the chest	_____	_____	_____
2. Rides a tricycle	_____	_____	_____
3. Hops on both feet several times without assistance	_____	_____	_____
4. Throws a ball five feet with accuracy	_____	_____	_____
5. Climbs up a slide and comes down	_____	_____	_____
6. Climbs by alternating feet and holding on to a handrail	_____	_____	_____
7. Stands on one foot and balances briefly	_____	_____	_____
8. Pushes a loaded wheelbarrow	_____	_____	_____
9. Runs freely with little stumbling or falling	_____	_____	_____
10. Builds a tower with nine or ten blocks	_____	_____	_____

Level IV (approx. age 4)			
1. Balances on one foot	_____	_____	_____
2. Walks a straight line forward and backward	_____	_____	_____
3. Walks a balance beam	_____	_____	_____
4. Climbs steps with alternate feet without support	_____	_____	_____
5. Climbs on a jungle gym	_____	_____	_____
6. Skips haltingly	_____	_____	_____
7. Throws, catches, and bounces a large ball	_____	_____	_____
8. Stacks blocks vertically and horizontally	_____	_____	_____
9. Creates recognizable block structures	_____	_____	_____
10. Rides a tricycle with speed and skill	_____	_____	_____

Level V (approx. age 5)			
1. Catches and throws a small ball	_____	_____	_____
2. Bounces and catches a small ball	_____	_____	_____
3. Skips on either foot	_____	_____	_____
4. Skips rope	_____	_____	_____
5. Hops on one foot	_____	_____	_____
6. Creates Tinkertoy and block structures	_____	_____	_____
7. Hammers and saws with some skill	_____	_____	_____
8. Walks a balance beam forward and backward	_____	_____	_____
9. Descends stairs by alternating feet	_____	_____	_____

TABLE 4.5   FROST-WORTHAM DEVELOPMENTAL CHECKLIST (cont.)

Dramatic Play: Preschool

	Color Code: Purple		
Level III (approx. age 3)	**Introduced**	**Progress**	**Mastery**
1. Imitates grownups (plays house, store, and so forth)	_____	_____	_____
2. Expresses frustrations in play	_____	_____	_____
3. Creates imaginary playmates	_____	_____	_____
4. Engages in housekeeping	_____	_____	_____
5. Paints and draws symbolic figures on large paper	_____	_____	_____
6. Builds simple structures with blocks	_____	_____	_____
7. Uses transportation toys, people, and animals to enrich block play	_____	_____	_____
8. Imagines any object as the object he or she wants (symbolic function)	_____	_____	_____
Level IV (approx. age 4)			
1. Role plays in the housekeeping center	_____	_____	_____
2. Role plays some adult occupations	_____	_____	_____
3. Participates in dramatization of familiar stories	_____	_____	_____
4. Uses puppets in self-initiated dialogues	_____	_____	_____
5. Differentiates between real and make-believe	_____	_____	_____
6. Pretends dolls are real people	_____	_____	_____
7. Constructs (paints, molds, and so forth) recognizable figures	_____	_____	_____
8. Participates in finger plays	_____	_____	_____
Level V (approx. age 5)			
1. Role plays a wide variety of roles in the housekeeping center and in other centers	_____	_____	_____
2. Role plays on the playground	_____	_____	_____
3. Role plays a variety of adult occupations	_____	_____	_____
4. Recognizes that pictures represent real objects	_____	_____	_____
5. Participates in a wide variety of creative activities: finger plays, rhythm band, working with clay, painting, outdoor play, housekeeping, singing, and so forth	_____	_____	_____
6. Produces objects at the carpentry table and tells about them	_____	_____	_____
7. Produces art objects and tells about them	_____	_____	_____
8. Searches for better ways to construct	_____	_____	_____
9. Builds complex block structures	_____	_____	_____

TABLE 4.6 PLAY OBSERVATION FORM

Child: _____   Age: _____

Date: _____

Place: _____

COGNITIVE PLAY

		Functional (Practice)	Dramatic (Symbolic)	Organized Games (Games with Rules)
SOCIAL PLAY	Solitary			
	Parallel			
	Group			

	Unoccupied	Onlooker	Transition	Aggression
NON-PLAY				

	Exploratory	Constructive	Rough and Tumble	Chase Games
OTHER				

TABLE 4.7   PLAY AND NON-PLAY CATEGORIES

Types of Behavior	Child's Behavior
Cognitive	
Functional	Repetition of actions for the fun of it
Dramatic or symbolic	Substitution of an imaginary situation or object in pretend play situations
Games with rules	Acceptance of prearranged rules and adjustments to them in organized play
Social	
Solitary	Child plays alone and independently
Parallel	Child plays *beside* rather than *with* other children
Group	Child plays with another child or group of children striving to attain a common goal
Other	
Exploratory	Child seeking sensory information or stimuli
Constructive	Manipulation of objects to construct or create something
Rough and Tumble	Play fighting or playful physical activity
Chase Games	One or more children planning to chase or actually chasing another child or children
Non-Play	
Unoccupied	Child is not playing. Watching anything of momentary interest
Onlooker	Watching other children play. May converse with players but does not participate
Transition	Preparing for or moving from one activity to another
Aggression	Real fighting—with intent to hurt or defend

	DRAMATIC
Group	(1) Preparing a meal

the adult (teacher)? Were any special needs observed (e.g., poorly developed motor or social skills)? What suggestions would you make for teacher involvement?

STUDYING OUTDOOR PLAY ENVIRONMENTS*

Another of the critical beginning points for enhancing children's play is the analysis of the outdoor play environment. The result of this analysis can be a useful tool in planning for playground improvement. The Playground Rating

*Excerpted from Frost J.L. (1986). "Planning and Using Children's Playgounds" in *Play: Working Partner of Growth*, (ed.) J.S. McKee. By permission of the Association for Childhood Educational International.

System (Table 4.7) provides detailed information about the existing state of the playground and is also a basis for developing a master plan for improvement. It is divided into three major areas: (1) the contents of the playground, (2) the safety of the playground, and (3) the functions (play activities) provided by the playground. Following analysis, using the Checklist, the first priority should be correcting any observed safety defects, then a master plan (Chapter 6) should be developed to improve the physical content and play activities. The following section summarizes the dimensions to be assessed.

What Should Playgrounds Contain?

The best playgrounds are never finished. Rather, they are constantly changing as new challenges replace old ones and as play equipment and materials are used in fresh combinations. For additional variety, growing things are introduced in nature and garden areas and children create their own structures in the building areas.

Although most items on the playground should be flexible and portable, a major exception is the *superstructure*, a relatively fixed combination of small decks (4–6 ft. wide) linked together with challenging apparatus (e.g., steps, clatter bridges, ramps) which provide routes to and from a variety of exercise options or activity devices (e.g., slides, fireman's poles, trapeze bars, climbers). The superstructure combines in one area most of the challenges of a conventional playground comprised of unlinked apparatus. The linkage of play/exercise apparatus is accomplished through use of modular equipment. Using a basic 4 ft. × 4 ft. to 6 ft. × 6 ft. deck as a starting point, up to 4 activity devices can be attached, 1 to each of the 4 sides. Complexity is increased by linking one deck to another with each additional deck offering four new options. The superstructure can be modified to accommodate growing enrollments, changing age groups, and developmental needs. Some manufacturers are offering superstructures with considerable flexibility, featuring structures that require no foundations in earth or concrete, decks that can be readily raised or lowered, and activity devices that can be moved from deck to deck.

The superstructure is one of two relatively large, fixed structures on modern playgrounds. The second is a swing set. This may be attached to the superstructure or it may be placed in a corner or end of the playground out of the line of direct traffic. Several types are available, including conventional swings with pliable strap seats, tire swings mounted on swivels for 360° rotation and movement, and "exerglide" type swings that require upper body exercise for propulsion.

All climbing and moving equipment is installed over sand or an equivalent resilient surface for safety and increased playability. Sand is a favorite play material of young children and its advantages far outweigh any problems of sticking to clothing, carrying into classrooms, or introducing health risks from animal contamination. Consultation with medical doctors, nurses, and playground directors reveals that risks from animal contamination are exaggerated. As one physician put it, "Health risks from chewing on pencils or playing on indoor classroom carpets are greater than playing in sand, which is exposed to natural cleansing agents, wind, rain and sunshine." The play value of sand is enhanced by the provision of a second fluid material, water, and this is further enhanced by the providing sand and water play materials—buckets, pans, shovels, and strainers. The undersides of well-designed superstructures are favorite sand/water play areas, as well as sites for various dramatic play activities. A crucial principle in design of play environments is illustrated here. Equipment and materials zoned in close proximity can increase challenges, multiply play activities, and enhance learning opportunities, while increasing socialization.

A feature of every good playscape is one or more facilities for storing play support materials and wheeled vehicles (tricycles, wagons, wheelbarrows), traffic signs, tools, building materials, benches with vises, and sand and water play materials. The storage facility is linked by a ramp to the wheeled vehicle track which poses various challenges (hills, curves, intersections, tunnels), takes children near interesting views (gardens, woods beyond the fence), and links to support structures such as multiple-function play houses that become gas stations, grocery stores, or garages. Several important linkages have been discussed: decks to decks, decks to activity devices, superstructures to sand and to water, sand and water to sand and water play equipment, storage facility to wheeled vehicle tracks, wheeled vehicle tracks to play houses.

The superstructure is designed primarily for exercise play but, with attention to design and provision of support materials, it also supports dramatic or make-believe play. The dramatic play function of superstructures is further enhanced by placing large dramatic play structures such as boats and cars close to one another. The best location for these items is just outside the superstructure sand area. Cars and boats should be properly stripped: remove upholstery and glass, remove doors, secure the hood and trunk lids, smooth all sharp and jagged parts, and repaint the vehicle. Functional parts such as steering wheels and gear shift levers should remain intact. As dramatic play is initiated in the car or boat and more children become involved, the activity expands to incorporate more than one play structure, frequently including the superstructure. Thus the value of linking the major dramatic play structures with the superstructure becomes obvious.

Unfortunately, some of the most meaningful play activities, from a development and learning perspective, are not supported by adults. Most school administrators reject stripped cars or boats as "unsightly" or "junk yards," but those willing to experiment usually become firm advocates fo such play materials. One of the most important forms of play, construction play, is disregarded by most schools and child care centers. A construction area should be available near a storage facility containing tools (high quality saws, hammers, nails, screwdrivers, screws, wrenches, bolts, shovels), scrap lumber (soft wood such as pine, cedar, or fir), and workbenches with vises. Construction play must be carefully supervised and basic skills (sawing, nailing) should be *taught* by skilled adults.

Natural features are also important qualities of playgrounds. They should contain nature areas, flat grassy areas for organized games, mounds and hills for challenge and excitement, trees and shrubs for shade and beauty, gardens, and animal habitats and live pets that children tend. The prevailing practice of considering such features to be secondary in importance to manufactured exercise devices is a grievous error. The natural features allow a wide range of learning opportunities not available from other playground options.

How Can Playgrounds be Made Safer?

A great deal has been learned in recent years about playground safety. The most complete data on injuries, fatalities, and equipment implicated in injuries and fatalities are available from the National Electronic Injury Surveillance System (NEISS). The Consumer Product Safety Commission has been instrumental in developing guidelines for playground safety. The bibliography includes some of the most important documents on playground safety.

The most common cause of deaths and injuries (70–80 percent of all cases) on public playgrounds (schools and parks) is falling onto hard surfaces (concrete, asphalt). An effective remedy is simple and inexpensive; install 8–10 inches of sand or an equivalent resilient surface (pea gravel, bark mulch, shredded tires) under and around all moving equipment (e.g., swings and rotating devices). A retaining border is needed for this material and it must be replenished frequently, particularly in heavy-use areas such as under swings and at slide exits.

Parents are now suing play equipment manufacturers, schools, and cities (city parks) for injuries sustained by children on playgrounds. The judgments against these groups are increasing, as are the monetary sums awarded plaintiffs. A common element in a number of lawsuits leading to judgments favoring plaintiffs is the long-term availability of safety guidelines that are commonly violated by manufacturers, equipment installers, and playground maintenance personnel.

Examples of injuries and fatalities leading to lawsuits known to the writer include crushing of legs in the undercarriage of revolving mechanisms, amputation of fingers in shearing mechanisms and exposed gears, apparent suffocation from entrapment of the head in guard rails, ruptured body organs and concussions in falls from equipment onto hard surfaces, severe punctures and cuts from exposed bolts, electrocution from accessible electric equipment, severe burns (requiring plastic surgery from exposure to bare metal decks and slides), and drowning in improperly fenced pools of water. This partial list illustrates cases that could have been prevented by adherence to common guidelines on design, installation, and maintenance.

Entrapment of body parts, particularly the head, is an all too common playground hazard. Hangings are a common cause of fatalities in back-yard playgrounds. These appear to be caused by faulty design, protruding parts, and exposed bolts that entrap clothing. Back-yard play equipment may be improperly installed and poorly maintained, leading to broken parts, collapse of structure, or breaking of swing swivels. Children may be unsupervised for long periods of time in back-yard playgrounds so the child who is accidentally suspended by the head or neck does not have the immediate adult assistance usually available at school playgrounds. Other entrapment areas are frequently found between guard rails on decks, between clatter bridges and decks (bridge cables loosen with use), and between the rungs of ladder-type climbers. Depending on the head dimension of the smallest users, spaces between railings, rungs, or angles should not fall between about 3½–9 inches. Allowance must be made for coat ponchos that can contribute to entrapment.

Most manufacturers design some equipment exceeding reasonable vertical fall heights that can be accommodated by a prescribed resilient surface (e.g.,

Special facilities and materials include:

FIGURE 4.8 Sand play areas

FIGURE 4.9 Shaded outdoor spaces for organized activities

FIGURE 4.10 Storage for toys and other materials

FIGURE 4.11 Tracks for wheeled vehicles

FIGURE 4.12 Water fountains

FIGURE 4.13 Pipe-telephone booths

FIGURE 4.14   Music (drums) area

FIGURE 4.15 Water play/nature areas

8–10 inches of sand). There appears to be no logical reason for constructing play equipment with climbing heights over 6–8 ft. A broad category of hazards includes sharp edges, exposed bolts, protruding elements, pinch points, broken parts, and toxic materials. These may be the result of poor design or improper installation or maintenance. All of the above hazards are considered in the Playground Rating System.

What Should Playgrounds Do?

First and foremost, playgrounds should stimulate play, for the values of play are widely documented by researchers and acknowledged by professionals who work with young children. Play is fun, active, spontaneous, self-initiated, and challenging, and it is closely linked to learning and development. The playground is merely a stage where children act out, spontaneously and freely, the events that touch their lives and simultaneously develop durable, resilient bodies through movement. In contrast to bad playgrounds, good playgrounds increase the intensity of play and the range of play behavior. More and broader language is produced on good playgrounds and children engage in more "ing" behaviors—running, climbing, sliding, crawling, jumping. Bad playgrounds limit play behavior, restrict language, reduce physical movement, and create behavior problems.

Playgrounds should promote learning and development. Play enhances both convergent and divergent problem-solving and it allows better performance on tasks requiring divergent creative thought. Dramatic or symbolic play contributes to a range of developmental virtues including communication, sex-role development, cooperation, perspective-taking ability, creativity, and social and interpersonal problem-solving skills. Skills arising from dramatic play involve the ability to consider various roles simultaneously, to distinguish between literal and nonliteral roles and activities, and to perform well on classification and spatial perspective-taking tasks.

The playground should stimulate the senses through a rich array of textures, colors, and forms. It should nurture curiosity through a rich ever-changing environment. Portable materials, growing things, and live animals are the truly flexible elements of a play environment. Portable materials can be used in an unlimited number of play activities; plants change as they grow and with the seasons; animals grow and change, show their personalities, get sick, give birth, eat and drink. The playground should be fun, a place to escape from routine mental fatigue and boredom, a place to relax and enjoy.

The playground should support the child's basic social, physical, and cognitive needs. It should be comfortable, scaled to the child's size, yet physically and intellectually challenging. It should provide for all the forms of cognitive play (exercise, dramatic, construction, organized games) and social play (solitary, cooperative), consistent with the developmental stages of the children. It should encourage and allow interaction among children, materials, and adults. The environment must be dynamic, providing graduated challenge—and it must be continuously changing. The best playgrounds are never finished.

TABLE 4.8 PLAYGROUND RATING SYSTEM* (AGES 3–8)

Instructions:
Rate each item on a scale from 0–5. High score possible on Section I is 100 points, Section II is 50 points and Section III is 50 points, for a possible grand total of 200 points. Divide the grand total score by 2 to obtain a final rating.

Section I. What does the playground contain?
Rate each item for degree of existence and function on a scale of 0–5 (0 = not existent; 1 = some elements exist but not functional; 2 = poor; 3 = average; 4 = good; 5 = all elements exist, excellent (function).

_____ 1. A hard-surfaced area with space for games and a network of paths for wheeled toys.

_____ 2. Sand and sand play equipment.

_____ 3. Dramatic play structures (playhouse, car or boat with complementary equipment, such as adjacent sand and water and housekeeping equipment).

_____ 4. A superstructure with room for many children at a time and with a variety of challenges and exercise options (entries, exits and levels).

_____ 5. Mound(s) of earth for climbing and digging.

_____ 6. Trees and natural areas for shade, nature study and play.

_____ 7. Zoning to provide continuous challenge; linkage of areas, functional physical boundaries, vertical and horizontal treatment (hills and valleys).

_____ 8. Water play areas, with fountains, pools and sprinklers.

_____ 9. Construction area with junk materials such as tires, crates, planks, boards, bricks and nails; tools should be provided and demolition and construction allowed.

_____ 10. An old (or built) vehicle, airplane, boat, car that has been made safe, but not stripped of its play value (should be changed or relocated after a period of time to renew interest).

_____ 11. Equipment for active play: a slide with a large platform at the top (slide may be built into side of a hill); swings that can be used safely in a variety of ways (soft material for seats); climbing trees (mature dead trees that are horizontally positioned); climbing nets.

_____ 12. A large soft area (grass, bark mulch, etc.) for organized games.

_____ 13. Small semi-private spaces at the child's own scale: tunnels, niches, playhouses, hiding places.

_____ 14. Fences, gates, walls and windows that provide security for young children and are adaptable for learning/play.

_____ 15. A garden and flowers located so that they are protected from play, but with easy access for children to tend them. Gardening tools are available.

_____ 16. Provisions for the housing of pets. Pets and supplies available.

_____ 17. A transitional space from outdoors to indoors. This could be a covered play area immediately adjoining the playroom which will protect the children from the sun and rain and extend indoor activities to the outside.

_____ 18. Adequate protected storage for outdoor play equipment, tools for construction and garden areas, and maintenance tools. Storage can be separate: wheeled toys stored near the wheeled vehicle track; sand equipment near the sand enclosure; tools near the construction area. Storage can be in separate structures next to the building or fence. Storage should aid in children's picking-up and putting equipment away at the end of each play period.

_____ 19. Easy access from outdoor play areas to coats, toilets and drinking fountains. Shaded areas and benches for adults and children to sit within the outdoor play area.

_____ 20. Tables and support materials for group activities (art, reading, etc.).

Section II. Is the playground in good repair and relatively safe?

Rate each item for condition and safety on a scale of 0–5 (0 = not existent; 1 = exists but extremely hazardous; 2 = poor; 3 = fair; 4 = good; 5 = excellent condition and relatively safe yet presents challenge).

_____ 1. A protective fence (with lockable gates) next to hazardous areas (streets, deep ditches, water, etc.).

_____ 2. Eight to ten inches of noncompacted sand, wood mulch (or equivalent) under all climbing and moving equipment, extending through fall zones and secured by retaining wall.

_____ 3. Size of equipment appropriate to age group served. Climbing heights limited to 6–7 feet.

_____ 4. Area free of litter (e.g., broken glass, rocks), electrical hazards, high voltage power lines, sanitary hazards.

_____ 5. Moving parts free of defects (e.g., no pinch and crush points, bearing not excessively worn).

_____ 6. Equipment free of sharp edges, protruding elements, broken parts, toxic substances, bare metal exposed to sun.

_____ 7. Swing seats constructed of soft or lightweight material (e.g., rubber, canvas).

_____ 8. All safety equipment in good repair (e.g., guard rails, signs, padded areas, protective covers).

_____ 9. No openings that can entrap a child's head (approximately 3½–9 inches). Adequate space between equipment.

_____ 10. Equipment structurally sound. No bending, warping, breaking, sinking, etc. Heavy fixed and moving equipment secured in ground and concrete footings recessed in ground. Check for underground rotting, rusting, termites, in support members.

Section III. What should the playground do?

Rate each item for degree and quality on a scale of 0–5 (0 = not existent; 1 = some evidence but virtually nonexistent; 2 = poor; 3 = fair; 4 = good; 5 = excellent). Use the space provided for comments.

_____ 1. Encourages Play:
Inviting, easy access
Open, flowing and relaxed space
Clear movement from indoors to outdoors
Appropriate equipment for the age group(s)

_____ 2. Stimulates the Child's Senses:
Change and contrasts in scale, light, texture and color
Flexible equipment
Diverse experiences

TABLE 4.8 PLAYGROUND RATING SYSTEM* (AGES 3–8) (cont.)

_____   3. Nurtures the Child's Curiosity:
           Equipment that the child can change
           Materials for experiments and construction
           Plants and animals

_____   4. Supports the Child's Basic Social and Physical Needs:
           Comfortable to the child
           Scaled to the child
           Physically challenging

_____   5. Allows Interaction Between the Child and the Resources:
           Systematic storage that defines routines
           Semi-enclosed spaces to read, work a puzzle, or be alone

_____   6. Allows Interaction Between the Child and Other Children:
           Variety of spaces
           Adequate space to avoid conflicts
           Equipment that invites socialization

_____   7. Allows Interaction Between the Child and Adults:
           Easy maintenance
           Adequate and convenient storage
           Organization of spaces to allow general supervision
           Rest areas for adults and children

_____   8. Complements the Cognitive Forms of Play Engaged in by the Child:
           Functional, exercise, gross-motor, active
           Constructive, building, creating
           Dramatic, pretend, make-believe
           Organized games, games with rules

_____   9. Complements the Social Forms of Play Engaged in by the Child:
           Solitary, private, meditative
           Parallel, side-by-side
           Cooperative interrelationships

_____   10. Promotes Social and Intellectual Development:
           Provides graduated challenge
           Integrates indoor/outdoor activities
           Involves adults in children's play
           Regular adult-child planning
           The play environment is dynamic—continuously changing

*Joe L. Frost © 1977; revised © 1985, 1990.

REFERENCES

Bailey, N. (1933). Mental growth during the first three years. A developmental study of sixty-one children by repeated tests. *Genetic Psychology Monographs* 14.

Barnes, K. (1971). Preschool play norms: A replication. *Developmental Psychology* 51:99–103.

Bergen, D. ed. (1987). *Play as a Medium for Learning and Development: A Handbook of Theory and Practice.* Portsmouth, New Hampshire: Heinemann.

Blurton-Jones, N.G. (1972). Categories of child-child interaction. In N.G. Blurton-Jones ed. *Ethological Studies of Child Behavior* (pp. 97–129). New York: Cambridge University Press.

Buhler, C. (1935). *From Birth to Maturity.* London: Routledge and Kegan Paul.

Buhler, K. (1937). *The Mental Development of the Child.* London: Routledge and Kegan Paul.

Howes, C. (1980). Peer play scale as an index of complexity of peer interaction. *Developmental Psychology* 16:371–372.

Isaacs, S. (1933). *Social Development in Young Children: A Study of Beginnings.* London: Routledge and Kegan Paul.

Iwanaga, M. (1973). Development of interpersonal play structure in three, four, and five year-old children. *Journal of Research and Development in Education* 6(3):71–82.

Johnson, J.E., Christie, J.L., & Yawkey, T.D. (1987). *Play and Child Development.* Glenview, Ill.: Scott, Foresman.

Moore, N., Evertson, C. M., & Brophy, J. E. (1974). Solitary play: Some functional reconsiderations. *Developmental Psychology* 10:830–834.

Myers, J. (1985). Perceived and actual playground equipment choices of children. In Frost, J.L. & Sunderlin, S. eds. *When Children Play.* Wheaton, Maryland. Association for Childhood Education International.

Parten, M. (1932). Social participation among preschool children. *Journal of Abnormal and Social Psychology* 27:243–369.

Pelligrini, A.D., & Perlmutter, J.C. (1987). A reexamination of the Smilansky-Parten matrix of play behavior. *Journal of Research in Childhood Education* 2:89–96.

Piaget, J. (1962). *Play, Dreams, and Imitation in Childhood.* New York: W.W. Norton.

Rubin, K. (1982). Non-social play in preschoolers: Necessary evil? *Child Development* 53:651–657.

Rubin, K.H., Maioni, T.L., & Hornung, M. (1976). Free play behaviors in middle and lower class preschoolers: Parton and Piaget revisited. *Childhood Development,* 47:414–419.

Rubin, K.H., Watson, K., & Jambor, T. (1978). Free play behaviors in preschool and kindergarten children. *Child Development* 49:534–536.

Saracho, O.N. (1987). Cognitive style characteristics as related to young children's play behaviors. *Early Child Development and Care* 25:163–179.

Seagoe, M. Y. (1970). An instrument for the analysis of children's play in an index of degree of socialization. *Journal of School Psychology* 8(2):139–144.

Smilansky, S. (1968). *The Effects of Socio-dramatic Play on Disadvantaged Preschool Children.* New York: John Wiley.

Smilansky, S., and Shefatya, L. (1990). *Facilitating Play: A Medium for Promoting Cognitive, Socio-Emotional and Academic Achievement in Young Children.* Gaithersburg, Maryland: Psychosocial and Educational Publications.

Sponseller, D.B., & Jaworski, A.P. (1979). *Social and Cognitive Complexity in Young Children's Play: a Longitudinal Analysis.* (ERIC Document Reproduction Service No. ED 171 416).

Sullivan, H. S. (1953). *The Interpersonal Theory of Psychiatry.* New York: W. W. Norton.

Valentine, C.W. (1942). *The Psychology of Early Childhood.* Cleveland, OH: Sherwood.

Wagner, B.S., & Frost, J.L. (1986). Assessing play and exploratory behaviors of infants and toddlers. *Journal of Research in Childhood Education* 1:27–36.

Winter, W.M. (1985). Toddler play behviors and equipment choices in an outdoor play environment. In Frost, J.L. & Sunderlin, S. eds. *When Children Play.* Wheaton, MD: Association for Childhood Education International.

Yawkey, T.D. (1990). the role of adults in children's play. In S.C. Worthan and J.L. Frost eds. *Playgrounds for Young Children* (pp. 167–189). Reston, VA: American Association for Leisure and Recreation.

"The more playgrounds the fewer the hospitals, asylums and prisons."[1]

5

The Evolution of American Playgrounds

Formal playgrounds for children are available typically in four places—city parks, elementary schools, preschools, and back yards. These locations contain playgrounds that differ substantially from one another in provisions for materials and equipment, layout of the environment, play supervision or leadership, provisions for safety and child development, and in philosophy. The one common feature is that the respective sponsors intend that their playgrounds be used by children. Because of public access and availability, any given child might use playgrounds in *all* these locations on a frequent or infrequent basis.

Playground sponsors of city parks and recreation departments, public schools, private preschools, and parents hold differing views of play and consequently develop a range of playground types. Just how these differing points of view developed historically and how they influenced playgrounds is quite a story. The following section will trace the evolution of school and park playgrounds. Backyard play areas are generally stereotypical assortments (there are marvelous exceptions) of cheap, combination slide, swing, climber sets, purchased at K Mart, Sears, or Toys R-Us, and will not be included in this history. This is not to imply that backyard playgrounds are unimportant—quite the contrary—but until recently, their history could be characterized as shallow and uninspired.

---

[1] E.B. Mero (1908). *American Playgrounds: Their Construction, Equipment, Maintenance and Utility.* Boston: American Gymnasia Co.

FIGURE 5.1 *The first organized playgrounds in the United States were the outdoor gymnasiums of the early nineteenth century. (Photo from Mero 1908)*

It is generally believed that American playgrounds originated with the German inspired "sandgartens" of Boston in 1887. Indeed this event was the beginning of the "playground movement" of the late nineteenth and early twentieth centuries, but the roots of the sandgarten and the early American playground movement extend well beyond the sandgarten to early nineteenth century Germany.

Under the influence of Rousseau, Gutsmuth introduced outdoor play and exercise training in Schnepfenthal during the first decade of the nineteenth century. In 1812 his ideas were extended in the Jahn gymnastic associations by Katharinium, Corninus and Koch, who organized the first system of school play (Koch 1908). The principal motive for vigorous outdoor play was to offset the "grave dangers which threaten physical and mental health through this increasing tendency toward city life" (p. 325). The emphasis was placed on physical development over mental development, despite the teachings of Rousseau about the value of play for mental, social, and moral development. Developing the muscles of the body and the organs of respiration through physical exercise was a long-standing tradition of the German people.

THE OUTDOOR GYMNASIUM

The earliest available record shows that a crude outdoor gymnasium was started without supervisor or instructor in 1821 at the Latin School in Salem, Massachusetts (Mero 1908). Mero attributes the initial inspiration for this outdoor gymnasium to New England physical training sources. But at least two events suggest probable German influence; first, the chronological proximity of initial development of the German and American sites and, second, the establishment of a plat of ground at the Round Hill School in Northampton, Massachusetts, in 1825 for play and gymnastics using German-type apparatus and supervised by Dr. Charles Beck, a former student of Jahn in Germany (Mero 1908).

Following this early development of outdoor gymnasia in Germany and America, the next events of historical significance took place in the last quarter of the nineteenth century. Froebel extended the influence of Rousseau, Pestalozzi, and Luther in Germany in making valid what the Germans called the "developing method" (Froebel 1887, P.V.), and in regarding play as ". . . the highest phase of child development" (p. 54). Play of the young child, he said, . . . is highly serious and of deep significance . . . plays of childhood are the germinal leaves of all later life" (p. 55). Froebel set the stage for changing the emphasis on play as valuable merely for physical development to emphasizing play as the care of total development of the child. Thus the stage was set for the invention of a "child development playground" to complement and extend the "physical fitness playground."

THE SANDGARTEN

During the 1880s a political leader, Von Schenckendorff, placed heaps of sand in the public parks of Berlin where children were allowed to play (Sapora & Mitchell 1948). Dr. Marie Zakerzewska, an American visitor to Berlin, wrote of her observation on these playgrounds to the chairman of the Massachusetts Emergency and Hygiene Association (Playground and Recreation Association of America 1915). That same year (1886) piles of sand were placed in the yards of the Children's Mission on Parmeter Street in Boston. The first organized and supervised playgrounds for *young children* in America were created and the first serious play movement in this country was initiated.

G. Stanley Hall was so impressed by the educational value of sand that he wrote a delightful little book, *The Story of a Sand-Pile* (Hall 1897), in which he related the story of two boys, Harry and Jack, whose parents had dumped a pile of sand in their back yard. This sand pile at once became, as disciples of Froebel would have expected, a bright focus of attention. So much so, in fact, that "all other boyish interests gradually paled" (p. 3). Wells, tunnels, hills, roads, bridges, ponds, bays, and islands all developed as part of a community

FIGURE 5.2 The German-inspired sandgartens in Boston marked the beginning of the playground movement for young children. (Photo from Mero 1908).

within which representational play abounded. Industrial training, mercantile pursuits, law enforcement, topological imagination, and valuable civic training were accomplished through play. Boys of all ages were quite alive in fictitious activity up until about age 15 when the sand pile began to lose its charm. The benefits were so great that, in the opinion of the parents, they had been "of about as much yearly value to the boys as the eight months of school" (p. 18).

The following chronology of early American playground development outlines events of historical significance during the earliest period of playground development.

CHRONOLOGY OF EARLY AMERICAN PLAYGROUND DEVELOPMENT*

1821–	First outdoor gymnasium at the Salem, Massachusetts Latin School
1825–	First outdoor playground and gymnasium with supervision and instruction, Round Hill School, Northampton, Massachusetts
1826–	First public outdoor gymnasium in Washington Garden, Boston
1825–1872	Period of relatively little activity
1872–	First legislative action recognized to purchase land for playgrounds, Brookline, Massachusetts
1876–	First park playground, Washington Park, Chicago
1887–	First state law authorizing small parks, New York City
	First sandgartens established in Boston, marking the beginning of the playground movement
1889–	First free, equipped, supervised outdoor gymnasium for public use, Charlesbank, Massachusetts (for men and boys)
1890–	First New York City playground
1893–	First Providence, Rhode Island, playground
1894–	First Chicago playground with modern equipment, Hull House
1896–	Northwestern University, Chicago, opened extensive scale playground, equipped with apparatus. First Minneapolis playground, by Improvement League, in school yards.
1898–	First Minneapolis playground, by Improvement League, in school yard
	First Denver playground, by women's club, on borrowed land
1899–	First municipal playground, in New York City, resulted from laws of 1895
1903–	Creation of the South Park, Chicago, recreation center idea
1904–	Formation of the Department of Public Recreation of the American Civic, the first organized national effort on behalf of playgrounds.
1905–	Opening of the first of the South Park recreation centers, Chicago
1906–	Play festival and field day for country children (Organization of the Playground Association of America), New Paltz, New York
1907–	First outdoor play festival, at Chicago on closing day of the first convention of the Playground Association of America

*Adapted from Mero, E.C. (1908) *American Playgrounds: Their Construction, Equipment, Maintenance and Utility*. Boston: American Gymnasia Co.

1908–   Beginning of extension work by the University of Missouri Department of Physical Education to spread playgrounds and physical training to all towns and cities in Missouri. Playgrounds Congress by the Playground Association of America, New York City.

THE DEVELOPMENTAL PLAYGROUND: KINDERGARTENS AND NURSERY SCHOOLS

Fredrich Froebel, the originator of the first kindergarten in Germany in 1837, assigned great educational significance to play and developed his curriculum and materials around combined play and work. In his gifts and occupations he formed a living connection between the two contrasts, using play to lead naturally and gradually into work, securing spontaneity and freedom for both. His "gifts," consisting of such objects as balls, cylinders, cubes, and blocks, were to be handled, examined, counted, measured, and so on. They were for the exploration of meaning. The "occupations" involved such activities as paper cutting and folding, weaving, stringing, and painting and were valuable for practicing skills and creating (Froebel 1887).

Froebel's outdoor playgrounds (Froebel 1887:111) were nature itself. Children built canals, dams, bridges, and mills in the streams; cultivated gardens and fruit trees; tended plants and flowers; observed beetles, butterflies, and birds; explored old walls and ruined vaults; and cared for pets. Open areas were provided for running, wrestling, ball games, and games of war. He proposed that fathers provide the same activities for their boys (Froebel did not overcome the gender stereotypes of his time) and that, "Every town should have its own common playground for the boys" (1887:114). The plight of children in cities was recognized by Froebel. He believed that they were deprived of the rich opportunities for physical, intellectual, and moral growth through play that were available for the children of the country. "Scientific, educational, Christian philanthropy has no better field of operation than in providing ample playgrounds in cities . . ." (Hughes 1897:152).

Froebel (Hughes 1897) credited visits to Pestalozzi's school for his growing awareness of play as an educational influence and the open air and nature as a powerful force in strengthening "the intelligence and the soul as well as the body" (p. 121). Reformers before him (Plato, Aristotle, Solomon, Quintilian, Luther, Locke, Schiller, Richter) delved into the significance of play in mind development, character formation, and physical training, but Froebel was the first to make extensive applications in practice. He also predated modern science in proposing a unity between physical culture and mind development (p. 129). He believed that play was more valuable than physical culture for in play the child thinks for himself while in formal physical culture the mind merely conveys the message of someone else to the motor system.

Some of the kindergartens in the United States responded to Froebel's pleas for "self activity" by adding swings, seesaws, climbing poles, and various toys to their play environments and by proposing programs dominated by free play (Blow 1909:158). The gifts and occupations were offered as incentives and a motley array of play things such as bean bags, wooden soldiers, tools, and footballs were added. The didactic qualities of the gifts and occupations were thus diluted or forgotten.

By the turn of the twentieth century kindergarten educators were torn between two camps: the school of Froebel and the progressive, scientific school of Dewey. Leaders of the two sides engaged in bitter debates at conferences of the International Kindergarten Union. A Committee of Nineteen was established in 1903 and charged with formulating a contemporary statement about kindergarten education. A conservative view (Froebel) was written by Susan Blow Froebel's greatest American interpreter; (Baker 1937:14), a progressive view (Dewey) by Patty Smith Hill, and a middle-of-the-road view by Elizabeth Harrison.

The ensuing reports (International Kindergarten Union 1913), though differing in their view of program process and substance, solidified the role of play, games, and play materials in kindergarten education and reconfirmed the importance of integrating rational modes of the teacher with the child's natural instincts. Purely "free play," they agreed, was not sufficient for optimum child development. Even William Heard Kilpatrick, a disciple of Dewey and critic of Froebel, supported Froebel's use of games in education and predicted that, "The school of the future will make even more thorough-going use of games and play" (Kilpatrick 1916:156).

By the end of the first quarter of the present century the textbooks for normal schools and teacher's colleges included brief sections on play, games, and play materials and apparatus. Parker and Temple (1925) described several types of play for four to seven year olds. Play for physical control included free movement play, play with apparatus, and play with toys. In addition to natural features (e.g., trees for climbing and swinging), playgrounds contained swings, slides, springboards, low trapeze, climbing ropes, ladders, see-saws, balls, and space for games. Such equipment, including swings, seesaws, and climbers, were commonly installed in gymnasiums and in classrooms. Some were portable, allowing movement between the classroom and the playground.

The typical American kindergarten of this period was generally better equipped and contained fewer children than the primary classroom. From its beginning the kindergarten had been stocked with an abundance of material while the traditional first grade classroom materials were limited to materials for reading and writing. The play views of Froebel, after which America's first kindergartens were borrowed, had not influenced the existing primary school. Unfortunately, as kindergartens grew in numbers and were increasingly integrated into public schools, these early advantages were diluted by more "academically oriented" points of view. The emerging nursery schools for five-year-olds and younger, on the other hand, maintained their independence from public schools. The child development tradition, strengthened through the child study movement of the early 1900s (Frost & Kissinger 1976:52) continued until the present day and the young child's right to play was preserved and enhanced by a rich array of play materials and equipment in leading kindergartens.

Beginning in about 1900, an American kindergarten leader, Anna Bryan, principal of the training school of the Chicago Free Kindergarten Association, began experimenting with materials such as hammer and nails, pasteboard boxes, wood, and wire to supplement and/or supplant Froebel's occupations (Parker & Temple 1925). The Chicago example was picked up by others throughout much of the country, leading to the establishment in 1925 of an extensive array of play and work/play materials for indoor and outdoor use.

Materials for woodworking
Materials for paper construction
Sewing and weaving materials
Modeling materials
Toys for dramatic play
    Playhouse, doll furniture, housekeeping toys, carts, wagons, trains, boats, toy animals, toys for playing store
Toys and apparatus for physical activity
    Rubber balls, bean bags, rocking horses, slides, swings, trapeze, swinging-ropes, seesaws, bars, springboards, ladders, sand piles

The nursery school movement developed separately from the kindergarten movement and was influenced by Rachel and Margaret Macmillan in England. They were contemporaries of Dewey and were influenced by the French psychiatrist Sequin, who also influenced Montessori's ideas on sensory education. The Macmillans believed that the whole child—social, emotional, mental, physical—should be nurtured, and established activities that are still in use today: personal hygiene, plant and animal care, indoor and outdoor segments, and the use of music, sand, and water.

In 1970, Abigail Eliot, a social worker and student of the Macmillans in England, opened the Ruggles Street Nursery School in Boston, drawing from the work of Froebel, Dewey, and the Macmillans (Osborn, Logue, & Surbeck 1973:17). In rapid succession others opened around the country.

The Harriet Johnson Nursery School, started by Lucy Sprague Mitchell in New York City, was typical of the better nursery schools of the era and was among the pioneer schools for toddlers (18 months to 3 years). The essential spaces were large indoor and outdoor play spaces, sleeping quarters, a kitchen, and toilet. The playground extended over the roofs of two houses with a 17-ft. × 18-ft. area of pebble surface, 8 inches deep, with a concrete border, and the remainder surfaced with tile. The cement sandbox was fitted with a water-proof cover (Johnson 1924).

Similar to the better kindergartens of this period, much of the play apparatus was used both indoors and outdoors, with large equipment such as slides and stairs being replicated rather than transported. The outdoor materials were: slide, two low swings, see-saw, two saw horses, two large packing boxes, boards, ladder, steps, sandbox, pails, spoons, trowels, shovels, perforated sink shovels, small pans and cups, skylight peak (used for climbing), three movable steps, two kiddy cars, large express wagons, small trailer cart, brooms, rubber balls, basketball, hammers, nails, lumber for nails, and workbench.

The indoor materials were: small tables, chairs and benches, adult chairs and table, large ironing table, slide, gymnasium mat, block chest, blocks, Montessori Pink Tower, Montessori Brown Stair, Milton Bradley cubes, nested boxes, Montessori cylinders, wooden dolls, large doll's bedstead, flatirons, covered boxes, extra wheels and axles, rubber balls, plasticene, drawing paper and crayons, Swiss tuned bells, musical bells, wooden tone bars, sand bar, sandpaper covered boards, piano, wooden paving blocks.

Even from contemporary perspectives the total array of play materials and certain of the program practices were impressive. Program practices included extensive periods outdoors; indoor-outdoor integration of activities; provision of many portable, creative materials (loose parts); and re-arrangement of apparatus for encouraging various play activities. The leaders understood that play has a central role in child development. History shows that the public elementary schools have never understood or accepted this basic principle and their playgrounds reveal this void to the present time. As a case in point, the playground at the leading 1920s nursery school was far superior to virtually all public education school playgrounds of the 1980s!

Not unlike public parks and public school personnel, nursery school and kindergarten workers appeared to give little regard to safety. The descriptive report (Johnson 1924) of the Harriet Johnson Nursery School made no mention of playground safety. Photographs reveal a range of conditions that are now known to be hazardous: excessive heights—walls, steps, play equipment—ladders positioned over concrete, swings with heavy wood seats, inverted angles on slide allowing head entrapment, equipment in fall zones under decks and slides. To their credit, it appears that news about injuries from falls onto hard surfaces had reached the Johnson Nursery School people, for their outdoor slide was installed in their sole pebble-filled space—probably for protection in falls.

In the *Journal of Education* for 1826, Wilderspin (Iowa Child Welfare Research Station 1934) predicted that in light of their obvious value, schools for children under five would soon spread to every corner of the land. But while kindergartens, primarily for children over five, had spread throughout the United States by 1930, there were fewer than five hundred nursery schools. By this time the International Kindergarten Union had been revamped to form the Association for Childhood Education International (ACEI). This organization included preschool education in its broad educational focus, but the new National Association for Nursery Education (now National Association for the Education of Young Children, NAEYC) was devoted entirely to education and development of the preschool child.

A fundamental tenet of these two organizations, relative to young children and preschool education, was that the old criterion of age of entrance and ability to master basic techniques of reading, writing, and arithmetic were no longer in accord with fundamental aims of education. The full range of development—physical, emotional, social, intellectual-influenced educational goals, and play—was assigned a central role. Both ACEI and NAEYC have remained faithful to these early commitments in their full range of publications, conferences, and membership activities and services. Indeed, both organizations recently published books on play and play environments (Frost & Sunderlin 1985; Fein & Rivkin 1986; McKee 1986).

In 1921, the first university laboratory school for preschool children was opened at the University of Iowa (Iowa Child Welfare Research Station 1934). Thirty-two children, ages two to five, were enrolled. Within a decade the enrollment had increased to 95. The two- and three-year-olds played on one playground and the fours and fives on another. The indoor and outdoor play environments for the younger children were very similar to those of the Johnson Nursery School except that the University of Iowa outdoor playground was in a natural grassy area with plants and trees rather than on rooftops and included a jungle gym, playhouse, and wading pool. Both of the University of Iowa playgrounds of the 1920s reflected the influence of manufacturers, with the inclusion of jungle gyms, and for the older children, a massive, heavy-duty steel slide-swing apparatus.

The publications of Patty Smith Hill, Professor and Director of the Department of Kindergarten-First Grade Education at Teachers College, Columbia University, and the teachers of kindergarten and first grade at the Horace Mann School in New York were highly influential in promoting healthy, developmentally oriented practice in schools and in promoting play. Beginning in 1905 in the Speyer School of New York City, directed by Luella Palmer, they spent many years of study and experimentation to develop a curriculum which was published in 1923 (Hill et al. 1923). Relying extensively upon the work of Dewey, Thorndike, Gesell and other noted psychologists, they upstaged President Lyndon Baines Johnson by proposing a "Great Society" for children. Like their contemporaries, before mentioned, they utilized a rich assortment of play/learning activities and materials indoors. These included block building, manipulative toys, sand, industrial and fine arts, doll play, and household arts.

Outdoors the children were given first-hand contact with animals, plants, and forces of nature. They planted and cultivated gardens, cared for animals, examined rocks and minerals, experimented with light, weather, fluid materials, and fire, and took excursions to points of interest both on and off campus. Thus, while Dewey was credited for their philosophy, Froebel clearly influenced their playgrounds. As a matter of special interest it is in written accounts of the Horace Mann School (Garrison 1926) that the present writer saw the earliest accommodation by nursery school-kindergarten specialists for merry-go-rounds and giant strides.

Luella Palmer herself was sufficiently enthusiastic about play to write a book on the subject—*Play Life in the First Eight Years* (1916)—in which she proposed a comprehensive program of play activities for children. This book contained the only reference the present writer located revealing a link between the nursery-kindergarten or early childhood movement to the work of the American Playground Association, which was to become so influential in the development of public school and park playgrounds (Palmer 1916:250, 255). Palmer echoed the Association's concerns for the social ends of play-cleanliness, politeness, formation of friendships, obedience to law, loyalty, justice, honesty, truthfulness, and determination. Her play environments reflected these ideals as well as the physical and mental benefits of a playground.

The reader should be aware that the innovative playgrounds described here were well advanced compared to those in most nursery schools and kindergartens across the country. A national survey published by the 1930 White House Conference on Child Health and Protection (Rogers 1932) revealed "considerable need" for play spaces, research, and standards of leadership. The report stressed the seriousness of neglecting opportunities for play: "Since play forms the chief, indeed the only, activity of the preschool years, it follows that the neglect of the recreation and physical education of the preschool child constitutes a serious flaw in any system of child care and protection" (p. 121).

Although preschools of the post-1920s era were influenced in varying degrees by commercial manufacturers and traditional primary schools, the best of the lot continued to subscribe to play and playground practices established by early leaders. The post-1920s writers in the early childhood field continued to extol the virtues of play for child development and introduced limited novel ideas of safety and playground development. Foster and Headley (1936) called for soft surfacing such as grass and tanbark. Foster and Mattson (1939) prescribed concrete footings for fixed apparatus, and the substitution of screws for nails to prevent wobbling, and the avoidance of sharp edges and metal subject to rust. They were yet to discover flexible, lightweight swing seats (wood was universally used), but they substituted chains for ropes (which were subject to breaking) and they proposed hanging an automobile tire from a rope for swinging. Their awareness of the dangers inherent in excessive heights led them to propose that no nursery school slide be higher than five and a half feet and it should have a discharge chute at the end for slowing descent. For large apparatus (swings, slides, seesaws, jungle gyms) they called for close supervision and they prescribed covers to keep sand areas clean.

The nursery school-kindergarten leaders of the 1940s and 1950s had refined their perspectives about health and safety during play. Paved areas were proposed for wheeled vehicles; gates and fences were child-proofed; asphalt was considered dangerous under climbing equipment; a combination of surfaces was proposed for various play activities; and semi-shelters and shelters were suggested for play under various conditions of climate (Landreth & Read 1942). Leavitt (1958) proposed the addition of horizontal ladders and tire or canvas swing seats.

THE PHYSICAL FITNESS PLAYGROUND: PUBLIC SCHOOLS AND PUBLIC PARKS

The outdoor gymnasia of the early 1800s had succumbed to lack of interest by 1830, and only a handful were established over the next half century. During the 1880s playgrounds for young children (infants to kindergarten age) grew in popularity and observers noted that, "Even big boys hung around and looked wistful," at the creative activities and play spaces of young children (Playground and Recreation Association of America 1915:3). Consequently the first free equipped and supervised public outdoor gymnasium for "men and boys" (older and younger boys) was opened in Charlesbank, Massachusetts, in 1889 and the Columbus Avenue Playground for mixed age groups was opened in Boston in 1900. By 1909, a Massachusetts law required all towns of 10,000 to establish public playgrounds (Playground and Recreation Association of America 1909:19; Mero 1908:242) and cities around the country were involved in the "playground movement."

The sand-pile work was so successful that the city of Boston placed sand piles on school yards for use during vacation periods. The second year kindergarten instructors were placed in charge of sand play during school periods. The city then installed sand play areas in city parks, including the before-mentioned Charlesbank open-air gymnasium and children of all ages were playing on the same playground—but with separate areas to keep older boys and girls from playing together.

Despite the growing interest in play and playgrounds during the first decade of the present century, most public school yards were virtually unchanged. In 1913, Henry Curtis (1913) authored a U.S. Bureau of Education Bulletin lamenting this fact. A sign on the side of a school building in Arkansas stated, "Fifty dollars fine for anyone trespassing on this yard after school hours" (p. 5). This represented the near universal attitude that school yards were primarily for the use of the janitor; they were surfaced for his convenience and used according to his desires. Curtis stated, "I do not know that there are any cases where he has used it to raise potatoes and the family vegetables but he might nearly have done so for any advantage that has come to the school or the children" (p. 5).

Curtis recommended that American schools provide larger yards for children's play, that they put them in a condition to be used, that they provide play equipment, and that they put someone in charge. Further, he stressed organized play on school grounds after school, on Saturdays, and during summer vacations. He cited the school yards of Gary, Indiana, for their imaginative work. Gary provided a play teacher in the yard or the gymnasium from 8 a.m. until 5 p.m., and from 7 until 9:30 each evening, for six days a week throughout the year.

Similar to most of today's public schools playgrounds, those in Gary were hopelessly inadequate for play (primarily exercise equipment) and extremely hazardous. Photographs and written descriptions reveal apparatus climbing heights well over 15 feet, and hard surfaces under equipment. The merry-go-round had an open center with cross braces, allowing intrusion of arms and legs. Curtis himself recognized many of the hazards. The sand for younger children's play should be kept in a sanitary condition. The see-saw was a frequent source of accidents and disputes. Curtis knew of "Half a dozen broken arms resulting in a week from a new set of poorly made seesaws" (1913:26). However, he did not hesitate to recommend 15-foot slides made of wood (to prevent burns and rust). The slide should be detachable so it could be taken in out of the rain. The tall swings took up too much room and were too dangerous for the younger children. Children being hit by a swing in motion, "Will certainly be seriously injured and may be killed" (p. 27). Consequently, Curtis recommended that swings not be over 8–10 feet high, that they be placed in a remote corner of the yard and fenced, that a piece of rubber hose be nailed to the side of the wood swing board to deaden the blow if a child is struck, and that the swing seats themselves be made of lightweight materials. Like swings, the giant stride should be placed in a corner of the school yard. Since the chains and steel ladders were dangerous, Curtis suggested that they be replaced by rope and wood. Despite such early warnings, original-type giant strides remain on some playgrounds and at least one manufacturer still sells a modified all-steel version.

By 1909, the vision of play proponents had expanded beyond the mere "physical fitness" focus to a much broader perspective. The Playground Association of America (PAA) (1909, 1910) identified the social ends of play; cleanliness, politeness, formation of friendships, obedience to law, loyalty, justice, honesty, truthfulness, and determination. These lofty views of idealists and romanticists, however, were tempered by the more rational views of some educators. Luella A. Palmer, assistant director of kindergartens in New York City, aptly wrote that play develops bodily organs, develops keen and quick thought, widens mental horizons, and promotes social development (Palmer 1916)—modern thoughts indeed!

THE PLAY MOVEMENT AND PROFESSIONAL ORGANIZATIONS

The "play movement" of the early 1900s was influenced by several factors; early theories of play, the new psychology which was focusing away from the course of study to the child himself, an emerging philanthropic spirit, concerns for child welfare and safety, and influences of the German physical play movement (Curtis 1977). The influence of Froebel so richly expressed through the establishment of sandgartens and kindergartens appeared to have been diluted by the broad range of recreation interests among the organizers of the first American organization devoted to play and playgrounds.

By 1905, 35 American cities had established supervised playgrounds. In that same year Chicago opened 10 small recreation parks at a cost of $5,000,000. These parks, designed for indoor and outdoor year-round recreation by people of all ages, were hailed by President Theodore Roosevelt as "the most notable civic achievement of any American city" (Knapp & Hartsoe 1979:28). Several recreation innovators, including Curtis Lee and Luther Gulick, recognized the need for a professional organization to provide effective implementation and coordination of municipal recreation. Following a series of negotiations the Playground Association of America was formed in 1907, with Luther Gulick as president and Jane Addams, Joseph Lee, Henry Curtis, and Seth Stewart as officers. The executive committee was comprised of 27 members from 10 cities. Stewart assumed the role of publishing a monthly periodical, *The Playground*, which remains a rich source of early play and playground information. To further illustrate the mood of the country about play, the new organization received a reception in the White House, hosted by President Roosevelt, to initiate the new organization.

During ensuing years the playground idea was spreading rapidly. In 1907 only 90 of the cities with populations of more than 5,000 had playgrounds; this figure jumped to 187 in 1908 and to 336 by the end of 1909. By mid-1910, with as many as 50 letters of request for assistance pouring into PAA offices daily, its leaders recognized that the term "playground," connoting children's play, was too narrow to represent the increasingly broad conception of recreation. Consequently PAA was changed to Playground and Recreation Association of America (PRAA), the journal was retitled, *Recreation*, and the constitution was revised. Although the PRAA leaders were successful in widening the concept of leisure and recreation, the emphasis of the organization rapidly shifted from play and playgrounds to a wide range of social work, recreation, and civic affairs. The field of play has not regained its early momentum to the present time.

In 1914 contributions to PRAA were eight times higher than in 1909. The PRAA, however, had so expanded its services that its finances were not sufficient. The following years, marked by war and depression, saw declining revenues and staff cuts. Nonetheless, by 1916 the Association had successfully guided American cities from informal "play" to public "recreation." The PRAA yearbook roster of activities carried on in city play programs and school recreation centers included over a dozen activities, such as Boy Scouts, not listed in 1910 (Knapp & Hartsoe 1979).

In 1930, even by PRAA definitions, less than one fifth of American school age children had access to playgrounds. The interests of the organization had continued to expand to match broadening recreation and leisure pursuits of citizens. The stock market crash of 1929 and the following depression resulted in increased leisure for many Americans. The PRAA took steps to gain public support for an even broader conception of recreation. The name change, PRAA, to National Recreation Association (NRA) in 1930 "finally removed the by-then restrictive term 'playground' from the title of the Association" (Knapp & Hartsoe 1979:104). Thus another nail was driven into the coffin of children's play.

Between 1906 and the end of 1965 the Association expended $45,979,355 for the advancement of play and recreation. NRA had developed over 2,000 affiliated recreation and park agencies and over 4,000 individual service associates. Amazingly, the Association's programs continued to expand including such areas as performing arts, personnel services, training institutes, consultation, research, site visits, the ill and handicapped, public information, correspondence (43 countries in 1 year), and publications. Despite this broad range of services, (most carried on in reduced fashion since 1907) some critics thought the Association was too narrow in its focus. The editor of *Youth Leaders Digest* claimed that NRA was still mainly a playground association!

Once again, limited resources and a desire to serve an ever-broadening field of recreation led the NRA and several other related organizations—the American Institute of Park Executives, American Recreation Society, National Conference on State Parks—to propose a merger. Consequently the National Recreation and Park Association was formed in January 1966.

Despite substantial achievements in the broad areas of leisure and recreation, the Association's achievements in children's play are largely limited to the 1907–1930 period. Their influence on children's play at the present time is negligible and disappointing.

PERIODS OF PLAYGROUND DEVELOPMENT

The history of playground development in America can be divided into broad time spans characterized by types and range of play equipment. These eras are the Manufactured Apparatus Era, the Novelty Era, and the Modern Era.

The Manufactured Apparatus Era

In 1910, the Playground Association of America's Committee on Equipment published recommendations for supervised public playgrounds (Playground Association of America 1910). By this time manufacturers of gymnastic and play apparatus were promising to settle playground problems ". . . with a scheme of material appliancies." Iron, steel, and wood were featured in the catalogs of manufacturers who were credited with "rendering distinguished service as a propaganda agency in the American playground movement" (p. 272).

The prescribed apparatus for girls of all ages and for boys under 10 years of age included; sand court; 4 rope swings, 10 feet high; 1 sliding board; 2 giant

FIGURE 5.3 *The manufactured appliance era of the early 1900s was a period of invention of apparatus for sale by commercial companies.*

strides; 2 teeter boards or teeter ladders; 4 sets of ring toss or quoits; and a supply of balls, bats, nets, bean bags, and similar materials. The area was to be about 100 × 200 ft. with a capacity (average occasion) of 150 to 200 children. The cost of apparatus totaled about $200.00

Play leadership was considered essential for supervision, organization, and administration of the playground during this early period (1910). Such accessories as toilets, drinking fountains, shaded areas, seating areas, shelter and storage rooms, landscaping, maintenance equipment, lighting, and water taps for sprinkling the playground were recommended. The advantages of steel versus wood apparatus were considered—wood rots and splinters, while steel is too hot on hot days and too cold on cold days and deteriorates in certain areas. These concerns are yet to be resolved.

Manufacturers and inventors were increasingly influencing playground developers. Drawings, photographs, and written descriptions of equipment during this era reveal major hazards; excessive heights, shearing actions in rotating equipment, heavy moving objects (swings, trapeze rings) with battering ram effects, crowded conditions, and hard surfacing under equipment (Frost 1986).

The first quarter of the present century was one of optimism and expansion. Attitudes toward play were changing as religious convictions against play and ignorance of child development gave way to an emerging awareness that play was essential for children's development (Lehman & Witty 1926; Lee 1927; Lloyd

1931). The impact of these beliefs, however, were scarcely to be seen in actual playground designs before the mid-1900s.

With the advent of motor vehicles, urban children were in increased danger of being injured or killed while playing unsupervised in city streets. Consequently, playgrounds were developed in parks, schoolyards, backyards, vacant lots, high density housing areas, and in streets closed for play (Stevens 1926; Jenkins 1934). Separate recreation programs for boys and girls continued and separate parks and playgrounds were maintained for black citizens.

Manufacturers continued to build traditional slides, swings, merry-go-rounds, jungle gyms, giant strides, and see-saws with minor variations to attract purchasers. The Medart Ocean Wave rotated and rocked simultaneously; the ball-bearing Flying Swing rotated as two children swung at each end; the Merry-Whirl swing was a combination merry-go-round and swing.

The Great Depression of the 1930s saw increased emphasis on recreation for unemployed youth and adults with sports fields sharing space with playgrounds. Coeducational activities for young adults and mixed gender play of children developed and became popular by World War II. Play and recreation specialists recommended smaller equipment for young children and separate zones for specified categories of apparatus (National Recreational Association 1934).

During the war years of 1941 through 1945, metal was diverted to the war effort and there was virtually no change in playgrounds. The post-war period saw the re-emergence of equipment manufactured during earlier decades.

The Novelty Era

The 1950s and 1960s were the most innovative periods in playground development since the turn of the century. By this time the "playground movement" had become essentially a "recreation movement" insofar as public parks and public schools were concerned. Physical fitness, aesthetic quality, and manufacturability motives were clearly emphasized over child development concerns despite an avalanche of imaginative designs by inventors, handy-men, and manufacturers (Musselman 1950, 1956; Shaw & Davenport, 1956).

Parents Magazine, the Museum of Modern Art and Creative Playthings, Inc., sponsored a nationwide competition for play sculptures designed to exercise the imagination of children (National Recreation Association 1954). The application of four basic criteria—aesthetic quality, play value, safety, and manufacturability—guided the selections. First place and $1,000 went to a painter from New York City who presented a series of square, block houses, five feet tall, with windows, ladders, climbing ropes, peek holes, and an "attractive color scheme." In the main, play sculptures were free-standing, molded, concrete forms utilizing tunnel mazes and a labyrinth of spaces and shapes. Essentially, they were abstract, fixed, lifeless, and resistant to change, movement, or action by children. Although the motives were worthy, play sculptures were frequently more appealing to adults than to children. The advocates of novelty or fantasy structures claimed that their motive was to compensate or substitute for the standard *municipal playground* with its paved surface, fence, and classic equipment—slide, sand, swings, and jungle gym–and the *amusement park concept* such as the famed

FIGURE 5.4 The "novelty era" of the 1940s and 1950s featured devices intended to appeal to the imagination—space ships, animal structures, etc.

Tivoli Gardens in Copenhagen focusing upon "amusement for amusement's sake" (Nichols 1955). They acknowledged the contributions of a third type of playground, the *nursery play yard*, praising its spontaneity and interesting materials, but opined that the modern concrete "air raid shelters" and "foxholes" of the *sculptural playground* would not have been possible in the early 1900s when the nursery play yard emerged. Finally, they concluded that all four types of playgrounds contribute to the mind, social, and leisure needs of children.

During the novelty era, a number of cities engaged in imaginative playground development. In the period of 1952 to 1956, Philadelphia's recreation department redeveloped 60 playgrounds, parks, and squares, with each playground tailored to the needs of the neighborhood (Crawford 1956; National Recreation Association 1959). Unique elements included toy lending, play street (streets closed off for playgrounds), theme playgrounds, and sculptured play equipment. Bellevilee, New Jersey's "improvised play community" featured component parts of concrete sewer pipes, railroad ties, a slide chute, corrugated iron pipe, balance beam, railroad track, and a horizontal ladder, "arranged so as to make each child's actions affect the other" (Cook 1956). The parks and recreation department of San Mateo, California, changed their "drab playground" to a "bright, gay one, filled with happy youngsters," by installing a sandbox painted in different colors; cement culverts, each painted a different color; a drinking fountain, painted red and blue; tables painted different colors; and an equipment hut, painted to represent a carousel, including nursery rhyme characters—all done to give the children something they could associate with their "dream world thoughts" (Shaw & Davenport 1956).

Not to be outdone, such developments as these were followed in rapid succession by numerous others. A "Dennis the Menace" playground designed by Hank Ketcham, the creator of the "Dennis the Menace" cartoons, was constructed in Monterey, California (National Recreation Association 1957). The East Orange, New Jersey Recreation Commission purchased two 14-foot cabin cruisers, constructed a lighthouse out of cinder blocks, built a jetty and dock from telephone poles, and added sand to create a "nautical playground" (National Recreation Association 1958). The Los Angeles Park Department's Recreation Improvement Committee designed, built, tested, and then put onto playgrounds for the supreme test. A wide array of equipment including western theme villages, novel slides, multiple purpose exercise equipment, and theme equipment such as sharks and octopus rockers (Frederickson 1959). By the early 1960s, rocket play structures inspired by Sputnik were springing up around the country (National Recreation Association 1960). Leading play equipment manufacturers predicted the future (National Recreation Association 1962). Action-oriented equipment would remain a critical priority; steel would continue to be the chief construction material for exercise equipment; plastic would predominate over concrete in play sculptures and in time would replace steel in many applications; plastic molding over steel frames would add color and variety; play sculptures would become more popular and swings in the shape of animated characters would be developed; equipment would be designed with definitive age groups in mind and equipment would be lower in height and placed in playground pits filled with gravel topped by tanbark. From a 1988 perspective, these predictions have proven to be surprisingly accurate. They did, however, fail to predict the popularity of wood equipment during the 1970s and 1980s; the inherent hazards in animal-type swings and the widespread ignorance about and resistance to providing resilient surfaces under play equipment.

Most commercial manufacturers were still advertising the same type of metal apparatus that had been available for decades. However, by 1962, commercial play equipment had entered the age of fantasy. Many climbing structures, slides, swings, and seesaws now resembled rockets, stagecoaches, ponies, turtles, and other fanciful objects and creatures. Complex climbing structures that combined

FIGURE 5.5 *Despite the advances in playground and equipment design, most American playgrounds are sterile, barren, hazardous places.*

more than one play event were being produced, but were very simple compared to the large multi-function structures that would be a central focus of play environments in the 1970s and 1980s.

The Modern Era

During the 1970s and 1980s, modular wood equipment featuring decks and attached play options was popularized by manufacturers such as Columbia Cascade, Big Toys, Landscape Structures, Mexico Forge, and Iron Mountain Forge and spread to other manufacturers. During the 1980s, powder coated metal equipment featuring modular designs became increasingly popular (see Beckwith 1985). These structures facilitated a wide range of designs incorporating complexity, linkage, and challenge. Space-age plastics lent color and resiliency to play structures and reduced the likelihood of burns from skin contact with bare metal in the hot sun and the likelihood of children's tongues sticking to bare metal in freezing climates.

Beginning in the early 1970s, the U.S. Consumer Product Safety Commission manufacturers and consumers began to reconsider playground safety. This interest was influenced by public awareness of playground injuries and fatalities and a growing number of lawsuits, climaxed by a $9.2 million judgment (Sweeney 1985) favoring a Chicago child injured in a fall from a slide and by a $30 + million dollar judgment in New York City.

A fundamental concern of play professionals is the tendency of playground designers and consumers to overspecialize. Manufacturers tend to emphasize large, expensive play structures while underemphasizing portable materials and development of the total environment. Architects frequently design impressive natural environments of high aesthetic appeal while selecting hazardous, fixed, uninspiring equipment. Educators follow tradition in establishing playgrounds and, thus, perpetuate decades-old designs that are hazardous and have limited value for child development. American public school playgrounds, as revealed in a recent national survey (Bruya & Langerdorfer 1988), are a national disgrace, light years apart from the compelling play environments of our most visionary thinkers. Public park playgrounds follow essentially the same patterns as the public schools—hazardous and ill-suited to the developmental needs of children. Although generally deficient, preschool playgrounds have profited over the years from leadership of professionals firmly grounded in principles and practices of play and child development, leading back to the early Froebel and Dewey schools.

Americans are beginning to understand the vast differences in the way things are and the way they ought to be in the domain of children's play and play environments. Just how to bring practice abreast of theory and research is the subject matter of the following chapter.

FIGURE 5.6 *Manufactured equipment of the "modern era" emphasizes modular construction, activity linkages, a range of activity options, and safety.*

CONCLUSION

The most frequent locations of formal outdoor playgrounds for children are public parks, elementary schools, preschools (child care centers), and back yards. Most of these have public access and a wide range of children play there.

American formal playgrounds emerged from two events: one, the German-inspired outdoor gymnasia of the early 1800s, led to the development of public park and public school playgrounds, primarily for older children. The German-inspired sandgartens of Boston in the late 1800s were the forerunners of playgrounds for very young children. The outdoor gymnasia carried a physical fitness tradition and the sandgartens a developmental tradition. These separate play environment types and traditions, with modifications, endure today.

Since the establishment of early American playgrounds, the movement has passed through several eras; the manufactured apparatus era, characterized by heavy-duty steel and wood devices, devoted to exercise play; the novelty era, featuring theme equipment intended to exercise both the body and the imagination; and the modern era, with modular wood and vinyl-coated steel equipment intended to increase safety, complexity, and play value. Throughout these eras, a few playground sponsors, primarily in child development centers, have created and maintained highly imaginative, flexible play environments designed to foster the various areas of child development.

Despite the advances in design, most American playgrounds remain sterile, hazardous, and unimaginative. The next chapter addresses these problems and offers guidelines for refinement and improvement.

Portions of this chapter have been reprinted from Frost, J.L. (Winter, 1989), "Play Environments for Young Children in the U.S.A.: 1800–1990." By permission of the Editors of *Childrens' Environments Quarterly.*

REFERENCES

Baker, E.D. 1937. *The Kindergarten Centennial: 1837–1937.* Washington, D.C.: Association of Childhood Education International.

Beckwith, J. 1985. Equipment selection criteria for modern playgrounds. In *When Children Play,* eds. J.L. Frost & S. Sunderlin. Wheaton, MD: Association for Childhood Education International.

Blow, S. 1909. *Educational Issues in the Kindergarten.* New York: D. Appleton.

Bruya, L.D., & Langendorfer (eds.) 1988. *Where Our Children Play: Elementary School Playground Equipment.* Washington, D.C.: American Alliance for Physical Education, Health, Recreation, and Dance.

Butler, G.D. 1958. *Recreation Areas: Their Design and Equipment.* (2nd ed.) New York: Ronald Press.

Cook, R.E. 1956. An improvised play community. *Recreation* 49(4):172–174.

Crawford, R.W. 1956. A new look for Philadelphia. *Recreation* 49(9):322–323.

Curtis, H.S. 1977. *The Play Movement and its Significance.* Washington, D.C.: McGrath Publishing Company and the National Recreation. (Original work published 1917.)

Curtis, H.S. 1913. *The Reorganized School Playground.* Washington, D.C.: U.S. Bureau of Education, No. 40.

Fein, G., & Rivkin, M. (eds.) 1986. *The Young Child at Play.* Washington, D.C.: National Association for the Education of Young Children.

Foster, J.C., & Headley, N.E. 1936. *Education in the Kindergarten.* New York: American Book Company.

Foster, J.C., & Mattson, M.L. 1939. *Nursery School Education.* New York: D. Appleton-Century.

Frederickson, W., Jr. 1959. Planning play equipment. *Recreation* 52:186–189.

Froebel, F. 1887. *The Education of Man.* W.N. Hailmann, trans. New York: D. Appleton.

Frost, J.L. 1986. Children's playgrounds: research and practice. In *The Young Child at Play: Reviews of Research, Volume 4.* (eds.) G.Rein & M. Rivkin. Washington, D.C.: National Association for the Education of Young Children, pp. 195–212.

Frost, J.L. & Kissinger, J.B. 1976. *The Young Child and the Educative Process.* New York: Holt, Rinehart & Winston.

Frost, J.L., & Sunderlin, S. (eds.) 1985. *When Children Play.* Wheaton, MD.: Association of Childhood Education International.

Garrison, C.G. 1926. *Permanent Play Materials for Young Children.* New York: Charles Scribners Sons.

Hall, G.S. 1897. *The Story of a Sand-pile.* New York: E.L. Kellogg.

Hill, P.S., Burke, A., Conard, E.U., Dalgliesh, A., Garrison, C.G., Hughes, E.V., Rankin, M.E., & Thorn, A.G. 1923. *A Conduct Curriculum for the Kindergarten and First Grade*. New York: Charles Scribner & Sons.

Hughes, J.L. 1897. *Froebel's Educational Laws for All Teachers*. New York: D. Appleton.

International Kindergarten Union 1913. *The Kindergarten: Reports of the Committee of Nineteen on the Theory and Practice of the Kindergarten*. Boston: Houghton Mifflin.

Iowa Child Welfare Research Station. 1934. *Manual of Nursing School Practice*. Iowa City, IA: State Universty of Iowa.

Jenkins, A.L. 1924. Public playgrounds versus highway perils. *The Playground* 18(3):155.

Johnson, H.M. 1924. *A Nursery School Experiment*. New York: Bureau of Educational Experiments.

Kilpatrick, W.H. 1916. *Froebel's Kindergarten Principles*. New York: Macmillan.

Knapp, R.F. & Hartsoe, C.E. 1979. *Play for America: The National Recreation Association 1906–1965*. Arlington, VA: National Recreation and Park Association.

Koch, K. 1908. Folk and child play. Report of the Central Committee on Folk and Child Play in Germany (trans. from German by A. Osten). *American Physical Education Review* 13:325–334.

Landreth, C., & Read, K.H. 1942. *Education of the Young Child*. New York: John Wiley.

Leavitt, J.E. 1958. *Nursery-kindergarten Education*. New York: McGraw Hill.

Lee, J. 1927. Play, the architect of man. *The Playground* 21(9):460–463.

Lehman, H.C. & Witty, P.A. 1926. Changing attitudes toward play. *The Playground* 20(8):436–438.

Lloyd, F.S. 1931. Play as a means of character education for the individual. *Recreation* 24(11):587–592.

McKee, J.S. (ed.). 1986. *Play: Working Partner of Growth*. Wheaton, MD: Association for Childhood Education International.

Mero, E.B. 1908. *American Playgrounds: Their Construction, Equipment, Maintenance and Utitlity*. Boston: American Gymnasia Co.

Musselman, V. 1950. What about our playgrounds? *Recreation* 44(4):5.

——————. 1956. Firming the foundations. *Recreation* 49(2):62.

National Recreation Association. 1954. Play sculptures for playgrounds. *Recreation* 47(8):500–501.

——————. 1957. 'Dennis the Menace' playground. *Recreation* 50:136–137, 151.

——————. 1958. Imagination visits the Playground. *Recreation* 51:106–108.

——————. 1959. Designs for play. *Recreation* 52(4): 130–131.

——————. 1960. Playgrounds in action: 1960. *Recreation* 53:154–156.

——————. 1962. Playground equipment: Today and tomorrow. *Recreation* 52:186–187.

Nichols, R.B. 1955. New concepts behind designs for modern playgrounds. *Recreation* 48(4):154–157.

Osborn, D.K., Logue C., & Surbeck E. 1973. *Significant Events in Early Childhood Education*. Athens, GA: Early Childhood Education Learning Center, University of Georgia.

Palmer, L.A. 1916. *Play Life in the First Eight Years*. New York: Ginn.

Parker, S. & Temple, A. 1925. *Unified Kindergarten and First-grade Teaching*. New York: Ginn & Company.

Playground Association of America. *Proceedings of the Third Annual Congress of the Playground Association*, 3(3).

——————. 1910. Report on the committee on Equipment. *The Playground* 4(1):270–284.

Playground and Recreation Association of America. 1909. *Proceedings of the Third Annual Congress of the Playground Association* 3:2–24.

——————. 1915. A brief history of the playground movement in America. *The Playground* 9(1):2–11, 39–45.

Rogers, J.E. 1932. *The Child and Play: Based on the Reports of the White House Conference on Child Health and Protection*. New York: The Century Co.

Sapora, A.V., & Mitchell, E.D. 1948. *The Theory of Play and Recreation*. New York: Ronald Press.

Shaw, R.H., & Davenport, E.C. 1956. A playground that pleases children. *Recreation* 49(11):445.

Stevens, M. 1926. Play streets. *The Playground* 20(4):219.

Sweeney, T.B. 1985. Playground injuries. *Case and Comment*. (July–August)

"Too much money and uninformed thought is often spent on fixed play apparatus. It must not be forgotten that this is only furniture and no matter how ingenious it may be, it alone does not make a playground."[1]

6

Fundamentals Of Playground Development

Changing patterns of American families, particularly increasing proportions of one-parent families and working mothers, are gradually leading to shared, community responsibility for children. There is no single, simple pattern for child care, no single form of schooling, and no simple solution to providing for the play needs of children. Families, family-care centers, daycare centers, public and private schools, churches, and community parks and recreation agencies share the responsibility. All of these groups, sometimes working together but usually working alone, construct playgrounds.

Adult-made playgrounds can be classified into four types: traditional, designer or contemporary, adventure, and creative or adapted (Frost 1978).

The *traditional* playground is typically a flat, barren area equipped with steel structures, such as swings, slide, seesaws, climbers, and merry-go-round, fixed in concrete and arranged in a row. The equipment is designed for exercise play exclusively. The *designer* or *contemporary* playground is typically designed by a professional architect or designer using manufactured equipment, usually wood, and expensive stone and timber terracing. It is intended to have high aesthetic appeal for adults. The *adventure* playground is a highly informal playground, within a fenced area, stocked with scrap building material, tools, and provision

---

[1]Arvid Bengtsson (1974). *The Child's Right to Play*. Sheffield, England: International Playground Association, p. 88.

133

for animals and cooking. One or more play leaders are available to assist children as needed. The *creative* or *adapted* playground is a semiformal environment combining features of the other types to meet the needs of a specific community or school. It often represents a compromise or adaptation of highly formal playgrounds and the junk or adventure playground. A wide range of manufactured and handmade equipment and loose materials is adapted, depending on availability and the play needs of children.

Traditional playgrounds remain the most prevalent type, but contemporary playgrounds are gaining ground, particularly in public parks. Unfortunately, adventure playgrounds are generally unacceptable to most American adults. Creative playgrounds are growing in popularity, especially in preschools.

The development of traditional playgrounds follows patterns essentially established over the decades. The primary motives for selecting equipment are exercise (running off steam), durability, and ease of maintenance. The motives for contemporary playgrounds are frequently the same as for traditional playgrounds with the addition of aesthetic appeal (to the adult eye). The motives for adventure and creative playgrounds are more frequently broadly based, drawing from contemporary theories, child development theory, and, more recently, research on children's play and playground behaviors.

In conducting research, we do not label or regard play environments as "good" or "bad" in advance but consider the variables and hypotheses to be studied and identify existing environments or create environments in which to conduct the research. These environments may, indeed, be labeled (e.g., adventure playgrounds, traditional playgrounds, contemporary playgrounds, environmental yards, tot-lots or x and y play yards), but it is the specific variables studied, not the global type that are relevant in research and practice. Indeed every outdoor play environment is unique. For example, the adventure playgrounds of Scandinavia differ dramatically from setting to setting. One must examine the individual characteristics of each environment to determine its true nature. The student of play and play environments must explore beyond the typologies of convenience and examine the specific elements of play and play environments that influence children's development.

CONTRASTING PLAY ENVIRONMENTS

While there has been a moderate amount of research concerning the functional relationship between play and play objects (toys), there has been scant research pertaining to the relationship between children's play and the design of playgrounds. However, since playgrounds may be viewed as a collection of large play objects in close proximity to each other, it seems reasonable to assume that the novelty and complexity of playgrounds would effect children's play much as toys do. Is this indeed the case?

Many years ago, Johnson (1935) studied the effects on children of varying the amount of play equipment. As the amount of equipment increased, the amount of motor play and play with materials increased, while the amount of undesirable behavior (hitting, arguing, teasing) and social play decreased. As the amount of equipment decreased, there was a corresponding decrease in gross motor play and an increase in the number of social contacts and social conflicts.

Thus it appears that increasing the complexity or variety of equipment has a positive effect on behavior. The author's observations support this assumption. Poorly equipped or sparsely equipped playgrounds force children to ramble aimlessly about, getting involved in conflicts and frequently leading to difficulties with teachers. On the other hand, there are relatively few conflicts or discipline problems on the best playgrounds we have seen.

Perhaps the most extensive series of studies on children's play behaviors and equipment choices in outdoor play environments have been conducted at the University of Texas at Austin during the past two decades. Abbreviated versions of many of these studies are available in Frost and Sunderlin (1985). These studies were initiated by the Texas State Survey of Public School Playgrounds (Vernon 1976), in 1974 and 1975. Several of the studies used the four playground categories described—traditional, designer/contemporary, adventure, and creative. Frost and Campbell (1977) and Campbell and Frost (1985) compared the play behaviors of second grade children in two types of play environments–traditional and creative—using adaptations of the Piaget-Smilansky cognitive play categories and the Parten social play categories described in detail in Chapter 1. For contrast they selected an existing traditional playground (see-saw, merry-go-round, swings, slide, and climbing bars) and they built a more varied creative playground including a play house, wheeled vehicle area, sand and water areas, storage for movable parts, and a variety of handmade climbing and swinging structures. Fifty second-grade children engaged in free play for 30 minutes a day for 10 weeks, alternating between the 2 playgrounds every other day.

The frequency of cognitive play differed across the two environments. Functional or exercise play was significantly higher on the traditional playground, consuming more than three-fourths (77.9%) of the play there versus less than half (43.7%) of the play on the creative playground. More dramatic play was observed on the creative (39%) than on the traditional (2%) playground. More constructive play took place on the creative playground, while more games with rules occurred on the traditional playground. Significantly more parallel play took place on the traditional (29.5%) than on the creative (12.6%) playground. The presence of different materials and equipment on the two playgrounds had a marked effect on all play categories. Results of this study support the contention that environment has a significant effect on behavior (Gump 1975) and that settings in which events and behavior occur have inherent regulatory features (Prescott, Jones, & Kritchevsky 1972).

The wider selection of equipment on the creative playground appeared to stimulate more solitary play, leading children to play apart from others or on separate equipment. However, in this solitary play, children exhibited a range of cognitive activity, an observation that lends support to the position of Moore, Everston, and Brophy (1974), who resist the assumption that solitary play should be categorized lower in hierarchical order than other cognitive forms of play.

The diversity of dramatic and constructive play materials and equipment on the creative playground clearly stimulated these forms of play, whereas their absence on the traditional playground resulted in more functional, parallel play and games with rules, a finding similar to that of Frost and Campbell (1985).

These findings for second grade children support Strickland's (1979) study of third grade children. He found that in comparing a traditional to a creative playground, the latter was more often chosen for dramatic play by both boys and girls. He added the intriguing observation that on the creative playground children *were* the characters in dramatic play and actually acted and talked out roles, while on a traditional playground they merely talked them out. Key materials in these dramatic play sequences were the loose or transportable items (spools, tires, boards, sand, wheeled vehicles) available on the creative playground but absent on the traditional playground.

Availability of equipment and materials also affects form, intensity, and nature of play. Frost and Campbell (1977) and Campbell and Frost (1985) found that second grade children prefer action-oriented to static equipment. On a conventional playground children selected action-oriented swings, merry-go-rounds, and seesaws over fixed apparatus and slides. On a creative playground, play houses (supplied with movable props for dramatic play) were the most popular equipment, followed by movable materials and a boat that could be rocked by the children to simulate sea travel. On a creative playground the play was spread over a wide range of equipment. Conversely, the equipment on a traditional playground was primarily fixed and limited in variety. On a creative playground, equipment designed for functional play (slides, climbers, swings) was selected for play less than one fourth of the time while equipment or materials designed for dramatic play (sand, loose materials, boat, and car) were selected for more than half of the play.

Expansion of the above studies to include a broader age group, 5- to 8-year-olds, resulted in even more startling findings (Frost & Strickland 1978). When given free choice of three playgrounds constructed adjacent to one another, children selected a creative playground 64% of the time, a traditional playground 23% of the time, and a special manufactured, fixed, multipurpose structure advertised as a complete playground 13% of the time. An interesting sidelight is that the costs of the playgrounds, respectively, were $500, $2,500, and $7,000.

Some general conclusions were: (1) action oriented equipment (equipment that moves) is preferred by children; (2) equipment designed primarily for exercise play is not sufficient to provide for the wide range of children's developmental play needs; (3) children prefer equipment that can be *adapted* to their play schemes; (4) among equipment tested only one type, loose parts, had equal appeal to children across all grade/age levels; and (5) inexpensive play environments can be superior to expensive ones.

Similarly, obstacle course equipment arranged in a circular pattern and designed for movement through a series of gross-motor challenges may not function as intended in free play situations (Frost & Vernon 1976). When 200 6- to 8-year-old children were observed daily for 8 weeks during free play, with access to an adjacent creative playground and obstacle course of 10 different structures, only two 6-year-olds and four 7-year-olds used the obstacle course in the manner for which it was designed: to complete the circle while attempting each challenge in turn. It appears that obstacle courses are unsuitable for free play, but may have value for directed activity such as physical education classes.

In contrast to traditional equipment and obstacle courses, contemporary super-structures feature a wide range of motor functions and play possibilities combined into one interlinking structure, thus increasing complexity and challenge. A single unified super-structure provides most of the play opportunities of a traditional playground and does so in one relatively small area. In addition, play and safety are enhanced by the addition of sand underneath and around the structure (Frost & Klein 1979, 1984), variety in play behaviors is stimulated (Bowers 1976), and time at play and peer interaction are increased (Bruya 1985).

Super-structure value is further enhanced by the provision of loose parts or transportable materials that can be used under and around the super-structure for dramatic and constructive play (Frost & Klein 1979; Strickland 1979). Indeed, an abundance of loose or transportable materials seems to be the nucleus of a good playground because these items offer flexibility, diversity, novelty, and challenge and are readily adaptable to use in conjunction with fluid materials, such as sand and water, as well as with fixed structures (Frost & Strickland 1978; Strickland 1979; Frost & Klein 1979; Noren-Bjorn 1982).

A creative outdoor playground, featuring a variety of fixed and movable equipment, influences play differently than does a typical nursery school indoor environment (Henniger 1977). The outdoor environment stimulates social play as frequently as the indoor environment. Results from Henniger's study, as well as others in the University of Texas project, show that with the right equipment and careful teacher planning and encouragement, any desired type of play can be stimulated in the outdoor environment and that the outdoor environment has advantages over the indoor for certain types of play and for certain children.

In particular, the indoor environment fostered more dramatic play for girls and younger children, while the outdoor environment stimulated nearly all of the functional play of both boys and girls. Older boys performed most of their dramatic play outdoors, a finding that supports Sanders and Harper (1976). Culture and environment appear to influence differences in the behavior of boys and girls (Lee & Voivodas 1977). These factors appear to have been involved in these studies, which revealed sex differences for all groups studied, ages 4 through 8. In the Campbell and Frost (1985) study, boys engaged in dramatic play on the creative playground about twice as frequently (45% of total play) as did girls (28% of total play). Bell and Walker's (1985) study of 3-, 4-, and 5-year-olds revealed that boys dominated play on the super-structure, boat, and play house, while girls controlled a separate portion of the playground containing an open air log cabin and swings.

ADVENTURE PLAYGROUNDS

The research on playgrounds shows that traditional, fixed playgrounds are poor places for children's play from both safety and developmental perspectives (Hole 1966). Holme and Massie (1971) note that traditional playgrounds suffer from low use rates compared to alternative play places, such as roads and lots, not designed as playgrounds. Traditional playgrounds have low attendance rates compared to contemporary or adventure playgrounds (Hayward, Rothenberg, & Beasley 1974) and creative playgrounds (Frost & Campbell 1977; Frost & Strickland 1978). Adventure playgrounds are popular in certain European countries but not widely accepted in the United States. Yet Vance (1977) reported data from 14 agencies in 5 states showing that adventure playgrounds were superior to conventional playgrounds: They were less expensive to maintain; community participation was greater; and the number of injuries was about the same or lower.

Hayward, Rothenberg, and Beasley (1974) compared the play activities at traditional, contemporary, and adventure playgrounds.

At each of the playgrounds the 6- to 13-year-old group made up a greater part of the playground population at the adventure playground (45%), while this school-age group was only a minor proportion of the total number of users at the traditional playground (21%) and the contemporary (22%) playground. At the traditional playground and contemporary playground, adults were the most predominant age group (40% and 35% respectively), while preschool children were the most predominant group (30% and 35%) at the adventure playground.

The most used piece of equipment on the traditional playground was the swing, followed by the wading pool. On the contemporary playground the sand areas were most widely used, followed by the mounds and slides. At the adventure playgrounds, the clubhouse area was the most used. The slides on the traditional playground were rarely used by any age group, while the slides on the contemporary playground were used heavily. The one small and two large slides at the contemporary playground allowed a variety of ways of climbing to the top. One slide purposely had bumps in it; there was sand and water nearby which could be applied to the surface of the slide, and more than one child could slide down side-by-side.

Another interesting aspect of this study pertained to the nature of verbal interactions between children. At the traditional and contemporary playgrounds, conversations focused primarily on equipment use and mutual play activities. In contrast, at the adventure playground children's conversations reflected a broader focus than the immediate setting and dealt with a wide variety of topics pertaining to their lives outside the playground. The author hypothesized that perhaps the opportunity for small groups of children to achieve some degree of privacy in their clubhouses led to some of this diversity.

There were also significant differences in the length of time children spent at each of the playgrounds. Children stayed the shortest lengths of time at the traditional playground, the next longest at the contemporary playground, and the longest at the adventure playground (median length of stay in minutes = 21, 32, 75, respectively).

The ambiguity of the adventure playground offered the children a potential setting in which to define self as well as space. It offered a selection of loose parts (e.g., tires, wood, tools, paint, plants, seeds, and the like) which supplied part of the potential for children to define their own activities. Thus, an important difference in the meaning of the environment to the users was that the built playgrounds were planned by others, they were permanent, and the potential for original combination was minimal; at the adventure playground, the form was created by the users and was only as permanent as they chose it to be (Hayward et al. 1974:166).

The adventure playground with its collection of loose parts was by far the most popular of the playgrounds. This setting allowed the children to create their own form and structure and level of complexity.

In sum, the growing body of evidence points to a play environment for young children that contains a variety of both fixed, complex equipment and simple, transportable materials. Large, fixed structures cannot be readily manipulated or modified by children so complexity must be built in by design. On the other hand, movable materials or loose parts can be manipulated and arranged by children in almost unlimited fashion. Because preschool children are able to create characters and situations through mental imagery, props or materials need not be theme specific or suggestive—raw materials such as sand, water, tires, lumber, and spools serve quite well.

Creative and adventure playgrounds, with provisions for various forms of social and cognitive play, clearly surpass conventional and contemporary playgrounds in play value. With attention to safety guidelines (Frost & Henniger 1979; Consumer Product Safety Commission 1981a, b; Henniger, Strickland, & Frost 1982), adventure playgrounds can be reasonably safe while ensuring challenge and variety. Such playgrounds also accommodate extra features that greatly enhance play and learning—animals, nature areas, digging and construction areas, cooking, and organized games—a far cry from the fixed, single function, exercise-oriented equipment of the early playgrounds and their present-day copies.

Whether the concern is for the development of a backyard playground for two or three children, a public school playground for children in early childhood education, a private nursery school playground for infants and toddlers, or a public park playground for all age groups, toddlers through old age, attention to certain needs is, in most cases, fundamental. These needs are selecting and preparing the site, selecting permanent equipment, and zoning the playground.

SELECTING AND PREPARING THE SITE

Not so many years ago American children grew up in a relatively uncomplicated, uncrowded environment, largely rural, with ready access to natural terrain—woodlands, creeks, wild animals, hills, rocks, grass—and an extended family of adults who encouraged movement, exploration, and responsible work roles. It was easy to play, for healthy children need only opportunity and interesting objects. Play is as natural for children as flying is for birds. And nature extends beyond the play motive of children to their play objects. It is quite a challenge for modern adults to equal the natural playscapes and the more natural human relationships that existed for children during the Colonial period. Today's adults must compete with television, traffic, concrete, limited space, bureaucracies, playground tradition, and the bulldozer mentality afflicting many administrators, planners, and builders.

To get right to the point, the primary, and in the long run most economic criterion for the provision of a creative playscape is to retain the original natural features of the site. From the initial conception of a building or area that will accommodate children, no effort should be spared to prevent the destruction of hilly terrain, trees, grass, top soil, and streams. Fortunately, more and more people are becoming conscious of the need but far too few are doing anything about it. Parents and teachers must apply pressure on groups such as school boards to guard against the wanton practice of demolishing many acres of natural terrain for each relatively small school building. This can be done through organizations such as Parent Teacher Associations. Win this battle and the playground is well underway. Except for space for the buildings and organized games, the rule is firm—not an unnecessary tree, not a yard of top soil is to be moved. The appropriate clearing of underbrush (such as poisonous plants) can be done carefully and by plan after the builders have completed their work. Local environmentalists (garden clubs, science centers) are usually eager to assist in proper preservation and development of such sites. Children themselves can and should be deeply involved in such activities. After all, it is their site too.

Unfortunately, most playground development projects get underway long after the site has been cleared and considerable additional expense and effort is required to make the playground a creative place for children. Several factors enter into planning, not necessarily in the order to be discussed.

Space

There is no simple rule of thumb for determining the optimum space for a playground. Such factors as numbers of children, type of soil, type and number of natural features (e.g., trees and streams), and types of structures available tend to influence the user/space ratio. It is not realistic to assume that a playyard that will accommodate 30 children at one time will do so repeatedly for group after group throughout the day. If grassy areas are desired, there can only be so many small feet per time unit. Some soils support grass better than others and some grasses are more resistant to traffic than others. Further, in extremely limited spaces multiple-platform climbing structures and dirt mounds effectively increase play area per child without in creasing yard area. A very general approximation is that some areas of grass can be retained and appropriate equipment can be provided for 4- to 8-year-old children on spaces of 75 to 100 square feet for each actual child user per day. This means that a playyard of 5,000 to 10,000 square feet would accommodate 100 to 300 children using the area in groups of 20–60 for 30 minutes to 1 hour each day. Obviously, infants and toddlers require less space and 8- to 12-year-olds require much more space for organized games such as baseball, tennis, and basketball.

We have seen very good playyards with extremely limited space and should point out that clever design and use patterns can compensate for limited space. This is particularly important in cities where space is scarce and expensive.

Ground Cover

The most desirable ground cover for the open spaces on a playground is grass. It is highly desirable for organized games. In selecting or organizing the site, one of the initial tasks is to select a relatively level area for this purpose. In most contexts this portion of the playground requires least supervision and can be located in an area farthest from the building. If grass is already present, the required care may be simply periodic watering and fertilizing. The grassy area requires the same tender loving care that well-to-do suburbanites give to their lawns. In most parts of the country a thorough soaking every Friday afternoon during dry periods will provide the needed moisture and will allow time for sufficient drying before children arrive on Monday. Fertilizer should be applied according to the recommendations of experts (nursery operators, etc.) in the locale. Generally, three to four applications each year are appropriate. Application at the beginning of holiday periods followed by soakings with water will allow the fertilizer to dissipate into the ground before children begin using the area.

If the area must be seeded or sodded, a thick bed (8–12 inches) of rich top soil should be spread evenly over the area to encourage future dense growth. The area must be declared off limits or fenced until heavy growth has begun. While equipment and labor are available for preparing the top soil, it is wise to inquire about the installation of a sprinkler system for the area. This greatly reduces the work and cost of caring for the grass in future years.

The type of grass to be used varies from region to region but the best all-around variety (cost, appearance, durability, disease resistance) is usually the most common type found on lawns in the local area, generally some type of Bermuda or St. Augustine. Seeding may be done if time is not an important factor. Strip sodding, like seeding, is relatively inexpensive but requires a full growing season to form a solid blanket. Blanket sodding is more expensive but it is the most rapid way to secure a complete ground cover. In addition, blanket sodding of the entire area in question prevents erosion under usual conditions and limited use of the area can begin in three or four weeks.

It will not be possible or desirable to retain grass on certain areas. All areas within the fall zone (6 to 10 feet) of moving and climbing equipment must be covered with a highly resilient material such as sand, tanbark, or small pebble gravel. We have found common concrete sand to be appropriate for this purpose. It is inexpensive and provides a reasonable degree of protection when children fall from equipment. Since such material tends to scatter easily, retaining walls must be provided. These can be formed with landscaping timbers, or properly designed concrete according to designs to be described later. If sand is used it should be 12 inches deep and periodically re-spread to ensure coverage in areas of greatest use. Manufactured pads of rubber or other resilient material can be used but the expense is great.

Finally, certain areas can simply remain dirt or mud areas for digging, water play, or gardening. These should be located near a water hydrant. No particular care or maintenance is involved in a mud or digging area. Provided with some simple tools (shovels, etc.), children will know what to do.

Drainage

Ideally, the playyard will slope gently away from the building, gutters will be properly installed on the adjacent building to channel run-off water away from the play area, and steep, sloping areas will have enough vegetation to prevent erosion. Steps to correct drainage problems should be taken before zoning and constructing play equipment. Low areas where water collects and settles should be filled with top soil. If water runs toward the building, dirt fill should be placed to reverse the direction of flow or drainage tile can be installed, perhaps with the advice of a parent who specializes in such work. Permanent equipment should not be installed in low areas for steady pounding of feet will accentuate the ground depression and create a catch basin for water and mud.

Areas for water play should have a natural slope to an outlet for run off. A ditch outside the playyard, or a drainage pipe with a ventilated cover, are sufficient for this purpose. Since water and sand play tend to go hand-in-hand, the sand play areas are located near a hydrant. Of course, equipment for house play, especially cooking, also fit within this general play area.

Additional Site Preparation

Certain additional preparation of the site may be desirable. If the site is flat, truckloads of dirt can be hauled in and graded into low, rolling inclines for wheeled vehicle (tricycles, etc.) paths. Great care should be taken to ensure that the inclines are not so steep that tricycles pick up dangerous rates of speed. A grade of 12 running feet from beginning (top) to end (bottom) should not exceed approximately 10 degrees in slope. The longer the slope the smaller the degree of rise should be. This means that the hill would not exceed about three feet in height (measured vertically from level ground).

Steeper hills can be constructed during this preliminary stage. Plastic culverts that are three feet in diameter can bridge hill to hill and also serve as tunnels for imaginative play. Tunnel length should be kept sufficiently short for clear, unobstructed vision and of sufficient diameter to allow easy entry by adults. The greater the diameter, the greater the allowable length. Hills are made more inviting and functional by the addition of slides and of steps constructed from railroad ties.

The site preparation stage is the best time to provide one or more drinking fountains and hydrants. These should be located next to the building or fence, out of the line of traffic, and away from active play areas. Usually, a water line already exists in a convenient location. This is also the best time to install plumbing for additional bathrooms that might be added in the future. Some schools build storage sheds sufficiently large to accommodate facilities for both boys and girls. Separate facilities in buildings designed for the purpose are common in community parks.

If the playground is to accommodate older children, selected areas are leveled and prepared during this early stage for the installation of asphalt or concrete areas for organized games.

SELECTING PERMANENT EQUIPMENT

Once the site preparation is complete, attention is directed to selecting and installing permanent equipment such as fencing and storage.

The Fence

A fence must be constructed around playgrounds for children through the primary grades and also for older children if play space is immediately adjacent to a hazard such as water, a busy street, or a drop off (ditch, wall, etc.). The fence should be at least four feet high, with gates that can be locked or secured from opening by young children. (Very young children do not always remember rules or admonitions about wandering away.) The fence can be constructed from chain link or other materials such as wood. Basic chain-link fences cost about half as much as wood fences, with wide variations in cost reflecting geographical areas of the country, difficulty of installing posts in the ground, and the irregularity of terrain. *A special precaution*: If play areas for very young children (2–6 are adjacent to ponds or pools, *extreme* care must be exercised, e.g., tall fences, secured gates.

Gates for walk through (three to four feet wide) should be installed in appropriate traffic areas such as entry to buildings and entry to adjacent open spaces that will be used for organized games. An additional gate (12 feet wide) is needed for truck delivery of sand and other materials or equipment. A path leading to sand pits and other areas to be served by trucks must not be obstructed with permanent equipment.

In addition to providing a measure of safety, the type of fence selected will determine what children will be able to see and, to some extent, what they will hear. Solid wood fences (use cedar or redwood for durability) cut down traffic or other undesirable noise to some extent but, simultaneously, they may also prevent the children from viewing activities relevant to conceptual development. So the developer should examine carefully the range of visual and auditory stimuli available when deciding on the type of fence to be constructed. Regardless of the type selected, growing plants should be used to overcome the barren effect and to provide visual and auditory boundaries as needed. Their care becomes the children's responsibility through cooperative planning with adults.

Storage

Storage facilities are an absolute requirement for good playgrounds for young children because "loose parts" (Nicholson 1971) are the major content for young children's play. The most valuable, creative materials are those that children can make an impact on. They can move them, build with them, stack, arrange, tear down, and rearrange them, use them as props for imaginative play, create their own structures for gross motor activity, and even incorporate them into games with rules. In short, every major form of play uses loose parts. The creative applications of most fixed structures are far more limited.

The location of storage facilities is critical. If children and/or teachers must carry everything from the classroom for each play period, it is doubtful that a wide range of play activities will be accommodated. Storage must be directly accessible to the outdoors for outdoor equipment. Ideally there will be several facilities, each serving the particular area of the playground that best accommodates the use of the equipment stored there. For example, wheeled vehicles are stored adjacent to the bike paths, sand and water play equipment near the sand and water areas, construction materials and carpentry tools near the designated for construction play, gardening tools and pet supplies near the farm area, art supplies near the creative arts area, and so on. Several smaller storage bins are usually preferable to a single large storage house because it is easier to organize and locate the contents and less carrying of equipment is required.

The type of facility is a matter of choice. We prefer wooden bins or buildings constructed from rough cedar because of their natural appearance. Application of exterior sealer or a natural stain is all the treatment needed, for cedar is extremely resistant to decay. Series of hooks and shelves are arranged to accommodate the type of equipment being stored and to make it easy for the children to locate, remove, and return it. Teachers or adults do not put away equipment for children. They plan with children for the cleanup that follows each play session.

FIGURE 6.1 *Storage facilities are indispensable for children's play, for loose, portable materials are the major content of their play.*

Wheeled Vehicles
tricycles
wagons
wheelbarrows
fire engines (pedal cars)
road signs
spare parts

Sand and Water Play
shovels
rakes
assorted containers
screens
cooking utensils
water hoses
funnels
soap bubbles

Assorted Toys
hula hoops
lemon twist
can stilts

Construction
assorted wood blocks
interlocking plastic blocks
Coke crates
lumber
saw horses
wood
cable spools
plastic electrical spools
packing crates
assorted tires

Dramatic
folding chairs and table
sheets of plastic
dress-up clothes
refrigerator boxes (folded)
puppets
puppet stage
parachute
mats
folding screens

Nature
animal feed
bird feeders
nets
magnifying glasses
binoculars
gardening tools
seeds
watering hose

Creative Arts (optional indoors or outdoors)
paints
brushes
art paper
clay
pottery wheel
handicraft materials
assorted art supplies
rhythm band instruments

Carpentry
hammers
saws
screwdrivers
nails, nuts, washers, bolts
wrenches
carpentry table
vise
paint and brushes
scrap lumber
clamps
brace bits
sandpaper
portable tool kit

Alternative types of storage facilities include aluminum, steel, or wood pre-fabricated buildings commonly sold along major thoroughfares of American towns and cities. Prices begin at $800 to $1000 for an 8' × 8' building (1990) and go up depending on size and type of material and construction. These are usually water tight but somewhat less durable and attractive than a custom-constructed storage shed. A second alternate type is the relatively flimsy sheet metal, pre-fabricated shed sold by department stores at about $400 each (8' × 10'). The major difference between this type and those mentioned above is the absence of wood framing and the resulting weakness of construction. These should be considered for temporary use only. A third alternative is modification of packing crates (adding a door and roof,) to form a series of sheds to be placed in select areas. Properly prepared and maintained, these can serve quite effectively for several years.

Playground developers may have their structures branded "eyesores" or "public nuisances" by the neighborhood busybody or the community fathers. The simple way to avoid this is to involve the community from the beginning. People are not likely to reject a project they understand and help develop. Every public playground should be a community or, at least, a neighborhood project. The involvement of children is a must because they throw themselves into playground construction with unbelievable interest and energy. Involvement also cuts down the possibility of vandalism. The list on the previous page is a sample list of materials frequently found in storage structures.

ZONING THE PLAYGROUND

At last, preliminary work is at an advanced stage and it is time to begin the construction and installation of equipment according to a previously planned format which we refer to as zoning the playground. Zoning is a critical step for it is in this process that one's philosophy and factual knowledge of play are clearly revealed. We believe that there are certain universal forms of play, de-velopmental in nature, that occur naturally and spontaneously when children have freedom to move and interesting objects to explore. These forms, described in detail in Chapter 4, are commonly categorized as social or cognitive. The social forms are solitary, parallel, associative, and cooperative. The cognitive forms are functional or exercise, constructive, dramatic or symbolic, and games with rules or organized games. Each form is important in the enhancement of social, cognitive, and motor development.

Play Development and Zoning

An understanding of play development is essential for effective playground zoning. If children are to have the tremendous developmental advantages af-forded by play, the environment must be capable of stimulating and supporting every form of play naturally engaged in by the participating children. For the early childhood context (ages three to eight) this means every form.

The various forms of social play are accommodated by the provision of private, out-of-the-way places for quiet solitary play or for reflecting and observ-ing, and a variety of places for cooperative and sociodramatic play. There are times when all children will prefer to be alone. The fact that play is essentially developmental in nature, that children engage in solitary play before they grow into cooperative play, does not mean, necessarily, that the seven-year-old who chooses to play alone is socially retarded. Children do not give up earlier forms of play as new forms are learned; rather they build new, more interesting, or more advanced features into a particular form. The solitary three-year-old stacks his blocks indiscriminately while the solitary eight-year-old builds elaborate castles, garages, and space stations. Gradually the child with many opportunities to interact with other children in free play contexts will develop more socialized behavior. The solitary play of the two- to three-year-old will phase into parallel, associative, and eventually the cooperative play of four- and five-year-olds. The accessibility and arrangement of playground equipment influences this development. Barren or dead areas, predominance of fixed equipment, relative absence of loose parts, restriction of play flow, and lack of natural materials hamper development by restricting the range of child-to-child interactions.

Provision for optimal social development is linked to provision for optimum cognitive development. The functional play of infants and toddlers is frequently carried on in solitary but often with an adult figure. A great deal happens during this social interaction and it works in two directions. Mother is socializing baby into childhood and baby is socializing mother in motherhood. The fantastic range of messages being conveyed through primitive verbal utterances and body language have their effect on both individuals. Baby and mother play because it is intuitively and biologically right to do so. The motive is intrinsic. In their game of peek-a-boo or shake-the-rattle, primitive functional-cooperative play is the vehicle or process for social and cognitive development and the object in question is the content of their play. Social and cognitive, indeed motor activities too, become one piece in the complex play and development act. The play environment for one form of development sustains and lends force to other forms even in infancy.

Just as the social forms of play merge into one another as development proceeds (simpler forms integrated into more complex forms), the cognitive forms are seen to become more complex and differentiated with the advanced development of the child. Dramatic play can and usually does incorporate both functional and constructive play. Frequently the observer must listen carefully to the language of the children to determine what form is going on. Stacking a set of blocks and spools next to the bike path may be interpreted as mere constructive play until one overhears a plan to use the structure as a gas station and incorporate it into the play of drivers passing by—all with their knowledge of course! Sociodramatic play, incorporating constructive play, is going on.

Some Factors to Consider

There are certain fundamental factors to consider in equipping and zoning the playground. First, *simple, single-function structures are generally not as useful as complex, multiple-function structures*. Simple structures can be arranged, of course, to form complex structures. If loose parts are plentiful, children will do this without prompting by adults. For example, the large fenced platform on a simple slide becomes a complex structure when children stock it with dramatic play

FIGURE 6.2 Simple, single-function structures are not generally as useful as complex, multiple-function structures.

props. The same slide can be made complex when adults attach a swivel and horizontal tire swing to the understructure.

Second, *there must be a sufficiently broad range of equipment to accommodate every form of play naturally engaged in by available children.* For exercise or gross motor activity: climbing structures, swings, loose parts such as tires, cable spools, stacking materials, etc. For constructive play: carpentry tools, blocks, lumber, dirt, sand, etc. For dramatic play: wheeled vehicles, play houses, crates, road signs, kitchen equipment, pots and pans, dirt, sand, water, dress-up clothes, etc. For organized games: balls, nets, paved and grassy areas, etc.

Third, *structures and equipment are arranged for integration of play between structures.* Dramatic play frequently has a mushrooming effect. As exciting activities begin to form, others join in and are taken up in the action. The activity gains intensity and begins to spill over to adjacent areas or structures. We observed the drama of a pirate ship being played out in a old boat. The captain sat on the front while the crew rocked the boat back and forth in the heavy seas. Sharks arrived and one enterprising fellow ran to a nearby pile of large plastic spools and, assisted by a volunteer, carried a half dozen or so back to the boat where they were thrown overboard to feed and appease the angry sharks. Land was sighted and half the pirates disembarked to set up quarters in an adjacent platform structure that became the home base for pirates entering and leaving town. The close proximity of these structures and parts allowed a smooth, natural integration with play theme, generating wider involvement and creativity in language, purpose, thought, and action. Although dramatic play can and does take place at one point or another on almost every structure on the playground, it is more likely to be fostered by certain equipment and this equipment should be zoned into a relatively compact but functional area. The same principle applies to gross motor and construction play, to organized games, and to work/play activities such as gardening and animal tending.

Fourth, *these play zones should be defined by boundaries that set them apart functionally and visually and integrate them spatially with adjacent zones.* These boundaries may take numerous forms: the low horizontal, landscape timbers bounding the huge sand pit encircling the array of climbing, sliding, and swinging structures; the staggered array of vertical timbers bounding a portion of the dramatic play area, with an opening and low, stepping column extensions leading into the construction area; the one-third buried vertical truck tires forming a tunnel to offer a choice (with the path) from the dramatic play structures to the nearby sand and water areas, and so on. Thus, two broad functions are achieved: one, the nature of the structure itself tells the child what it can be used for; and, two, the proximity and spatial arrangement of adjacent structures with their boundaries stimulates and directs the child visually, motorically, and cognitively, leading to diversity and creativity. The designers of Disneyland and Disney World must have had such concepts in mind when they arranged the various entertainment areas of their glittering funscapes.

Fifth, *space should be arranged to invite movement within zones, between zones, and between points of entry and exit.* In most enclosed playyards there will be three gates: one for service entrance and two for people. The service gate is positioned for unobstructed access from a street and ready access to areas of the playground where service will be needed, such as sand for sand areas, etc. One of the people gates is conveniently located for entry and exit into the building (school), and the other is usually located all the way across the playyard to allow exit to retrieve wayward equipment, such as balls, and/or for access to adjacent areas, such as open space for organized games or a nature area. An individual would be able to follow a more or less direct path along the triangle formed by these three gates.

Once inside the play area, children should find challenge and alternate access to any of the play zones. The open space, the visual boundaries, and the lines of invited movement (e.g., balance logs) carry them naturally from one zone to another. It should be noted that equipment for invited movement between zones does not replace open space. Children are merely given a choice of whether to walk, run, or climb through a tunnel, over steps, or walk a balance beam from one zone to another.

With regard to movement on equipment proper, a similar principle is used. As children contemplate a complex climbing structure, they may find a number of access routes—arch climber, ladder, suspended rope, or tire climber. Upon gaining access they may have numerous exit possibilities—all of the entry points plus a slide or fireman's pole. Further, they find various on-equipment play possibilities: areas for privacy, dramatic houseplay, or mastering built-in climbing obstacles. Such a complex structure occupies a central position in the gross motor zone and is often called a superstructure.

Zoning for Individual Differences

When children of widely varying ages or developmental levels (for example, infants through eight- to nine-year-olds) are occupying the same general play area, certain modifications are built into the zoning arrangement. Infant and toddler areas are fenced off from older children's areas, but within the infant-toddler area certain zones are created. Gerry Fergeson of Pacific Oaks College starts her youngest infants in a relatively simple zone that is adjacent to gradually more difficult ones according to the motor skills involved. These zones are bridged by series of steps or staggered surfaces and a tunnel. As infants gain motor skills they gradually begin to explore and eventually master these boundaries. Soon they become active in more complex zones.

The "graduated" principle can also be applied to individual play structures. Increasing the difficulty factor involved in scaling a climbing structure decreases the number of children able to try or succeed. Installing steps or platforms at successively wider intervals, allowing access only by a rope climber, and so on, effectively regulates activity. This also builds in a safety factor by prohibiting access to areas too high for younger children. Some considerations about zoning and equipment design for handicapped children will be treated in a following section.

Work/Play Areas

Additional outdoor zones or areas are created (especially in warmer climates) for activities not quite meeting the definitions of free play or those for the teacher-directed, didactic activities of the classroom. We choose to call these work/play zones. They allow the teacher to integrate outdoor work/play activity with the indoor curriculum—creative arts, science, math, and social studies. We will not attempt to name or discuss all the possibilities but will identify some of the more common ones.

A relatively full range of creative arts activities can be conducted outdoors. The most convenient location for this may be directly adjacent to the indoor environment. This location facilitates the flow of art materials between the indoors and the outdoors. It is more likely to be near a ready source of water and, perhaps most importantly, this location allows for free movement of activity—the

FIGURE 6.3 Classroom walls that open to the out-of-doors allow for integration of indoor-outdoor activities.

FIGURE 6.4 *A full range of creative, work/play activities can be conducted out-of-doors.*

FIGURE 6.5 *Children need to observe and interact with animals in their natural habitats.*

indoor-outdoor continuum. This is particularly enhanced by the provision of direct openings between the classroom and the playground. There are no readily identifiable limits to the range of creative arts activity that can be conducted outdoors. Weather is perhaps the most crucial factor. The variety may include painting, pottery, sculpture, handicrafts, weaving, music, drama, and dance.

The possibilities for science activity are virtually endless. Corrals and pet houses allow children to care for their own animals. A great deal of cooperative planning can be conducted with children about the proper care of animals. Too many school-related pet projects are exercises in animal abuse. In many areas wild animals such as birds, squirrels, and deer can be attracted by locating feeders near the play area. Areas for gardening and growing plants and flowers

Animals	**Forest and Plants**	**Other**
Corrals	Vegetable garden	Weather Station
Feeders	Local flora	Photography
Cages	Climbing trees	Preserving historical sites
Bird bath	Rock and fern garden	
Fish Pond	Natural trail	
Observation shelter	Marsh and pond	
Bird houses	Picnic site	
Habitat Area	Compost area	
	Amphitheater	

are essential to every school-related playground. Children can learn basic principles of forestry, geology, and ecology by caring for a wild area of woodland, ponds, streams, and native wildlife. Social science concepts are developed through the establishment of small villages, streets, stores, signs, and the use of vehicles. These and additional possibilities are in the list above.

CREATING MAGICAL PLAYSCAPES[2]

All too commonly, despite the best intentions of adults who influence, design and build playgrounds, the results are sterile, uninspired, and inappropriate for children's play. We have entered an era where manufacturers are offering ever more expensive and elaborate, high-tech play structures, often viewed as the "complete playground." Parents and professionals, intent on improving play places for children, subscribe to the temptation to solve play problems and needs with a quick, easy, fix—call the local play equipment representative and pick a glossy, new play structure for the back yard, the child care center, school, or public park, and resolve your guilt and concern. Throughout this entire process, no one reflects on playscapes through the eyes of the child or devotes the thought and time needed to make play environments vibrant, child-centered places.

What are the qualities of magical playscapes for children—playscapes that transcend the usual and become vibrant, enchanting, magical places? We can create *with* children such places if we are willing to engage in child-like reflection and set aside preconceived notions that children's playscapes are merely collections of materials. Toward this end, twenty design principles are geared to the child's perspective.

- *Changes of Scale*: Three scales—the miniature, the child-sized, and the colossal—extend children's capacities and sense of personal power (e.g., models, tiny animals, child-sized trains, dinosaurs).
- *The Suggestion of Other Beings*: Children gain a sense of power by hearing stories about small versions of themselves—brownies, pixies, fairies—and a sense of magic is felt in a place inhabited by them (e.g., Santa's workshop, cozy garden setting for reading stories).

[2]This section was adapted from J. Talbot & J.L. Frost. (1989). Magical playscapes. *Childhood Education* 66:11–19. By permission of the Association for Childhood Education International, 11141 Georgia Avenue, Suite 200, Wheaton, MD. Copyright © (1989) by the Association.

- *Realness*: Children prefer the real to the sham—the degree of detail, the link to known entities, the functional qualities—all endow the user with special capabilities (e.g., real fire engines, tools).
- *Archetypal Images*: Childhood values myths, fairy tales, and their symbols. These are universally employed in children's art and in their symbolic play (e.g., stars, moon, trees).
- *Sense of "Placeness"*: Magical places have a certain atmosphere, a mood—setting place, an ambience, a special atmosphere, that set them apart from the everyday world (e.g., amphitheater, garden containment, fireplace).
- *Open-endedness*: Shapes with meanings that are not well-defined lend themselves to many interpretations. Such objects are open to many uses and give children the power to say what they will be or do (e.g., cardboard boxes, building blocks).
- *Nature and the Elements*: Make sure that the playscape opens up possibilities to interact with nature and its elements—earth, air, fire, and water. Nature offers levels of meaning far beyond the artificial or manufactured (e.g., gardens, orchards, groves, streams).
- *Line Quality and Shape*: The line quality of playscapes can be enhanced by considering arches, curves, cloud shapes, hanging shapes, and topsy-turvy (e.g., arched doorways, mobiles, rolling hills).
- *Sensuality*: Places that engage the senses—rich color, fragrances, pleasant sounds, engaging textures, varied light qualities—heighten the enchantment and meaning of any experience (e.g., blooming flowers, chimes, sensory walks).

Magical playscapes allow the child to experience:

FIGURE 6.6 *Changes of scale—the miniature . . . the child-sized and the colossal . . .*

FIGURE 6.7 *Sense of placeness . . .*

FIGURE 6.8 Nature and the elements . . .

FIGURE 6.9 Line quality and shape (design by James Talbot)

- *Layering*: Objects or views that are "framed" by layers of foreground materials heighten sense of depth and feeling of richness and increase the degree of complexity (e.g., vegetation, walls, hills).
- *Novelty*: Rarity, unusualness, unpredictability, and incongruity expand children's perceptions of the world and lend a sense of specialness (e.g., totem poles, tire animals, pipe telephone systems).
- *Mystery*: Children love surprises and discovery. Consider how the playyard might remain a bit secret and obscure (e.g., nooks, crannies, enchanted forest).

FIGURE 6.10 *Sensuality* . . .

FIGURE 6.11 *Connection with other times, other places* . . .

- *Brilliance*: Young children are delighted with sparkling, gleaming, glittering surfaces. Playyards can contain mesmeric qualities of such things (e.g., mirrors, tile, light reflecting prisms).
- *Juxtaposition of Opposites*: A certain epic quality, a largeness of purpose, is suggested when opposites are at play with each other (e.g., hard/soft surfaces, rounded/straight lines, sunlight/shadow, contrasting and complimentary colors).
- *Richness and Abundance*: Very little can be created in a vacuum. Children need an environment rich in possibilities with no sense of scarcity (e.g., storage, building supplies and tools, vegetation, events).
- *Connection with Other Times, Other Places*: Age and history bestow a magical aura. Age implies an unknown quality that leads to speculation and expanding imagination (e.g., preserving old trees on the playground, old building materials, Chinese sculptures).
- *"Is-ness"*: Not everything in the playyard needs to be functional. Add something with no other purpose than to express a meaning beyond utility and reasoning (e.g., a flower garden, a tree hanging, a graphic design).
- *Loose Parts and Simple Tools*: Add materials that allow the child to transform mere junk into personal creations and wonderlands (e.g., tools, scrap materials).

FIGURE 6.12 The illusion of risk . . .

FIGURE 6.13 Doing nothing . . .

- *The Illusion of Risk*: Peak experiences during moments of apparent risk place the mind in a state of alertness, resourcefulness, and expectancy. Mastering perceived threats results in growth spurts and affirmations of personal power (e.g., hillside slides, guided use of fire, wilderness adventure hikes).
- *Doing Nothing*: Substitute recess, free time, leisure, and fun for tightly structured lessons, practices, schedules, and television. Give kids time for messing around with valued friends in enchanting places.

FIGURE 6.14 *Children can help design their own playgrounds.*

FIGURE 6.15 *Do-it-yourself playground projects should include leaders who are well-trained in play-value and safety.*

Assessing the Playground

In playground development a master plan should be prepared in advance. A site plan and a three-dimensional model ensure that critical elements are included, that space is used efficiently, and that proper zoning is arranged. In addition to such composite plans, assessment of three major elements, using the Playground Rating System (Chapter 4), is essential. These elements are: (1)

contents of the playground, (2) safety of the playground, and (3) play value (What should the playground do?). The Playground Rating System organizes the various playground development fundamentals discussed in this chapter and the playground safety fundamentals in Chapter 9. It can be applied to the site plans and three-dimensional model before playground development begins, as development proceeds, as a final check, and periodically thereafter as new ideas are incorporated. *The best playgrounds are never finished*, but change and grow with the creative energies of children and playleaders.

CONCLUSION

Playgrounds are developed for children in a wide variety of contexts, but there are common fundamentals of design that should be taken into account.

A great deal of later effort can be avoided by careful selection and preparation of the site. Ideally, planners of public buildings such as schools and apartments will include the playground in original site plans long before buildings are started. This activity should be done with careful attention to preservation of natural terrain—shrubbery, streams, and trees. Preliminary planning also takes into account child/space ratios, ground cover, drainage, and site preparation.

Before play equipment is placed on the site, permanent equipment is installed. This includes the fence, storage facilities, water lines, water fountains, and hard-surfaced areas such as wheeled vehicle paths and areas for organized games. In some areas, artificial structures for shade will also be built.

Following these steps the playground is zoned to provide for the range and arrangement of equipment to be used. Some major factors taken into account are: (1) providing complex, for integration of play across two or more structures, (2) providing a sufficient variety of equipment to allow every form of play naturally engaged in by the children, (3) arranging structures and loose equipment to allow for integration of play across two or more structures, (4) defining play zones by functional and visual boundaries that allow the integration of zones, and (5) arranging space to allow and invite movement within zones, between zones, and between points of entry and exit.

The playground is also zoned to accommodate special needs. Individual differences in ability are taken into account, allowing various age groups and ability levels to use the area. Zones are created to facilitate work/play such as creative arts and natural activities. These activities are arranged to allow a smooth uninterrupted flow of indoor-outdoor participation. In sum, the content of play yards, their safety, and their play value are all important elements for children's play.

Finally, special consideration should be given to making playscapes magical, enchanting places. These special touches are intended to transform mundane, over-slick, sterile playyards into places that invite, challenge, and satisfy—places that transcend the ordinary and allow children to create, wonder, and, consequently, to grow.

Portions of the section on "Contrasting Play Environments" were adapted from Frost, J.L. (1986). "Children's Playgrounds: Research and Practice." In G. Fein and M. Rivkin (Eds.). *The Young Child at Play*. By permission of the National Association for the Education of Young Children.

REFERENCES

Bell, M.J., & Walker, P. (1985). Interactive patterns in children's play groups. In (eds.), *When Children Play J.L. Frost & S. Sunderlin. Wheaton, MD: Association for Childhood Education International.*

Bowers, L. (1976). *Play Learning Centers for Pre-school Handicapped Children.* Tampa, FL: University of South Florida.

Bruya, L.D. (1985). The effect of play structure format differences on the play behavior of preschool children. In (eds.), *When Children Play* J.L. Frost & S. Sunderlin. Wheaton, MD: Association for Childhood Education International.

Campbell, S., & Frost, J.L. (1985). The effects of playground type on the cognitive and social play behavior of grade two children. In (eds.), *When Children Play*, J.L. Frost & S. Sunderlin. Wheaton, MD: Association for Childhood Education International.

Consumer Product Safety Commission. (1981a). *A Handbook for Public Playground Safety: Volume 1. General Guidelines for New and Exiting Playgrounds.* Washington, DC: U.S. Government Printing Office.

————. (1981b). *A Handbook for Public Playground Safety: Volume 2. General Guidelines for New and Exiting Playgrounds.* Washington, DC: U.S. Government Printing Office.

Frost, J.L. (1978). The American playground movement. *Childhood Education*, 54(4):176–182.

Frost, J.L., & Campbell, S. (1977). *Play and Play Equipment Choices of Young Children on Two Types of Playgrounds.* Unpublished ms., The University of Texas at Austin.

Frost, J.L., & Campbell, S.D. (1985). Equipment choices of primary age children on conventional and creative playgrounds. In (eds.), *When Children Play*, J.L. Frost & S. Sunderlin. Wheaton, MD: Association for Childhood Education International.

Frost, J.L., & Klein, B.L. (1979). *Children's Play and Playgrounds.* Boston: Allyn & Bacon. (1984). Playgrounds International, P.O. Box 33363, Austin, TX 78764.

Frost, J.L., & Strickland, E. (1978). Equipment choices of young children during free play. *Lutheran Education* 114(1):34–46.

Frost, J.L., & Sunderlin, S. (eds.). (1985). *When Children Play.* Wheaton, MD: Association for Childhood Education International.

Frost, J.L., & Vernon, L. (1976). *Movement Patterns of First and Second Grade Children on an Obstacle Course.* Unpublished ms., The University of Texas at Austin.

Gump, P.V. (1975). Ecological psychology and children. In (eds.) *Review of Child Development*, E.M. Hetherington. (vol. 5), Chicago: University of Chicago Press.

Hayward, D.G., Rothenburg, M., & Beasley, R.R. (1974). Children's play and urban playground environments. *Environment and Behavior*, 6(2):131–168.

Henniger, M. (1977). *Free Play Behavior of Nursery School Children in an Indoor and Outdoor Environment.* Unpublished doctoral dissertation, The University of Texas at Austin.

Henninger, M., Strickland., & Frost, J. (1982). X-Rated playgrounds; issues and developments. *Journal of Physical Education, Recreation, and Dance*, 53:72–77.

Hole, V. (1966). *Children's Play on Housing Estates.* London: HMSO.

Holme, A., & Massie, D. (1971). *Children's Play: A Study of Needs and Opportunities.* London: Michael Joseph.

Johnson, M.W. (1935). The effect on behavior of variation in the amount of play equipment. *Child Development.* 6:56–68.

Lee, P.C., & Voivodas, G.K. (1977). Sex role and pupil role in early childhood education. In (ed.) *Current Topics in Early Childhood Education*, L.G. Katz. Norwood, NJ: Ablex.

Moore, N.V., Evertson, C.M., & Brophy, J.E. (1974). Solitary play: Some functional considerations. *Developmental Psychology*, 10:830–834.

Nicholson, S. (1971). The theory of loose parts. *Landscape Architecture.*

Noren-Bjorn, E. (1982). *The Impossible Playground.* West Point: Leisure Press.

Prescott, E., Jones, E., & Kritchevsky, S. (1972). *Day Care as a Child-Rearing Environment.* Washington, DC: NAEYC.

Sanders, K.M., & Harper, L.V. (1976). Free play fantasy behavior in preschool children: Relations among gender, age, season and location. *Child Development*, 47: 1182–1185.

Strickland, E.V. (1979). Free play behaviors and equipment choices of third grade children in contrasting play environments. Unpublished doctoral dissertation, The University of Texas at Austin.

Talbot, J. & Frost, J.L. (1989). Magical playscapes. *Childhood Education*, 66:11–19.

Vance, B. (1977). The president's message. *American Adventure Play Association News*, 1(4):1.

Vernon, E. (1976). *A Survey of Preprimary and Primary Outdoor Learning Centers/Playgrounds in Texas Public Schools.* Unpublished doctoral dissertation, The University of Texas at Austin.

"All play moves and has its being within a playground marked off beforehand either materially or ideally, deliberately or as a matter of course."[1]

7

Alternate Routes to Playground Development

During the past decade, unprecedented growth has occurred in the variety and quality of playground equipment and overall playground design. A growing number of designers and manufacturers have sharpened their awareness of children's play needs and have set out to provide developmentally sensitive and safe playgrounds.

Unfortunately, a number of designers and manufacturers have not taken advantage of the rich educational literature, conferences, and workshops, and continue to advertise and market outmoded, hazardous equipment. Perhaps in no other category of consumer products is the old maxim, "Let the buyer beware" more accurate than in the play equipment industry. As an aid to the potential consumer/purchaser, a sampling of the viewpoints and products of visionary designers/builders/manufacturers are represented here. The group includes individuals who organize communities to build their own playgrounds, those who provide comprehensive, custom building services, and major manufacturers. This sampling of innovative, visionary activity is not exhaustive. A growing number of designers are entering the playground field and more and more manufacturers are improving their products.

---

[1]Johan Huizinga (1950). *Homo Iudens: A Study of the Play Element in Culture.* Boston: The Beacon Press, p.10.

CUSTOM DESIGNERS/BUILDERS

Grounds for Play, Inc.[2]

Grounds for Play, Inc. approaches the playground as a total system—one whose components function interdependently. This interdependency is critical along three dimensions: *integrating* the elements of the playground internally, *coordinating* the design of the playground with overall programmatic goals, and *adapting* the design of the play equipment to the specific characteristics of the playground. INTEGRATE: A well-designed playground orchestrates the movement of children and their play episodes so that play functions to develop physical, cognitive, social, and emotional needs. COORDINATE: Further, the design of the play area must seek to maximize the relationship between the indoor learning environment and the outdoor learning environment so that program goals are clearly evident in the playground. ADAPT: Finally, the playground must be designed with consideration given to the physical area set aside for play.

In keeping with the above, our systematic approach to playground planning results in a unique design for each play area, for not two programs—and certainly no two playground sites—are exactly the same. The "pick a piece of equipment from this page" approach to playground development does not lead to a cohesive, functioning play environment that maximizes children's total development while

FIGURE 7.1 *The playground is a total system—one whose components function interdependently.*

[2]Script and photo courtesy of Eric Strickland and James Dempsey, Grounds for Play, Inc.

at the same time spending hard-to-come-by funds wisely. By using consumer input, the program is systematically analyzed—its participant group, its goals, and the play area from overall size to the most minute detail—in order to develop a plan for the playground. The outcome is a comprehensive design that allows for implementation immediately as a single project or in a series of well-coordinated phases. In either case, utilizing the comprehensive plan means that when the playground is completed, it will function as a fully integrated environment to promote total child development.

Most playgrounds have equipment which promotes some types of physical development moderately well. The aim of Grounds for Play is to provide for **physical development** in the broadest possible sense from gross-motor to fine-motor skills, from stretching and balance to cardiovascular stimulation. The equipment includes activities designed to increase grip and finger strength, and to promote eye–hand coordination, eye–foot coordination, upper body strength, and kinesthetic awareness. All of these derive from well designed equipment for exercise play.

But exercise play is only the tip of the iceberg. Children need other types of play to develop all of their abilities! **Intellectual abilities** develop through manipulative/creative play with water pumps, channels, sand play, art easels, and construction opportunities using loose parts.

Children develop emotionally through the creative activities mentioned above and through choosing play options that allow them to set goals and conquer appropriate challenges. **Emotional development** is also encouraged by providing non-specific dramatic play components such as playhouses and pretend vehicles. These props allow maximum flexibility for children to create their own environments. Research concludes that children work out many threatening experiences through dramatic play.

Social skills are practiced in dramatic play settings as well. Equipment for toddlers allows for play alone and in pairs which results in reduced conflicts. Older children are presented numerous opportunities for group play which emphasize language interaction (telephone systems), cooperation (tire swings), and problem solving (water play). Equipment is designed to assist "traffic flow" so that, as a child comes off one activity, an opportunity awaits to lead the child to another activity, and from there to still another. Such "loops" result in increased involvement with the equipment. Further, research indicates that these complex play designs increase language production and vocabulary. The bottom line is that complex, dramatic, and creative playgrounds are more fun.

For a sense of the range of development possible with Grounds for Play equipment, note the figure on page 160. The illustration is keyed to some of the abilities that should be developed in children.

Tire Playgrounds Inc., and MAXIDEX Play System[3]

Play is an integral part of the development of every human being, and a child will use every chance to play. However, generation after generation the play environment has been shrinking and now children are more limited in the play opportunities available to them.

[3]Script and photos courtesy of William Weisz.

FIGURE 7.2 *The public playground can serve as a man-made substitute for a natural environment.*

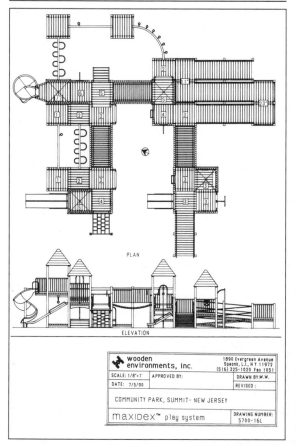

FIGURE 7.3 *Maxidex features a wide range of accessories to create a varied and stimulating playground.*

The public playground can serve as a man-made substitute for a natural environment. It allows the concentration of a large number of users into a small area and must accommodate children with greatly differing ages, abilities, disabilities, strengths, coordination, and social skills. The physical activities involved in play lead to improved gross motor development, coordination, and perception. Children explore, manipulate, and build, and thus learn about the physical properties of objects and their environment. Playing with others develops children's social skills and offers opportunities to act out various roles.

The public playground serves some of the child's fundamental play requirements as it functions as:

- **A public meeting place** where children of different backgrounds, ages, and abilities share in its use.
- **A stage** where children create roles, act out fantasies, imagine various settings.
- **An arena for competition** where children observe and try to out-do each other, make rules, break them, fight, and make up.
- **A forgiving testing ground** where children grow and develop their muscles, senses, and skills. Children want to test their new powers; therefore, risk-taking is an integral part of play. The playground has to balance challenging activities with adequate safety measures.

Incorporating these themes into a positive play experience requires a team effort between the playground designer, the people who initiate the playground, and those who will use it.

The role of the playground designer is to help educate clients about the nature of play and play environments, and to learn from them about the specifics of their population, site, and budget. Pre-existing conditions at the site have to be observed in order to better understand the site conditions, traffic patterns, accessibility, and current use. Various designs have to be considered with the active participation of all concerned.

MAXIDEX Play System

"MAXIDEX," a modular playground system, is the result of a four-year design process created with Wooden Environments Inc., located in Speonk, Long Island, New York.

"MAXIDEX" is 100% larger than the typical playground platform. It is based on a square grid, 55" × 55", centered on 5" × 5" posts. Platforms extend to the outside of the posts, thus covering an area 60" × 60". The decision to use an enlarged platform was an important step toward providing adequate space for activities and traffic in the playground:

— Sliding requires space to sit down at entrance to slide.
— Standing while using wall activities such as a steering wheel.
— Sitting on a bench.
— Standing and socializing in a small group.
— Standing and looking at other children.
— Moving through.

In order to allow for interesting layouts, double platforms and a 45- and 90-degree curved platform were designed. The curved platform breaks the monotony of the 90-degree grid and solves problems in difficult site configurations. All walls, sliding poles, safety loops, and vertical ladders are modular and interchangeable, using the same connections to the posts.

'MAXIDEX' provides numerous additional accessories, including special equipment to serve the needs of the disabled, to create a varied and stimulating playground. The "MAXIDEX" system complies with or exceeds all requirements published in the Consumer Product Safety Commission Guidelines.

By standardizing connections and simplifying the assembly process with factory pre-assembled components, the construction of a "MAXIDEX" playground is fast and easy. This approach has enabled many community groups to build safe, durable playgrounds with volunteer labor.

In order to be a successful substitute for the natural environment, the playground must provide settings similar to those found in nature. In nature we encounter a seemingly endless variety of physical features arranged in infinite combinations. Thus, when creating a layout for a playground, the designer should incorporate maximum variation in components and link them in carefully chosen patterns. For example, platforms at various heights can substitute for hills, trees and rocks. The more components used, the more permutations are possible in the ways they can be linked. By subdividing the playground into self-contained **activity loops**, solutions to design problems become evident. A well-designed activity loop can be linked to others, creating further permutations and interesting traffic patterns.

Each activity loop should contain all the components needed for a successful play experience. An example of a complete activity loop is a platform with a slide and a ladder, because it contains a "hill" with a "slope" to be climbed, a "plateau" on top, and a "slope" to slide down. The child can enjoy climbing up and sliding down repeatedly, a self-contained activity. An example of an incomplete activity loop is an overhead ladder between two platforms where the child swings from "branch" to "branch" between "trees." A complete activity loop should contain two different but parallel overhead activities so that a different play experience can be enjoyed in each direction. All activity loops can be enriched by providing secondary options, such as sliding poles, an alternate climbing unit, or a steering wheel.

In addition to activity loops that allow for energetic play to develop body strength and gross motor skills, a well-designed playground should also provide activity loops that allow for quieter interaction to develop social skills, imagination, and creativity. Most public playgrounds unfortunately do not provide access to free movable play materials, so children have to bring their own toys to the playground.

In order for a playground to be safe, the height of the platforms must be based on the ages and abilities of the users. Appropriate safety walls should be added when a platform is 36 inches or more above ground. As a rule, overhead activities should be attached to platforms 24 inches or lower and be connected to other activity loops instead of leading to a dead end. Since safety walls have no play-value, an alternative such as a cargo net, a wall with a steering wheel, or a sliding pole could be used instead. Thus the playground is safe and enriched at the same time.

Tom Jambor: Independent Designer/Builder: University of Alabama at Birmingham[4]

In 1976, I was introduced to Paul Hogan's book, *Playgrounds for Free*, and subsequently started designing school playgrounds using inexpensive materials and the community as a construction support system. With limited funds available, the concept of community people uniting to help design, construct, and maintain a playground has been, and still is, a very attractive school project.

FIGURE 7.4 With rope connections, children can transport themselves through a maze of trees, ledges, and standard structures in both planned and spontaneous play.

Over the years the "barn raising" approach and the procuring of needed materials through a people-who-know-people approach have not changed much, but my playground designs and thoughts about children's play have. While providing interesting play environments that draw children to them has always been a priority, the integrated tire, utility pole, and wood combinations usually constructed in an open flat area are now being linked to the foliage and contours of nature.

In 1982, under the influence and guidance of IPA colleague Asbjørn Flemmen in western Norway, I found the linkage that best integrated nature and man-made structure—rope!

It was an old, simple play component, but with renewed application. Horizontal, vertical and diagonal spans of 1½" diameter rope now link my structure designs with the natural de-

---

[4]Script and photos courtesy of Tom Jambor.

FIGURE 7.5 A good playground provides opportunities for growth, development, and learning for the total child.

sign of nature. With rope connections, children can transport themselves through a maze of trees, dirt/rock ledges, and standard structures in both planned and spontaneous play. With rope, and a little imagination, one can design a multitude of alternative play possibilities in a backyard or on a community/school play site.

Rope has become the key element in enabling this designer to provide skill levels that take on the developmental needs of children, for a single rope can be used in as many ways as there are children to use it. It provides play opportunities that grow with the ever-changing needs of children.

I feel strongly that *a playground must be challenging* if we expect children of any age to use it. Children are drawn to a potential play site because of the variety of play alternatives offered. As children congregate, it becomes a social entity and catalyst for involvement and children's subsequent development. A good playground provides opportunities for growth, development, and learning for the *total* child. With social interaction at its core, play aptly allows for an abundance of cognitive, emotional, and physical involvement that creates and encourages personal exchanges that enhance problem-solving, decision-making, and language use.

As we offer protections to our children through regulations and guidelines for playground design, we must remember that the playground is *for* the child, and that the child will play there only if his/her developmental needs can be addressed. The question "What is safe and what is unsafe?" must be coupled with the question "What is appealing and what is unappealing in the eyes of the child?". For without use by children, the playground need not be.

James Jolley: Independent Designer/Builder, Austin, Texas[5]

James Jolley has designed and built several dozen playgrounds in Florida and Texas. During 1987–1990 he traveled throughout Europe and Asia studying playgrounds and assisting in design and construction of numerous playgrounds. At the time this was written he was helping direct construction of playgrounds in India. His philosophy of playground development follows:

My basic philosophy is one based on "allowing." I think that space for children should be set up and provided in ways that allow children to be children in a total sense, where they can explore and experience themselves in a *hands on*, *non-restrictive*, and *safe* environment.

The environment must meet the developmental needs of each individual child so that he or she can explore and do in that environment what he or she feels a need to do. The environment should allow free exploration and interaction;

---

[5]Script and photos courtesy of James Jolley.

it shouldn't be an environment that acts upon the child (such as you get when you merely supply fixed equipment) but should allow the child to act on the environment. The child should have opportunities to make decisions and choices about not what he can do on the equipment but what he can do *with* the equipment. The equipment should have an interactive quality that can adjust or change to meet the child's needs from the child's perspective. There should be equipment, particularly for younger children with limited skills, that allows them to have experiences that they might not be able to safely create for themselves, i.e. high places, slides, different ways to travel or move through space or their environment.

The environment should be non-restrictive. The equipment or materials should be appropriate for children in terms of their developmental levels. Often environments seem to be designed with only one size of child in mind and yet a broad range of ages have access to them. Adult criteria for safety and beauty can be restrictive. For example, it is restrictive to place plants in an environment to such an extent that the plants become more important than what we will allow the children to do. Adults want the plants to survive so they create rules that restrict the movement of the children away from them without providing for the interaction of the child with the plants. Children need a wide variety of growing things in their play areas but the emphasis should be on play—not keep away. This can be done by providing enough space for both nature and children to exist.

The environment can also be restrictive in the sense of limiting the choices of play activities or behaviors that the children have to choose from. Not all children want to climb, swing, or slide at the same time—not all children can. Children's space should provide opportunities that offer a wide range of play choices and activities where they can open up and try a range of activities.

FIGURE 7.6 *Space for children should allow children to explore and experience in a hands-on, non-restrictive, and safe environment.*

There are numerous safety concerns relevant to playgrounds. A playground should be designed in such a way that children can have experiences and opportunities to test their physical boundaries. A playground that challenges and provides opportunities for risk taking shouldn't bring a child to the point of frustration or place her in life-threatening situations. The child should have a variety of outlets for choosing the level of difficulty he/she wishes to engage in. This is where the child can gain the self-confidence to try more challenging events. Internalizing such risks should offer a personal sense of adventure, not unrecognized physical danger. A playground that

FIGURE 7.7 *Children have limited opportunities to interact with the real, natural world.*

allows freedom of choice and a variety of play options is a playground where children can take ownership and feel safe.

I'm a firm believer in making the community an integral part of the process— in the design and implementation. I also feel children should be involved in the conception phase. Many would say that children don't know what they want, but if they are provided with inspiring spaces that will give them more opportunities to be creative, than they can help with the design process. We can help children think through the following: "what if?," "how about?", and "how can?." However, providing children with the opportunity to share ideas to solve problems does take time. In an environment for children we shouldn't look at only the product but at the processes that the particular space will provide. Children will grow and become problem solvers if designers can provide the appropriate outlets for such growth.

Children have limited opportunities to interact with the real, natural world in a safe way. In crowded cities, over-developed urban areas, and in crowded schools and child care centers, there is not sufficient space for children to do as they please (as in strict city parks where you can't dam up streams, climb the trees, or walk on the grass). We need to provide space that "allows" interaction, creativity, process, challenge, risk, adventure, growth, action, and all the elements the child needs while playing in the world of the adult.

Learning Structures, Inc.[6]

Christopher Clews is the inventor of a unique system of community participation in playground construction. With original designs, training workshops, and

specially designed assembly tools, he has provided a widely imitated model of successfully built playgrounds. Selected principles underlying his designs and construction follow:

- Children require a rich, stimulating, safe play experience for their development.
- Towns and schools rarely provide play leaders or offer organized outdoor supervision in the natural environment.
- Without creative leadership, the physical play environment must be stimulating, self-guiding, and self-regulating.
- Equipment offering a backdrop for children's discovery and adventure play is very expensive and doesn't get built in most schools or vacant lots.
- Limited by cost, what is purchased or built conventionally is often totally inadequate for the numbers of children wanting to use it. A well-

FIGURE 7.8 Use of volunteer labor and local materials make it possible to build the "Tire-Tanic" at an affordable cost.

[6]Script, photos, and design courtesy of Christopher Clews, President, Learning Structures, Inc.

FIGURE 7.9 The "Giant Octopus" with one-half tennis ball suction cups and Rockport lighthouse background.

designed structure for 10 becomes a very dangerous structure for 100.

- Use of volunteer labor and local materials makes it possible to develop an exciting, complex, multi-level, safe play environment at an affordable cost.
- The feeling of satisfaction and accomplishment from participating in a highly successful community event is the fuel that continues to power ever increasing numbers of volunteer playground builders.
- Over the past 15 years, Learning Structures, Inc. has developed a combination of organizational techniques and designs that have made it possible to build ever larger and more complex play environments in one weekend.
- Design ideas are solicited from the children and community members who will use the playground.
- Typically, each Learning Structures playground includes facilities for large muscle development, fantasy play, cognitive, development, and cooperative play.
- Specifically, most playgrounds include challenge courses; various fantasy play "sets" like animals, vehicles, hideouts, or castles; stages with gathering places; art and music equipment; and group swings requiring the cooperation of several children to set them in motion. Handicapped access and general seating is always incorporated.
- Materials include locally available lumber, chain, cable, hose, stainless steel, and bolts, all with a 20-year minimum life expectancy as a standard. Key wear joints are custom designed and supplied by Learning Structures, Inc.
- Construction is divided into 10 to 30 teams, with each team captain directing 3 to 8 team workers. Advance planning of all required materials and preparation of detailed assembly diagrams for each team are the keys to successful one or two day construction.
- A team captain's training session just prior to construction and several specialized tools and templates have further increased the safety and efficiency of construction.
- A complete checklist is produced along with every new design to help each community keep their new playground safe and attractive.

Neverland Play Designs[7]

When I design a space for children I am influenced by my own wide range of childhood memories: trees, fireflies, cartoons, snow, tulips, forts and clubhouses, Dr. Seuss books, orchards, tall grass, Uncle Remus, storefronts and displays, carni-

[7]Script and photos courtesy of James Talbot, owner and designer, Neverland Play Designs.

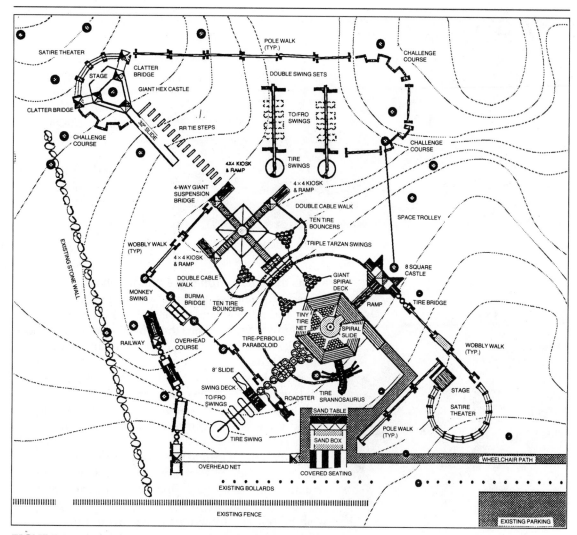

FIGURE 7.10 *The playground includes facilities for large muscle development, fantasy play, cooperative play, and cognitive development. (Design by Christopher Clews)*

vals, storybooks, twilight games, dank spaces under porches, Disney movies, Tarzan, Boy Scouts, vacant lots, the Little Rascals...it's the kind of list each of us have and it goes on and on. Because I and my family have traveled so much, my particular list has widened to include, for example: a double-decker bus in London, a walled rose garden in Casablanca, a Venetian gondola, the Alamo, a Venezuelan hammock, the cherry trees of Washington, D.C., the labyrinthine cobblestone streets of Ankara, Gaudi's Parque Guell in Barcelona....

As a kid I loved cartoons, comics, and illustrations, but I somehow felt cheated because they weren't *real* enough—I wanted to enter them, experience them in the round, have my own games and adventures in them. A favorite quote from J.M Barrie's *Peter Pan* (Barrie undated) goes, "... *you think the Neverland is*

FIGURE 7.11 *You think that Neverland is only make-believe . . . but this is Neverland come true.*

only make-believe . . . but this is the Neverland come true . . . very compact, not large and sprawly with tedious distances between one adventure and another, but nicely crammed . . . where all the four seasons may pass while you are filling a jug at the well . . ."

After completing Architecture School at Rice University I found myself, like so many idealists and romantics of my generation, facing a world of business and adults that I had strong reservations about. I gradually turned my talents towards creating small wonderlands and fantasy landscapes, places intended to hint at other worlds, bombard the senses, and reward those who like to explore. So began my company, Neverland Play Designs.

It has become so apparent to me that play is how children teach themselves and grow into their fullness, and that childhood cannot become just a training period for a career. *Our playscapes cannot be reduced to merely platforms and safe ways to access them.* I repeat this to myself daily. Despite the many improvements that have been made in terms of safety, details, and construction methods, I still find myself dissatisfied with the ambience and interest level of most play spaces—I wish there was a little more jungle in our jungle gyms, a little more play in our playgrounds, more variety, more caring and understanding, even a hint of anarchy—but above all, MORE MAGIC! When kids turn to drugs, TV, and vandalism, aren't they really just asking for more in their lives?

FIGURE 7.12 *Our playscapes cannot be reduced to merely platforms and safe ways to access them.*

My intent is to build playgrounds that are a joy to be in; fun places that are rich, open-ended, and adventurous. I might hang bells on a swing, impregnate a tunnel wall with aromatic oil, add a double-decker "Rocket" tire swing, install a "Whispermaphone," put up a hanging multi-tire "Jungle," fence off a "Konstruction Korral," or create a hill with tire climbing cliffs and painted ferrocement caves—who knows what will rear up it's head? My environments offer lots of "over-under-around-through" movement; they have unique visual imagery that is decidedly un-machine; and each one provides some combination of opportunities for exercise play, drama and imaginative play, construction, wheeled vehicle use, aloneness and togetherness, games, music, contact with nature and the Four Elements, growing plants, and directed learning.

Above all else I want my Neverlands to arouse a sense of magic, mystery, and wonder. I want them to hold secrets, intricacies, and precious things. They need to be enchanting and unconventional, the landscapes of dreams and day-dreams, exciting wonderlands that stimulate creativity and awareness. They must offer the promise that there is always more; that nothing is merely itself but can become something else, or be happily misused, or somehow blossom into the whole. I want them to somehow demonstrate the Oneness of all things and the truth that there is something nameless beyond time and space that need not be regarded with fear.

My personal process in creating play spaces centers around learning to give credence to and draw from the child within me, along with respecting and accessing my adult side. As the two grow and make friends, I see my Neverlands improving and gaining depth. When the places I build finally do reach a point, and I think they can, where they are *at least* as interesting as a wooded lot or barnyard, and as colorful as a Mexican street; when they actually do attract fireflies and frogs; when the kids in them can play hide-and-seek without running out of neat places to hide; when I find them planting flowers and bushes, and actually building their own castles—in other words, when I think there's some life in my children's environments, then I'll know a new beginning is in store.

INNOVATIVE MANUFACTURERS OF PLAY EQUIPMENT

BigToys, Tacoma, Washington[8]

BigToys see play as a child's foundation for development and as a catalyst for change and growth. BigToys are bold, innovative systems that encourage children to explore, discover, and learn. They invite and require imagination.

In every sense, BigToys help strengthen the physical, intellectual, emotional, and social skills our children need today, and must have for tomorrow.

BigToys' best example of a comprehensive playscape is the SB-6ab. A low, safe, two-phase structure especially for kindergarten through third grade (Figure 7.13).

PlayShells are unique components for building unique play experiences. They are assembled in an

FIGURE 7.13 *BigToys are bold, innovative systems that encourage children to explore, discover, and learn.*

---

[8]Script and photos courtesy of BigToys.

endless variety of ways to form climbing platforms and walls, sliding tunnels and chutes, and play spaces for crawling, hiding, socializing, and creative interacting. The colorful PlayShells are made of very durable molded polyethylene and are assembled with 1" galvanized steel tubing in a way that is extremely vandal resistant (Figure 7.14).

FIGURE 7.14 Playshells are assembled in an endless variety of ways.

Iron Mountain Forge, Farmington, Missouri[9]

Iron Mountain Forge manufactures Kid Builders, primarily for older children, and Kid Kubes, primarily for younger children.

Kid Builders combines a series of play events with platforms and decks creating a modular play structure. The more complex the playstructure, the more rewarding the play experience becomes.

Although primarily suited for 5 to 12-year-olds, younger children also can enjoy Kid Builders with proper supervision.

Kid Builders was originated by Jay Beckwith, a nationally recognized designer of safe, educational playgrounds for the past 20 years. Some unique features of Kid Builders follow.

- LARGER, SAFER DECKS
  Posts are full 48" center to center, providing 2275 sq. in. of usable, safe play area.
- BIGGER PLAY EVENTS
  We don't cut costs by reducing the width or length of our challenge ladders, track rides, or ring treks. They are all 48" wide by 12' long.
- DEEPER FOOTINGS
  Many parts of our country have deep frost levels. Iron Mountain Forge footings are a full 36" deep to avoid possible heaving. Not only do we ensure a well-built system above the ground, we make sure it's the best built product possible even where you don't see it, below ground.
- THICKER VINYL COATINGS
  Kid-friendly, non-pinching, slip resistant, long lasting vinyl coatings are applied a full ⅛" thick.
- KID-FRIENDLY SLIDES WON'T CUT OR BURN
  Soft and cool to the touch, plastic slides are a major advancement over

---

[9]Script and photos courtesy of Robert V. Barron, National Sales Manager, Iron Mountain Forge.

traditional steel. Color molded into industrial grade polyethylene, along with ultraviolet light stabilizers, Kid Builders' slides will endure even the harshest environments. They won't rust, fall apart, or develop dangerous jagged metal edges.

- SAFER, 6" DEEP SLIDES
  Kids don't necessarily play on slides the way we intended. That's why our slide sides are a full 6" deep. Deeper sides mean safer play and fewer accidents.
- MORE VIBRANT COLORS
  Kids choose play events because of shape, motion, and color. Kid Builders offers you a choice of blue, brown, and green posts with matching dome caps. Orange and tan polyethylene slides and bright orange safety rails and rungs visually alert the youngster to upcoming challenges.
- SUPERIOR POWDER COATING
  The longevity of powder coating is determined by the cleanliness of the metal to which it is bonded. Iron Mountain Forge uses a special cleaning process to insure the utmost adhesion. Rigorous test procedures, including salt spray adhesion and impact tests, prove the superiority of this coating.
- NON-SLIP CLAMP
  Kid Builders' clamps are adjustable for easy installation. Yet once you attach the roll-pin through the clamp and into the post, it becomes totally non-slip and safe.

STRUCTURAL MEMBERS

Vinyl Clad Steel Deck

What great shapes we're in! Squares, triangles, rectangles, hexagonal, and half hexagonal shapes are combined in multitudes of new, spectacular design concepts.

Vinyl Clad Steel Ramps

Is getting from here to there with total accessibility one of your concerns? Our vinyl clad steel ramp provides a durable non-slip surface. The addition of two hand rails at optimum height makes sure all children are given the opportunity to play.

Redwood Decks

The warmth of genuine California Redwood, furnished only in playground grade timbers. Enjoy the best of both worlds— the beauty of wood with the durability of steel upright posts.

Step Decks

One-, two-, and three-step decks are available in vinyl-coated steel or Redwood timbers. Use step decks for access for the younger child or those with special needs.

FIGURE 7.15 Kid Builders combines a series of play events with platforms and decks creating a modular play structure.

SWINGS

To/Fro Swing

Swings are not only the most popular event in any playground, but they also have educational value. The motion stimulates the balance system and improves both balance and vision. The use of vinyl-clad chain eliminates pinched fingers and the wrapping of swings over the swing beam. Swings are available with tot or belt seats, and may be attached to or placed independent of the play structure.

Tire Swings

Tire swings promote social and cooperative play, and provide the sensation of spinning. An extra-long horizontal beam eliminates collisions with the vertical support posts. Our tire swing has the heaviest bearing in the industry. Protected by a durable rubber boot, this automotive-type U-joint is the same as ones used on heavy-duty trucks. Vinyl clad chain eliminates finger pinching, and only new tires are used. Tire swings may be attached to, or placed independently of the play structure.

SLIDES

Plastic Wave Slide

Soft and cool to the touch, plastic wave slides are a major advancement over traditional steel slides. Color molding into industrial grade polyethylene, along with ultraviolet light stabilizers, ensure this slide will endure even the harshest environments. The 6"-high sides add an extra touch of safety.

Put the wave slide end for a double long ride and get a really great focal point for play. Better yet, make it double long and double wide and the play action really gets going! Slides promote self-confidence in children with more cautious play patterns (developing inner ear balance sense).

Spiral Slide

Nothing communicates the essence of a playground more than a spiral slide. It is always the center of attraction. Fast moving and challenging, the spiral slide helps children develop coordination and motor skills. Use a spiral slide to conserve space in close environments. Like all our slides, the color is molded in. Unlike metal spiral slides there are no sharp edges—ever! A sturdy steel center post supports this play event. Tunnel and bannister slides are also available.

Sliding Pole

A hearty play event designed to challenge even the seasoned playground veteran. It develops upper body strength, coordination, and equilibrium.

CLIMBERS

Three Rung Ladders

All ladders are made from coated steel pipe and include hand loops for added security.

Vinyl Clad Stairs

Accessibility is a critical issue on every play structure. Vinyl clad steps provide an easy access route for the child with low movement confidence and skill. Accompanied by rails made from coated steel pipe, 1⁵⁄₁₆" in diameter. The vinyl clad steps are vandal- and slip-resistant. The mesh design keeps dirt, water, or snow from accumulating.

Vinyl Clad Chain Net Climber

The "ouch" has been removed in this pinchless design which provides a unique and important challenge. Better than other climbers which are inflexible, the movement of our net builds necessary balance skill. Movement also makes it an interesting and significant learning situation, and since the unit is low to the ground, no hazard is present.

Arch Climber

The arch climber is an important learning station for several reasons. As the children climb, they adjust their center of balance as the angle changes. Considerable skill is also required in the transition between the deck and the climber. Two hand-rail loops are placed at this point to provide assistance to early learners. Promote agility and rhythm with an arch climber on your playstructure.

Curly Climber

A recent Iron Mountain Forge innovation, the Curly Climber is at once challenging yet safe. It stimulates the imagination of its young users; some use it like a ladder, others inch around the outside going around and around. Only Iron Mountain Forge builds a Curly Climber with just the right spacing between the curls to prevent head entrapment or climbing on the inside.

UPPER BODY DEVELOPMENT

Challenge Ladder

Unlike old-fashioned horizontal bars, the Iron Mountain Forge Challenge Ladder has rungs set at a slight angle to each other. Our design increases interest and difficulty without adding risk. It also reduces the tendency of children to skip bars. To reduce conflict, the challenge ladder is wide enough to be used by several children at a time. This play event is a great upper body developer!

Ring Trek

Ring Treks require even more skill than the Challenge Ladder. Success requires coordinated swinging and precision grasp, as well as strength. Excellent for developing upper body muscles, eye–hand coordination, and self-confidence.

"C"- or "S"-shaped Challenged Ladder

To make hand-over-hand even more interesting, both "C"- and "S"-shaped ladders are available. These provide routes with both narrow and wide rung spacing to accommodate a wide range of abilities. Their shape greatly reduces rung skipping. Unlike the ladders on other systems, the kid builders design is wide enough

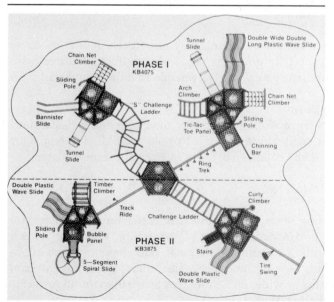

FIGURE 7.16 The more complete the playstructure, the more rewarding the play experience becomes.

for several children to use at once. The support posts are offset away from the path of travel to eliminate collision with equipment.

Track Ride

Track Rides have the same degree of movement difficulty as Ring Treks but require more strength. This event encourages cooperation of the children using this event. Unlike other systems, which use roller skate, or even steel wheels, Kid Builders track rides use nylon wheels which are oil impregnated for service-free durability. Custom-manufactured with special grooves, these wheels will not rub the sides of the track and are exceptionally smooth-rolling.

Parallel Bars

Simple in design, yet able to provide countless new ways to play. Some children will straddle the bars, others will try somersaults, still others will try gymnastic feats of strength. Even children with special needs will find a creative and safe way to play.

Turning Bar/Chinning Bar

Are you concerned with the physical stamina and upper body development of your youngsters? Add a turning bar/chinning bar combination to your play unit. We guarantee games of skill and challenge will evolve. Best of all, children will be developing strong, healthy bodies while hard at play.

BALANCE

Burma Bridge

Balance skills are generally forgotten in playground design. This sort of challenge is essential in the development of the inner ear balance sense (vestibular). Because it requires instantaneous adjustments both right and left, back and forth, Burma Bridges challenge both the beginner and expert players. Yet hazards are eliminated because the event is only a few inches above the ground cover.

Clatter Bridge

This event is an interesting way to link play structures. It is a low-level balance challenge, especially good for physically disabled children who need to develop ambulatory skills. It is available in either vinyl clad steel or redwood.

Curved Steel Balance Beam

All children need balance skills for healthy development, yet standard beams are often not challenging enough to hold a child's interest. Our curved design reawakens balance curiosity in even the expert player.

ENCLOSURES & ATTACHMENTS

Crawl Tunnel

In addition to building spiral awareness, the crawl tunnel also adds a sense of adventure and mystery to the playstructure. Crawling, which many educators identify as an important basic skill sometimes lacking in kindergarten children, now becomes fun. The square design of the Iron Mountain Forge Tunnel provides 28% more play space than round tunnels.

Bubble Panel with Steering Wheel

All children engage in fantasy play at one time or another. Just ask anyone who works with kids. Experience shows the bubble panel, which provides concave views of the world around him, with the steering wheel, which invites fantasy play, . . . one of the most used play events available.

Redwood Panel

Six vertical timbers of playground quality redwood provide an aesthetically pleasing safety barrier. The non-climbable panel utilizes polyethylene spacers to make sure that timbers cannot shift or allow entrapment.

Tic-Tac-Toe Panel

Education experts have said for many years that playgrounds need movable parts. The Tic-Tac-Toe Panel is a focal point for lots of social interaction and all of the language and relationship skills which arise from this sort of play. Pinching and climbing are eliminated by the use of round cylinders for the "X"s and "O"s.

Eight Bar Safety Rail

Eight evenly spaced vertical bars clearly state that Iron Mountain Forge takes the safety of your children very seriously. Non-climbable and without entrapment points, our safety rails make supervision easier.

PlayDesigns, New Berlin, Pennsylvania[10]

At PlayDesigns, we view our role as one of helping the child realize his potential for physical, emotional, and cognitive development. Children need opportunities to interact with an environment that is in harmony with their developmental levels and personality differences. Their style of learning is through play with others which can be augmented by well-designed equipment.

A comprehensive design team at PlayDesigns, with expertise in engineering and child development principles, applies the use of anthropomorphic data and guidelines for equipment manufacturers as set forth by the Consumer Product Safety Commission to create developmentally appropriate equipment for challenging, yet safe play. The aesthetics of equipment entice players to participate in physical activity as well as to engage in social learning play opportunities with others. Each piece of equipment has been designed to enhance a particular type of play experience that can be used alone or in conjunction with other equipment. Some examples are:

Climbers: The many levels invite bilateral climbing for both upper and lower body development as the child's manual dexterity and grasp is strengthened. Children can extend to higher levels at their own personal developmental progression.

FIGURE 7.17 Children's learning through play is augmented by well-designed equipment.

---

[10]Script and photo courtesy of Daly Miller, Play Designs.

Sturdy Riders (heavy-duty institutional tricycles): Children enjoy developing agility, muscular coordination, and balance while "motoring" these vehicles. Our vehicle group also includes a trailer for "hitching" to a trike, a wagon, and three specialty vehicles.

Slides: Children develop kinesthetic awareness during their downward flights. These are also available in *double wide*, to promote parallel play; *spiral*, adding the sensation of spiral motion; *tube slide*, which allows for experiencing gravity in an enclosed space; and *wave slide*, with added motion and complexity.

Swings: Old favorites that remain popular as they allow children the sensation of flight while they develop muscle coordination and balance.

Sand Play Area with Seats: A vital, creative element of the play environment, sand stands alone in play value or can be integrated with other play components.

Complex Unit Structures: These structures have a basic design of wood or pipe with added components of crawl tubes, slides, swinging bridges, steering wheels, store front counter, and various levels of platforms and accesses such as ramps, stairs, or chain nets. Components are linked together in desired design patterns to allow a smooth flow of sociodramatic and solitary play. Usually these unit structures are central to the outdoor play environment and can be coordinated in conjunction with other play components.

Activity Panels: These are unique to PlayDesigns. These weather-resistant panels each display an activity that extends outdoors the learning from indoors. Some examples are: A clock with hands that turn, a color wheel of primary colors that combine with the secondary colors, and a tic-tac-toe game with colored balls for markers. These panels can be added to the complex linked structures for added play value.

The variety of choices of equipment gives multiple opportunities for designing unique outdoor play environments. Components for outdoor play spaces are available to conform with specific space restrictions of facilities' outdoor play areas and climate as well as individual program goals, personal preference, and age of the children using the environment.

A properly designed outdoor play environment can be used most effectively by informed playground supervisors. It is recommended that play environment supervisors become educated on the safe use and proper maintenance of a play environment and the equipment on it. Children should also be instructed in rules that facilitate safe play that is also challenging. Well-designed equipment, proper maintenance, informed supervisors, and good play habits are all necessary to make play the healthy developing experience it should be.

Kompan, Inc., New Haven, Connecticut[11]

During the second half of the twentieth century there has been a major shift of the world's population away from the country and into urbanized centers. Today

---

[11]Script and photos courtesy of Mogens Jensen, Kompan, Inc.

FIGURE 7.18 *Kompan designs say, "This is a special item for a child",
bright, warm colors in softly rounded shapes.*

most of the world's children are born and grow up surrounded by human-built environments, and those elements of nature that are part of their daily lives are limited to ones that are allowed to survive in cities.

The modern-built city environment is a hard linear, metal, concrete, and glass world—a hard world in shades of grey and brown. To build a special micro-environment for children in such a setting is a very large challenge to modern culture. In response to the predominant characteristics of the adult-oriented city, Kompan has consciously provided furniture for the child's place that contrasts with the adult city-world. Their designs say "this is a special item for a child." Bright, warm colors in softly rounded shapes—evocative of flowers and children, of the softer, kinder side of city life—these are the hallmarks of the unique Kompan play furniture designs.

Good design and a high respect for children are integral elements in the Kompan concept. Kompan has been awarded a number of prizes and honors for good design and their design qualities are recognized world-wide. From these basic elements flow the many varied elements in the Kompan range of items for furnishing children's outdoor play areas wherever children and families gather in public spaces and institutions.

The predominant material used is wood; however, the wood is unlike that found in other wood playground equipment. Kompan quality woods—and they use a variety of different woods and wood products throughout their designs—are chosen to provide the strength and durability needed in urban public play-

FIGURE 7.19 *Good design and a high respect for children are integral elements in the Kompan concept.*

grounds and yet still offer the child some of the warmth and softness of nature. Children as well as adults can appreciate the feel of well-finished wood.

Kompan has pioneered many new techniques of working with woods in its drive to provide wood play furniture with none of the drawbacks and disadvantages found in other wood equipment. Kompan has invented ways of bolting and attaching to eliminate the problem of loose connections and the need for frequent retightening. Their dense, thick woods are difficult to burn and to vandalize. Their careful selection of finishes wherever the child's hand touches the furniture has eliminated the problem of slivers or other abrasion. These are some of the innovations found in the Kompan wood.

Why refer to Kompan as play furniture rather than using the more typical term "playground equipment"? The difference is in the Kompan design and the finish—everything about the Kompan play items is completed, ready to touch, all furnished for play. The appearance is much closer to items used to furnish living spaces than to equip factories or sports facilities. Thus, "play furniture" is a more appropriate term.

Quality is a prime consideration with Kompan. Public spaces such as parks and school yards need items that can withstand use by many children for many years. This requires durability, strength, and vandal resistance—characteristics that are found in materials classed as top quality. For example, Kompan carefully selects wood for characteristics of density, uniformity in density, and ability to weather well in all climates, and then applies high technology in the processes of working and finishing these woods. These are then combined with engineering and production techniques invented specifically for Kompan with the aim of increasing the durability of the product. Kompan is widely recognized as an innovator in working with wood and wood materials.

Safety is, of course, a subsection of quality for public spaces. All Kompan products are designed with meticulous care for the safety of the young child and the company has drawn on the best outside expertise in child safety on the playground to test and certify their products. The agency that does this has the longest practical experience in working for safety on the public playground. The care and attention to quality and to the details of good industrial design for children's play furniture is soon discerned on the playground by children, their parents, and the maintenance staff.

Bright, strong colors are one of the first characteristics noted in the Kompan designs. The use of color is carefully considered and controlled. The warm clear reds, oranges, and yellows which predominate are applied in selected patterns to clearly signal shapes and changes in spaces. These choices of colors and their application have been confirmed as correct by both the child user and by research on the interaction between children and color. The Kompan colors and shapes are clear signals to young children that this is a place for them, a place where they can be playful and lively.

In its work Kompan has deliberately chosen to focus on providing play furniture for young children. The reason for this is that the younger child needs the physical props of well designed and placed play furniture to fully develop their play. Older children who have had seven or eight years to develop both physically and intellectually are much more able to initiate and continue in play activities with a minimum of supplied props. This is not the case with young children. Further, Kompan has carefully studied its customer groups and has observed that in most modern cultures it is the young preschool-age child who actually visits and uses the playground with the greatest frequency—and they feel these spaces should have some furniture that welcomes these young children, that appeals to them, and fosters learning and development.

To offer children the best play value at every age and stage of development/ play interest, Kompan offers items designed for specific age groups. From Kompan there is no such thing as one item that serves all ages—for such an item would serve none well. Knowing children and children's play in great depth means that Kompan tries to match their products with stages of development and specific play interests of young children. Their aim is to offer the play environment designer a wide range of possible furnishings.

Child testing of new products is an important part of the development stage of Kompan items, prior to release on the market. If the kids don't like the item and it is not freely chosen by them as a place to play, then the design has failed the test. Child development experts on the staff at Kompan as well as outside consultants observe children at play on these test products and they suggest modifications and changes to improve the play value of the final design.

Kompan has placed a great deal of emphasis on social play, role play, and togetherness or nearness of the children in its product range—as well as on the physical play opportunities that children look for at the playground. Kompan has included social play based on the information from their staff of child development specialists that it is through play experiences that children develop skills such as how to interact with their peers or with children of other ages, develop their language skills, develop their imaginative abilities, and play out roles and activities they have observed. Further, children enjoy playing this way. Play value, in Kompan's assessment, depends on the degree to which the activities fostered by the setting fit with the child's interests and abilities.

Kompan's product range meets the play needs of most of the children in the community—about 90–95% of young children can enjoy their products if they are placed in an appropriately accessible environment. The designs allow children with less ability to enjoy joining into the play without any sense that they are limited to a "special" piece of equipment for use only by them.

New engineering technology applied to the Kompan design has eliminated the need for concrete anywhere in the Kompan installation— because "concrete and kids do not mix." The structural stability and integrity, however, remain. Sound engineering practices provide strong foundations but avoid the problems of concrete.

The community can enjoy the building of a Kompan playground for their children, and can get expert help from Kompan through a video and supervisory staff. Kompan is relatively easy to put up and the installation of a Kompan playground can serve as a good way to bring the neighborhood together—and to get to know the neighbors. With Kompan the sense of do-it-yourself gives such a positive community involvement in all stages including the installation; and achieves an attractive, playful, and enduring playground.

Children's Playgrounds Inc., Cambridge, Massachusetts[12]

Children experience so much more than adults are willing to admit that it is hard to see how any planned environment can provide them with sufficient challenge and space in which to grow. We believe no playground can compare with the rich and vital experiences of climbing a tree, fording a stream, digging a tunnel, and watching a cobbler mend a shoe, or replace the attention of wise and loving adults. Play equipment should be integrated into a diverse landscape

---

[12]Script and photos courtesy of Horst Henke, President, Children's Playgrounds, Inc.

FIGURE 7.20 *Play equipment should be integrated into a diverse landscape so children can have a bountiful access to nature.*

FIGURE 7.21 *The successful playground offers children a wide variety of challenges that lead them through a series of progressively more difficult tasks.*

so children have a bountiful access to nature and can move across terrain that is an experience in itself.

Our equipment is designed around a set of platforms which come in several basic sizes and 5 basic heights to have combinatorial possibilities that respond to the unique needs of each site, climate, community, and age group—including infant/toddlers and 10–14 years olds. In addition to platforms, as many as 60 components from which to create connecting links, and modes of entering and exiting a structure, satisfy children's needs to move and interact with a responsive environment. Most components are designed with a simpler version for younger children and a more difficult version for older ones, so all ages can do the same things, alongside each other, at their own performance levels. The modularity of the structures also ensures that they can be upgraded as circumstances dictate and money permits.

Psychologists agree that movement and activity are essential to children's development in general and intellectual development in particular. Children tire primarily by NOT being able to move about. The successful playground gives them a wide variety of challenges that lead through a series of progressively more difficult tasks, from simple to complex to super units, so they can go from beginner to master, utilizing an almost infinite range of movement possibilities. Since injuries rarely result from genuine challenge but rather from children's need for activity, we strive always to increase our equipment's number of movable parts, and to assiduously design and refine our hardware to be safe and capable of withstanding heavy use. Our components are intended to honor the range of movements children want and need to employ.

In addition to motoric challenges, many features such as built-in benches, steering wheels, play counters, playhouses, and inviting space under platforms which are not allowed to go to waste, encourage social and imaginative play. Large structures are notable for the range of ages they can support and for the way in which events are linked to create a sense of flow, so one movement or activity leads naturally and spontaneously to the next: a child climbs a mound to cross a bridge to slide down through a tunnel to go into sand or water. Because heights are developmentally important for perspective and cognitive mapping, we enjoy enabling children to climb safely high above ground and site our structures so a climb to the top provides a unique experience or view not possible at ground level. Ability to see through most spaces enables easy supervision and responds to the needs of young children for adult contact.

All structures can incorporate a rich complement of loose parts—ropes, pulleys, balls, etc.—and unstructured materials such as sand and water. The younger the child, the more critical his exposure to long, leisurely hours of invention with the rich sensorial qualities of sand, earth, clay, and water, on which he can create and impose structures of his own choosing. We have gone to great efforts to create sand and water units which are easily adaptable to outdoor public and school sites, at which children of all ages can stand, sit, or remain in a wheelchair to pump water, experiment with damming, streaming, and flow, with the assurance they will neither slip nor damage the surface beneath them.

Landscape Structures, Inc., Delano, Minnesota[13]

FIGURE 7.22 *The playground should be a challenging, safe outdoor learning environment, but also a community amenity that is easy to maintain and supervise.*

We at Landscape Structures Inc. feel that a playground should be a positive force in the development of a child and that it takes more than creative playground equipment to make it successful. A successful playground is not only a challenging, safe, outdoor learning environment, but also a community amenity that is easy to maintain and supervise. Because the playground must provide many years of service to the community, without major expense, it is important that the right steps be taken in its development. Short-circuit the process and you could pay for the mistakes for years.

[13]Script and drawings courtesy of Steve King, President, Landscape Structures, Inc.

Step 1. Site Analysis

The first step in the development of the playground is a careful analysis of the site. An assessment of the soil, surface drainage, utility locations, visibility, and accessibility of the potential location is essential. The ideal park is located in a highly visible area, yet far enough from residences so that the noise of children having fun is not disturbing. It is easily accessible to users, as well as maintenance and supervisory personnel. The soil is stable and well drained. It is away from any utilities and is not subject to flooding.

Step 2. Neighborhood Analysis

The second step in creating a successful playground is an analysis of the neighborhood. Neighborhood support and involvement are essential. Pride in "their" playground is one of the best deterrents to vandalism and one of the most important steps in creating a playground that will be an asset to the neighborhood for years. This involvement can take the form of neighborhood meetings/trips, individual surveys, or even a classroom project. In all cases, the designer should direct the discussions. He must be knowledgeable about products and materials so he can direct a useful discussion. These discussions could become detrimental if the neighborhood desires far exceed the budget and the neighborhood is not informed.

The designer should seek answers to such questions as: Where should the playground be located? What should it look like? What materials should be used? What kind of activities/apparatus should or should not be included? What type of safety surface should be used? Product literature from reputable manufacturers and field trips can be very helpful. General costs of a typical neighborhood play structure are shown. It is interesting to note that the safety surfacing can cost four or five times the cost of the playground equipment.

TYPICAL PLAYSTRUCTURE COSTS (1990 PRICES)

25–30 Children			
Playground Equipment	$ 9,000	$ 9,000	$ 9,000
Installation 35–40% of Equipment	3,500	3,500	3,500
Sand and Edger 40' x 50' area $1.00/SF	1,600		
Synthetic Mat and Base $6.00/SF		9,600	
Synthetic Mat and Base $25.00/SF			40,000
Total Cost	$14,100	$22,100	$52,000

Step 3. Equipment Selection

The most complicated and sometimes confusing job of the designer is the selection and recommendation of the specific design of equipment to use. For decades, prior to multimillion dollar law suits, the only concept used was one that segregated individual play events within a large paved area. Children waited in line to have an opportunity to go down the slide or to swing. Now, with emphasis on play as a learning experience, the "continuous play" concept is widely accepted by educators and playground equipment manufacturers alike. The concept is quite simple—connect large multi-level mainstructures with active play

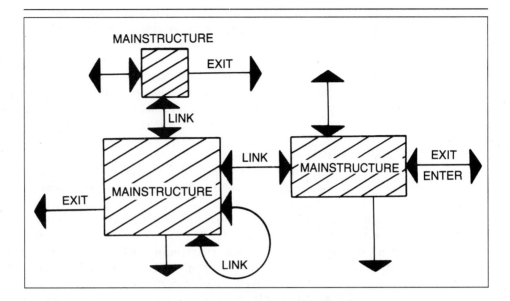

components. Provide a variety of ways to enter and exit this large connected playstructure and you have a structure that promotes continuous play challenges, not waiting lines.

A major benefit of this continuous play concept is that it requires little space to satisfy the needs of many. It encourages the social aspects of play while reducing the height ofequipment to safer levels. The result is a safer, more flexible and stimulating play experience than ever before.

The continuous play concept was originated by Landscape Structures Inc. in the late sixties. Now most manufacturers world-wide offer a similar play system in a variety of materials. Independent park planners/designers have also utilized the concept to develop a one-of-a-kind playground designed for a particular site. However, the number of these playgrounds has diminished substantially in recent years. This is due in part to the Consumer Products Safety Commission. They have issued complicated and, at times, confusing guidelines for the design of playground equipment. It is unrealistic to expect a designer to know all the technical data, thus exposing himself to undue liability. Also, both the designer and owner have found it less expensive to purchase pre-engineered and tested equipment from a reliable manufacturer. The quality and design flexibility of most of the continuous play systems offered by manufacturers make it easier for a designer to solve particular site problems.

Step 4. Play Value Analysis

With this new play concept came a number of new play events. These large multi-level mainstructures have made it easy to attach a variety of components to the same structure. Slides, poles, ladders; bridges, beams, etc. have been designed to attach to a variety of platform heights to satisfy most activity requirements of your playground. These playstructures can easily be expanded in the future. When selecting play events to include in your playground, it is important to understand the relative play value of each event. Each event can be assessed as to its active, social, and creative play value. An event that contributes to the development of a child's coordination, balance, and strength is high in "active play" value. Events that encourage group interaction or relationship play are considered high in "social play." Events that are high in "creative play" value provide an opportunity for children to use their imagination to shape and build their environments. All events offer some of each type of play, but usually emphasize one. In selecting play events, the safety and maintenance aspects must also be considered. As a general rule, moving events require more maintenance and are more likely to cause accidents than stationary events.

Step 5. Age Appropriateness

It is important to provide a variety of challenging yet safe play events for all age groups. It is unrealistic to think that one playstructure can safely satisfy the needs of children from 2–12 years-of-age. Their mental and physical characteristics and capabilities are substantially different. Generally speaking, a single playstructure can provide a safe play experience for children in a 4–6-year age range. For those under five years old, a maximum deck height of four feet is appropriate and no decks over six feet are appropriate in a public playground for any age. The only thing that increases with height is your risk.

A large single playstructure appropriate for a majority of the users (5–10-year-olds), combined with or adjacent to age appropriate independent play events for the 2–5-year-olds is a common solution.

Step 6. Equipment Details

Because so many of the new play systems offered by manufacturers look alike, it is necessary to study the minor differences to ensure that you get what you want and need. Until recently, the only type of material used in these play systems was wood. Now there are also systems in aluminum, steel, plastic, or a combination of these materials. The wood systems were easier to compare because a variety of woods were used, each with their own predictable characteristics. After using several types of wood, both treated and untreated, we have come to the conclusion that a high grade of heart Redwood is the best wood for these new playsystems. It not only looks better, but is resistant to rot without the use of toxic chemicals, is dimensionally stable, and has virtually no sap.

Steel and aluminum systems are not as easy to compare. They all will require less maintenance than wood. Aluminum will not rust but will dent easier than steel unless it has a heavier wall.

Structurally, all the systems will support the loads required of them. You will have to compare the little things. Do they offer all the play events you want? Do the various play events connect to the mainstructure in a safe and secure way with no awkward steps or spaces between? Do their swing chains and other metal parts have a resilient coating? Are there hazardous protrusions or sharp edges? Are there 38"-high barriers around platforms that are over 30" high? Are the connectors durable and vandal resistant? Are heavily used rungs or rails made of aluminum, or coated with a heavy vinyl coating? Compare the swing hangers, chains, and seats or tires. Also compare the delivery, installation, and relative maintenance costs.

Perhaps the most important part of the selection process is the experience and reputation of the manufacturer and his local sales representative. Do not be afraid to ask the representative for technical supporting data or samples, if necessary.

Step 7. Safety Surface

Perhaps the most important and potentially the most expensive part of the playground is the safety surfacing under and around the playstructure. The Consumer Product Safety Commission has identified falls to the surface as the single greatest hazard on the playground (accounting for 70% of all playground accidents). Their findings and recommendations have been summarized in their handbook. Selecting a fall-absorbing material for your playground is a complex problem. For years asphalt was the only surfacing under equipment. It was easy to maintain but not at all fall absorbing. Many cities and schools have found that out the hard way. Now a variety of surfaces is being used. The most common and least expensive of these is a 10–12" layer of loose natural material such as sand, bark chips, etc. Another choice that is increasing in popularity is synthetic surface systems. There are a variety of systems available commercially from premolded tiles to poured-in-place systems.

Perhaps the best way to compare these systems is by a careful analysis of technical test data available from each manufacturer. Generally speaking, these systems require less maintenance and are more expensive, cleaner, and, in some cases, more resilient than the loose materials; however, loose materials, such as clean, course sand do have play value.

No matter what type of surfacing used, it is important that it be placed in the best location to cushion as many falls as possible. The Consumer Product Safety Commission offers general guidelines in their publications: A surface system must withstand an impact of less than 200g when a test headform is dropped from the maximum fall height of the equipment.

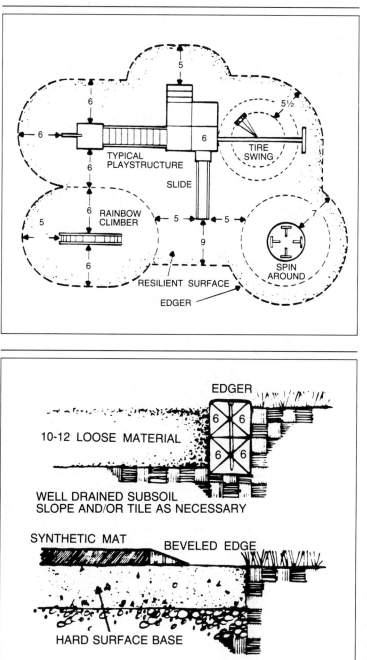

Generally accepted safety zones around common events are shown in the above sketch.

Step 8. Adjacent Areas
We have primarily discussed the design and development of a playstructure. To make a successful playground, the areas adjacent to the playstructure must also be considered. A bicycle parking area, a sitting area for parents and senior citizens, and a multi-purpose paved area for organized games should all be included in the design.

Step 9. Specifying the Design
If you follow the steps and procedures discussed herein, it will be easy to make specific recommendations with confidence as to the development of the playground. These recommendations can best be presented on a scale drawing. The drawing should show all improvements and pertinent dimensions and details necessary to make your recommendations clear. Once the drawing is prepared, and costs and other necessary supporting data gathered, a presentation to the neighborhood and city officials is necessary for approval.

Upon approval, the drawings and specifications are submitted to suppliers interested in supplying the products and services specified or equal products. A careful evaluation of the products and services offered as "equal" is an essential part of the designer's responsibilities. Approval and recommendation to purchase should come from the designer, the only one technically knowledgeable to make that decision. Too many times, ill-informed purchasers take the "low bid" and pay for it many times over. The playground is not the place to save a few hundred dollars—it is a long term and highly visible investment.

Step 10. Installation and Maintenance
The designer's job is not done until the improvements/equipment are installed according to the manufacturers' instructions. Perhaps nothing can be more detrimental to the success of a playground than a poor installation job. Once the playground is completed, a neighborhood party is a must.

The maintenance check list provided by the manufacturer should become part of the overall maintenance program of the park. Poor maintenance of the playground can be as detrimental as a poor installation job and is a primary cause for a least one-third of all playground accidents. If the neighborhood takes pride in their park, it will demand that it be maintained properly. Also, records of all meetings, approvals, decisions, and suppliers should be kept with the drawings for future reference.

Other Notable Designers

Although photographs were not secured, the author wishes to refer the reader to other designers whose works are making significant contributions to the improvement of play environments for children.

Robin Moore of North Carolina State University and Herbert Wong worked with children to create one of America's most imaginative play spaces for children —the Environmental Yard, in Berkeley, California. Conceptualized in 1971, the Environmental Yard was a research and development project demonstrating how an asphalted urban school yard can be transformed through the participatory process into a natural learning resource for children, parents, teachers, and neighbors. See Moore (1986) for elaboration.

Paul Hogan of Playground Clearing House, Inc., is affectionately regarded by his friends and co-playground designers as the "Father of the Community-built Playground Movement." He has worked with community groups (including children) world-wide to create inviting, creative, inexpensive playgrounds. A photographic sampling of his work is available in Hogan (1982).

Robert Leathers, a New York-based architect, and his staff design and build playgrounds in communities throughout the United States, using community labor, donations, and a range of salvaged and bought materials—tires, telephone poles, and lumber. His fantasy themes are very popular with both children and adults. See Chapin (1984) for a discussion of his work.

Popular magazines have featured the work of many of the designers included in this chapter; see Goldberg (1987); LaFarge (1988).

Gary Moore of the University of Wisconsin is one of the nation's most innovative and skillful architects of children's play environments. A sampling of his work is available in Moore (1985) and Moore, Piwoni, and Kennedy (1990).

CONCLUSION

Playgrounds that are reasonably safe and provide high levels of play value—challenge, novelty, flexibility, developmental appropriateness—can be constructed expensively or inexpensively, can use one or more varieties of basic building materials, and can be secured from a wide range of providers (builders and manufacturers). Some of the best playgrounds were inexpensive to construct and some of the worst were very expensive. The qualities of good playgrounds that are difficult to obtain inexpensively are durability and aesthetic qualities favored by adults.

The materials now in favor for constructing playground equipment are wood and powder-coated metal. (The author believes that space age plastics will become increasingly popular.) Both have advantages and disadvantages. The most frequently questioned qualities of wood are toxic preservatives, splinters, and durability; for powder-coated metal the common concerns are expense, aesthetic appeal, and possible rusting and deterioration (for non-aluminum and non-galvanized metals).

Most manufacturers continue to market playground equipment that violates Consumer Product Safety Commission guidelines (see p. 207), but those featured here are among those giving special attention to safety and play value. A growing number are turning to research (field tests, published research) and professional activity (conferences, workshops, task forces) for information on playground improvement. Some of the more promising advances are: making equipment appropriate to age and development of child users, providing direct help and printed resources to potential users, developing equipment that provides for flexibility (e.g., changeable panels, modifiable structures, free-standing equipment), providing follow-up safety services, training field workers (salespersons, representatives, installers, administrators), assisting in research and consumer education through sponsorship of research and workshops and providing educational materials, and assisting in standards development.

Some manufacturers are turning to university researchers for collaboration leading to refinement of play equipment and play environment designs. The author and Northwest Design Products Inc. (Big Toys) initiated a research project in 1991 intended to evaluate and redevelop play equipment and environments.

The playground equipment industry, during the early 1990s, is deeply involved in legal litigation, standards development, equipment modification, and expansion to meet unprecedented interest in redeveloping America's antiquated playgrounds. Public parks, public schools, preschools, and backyards are the major loci for this activity. If the present rate of change continues throughout the 1990s, children's playgrounds of the twenty-first century begin to reveal the magic that children need and deserve.

REFERENCES

Barrie, J. (undated). Peter Pan or the boy who would not grow up: the play.

Chapin, B. (1984). King of the playground. *American Way.* 17:124–127.

Goldberg, P. (1987). Great American playgrounds. *Child* June:62–65, 122–123.

Hogan, P. (1982). *The Nuts and Bolts of Playground Construction*. West Point, N.Y.: Leisure Press.

LaFarge, P. (1988). Why kids need playgrounds. *Parents* 63:124–128, 256, 258–260.

Moore, G. (1985). State of the art in play environment. In *When Children Play*, J. Frost & S. Sunderlin. Wheaton, MD.: Association for Childhood Education International.

Moore, G.T., Piwoni, J.L., & Kennedy D. (1990). Designing child care centers based on the children's environments pattern language: The Northern Michigan University Children's Center. *Childrens Environments Quarterly* 6:54–63.

Moore, R. (1986). *Childhoods Domain*. Dover, NH.: Groom Helm.

"The school yards of many of our cities are a disgrace to the systems to which they belong. . . . The school trustees apparently finish the school building and forget all about the playground . . ."[1]

8

History of Playground Safety in America

Since the initial period of rapid playground development in American cities, in the last decade of the 1800s, the issue of playground safety has been a subject of concern. Initially, a primary concern was that children be removed from the temptations and hazards of playing in the streets, but it was soon found that the new playgrounds themselves contained inherent dangers.

EARLY PLAYGROUNDS

As discussed in Chapter 5, the first playgrounds for very young children were sand play areas inspired by the sand gardens of Germany. Gymnasium equipment transported outdoors comprised the earliest playgrounds for older children. Mero (1908) illustrated serviceable equipment in use on playgrounds in various American cities in the early 1900s. For example, the approved equipment for children under six were sand bins with awnings for shade, sand buckets and shovels, bean bags, and low benches. The equipment for children 6 to 12 included giant strides, horizontal ladders (adjustable from 4 ft. 6 in. to 6 ft.), swings with four seats each (9 ft. high), tether poles, and teeter boards. More comprehensive playgrounds included basketballs, baseballs, and jumping ropes. For municipal

---

[1]Henry S. Curtis (1917). *The Play Movement and its Significance*. Washington, D.C.: McGrath Publishing Co., and the National Recreation and Park Association. pp. 121–122.

FIGURE 8.1 *The merry-go-round was invented by Tehurdore Worth. "Eighty children have been known to use it at a time." (Photo from Mero 1908).*

playgrounds, shelter houses with toilets, storerooms, shower baths, fencing and shrubbery, baseball diamonds, and tennis courts were prescribed.

During this same period, slides and merry-go-rounds were becoming common on playgrounds. The merry-go-round was invented by Theurdore Worth, formerly Superintendent of Parks in Hartford, Connecticut. Mero described it "...at once the most expensive simple piece of apparatus and the greatest economizer of space." It could be operated in 20 square feet of space by as many as 80 children at a time!

Judging from drawings, photographs, and written descriptions of equipment of this era, some of the major hazards were excessive heights (swings and trapeze bars 15 to 20 feet high, slides 10 to 15 feet high), merry-go-rounds with openings in the base to allow children to run inside the apparatus, swinging metal rings at body (head) level, crowded conditions (several hundred children at once), and hard surfacing under equipment. It is to their credit that early playground pioneers stressed high quality play leadership and supervision.

Even in this early period, a great deal of attention was given to surfacing. Mero suggested mixing equal parts of screened cinders and clay, spread one inch thick over coarse cinders and rolled to make an all-weather surface for the overall playground, excluding areas under equipment. He recommended that fine soft sand be spread a foot deep under the gymnasium, parallel bars, turning poles, see-saw, and jumping places. He prescribed hard surfaces under giant strides and swings to prevent holes from wearing in the surface. "A strip of cement side-walk about three feet wide under the swings works like a charm...About the best thing for the giant stride is a bed of screened cinders mixed with clay spread eight inches deep and packed solid (1908:82)."

Mero gave specific guidelines for the construction of equipment to ensure durability and safety. He suggested swing frames should be strong and secured by attaching them to planks buried one foot underground, and see-saw boards

FIGURE 8.2 Excessive heights were common in early playgrounds.

*FIGURE 8.3 Excessive heights are still
all too common in today's playgrounds.*

should be fastened securely to saw horses so they could not slip off or turn to the side and hit others.

Further elaboration was made by Arthur Leland in Mero's book (1908:79–90). He believed the following points should be considered in judging playground apparatus. (1) Is it safe? Will it run by itself or will it need supervision? The teeter ladder and the flying Dutchman were judged without elaboration as "interesting but somewhat unsafe." (2) Will it be interesting after the novelty wears off? Apparatus involving falling, swinging, or gliding" . . . take the place of foreign travel to the city child, and are intrinsically interesting." (3) Is the equipment simple, inexpensive, durable? From an administrative standpoint, the less adjustability and maintenance, the better. Wood and rope should be replaced by galvanized metal.

Leland gave detailed instruction for the construction of equipment. For example, equipment frames should be made of three-inch wrought iron pipe and set in concrete. Swing uprights should be 13 feet long. See-saw boards are to be made of good solid oak, 2 in. by 10 in. by 14 ft. long. Giant stride uprights are 4 ½ in. by 18 ft. To keep little tots from danger, he substituted swing seats made of two pieces of sole leather riveted together for the typical hardwood seats, perhaps America's first soft, flexible swing seats. Swings (gliders) made of wood, in which several persons sit opposite one another, were not recommended because of "the danger of accident."

By 1917, playground specialists were recognizing the miserable state of American playgrounds. Curtis (1917) called the playgrounds of many of our cities "a disgrace to the systems to which they belong" (p. 121). He believed that less than half were in useable condition—they were covered with brickbats, piles of ashes, and gullied by rain. He offered a common modern-day criticism, "The school trustees apparently finish the building and forget all about the playground." He lamented the fact that so many schools paved their playgrounds with brick: "I suppose that this surfacing must have been chosen by the janitor." (p.123) An ideal surface would be smooth, dry, springy, cool in the sun, non-slippery in the rain, and would not shock or bruise the children. "Probably we shall have to manufacture a surface for the playground as we do for the street before we get one that is entirely satisfactory." (p. 122)

EARLY PLAYGROUND STANDARDS

The first formal effort to develop standards for playground apparatus was apparently made by the Committee on Standards in Playground Apparatus, commissioned by the National Recreation Association (NRA). Seventeen recreation executives from 10 states prepared a statement (NRA:1931) which they considered to be a guide to communities in selecting playground apparatus. Essential elements for playground success were to:

1. Consider location, arrangement, and erection, regular inspection, supervision, designated apparatus zones, care of ground under apparatus, and instruction for use of equipment.
2. Specify preschool apparatus for the exclusive use of younger children.
3. Provide separate elementary age playgrounds for boys and girls (some believed that boys and girls could play together).

Minimum standards recommended by the Committee were:

Preschool Children	Chair swings (6)
	Sandbox (2 sections)
	Small slide
	Low climbing device
Elementary School Age	Swings (6, 12 ft. high)
	Slide (8 ft. high, 16 ft. long)
	Horizontal ladder
	Traveling rings or giant stride
	Balance beam
	See-saws (3–4)

The committee decided it was better to provide separate pieces of apparatus rather than the multifaceted gymnasium frame then popular on many playgrounds. Flying rings and trapeze mounted on the gymnasium frame were considered too dangerous and slides attached to the frame were too high. Whirling or revolving devices (e.g., merry-go-rounds) were judged to be of less value than the apparatus recommended and presented a greater hazard due to power generated in its use and the large number of children accommodated at one time. It was agreed that such apparatus could be installed only if it was properly constructed and supervised.

FIGURE 8.4 *The professional literature of the early 1900s questioned the safety of giant strides.*

Although not generally considered as playground apparatus, the committee also recommended equipment for basketball, volleyball, baseball, jacks, bean bags, horseshoes, building blocks, and handcrafts. They recommended playgrounds contain a shelter with toilet facilities, drinking fountains, grass plots and shrubs, gardens, and fencing. Sandboxes and handcraft areas should be shaded by trees or awnings. Benches should be available for mothers who come to the playground with small children. The surface of the playground should be even and smooth, hard enough to prevent footprint holes, yet soft enough to prevent injury by falls. Grass was considered to be the most desirable surface but not practical in high-use areas. The recommended surface was a subsurface of rolled cinders covered with loam, limestone screenings, or torpedo sand. Grass was recommended for major games and sports areas, and a year-round surface, preferably bituminous, for a year-round play section of the playground.

GUIDELINES FOR SURFACING: THE 1930s

In response to a request by recreation authorities the National Recreation Association (1931) appointed a committee of 11 recreation authorities from the United States to conduct a study of problems involved in surfacing children's playground areas. Information was collected on three areas: (1) surfacing materials, (2) methods of constructing and maintaining surfaces, and (3) cost involved. Their two-part report was published in the August, 1932, and September, 1932 issues of *Recreation* (formerly *The Playground*). Although the methodology of the study was not discussed in the final report, data on surfacing practices were reported

FIGURE 8.5 Giant strides are still in use in public playgrounds and can be purchased from equipment catalogs.

from more than 20 major cities with extensive playground experience. The committee inquiries and conclusions dealt with both playgrounds and specially surfaced courts used for games such as tennis and handball, with the dominant emphasis on the special games courts.

In general, the recommended desirable qualities of a play surface were resilience, good drainage, dust free, durability, nonabrasiveness, cleanliness, firmness, smoothness, utility, reasonable cost, and good appearance. The committee found a wide range of surfaces in use around the country: grass turf, sand-clay mixture, clay-torpedo grave-sand mixture, loam, agricultural slag, sand-clay-loam, crushed stone, limestone screenings, rock screenings, bituminous surfaces (various asphalt mixes), and concrete. Most of the surfaces were of combination materials and rolled to promote a smooth, even surface.

Recreation officials from the South Parks playgrounds in Chicago commented on their experience with surfacing. They found that cinders were too sharp, easily crushed into dust, and dangerous to the eyes. Crushed limestone, packed too solidly, created a dust problem and was "glaring in color." Torpedo gravel, or granite screenings, one stone deep over heavy black loam, was unsatisfactory. The loam cut through the gravel, creating a dusty, loose surface. The surface was treated with light road oil in an effort to control the dust, but a grimy condition ensued, blackening children and floors of buildings. Cork brick heaved in the winter; granulated slag hardened; and both were discontinued. After 25 years of experience the Chicago officials found a "satisfactory surface" consisting of 4 inches of yellow clay with a 3/16" topping of torpedo gravel and sand, rolled and compacted. Calcium chloride crystals were sprinkled over the surface to absorb moisture and eliminate dust.

Most recreation leaders agreed that concrete was not a satisfactory surface for general play because it lacked resiliency and was likely to "prove harmful to the feet of children." Most preferred asphalt surfaces since they were more resilient than concrete and easy to maintain.

The extensive report contained a brief section on surfacing under equipment. Special surfacing under and around such equipment as the horizontal bar, trapeze, flying rings, horizontal ladders, and at the foot of slides was recommended in order to avoid or reduce injury in the case of falls. The materials recommended were tanbark, sawdust, shavings, and sand. These materials were to be used alone or in combination and should be spaded and raked frequently. It was judged advisable to excavate the area a few inches and set planks on edge to contain the surfacing material.

The committee appears to have made two significant oversights. One, they over-emphasized the desirable qualities of bituminous surfaces and, two, they excluded certain equipment for recommendation for special resilient surfaces. They stated that regular playground surface (e.g., asphalt) is laid around such equipment as the see-saw, giant stride, and traveling rings since holes are worn in softer surfaces, which required frequent maintenance. Although they did not approve of concrete under swings, they reported several "successful" methods of surfacing including creosoted planks, gravel, and bituminous surfaces.

The recommendations of the NRA's Committee on Playground Surfacing set the standard for later playground designers and specialists. Six years after publication of the Committee's report, the NRA published *The New Play Areas:*

Their Design and Equipment (Butler 1938). The recommendations on surfacing were virtually identical to those of the Commission, indicating no measurable progress or change in attitudes or knowledge of the subject. Further, the minimum standards recommended for playground equipment by Butler in 1938 were identical to those made by the NRA's Committee on Standards in Playground Apparatus in 1931.

EARLY CONCERNS FOR LIABILITY

The playground developers of this early era were not swayed by the threat of lawsuits as they are today. Yet, as early as 1915, parents of a young boy sued the school board of Tacoma, Washington, over an injury their son received in a fall from a swing. The verdict required the school board to pay damages for the injury and resulted in the removal of play equipment from many schools in the state of Washington (Curtis 1917). Periodically over the years, similar patterns of injury/play equipment removal have been recorded in various areas of the United States.

By 1940, the subject of liability for recreation area injuries (including playgrounds), was of such interest that an address to California recreation workers titled, Safety Versus Lawsuits, was published in *Recreation* (Jacobson 1940). Based upon his knowledge of law and of numerous lawsuits during the 1930s, Jacobson made specific recommendations for safety aimed at reducing injuries and liability:

1. Purchase the best equipment obtainable and keep it in good condition.
2. Observe equipment in actual use. If defects are found, correct them. "You will find it impossible to convince a court or jury that a playground device is safe when injuries are proven to have occurred frequently upon it (1940:88)."
3. Develop a system of inspection, including prompt repair or dismantling of defective equipment.
4. Inspections should be according to a set schedule, some devices weekly, some monthly.
5. A printed inspection and repair form should be used for each piece of equipment specifying the inspection rules.
6. Records should be kept of all repairs with the nature of the work, dates, and names of the inspector and the person making the repairs noted.
7. Playgrounds should be carefully supervised by trained personnel.
8. Signs addressed to parents and guardians should warn specifically of any unsafe conditions in recreation areas (water hazards in park areas, etc.). Signs such as "Not Responsible for Accidents" are absurd. One cannot escape one's legal responsibility by a sign saying, in effect, that one chooses not to be obligated.

PLAYGROUND SURFACING: THE 1940s AND 1950s

The popularity and heavy use of playgrounds during the 1930s and 1940s inevitably led to extensive areas becoming hard packed with protruding rocks and "dust bowls." Entire school systems turned to asphalt as a substitute. (Grass turf, though considered the best general surface by many, was very difficult to retain in high use areas). Administrators and teachers appear to have been so eager to escape the dust bowl conditions of previous playgrounds that they heartily endorsed asphalt as the "ideal" play surface. In a California survey (Scott 1942), when asked: "Do you, in general, like or dislike the hard surfacing (asphalt) for playgrounds?," the response was: Like, 97; Dislike, 3; Uncertain, 3. They also endorsed asphalt as making it possible for greater use of playgrounds and as causing fewer accidents than before. It appears that no distinction was made in the survey for general play areas and areas under and around equipment. The dearth of careful, extensive studies of equipment and surface-related accidents/injuries appears to have allowed almost universal acceptance of asphalt as a general playground surface without due regard for surfaces under equipment.

One of the predictable consequences of this attitude was the later belief that ordinary equipment, such as swings and slides, was dangerous, inadequate, and breakable. Not realizing that surfaces and sloppy maintenance were probably greater contributors to accidents than equipment per se, designers introduced the concrete sculpture era (*Recreation* 1949; Hostvet 1950; *Recreation* 1954). This period was reputed for its intense interest in sewer pipes and concrete sculptures: the "whatnot," a set of concrete steps leading nowhere; the "dodger," a series of low concrete block walls arranged in maze-like fashion; the "rocket ship," made of concrete sewer pipes; the "concrete turtle"; and the concrete log," imbedded in concrete and raised off the ground for playing "Hi-Yo Silver." We were now seeing total disregard for (indeed, oblivion to) earlier concerns about hard surfaces on playgrounds. Concrete and asphalt, the pride of maintenance personnel and administrators, had carried the day over concerns of safety, creativity, and challenge. We are still fighting this legacy today.

Fortunately, not everyone during the 1950s subscribed to this "concrete affinity." In Europe the development of "junk playgrounds," later called adventure playgrounds, began to influence Americans. Commercial firms, spurred by the profit motive, were experimenting with safer playground surfaces. The Firestone Tire and Rubber Company (Moore 1951) developed a rubber powder playground surface material for installation on asphalt or concrete while the Goodyear Tire and Rubber Company (Polson 1951) developed pelletized rubber. It is unlikely that such materials, applied to a thickness of three-eighths of an inch, would provide acceptable protection in falls from equipment. However, they did set the stage for more effective, manufactured surfaces later on.

Predictably, the consequences of using hard surfaces under playground equipment was brought to public attention (*Recreation*1951). Injuries and fatalities on the school playgrounds of Los Angeles (Bradshear 1952; Zaun, 1952, 1955) led to public protest against the use of blacktop surfaces for elementary play areas. This criticism included a prediction that the school board would be indicted for involuntary manslaughter. By 1948–49, 190 elementary schools (60% of the total in the district) had been resurfaced with blacktop. Recommendations to the board of education were varied: inactivate all playground apparatus; remove all blacktop surfaces; and remove all playground apparatus.

Two studies were conducted; one resulted in a report by the school superintendent and a report by the Citizens' Advisory Committee on Playground Surfaces. The superintendent's report noted that all 50 American cities with populations over 200,000, 27 had blacktop surfaces under or around all, or a substantial portion of, playground apparatus. Ten of these cities had no playground apparatus. Nine of the cities had coverings other than blacktop; in four cases this was some form of hard surface. It is particularly revealing that *no more than* 5 out of 50 American cities had any form of resilient surface under or around equipment. There were no data to indicate the nature of the surfaces. Of 29 California school systems studied, only 1 (Long Beach) consistently used sand under equipment. The superintendent's report generally supported the use of blacktop and school principals overwhelmingly supported its use under equipment. The report concluded the major problem was not the type of surfacing but one of pupil instruction on use of equipment and adequate supervision . . . "teachers and supervisors and principals have found that blacktop hard surfacing actually promotes safety" *Recreation,* (1951:326)."

In contrast, the Citizens Advisory Committee Report concluded that playground apparatus activities are an integral part of the program and should be continued: shock-absorbing material should be placed under apparatus; supervision and instruction are essential; and studies are needed on the absorptive qualities (resiliency) of surfacing materials. Their additional conclusion that injuries in falls result from the manner in which the body strikes the surface, and not necessarily by the type of surface, may have influenced the outcome of a lawsuit against the city of Los Angeles involving the deaths of two children after falls on hard surfaced areas.

The city won the court case, with evidence that "how you land is more significant than what you fall on, in determining the severity of injury . . . "(*Recreation* 1952a). These Los Angeles-centered events stimulated schools, at least in California, to initiate experimentation with surfacing under apparatus. The Los Angeles school district installed rubber surfacing under equipment in 1955 (Butwinick 1974) and the Pasadena school system installed eight inches of sand under equipment, retained by prefabricated concrete curbs with rounded edges (*Recreation* 1952b).

MOVEMENTS TO MODERNIZE EQUIPMENT

During the 1950s and 1960s, an increasing number of playgrounds continued to reflect the imagination of adult designers and their concern for creativity in play. Earlier concrete sculptures were supplemented by boats to free landlocked children to "go down to the sea in ships," and horses (some mounted as swings) to appeal to the "cowboys and Indians of the 'horsey' set" (Skea 1958). Heavy animal seats with projectile-like noses and legs became battering rams, later responsible for many playground injuries. Many commercial firms still offer a wide selection of these hazardous swing seats. Such efforts to modernize playgrounds through provisions for imaginative play were indeed well founded philosophically. Conventional playgrounds provided for essentially one form of play-exercise. The spray pools, trains, igloos, sculptures, boats, stagecoaches, fire engines, and, later, rockets and space ships (*Recreation* 1959; Birkhead 1959; Hanson 1959; *Recreation* 1961) were serious efforts to enhance play but frequently resulted in potentially hazardous and uninspiring designs. Since only very limited research was available to guide them, the creations of adults tended to mirror adult conceptions of children's play choices. By the end of the 1960s, various groups concerned with safety were seeing that efforts to "modernize" playgrounds had not resulted in an acceptable degree of safety.

DEVELOPMENT OF SAFETY STANDARDS AND GUIDELINES FOR PLAYGROUNDS AND PLAYGROUND EQUIPMENT

In 1969, the chairman of the Committee on Accident Prevention of the American Academy of Pediatrics met with a group in New York to prepare voluntary standards for playground equipment (correspondence dated September 14, 1972, between the Accident Prevention Laboratory of the University of Iowa and the American Academy of Pediatrics). The purpose of this group was to "establish a nationally recognized safety standard for children's home playground equipment" (Committee on Accident Prevention of the American Academy of Pediatrics 1969). Their specifications were relevant to swinging, revolving, and rotating equipment and related apparatus. Primary concerns were with proper assembly, installation, location in respect to obstructions, exposed bolts, durability and strength of materials, manufacturer's testing procedures, materials for swing seats, and surface finishes. Although the draft of standards was sent out to members for comments, they were not adopted. Legislation was not proposed and the effort was abandoned in 1971.

The early playground developers were hampered in their quest for playground safety by the absence of comprehensive research data. This led to considerable confusion, especially with respect to appropriate surfaces. The overall effect was tacit acceptance for over a half century of asphalt and packed surfaces under and around play equipment. The introduction of the National Electronic Injury Survey System (NEISS) in 1972 was a milestone in playground safety (NEISS 1982). The system comprises a sample of hospitals (currently 72) that are statistically representative of hospitals with emergency departments in the United States and its territories. The NEISS provides national estimates of the number and severity of injuries associated with but not necessarily caused by consumer products including playground equipment that were treated in hospital emergency rooms.

Two separate actions intended to result in mandatory standards for playground equipment were initiated in 1972. First, the United States Food and Drug Administrations' (FDA) Bureau of Product Safety (BPS) issued a report, *Public Playground Equipment* (BPS 1972), that revealed a dismal picture of playground hazards and injuries in the United States. Playground equipment was ranked eighth on the Consumer Product Safety List. Second, the Food and Drug Administration requested that the Consumer Product Safety Commission (CPSC) support a study of public playground equipment done by the University of Iowa. The Iowa investigators (McConnell 1973) explored accident injury data prepared by the National Electronic Injury Survey System, the National Safety Council, and in-depth studies by the CPSC. They also utilized anthropometric data (ages of children and sizes of equipment) and data on behaviors of children (equipment misuse, horseplay) that contribute to accidents and injuries. This report influenced studies on anthropometric data and strength of children by the University of Michigan, and studies of playground surfaces by the Franklin Testing Institute.

School districts reacted in various ways to fatilities and injuries resulting from falls onto hard surfaces. For example, one large southern city removed all the swings from its elementary schools because too many children were being injured from falls on to the asphalt surfaces previously installed to reduce maintenance problems. Following the unfortunate death of a seven-year-old child in an elementary school playground, the Ogden, Utah, School District ordered over 10,000 square feet of manufactured safety turf for installation under playground equipment and made plans to modify certain equipment to make it safer.

During the same period of the Iowa Study, the Playground Equipment Manufacturer's Association was working in conjunction with a safety task force of the National Recreation and Park Association to develop proposed safety standards. Their draft, circulated by the Consumer Product Safety Commission (1973), was intended to be used by industry as a voluntary standard. In 1974, a member of this group, public school teacher Elayne Butwinick, petitioned the CPSC to exercise its authority under Section 7 of the Consumer Product Safety Act and began proceedings for consumer product safety standards for playground slides, swinging apparatus, and climbing equipment (Butwinick 1974).

Butwinick criticized the work of the CPSC Task Force " . . . I find the standards are being drawn up by industry with only token input by other members. The Task Force has only met twice, once in April of 1973 and once in October of 1973." She also revealed that the preliminary draft was already influencing industry. "The voluntary standards, with some modifications were being used by one company, Game Time by Toro, as a means of advertising their equipment." Butwinick goes on to claim that both the Game Time and the industry voluntary standards are inadequate because: (1) heavy swinging objects are excluded from coverage; (2) slide sides are dangerously low; (3) the danger of specific surfaces is excluded; and (4) performance tests are not utilized.

Butwinick supported her petition with reports showing that playground equipment ranked tenth in frequency among product categories by hospital emergency reports, third in a physician's survey, and twelfth in an insurance survey. She personally conducted 3 surveys involving accident reports of a recreation department (250 accident reports), and 2 area school systems, one having 3,425 accident reports in a single year with 656 involving playground apparatus, and the other having 419 playground apparatus accidents. The injuries included several fractured skulls, vaginal bleeding, a fractured shoulder blade, a near severed tongue, a crushed jawbone, kidney contusions, a fractured spine, teeth knocked out, and severe lacerations. To further support her petition, Butwinick detailed several fatalities resulting from head injuries incurred in falls onto paved surfaces; a 10-year-old in Rock City, Illinois, a 7-year-old in Ogden, Utah, a 9-year-old in Milwaukee, and a 6-year-old in Los Angeles. She noted that the death of the 6-year-old in Los Angeles in 1951 was the eleventh playground death in that school system over a 20-year period. In 1955, the system installed rubber surfacing under playground equipment and as of 1965, 10 years later, "had had no further fatalities."

Butwinick's surveys supported the findings of other investigators in identifying the most likely occurrences leading to injuries and fatalities: falling onto hard surfaces (especially asphalt and concrete); being struck by heavy swing seats (weighing from 2 to 59 pounds); entrapment in poorly designed equipment; and pinch and crush points on equipment. She noted that 85 percent of all accidents on climbing equipment involved falls. The fatalities she reported involving climbing equipment *all occurred on asphalt or pavement.* She cited a nationwide spot check of school business officials revealing that "60 per cent of today's school districts have blacktop under play equipment...."

Butwinick's petition was later endorsed by the Americans for Democratic Action and the Consumers Union. A second petition, submitted by Theodora Sweeney (1974), chairperson of Coventry School P.T.A. in Cleveland Heights, Ohio, was used by the CPSC in support of the Butwinick petition. Later in 1974, the CPSC decided that the Federal Hazardous Substance Act, rather than the Consumer Product Safety Act, was the appropriate legal mechanism for regulating playground equipment. The CPSC extended a call for proposals in the Federal Register to develop a standard to cover both home and public playground equipment. A contract was granted to the National Recreation and Park Association (NRPA), the only bidder. A committee of citizens and representatives from industry formulated a report, *Proposed Safety Standards for Playground Equipment* (NRPA 1976a; 1976b).

The NRPA report stimulated a great deal of controversy. Designers feared the standards would stifle creativity; industry was concerned that adoption would lead to high retooling expenses. The CPSC identified problems of inadequate technical rationale, validity, repeatability and reproductability of the test methods and the contracted with the National Bureau of Standards (NBS) for the technical work needed to revise the recommended standard. (CPSC 1979).

The NBS completed two reports (NBS 1978a, b) in 1978 and a third in 1979 (NBS 1979). The CPSC sponsors of the NBS studies decided to issue the NBS reports as handbooks rather than as mandatory regulations. "The variety of users and equipment, the diverse ways in which the equipment may be used, and the many non-equipment factors involved in overall playground safety clearly indicate that a mandatory equipment specification by itself cannot adequately address the problem of playground injuries" (CPSC 1979). However, before distributing the handbooks, the commission decided to request comment on the NBS reports from the general public. The call for proposals for this purpose was published in the Federal Register on October 4, 1979.

The author of this book responded to this call for proposals, conducted an analysis of the three NBS documents, and submitted a report (Frost 1980). It was found that the reports (and the handbooks published by the CPSC in 1981) did indeed reveal a great deal of useful information, yet they were not sufficiently refined to serve as a standard or as a handbook. Sections on testing equipment were too technical for many consumers; home playground equipment and equipment for preschool children were not included; and the most common playground surface, soil, was not subjected to impact testing. Perhaps the most serious fault was the general orientation to conventional, outmoded equipment. The illustrations represented bad design, unjustifiable expense, and excessive hazards, such as heavy wood and animal-type swing seats, restricted areas between moving parts, protruding elements, and excessive heights. There were no drawings or photographs of well-designed contemporary play-structures. The illustrations were generally of outmoded, single, or limited-function equipment such as narrow slide and ladder combinations with limited access and entry to promote one-at-a-time and stand-in-line play activity.

Despite these shortcomings, it should be acknowledged that the NBS reports and the handbooks, later published by the CPSC (1981a, 1981b), were the most extensive and thoughtful American safety guidelines for play equipment for about a decade. They represented a substantial amount of research and technical expertise and made major recommendations for playground and play equipment safety.

Recent Efforts to Develop Guidelines/Standards

On September 4, 1986, at the request of the CPSC, an organizational meeting was held by the American Society for Testing and Materials (ASTM) to initiate standards development for playground surfacing. ASTM is a non-profit corporation organized in 1989 for the development of voluntary consensus standards for materials, products, systems, and services. It provides a forum for producers, consumers, and numbers of government and academia to write standards for a wide range of consumer products. The playground surfacing committee met in regular sessions and completed an *eighth* draft on May 3, 1989. A surfacing standard was approved by the ASTM in June 1991.

During the last half of the 1980s and early 1990s several other groups were working on standards/guidelines for playground equipment. An ASTM committee developed a voluntary standard for home playgrounds which was approved in 1990. Yet another task force, the Public Playground Equipment Task Group, was developing standards for public playground equipment, including equipment for both school age and preschool children. A standard is expected to be approved in 1992.

The CPSC, during 1989, contracted with the Comsis Corporation to evaluate the technical rationale for the existing CPSC Playground Equipment Guidelines (1981 version) and to make recommendations for changes to the existing handbooks. Comsis prepared a document that appears to be the most comprehensive compilation of research on play equipment safety ever published. The document was submitted to CPSC in 1989 and sent out to field specialists in 1990 for review. A final draft (presumably) of CPSC Guidelines was distributed for review in June 1991. If the CPSC and the ASTM prepare and distribute separate standards, producers and consumers will undoubtedly be confused by conflicting criteria. Hopefully, these two national groups will collaborate to develop a common standard.

The issue of playground equipment standards is complicated further by the development of guidelines/standards by numerous other groups. The National Safety Council has adopted safety criteria, the American Academy of Pediatrics and the American Public Health Association in early 1990 prepared a draft standard that included both indoor and outdoor equipment for child-care facilities. In addition, many state department agencies responsible for regulating child-care centers have adopted safety guidelines (for an analysis of these see Wallach and Afthinos 1990). (All of these that the authors have reviewed are inadequate.) Some cities (e.g., Seattle) have developed extensive guidelines; a growing number of State Departments of Education are deliberating about the possible development of guidelines. State regulations for elementary schools are either non-existent or hopelessly inadequate (Wallach and Edelstein, 1991). If all of these (and other) groups initiate and enforce playground safety regulations, play equipment designers, manufacturers, installers, and groups responsible for maintenance and supervision will find themselves in legal, technical, bureaucratic log-jams of major proportions. The United States should follow the lead of European countries and develop collaboratively one set of standards for the entire country. The involvement of Americans, Canadians, and other interested groups with the European standards development group could *possibly* lead to a single world standard.

Common safety hazards in American public school and public park playgrounds:

FIGURE 8.6 *Asphalt under equipment*

FIGURE 8.7 *Open base rotating equipment*

FIGURE 8.8 *Heavy, "battering ram" swings*

FIGURE 8.9 *Crushing mechanisms*

RECENT RESEARCH ON PLAYGROUND EQUIPMENT AND SAFETY

During the late 1980s three national surveys were conducted by the Play Group of the American Association for Leisure and Recreation, which is affiliated with the American Alliance for Health, Physical Education, Recreation, and Dance. The first of these was a survey of American public elementary school playgrounds (Bruya & Langendorfer 1988), the second was a survey of American public park playgrounds (Thompson & Bowers 1989) and the third was a survey of American

TABLE 8.1   CPSC VIOLATIONS

	Head Entrapment	Clothing Entanglement Protrusions	Pinching Crushing Mechanism	Lacking Guard Rail	Heavy, Rigid Swings Seats	Insuf. Clearance Btwn Swings and Supports	Open Area In Base of Rotating Device
NO VIOLATIONS							
Company A							
Company B							
Company C							
LIMITED VIOLATIONS							
Company D		yes					
Company E		yes		yes			
Company F		yes		yes			
SOME VIOLATIONS							
Company G	?	yes		yes			
Company H		yes	yes	yes		yes	yes
Company I	yes	yes	yes	yes			
Company J		yes	yes	yes		yes	
Company K		yes		yes			
Company L	yes	yes		yes			
EXTENSIVE VIOLATIONS							
Company M	yes	yes	yes	yes		yes	
Company N	yes	yes	yes	yes			
Company O	yes	yes		yes		yes	
Company P	yes	yes		yes			
Company Q	yes	yes		yes			yes
Company R	yes	yes	yes	yes			yes
EXTREME VIOLATIONS							
Company S	yes	yes	yes	yes	yes	yes	yes
Company T	yes	yes	yes	yes	yes		yes
Company U	yes	yes	yes	yes			yes
Company V	yes	yes	yes	yes	yes	yes	
Company W	yes	yes	yes	yes	yes	yes	
Company X	yes	yes	yes	yes	yes	yes	

From Frost, J.L. (1990). "Playground Equipment Catalogs: Can they be Trusted?" Adapted with the permission of *Texas Child Care*, Texas Department of Human Services.

preschool playgrounds (Wortham & Frost 1990). The overall results reveal patterns of poor equipment design, faulty installation, improper surfacing, and poor and nonexistent maintenance. Public school playgrounds ranked lowest among the three locations (schools, parks, preschools) on measures of safety, but all three surveys found general patterns of neglect and inattention to safety.

In general, the playgrounds surveyed (over 700 including most States) were remarkably consistent with the hopelessly inadequate 1931 playground safety guidelines of the National Recreation Association (1931). The worst of the lot were accidents waiting to happen—unfit for children's play. Virtually all of the playgrounds surveyed violated one or more of the minimal safety guidelines of the CPSC.

Given the frequency of playground injuries (about 200,000) per year and the author's experience in legal litigation, where over 90 percent of the lawsuits involved violations of CPSC guidelines, a critical issue emerged. Were manufacturers in 1989 continuing to market playground equipment that violated CPSC guidelines? In an effort to determine the answer, the 1989 equipment catalogs of 24 companies distributing nationwide were analyzed (Frost 1990). Using catalog copy, equipment specifications, and first-hand inspection, the equipment was compared with CPSC safety guidelines (1981a, 1981b). The investigator's analysis was verified in blind analyses by two additional playground specialists with over 90 percent agreement.

The analysis revealed that much of the equipment available from manufacturers and distributors in 1989 violated CPSC guidelines. Only three companies had "no violations", nine additional companies had "limited violations" or "some violations." Most of these violations could be readily corrected. Twelve of the companies, or half of those surveyed, advertised playground equipment with "extensive violations" or "extreme violations." A portion of the results are illustrated in Table 8.1.

A growing number of equipment manufacturers/distributors are studying play and playground research and making extensive improvements in their products as revealed in Chapter 7. A continuing problem is the reluctance of some to remove old, antiquated, hazardous equipment from their product lines and focus on contemporary designs with extensive play value and reasonable safety features.

CONCLUSION

It is to the discredit and chagrin of contemporary school and public park officials that most American playgrounds, particularly public school playgrounds, still bear striking similarities to those of the early 1900s. The typical modern-day playground, with minor exceptions (e.g., deletion of most giant strides), is consistent with the National Recreation Association's 1931 guidelines. This is perhaps the single most striking indictment of the concern of adults toward the value of children's play and the safety of their playgrounds. Equipment of traditional design, such as swings, slides, seesaws, climbers, and merry-go-rounds, is the most common equipment in the United States.

Playground and play equipment designers, manufacturers, and consumers have reacted very slowly to research data and expert opinion about playground safety: soft, flexible swing seats were proposed in 1908; special resilient surfaces under and around playground apparatus were recommended by a major committee of the National Recreation Association in 1932; regular inspection and repair of equipment was recommended by writers in the early 1900s; the causes of injuries and fatalities on playgrounds have been extensively documented by research and the National Electronic Injury Survey System since 1972; and guidelines for playground safety have been developed in increasing frequency throughout the twentieth century. Despite advances in knowledge, much of the manufactured play equipment and most playgrounds remain hazardous and unsuited to children's developmental play needs.

Several professional organizations are now initiating research and development aimed at improving playground safety. In the late 1980s, a group of play specialists working under the sponsorship of the American Alliance for Health, Physical Education, Recreation, and Dance and the American Association for the Child's Right to Play conducted national surveys of elementary school playgrounds, public park playgrounds, and preschool playgrounds. For the first time comprehensive national data on the state of children's playgrounds were available, revealing a pattern of neglect and hazardous conditions.

A number of interrelated factors contribute to playground safety and will be considered in the following chapter. These are: (1) design of the total playground, including surfacing; (2) design of equipment; (3) installation of equipment; (4) maintenance of the playground; and (5) playground use, including play leadership and supervision. Finally, it must be acknowledged that the development of cognitive/motor skills of children are also important factors in promoting playground safety. The challenge to adults responsible for playgrounds is to ensure that children have convenient access to safe, yet challenging playgrounds, and that time and support for their use is assured.

REFERENCES

Birkhead, F.V. (1959). Saddle City. *Recreation* 52(4):132–133.

Brashear, E. (1952). "But-Suppose She Falls." *Safety Education*. (National Safety Council) 32(1):2, 5, 26.

Bruya, L.D., & Langerdorfer, S.J. (eds.). (1988). (Where Our Children Play: Elementary School Playground Equipment. Reston, VA: American Alliance for Health, Physical Education, Recreation, and Dance.

Bureau of Product Safety. (1972). *Public Playground Equipment*. Washington, DC: Food and Drug Administration.

Butler, G.D. (1938). *The New Play Areas: Their Design and Equipment*. New York: A.S. Barnes and Company (copyright, National Recreation Association).

Butwinick, E. (1974). Petition requesting the issuance of a consumer product safety standard for public playground slides, swinging apparatus and climbing equipment. Washington, DC: United States Consumer Product Safety Commission.

Committee on Accident Prevention of the American Academy of Pediatrics. (1969). "Proposed voluntary standard for children's home playground equipment." Evanston, IL: American Academy of Pediatrics.

Consumer Product Safety Commission. (1973). *Proposed Technical Requirements for Heavy Duty Playground Equip*-

ment Regulations. Washington, DC: The United States Consumer Product Safety Commission.

————. (1979). Public Playground National Bureau of Standards Reports and possible notification rules regarding surfacing. *Federal Register*, 44(4): 57352–57355.

————. (1981a). *A Handbook for Public Playground Safety. Volume I: General Guidelines for New and Existing Playgrounds*. Washington, DC: U.S. Government Printing Office.

————. (1981b). *A Handbook for Public Playground Safety. Volume II: Technical Guidelines for Equipment and Surfacing*. Washington, DC: U.S. Government Printing Office.

Curtis, H.S. (1917). *The Play Movement and It's Significance*. Washington, DC: McGrath Publishing Company and National Recreation and Park Association.

Frost, J.L. (1980). *Commentary: Public Playground Equipment*. Report presented to the Consumer Product Safety Commission, January.

————. (1990). Playground equipment catalogs: Can they be trusted? *Texas Child Care Quarterly*, 14:3–12.

Hanson, L.R. (1959). Our Playgrounds. *Recreation*, 52:134–135.

Hostvet, H. (1950). They Don't Have to Swing or Teeter. *Recreation* 44:(1).

Jacobson, W. (1940). Safety Versus Lawsuits. *Recreation*, 34:(2).

McConnell, W.H. (1973). *Public Playground Equipment*. Iowa City: College of Medicine. October 15.

Mero, E.B. (ed.). (1908). *American Playgrounds: Their Construction, Equipment, Maintenance and Utility*. Boston: American Gymnasia Co..

Moore, J.R. (1951) Boston Gets a Rubber Playground Surface. *Recreation* 44(9):517.

National Bureau of Standards. (1978a). *Suggested Safety Guidelines and Supporting Rationale for Public Playground Equipment*. Washington, DC: Consumer Product Safety Commission.

————. (1978b). *Suggested Safety Requirements and Supporting Rationale for Swing Assemblies and Straight Slides*. Washington, DC: Consumer Product Safety Commission.

————. (1979). *Impact Attenuation Performances of Surfaces Installed Under Playground Equipment*. Washington, DC: Consumer Product Safety Commission.

National Electronic Injury Surveillance System. (1982). *NEISS Data Highlights*. Directorate for Epidemiology, Consumer Product Safety Commission, Room 625, 5401 Westbard Avenue, Washington, DC 20207.

National Recreation and Park Association. (1976). *Proposed Safety Standard for Public Playground Equipment*. Arlington, VA: Consumer Product Safety Commission.

National Recreation Association. (1931). Report of Committee on Standards in Playground Apparatus (Bulletin 2170). New York: The Association.

Polson, A.E. (1951). Pelletized Rubber for Playground Surfaces. *Recreation*, 44(9):482–484.

Recreation. (1949). Unusual equipment. 43(1).

Recreation. (1951). Playground accidents prompt surfacing study. 45(6):324–327.

Recreation. (1952a). Experiments with surfacing under apparatus. 45(9):517–518.

Recreation. (1952b). Things you should know. 56(4):189.

Recreation. (1954). Play sculpture for playgrounds. 47(8):500–501.

Recreation. (1959). Designs for play. 52(4):130–131.

Recreation. (1961). Playground countdown. *Recreation*, 54(4):174–176.

Scott, W.L. (1942). Hard surfaced playgrounds meet with approval. *Recreation*, 36(4):241–242, 255.

Skea, G.M. (1958). Imagination visits the playground—1958. *Recreation*, 52(4):106–108.

Sweeney, T. (1974). Petition to the consumer product safety commission. Cleveland Heights, Ohio: Coventry School PTA, May.

Thompson, D., & Bowers, L. (eds.). (1989). *Where Our Children Play: Community Park Playground Equipment*. Reston, VA: American Alliance for Health, Physical Education, Recreation, and Dance.

Wallach, F., & Afthinos, I.D. (1990). *An Analysis of the State Codes for Licensened Child Care Centers*. New York: Total Recreation Management Services, Inc.

Wallach, F., & Edelstein, S. (1991). *Analysis of the State Regulations for Elementary Schools*. New York: Total Recreation Management Services, Inc.

Wortham, S.C. & Frost, J.L. (eds.). (1990). *Playgrounds for Young Children: American Survey and Perspectives*. Reston, VA: American Alliance for Health, Physical Education, Recreation, and Dance.

Zaun, C.G. (1952). It's not what you fall on: It's how you land. *Safety Education*. National Safety Council, 32(1):3–4.

Zaun, C.G. (1955). Four conclusions. *Safety Education*. (National Safety Council), 34(5):8.

"When our car has a funny tic, we rush it to the garage mechanic . . . We have trained inspectors to make sure our elevators run smoothly and safely. Every public fire extinguisher in America has a little tag on it with the inspectors' initials and date of last inspection. Our boiler rooms are protected by boiler inspectors, our airplanes protected by the FAA, our ships by the Coast Guard, ad infinitum, ad nauseum. How many years ago was your playground really inspected by a competent, well trained person? Why are our boats and elevators more important to us than our children?"[1]

9

The Nature and Prevention of Playground Injuries

Events in the United States leading to the publication of Consumer Product Safety Commission (CPSC) Guidelines for Playground Safety paralleled events in a number of other countries. As injury data were collected and publicized, an increasing number of organizations and consumer advocates called for standards or guidelines for the design, manufacture, installation, maintenance and supervision of playgrounds. In this chapter, injury data focusing primarily on the United States will be reviewed, with special attention to number of injuries, type of equipment involved, nature of injuries, and age groups involved.

PLAYGROUND HAZARDS: THE 1970s

The movement to improve play equipment and children's playgrounds during the 1970s was related to the growing body of data on playground injuries and deaths. Prior to the development of the National Electronic Injury Surveillance System (NEISS) in 1971, information on such accidents was available largely from independent small sample surveys and case studies (e.g., Franzen 1958; Dale et al. 1969; McFarland 1969; Watson 1969). Since methods of study and study sites differ across independent studies, it is difficult to make meaningful comparisons, but there are some general conclusions common to these independ-

---

[1]Hogan, P. (1988). *The Playground Safety Checker*. Phoenixville, PA: Playground Press.

ent studies: (1) falls were the most common factor contributing to injury; (2) the head, face, and neck were the body parts most frequently injured; (3) lacerations were the most frequent type of injury; and (4) young children were the most frequently injured group.

The National Electronic Injury Surveillance System Data

With the initiation of the National Electronic Injury Surveillance System (NEISS), an important new tool in the field of product safety came into use. NEISS is a national data collection system designed to determine the nature and scope of consumer product safety problems.

On July 1, 1972, NEISS, operated by the Consumer Product Safety Commission's (CPSC) Bureau of Epidemiology, was fully operational with a computer-based network of 119 statistically selected hospital emergency rooms located throughout the country (United States Consumer Product Safety Commission 1975). From this sample estimates are made of product-related (playground equipment) injuries treated in all hospital emergency rooms in the continental United States.

For 1974 NEISS estimated 117,951 playground injuries. Climbing equipment was most often associated with injuries on public playgrounds. This appears to be related to the frequency of falls from equipment.

> The most frequent hazard associated with playground equipment is falls, particularly from slides and climbing apparatus. Three-fourths of all the injuries (reported by NEISS) were falls to the ground (ground or artificial surface such as concrete and asphalt) or onto other equipment. (United States Consumer Product Safety Commission, 1975)

This 1974 data are generally consistent with that collected in previous years. In 1972–1973, falling from equipment compared to other factors resulting in injury occurred with a 3:1 frequency. There was little difference in this ratio between public and home equipment. In 60 percent of the cases the injuries occurred on the surface beneath the equipment: 43 percent on bare ground or gravel, 12 percent on concrete or asphalt, and 2 ½ percent each on sand and "safety turf" surfaces.

In August, 1978, NEISS estimated that during the previous year 167,000 persons were administered hospital emergency-room treatment nation-wide for injuries associated with public and home playground treatment (United States Consumer Product Safety Commission, 1978). These estimated injuries were broken down as follows: swings, 72,000; climbing apparatus, 45,000; slides, 25,000; seesaws and teeter boards, 8,000; unspecified equipment, 17,000. The report points out that of all injuries studied, three-fourths resulted from falls to the ground surface or onto other equipment.

PLAYGROUND INJURIES: THE 1980s

The Consumer Product Safety Commission estimates of playground injuries for the 1970s fluctuated widely, apparently because of sampling differences and methods of study. A decade of refining the NEISS system produced a more consistent pattern for the 1980's. The total estimated annual injuries ranged from

TABLE 9.1

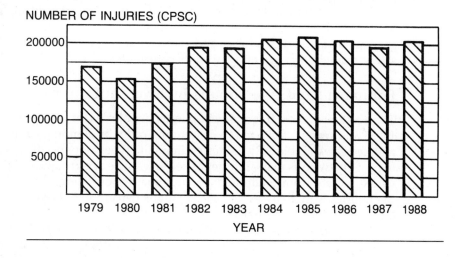

NUMBER OF INJURIES (CPSC)

**TABLE 9.2   EQUIPMENT INVOLVED IN INJURIES 1988
AND AGE OF CHILDREN (CPSC)**

	1988
SWINGS	76089
0–4	33.10%
5–14	59.80%
OLDER	7.00%
SLIDES	42806
0–4	48.10%
5–14%	48.90%
OLDER	3.10%
CLIMBING EQUIPMENT	57217
0–4	18.70%
5–14	78.50%
OLDER	2.80%
SEE-SAWS	9686
0–4	32.20%
5–14	63.00%
OLDER	4.80%
OTHER	16548
TOTAL	202346

154,828 in 1980 to 208,488 in 1985. The most recent data revealed 202,346 injuries for 1988. (Table 9.1)

In general terms, there was a steady increase in injuries during the first half of the decade but little fluctuation from 1984 through 1988. It is conceivable that growing awareness of injuries and safety guidelines, coupled with increases in safety-related literature and law-suits contributed to this leveling effect.

Equipment and Age Groups Involved in Injuries: 1980–1988

The equipment most frequently implicated in injuries for each year, 1980 through 1988, was swings, followed in descending order by climbing equipment, slides, and see-saws (Table 9.2). Other equipment (types not specified) was involved in roughly twice as many injuries as see-saws. The age groups of children injured varied widely from equipment to equipment. For swings about 33 percent of the injuries were to 0–4-year-olds, about 59 percent to 5–14-year-olds and about 8 percent to older children.

This pattern was consistent annually from 1980 through 1988. The annual pattern for climbing equipment was markedly different, with about 16 percent of the injuries to 0–4-year-olds and 81 percent to 5–14-year-olds. Remarkably, the frequency of injuries on slides was almost the same for 0–4-year-olds and 5–14-year-olds. We can only speculate as to the reasons for these similarities and differences. The availability of equipment and frequency of use by various age groups are undoubtedly implicating factors. The age categories used by NEISS should be modified to more accurately reflect developmental educational categories; e.g., 0–3 (infants and toddlers), 4–6 (preschool), 6–9 (primary), 9–12 (elementary), and above 12 (other).

Playground Injuries to Girls Versus Boys

The pattern of injuries in 1988 for girls versus boys shows that more boys are injured than girls on all types of equipment (Table 9.3). This pattern holds across the past two decades. Cultural expectations appear to be deeply implicated in this difference. From an early age boys are conditioned by parents, other adults, peer pressure, and television to be involved in outdoor games and sports and to engage in active motor activities. Girls are still influenced from an early age by traditional models and play materials that promote less active play, particularly in outdoor contexts. It is interesting to note (Table 9.4) that in the over-15 age category more females than males are injured.

Body Parts Injured

The 200,000-plus injuries in 1988 involved a wide range of body parts. Among specific body parts, the face and head were most frequently injured, followed by the wrist and lower arm. (Table 9.4) The head region (head, ear, neck, mouth, eyeball, face) led all categories with 82,461 injuries, followed by the arm region (finger, hand, wrist, lower arm, elbow, upper arm, shoulder) with 71,418 injuries. The leg region (toe, foot, lower leg, knee, upper leg) ranked a distant third with 31,769 injuries. Trunk, pubic region, and internal injuries accounted for most

TABLE 9.3   PLAYGROUND INJURIES BY SEX 1988 (CPSC)

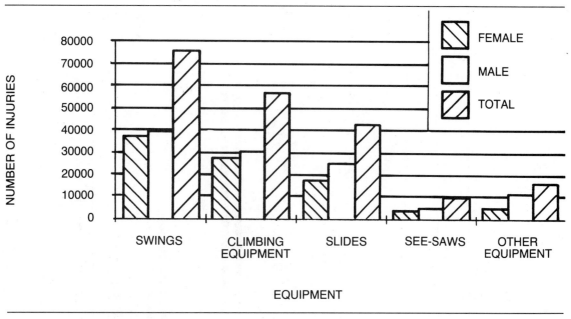

of the remaining injuries. These data, coupled with those showing that most injuries result from falls, reveal a pressing need to improve child protection by improving surfacing under and around equipment, limiting heights, and ensuring that equipment is of fall-free design. The head and upper limbs are at greatest risk in falls.

Playground Injury Diagnosis

Diagnosis of injuries in 1988 were, in order of most to least: fracture, laceration, concussion, strain/sprain, hemotoma, dislocation, puncture, dental injury, foreign body, avulsion, crushing, amputation, ingestion, hemorrhage/burns (tied). Diagnoses for remaining injuries (3,253) were not specified. Over half (110,177) of all injuries, contusions, abrasions, and lacerations can be classified as relatively minor, non-permanent, non-life threatening injuries. Fractures lead the list of serious injuries, accounting for over one-fourth of all injuries. Fractures to the arms and legs are by far the most common fractures, with the large majority to the arms.

INTERNATIONAL PERSPECTIVES ON PLAYGROUND INJURIES

An extensive analysis was conducted by King and Ball (1989) of playground injuries in Britain, Denmark, France, Italy, the Netherlands, New Zealand, Australia, Canada, and the United States. Among these countries there are similarities for the types of playground injuries resulting in hospital admission.

TABLE 9.4 BODY PARTS INJURED BY EQUIPMENT IN 1988 (CPSC)

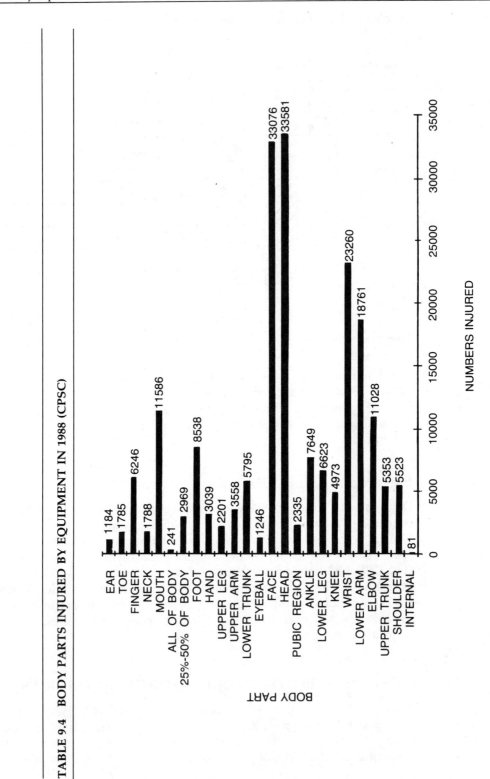

About 6 percent are attributable to skull fractures, 23 percent to concussion or intracranial injury, and 60 percent to long bone (arm/leg) fractures. There are about 3,000 to 4,000 playground accidents per 100,000 children annually. About 1,000 of these go to a hospital emergency room. Hospital admission rates are about 140 per 100,000 children.

World-wide (industrialized countries), serious long bone fractures are far more prevalent than *serious* head injuries, although head injuries, overall, are the leading types of injury. Head injuries are very prevalent among young children. Studies of falls show that head-first falls from heights of three or more meters onto rigid surfaces is "almost always likely to result in fracture or concussion." The lower bound for such injuries is about one meter (some U.S. data indicate six inches). King and Ball conclude that "the majority of playground accidents involve falls on the same level i.e., collisions, stumbling and tripping" (1989:page unnumbered), but the data they reviewed contradict this conclusion. A British National Association of Ladies Circles survey (King & Ball 1989:24) shows that 118 of 256 accidents were caused by falls from equipment. Only half this number (59) were caused by falls at the same level (collision with equipment and other children). A study by the Dutch Consumer Safety Unit, (King & Ball 1989:36) revealed that 177 of 326 accidents were caused by falls from heights and only 96 were caused by falls on same level and collision/pushing. A New Zealand study (King & Ball 1989:41) showed that 70 of 98 accidents resulted from falls from height. A Canadian study (p. 62) of 5,685 children concluded that 4,394 of the accidents were falls from heights and only 21 were falls on the same level. Perhaps the most comprehensive study ever conducted on playground accidents (Rutherford 1979 cited by King & Ball 1989: 69) found that 71 percent of 7,314 accidents resulted from falls to the surface (59 percent) and striking same equipment (12 percent).

In 1989 the United States Consumer Product Safety Commission's (1989) epidemology staff prepared a hazard analysis of injury data related to falls from all playground equipment:

> . . . the major findings of this analysis are: (1) that about 60 per cent of all playground equipment-related injuries (for both public and home equipment) are the result of falls to the surface below the equipment; (2) that 9 out of 10 of the "serious" injuries are associated with both public and home falls to the surface. (p.i)

The available evidence concludes overwhelmingly that falls from height account for most playground injuries. This conclusion lends urgency to current developments for improving surfacing around the under equipment.

In the 1989 report, CPSC used data on surfacing from a national survey of public school playgrounds (Bruya & Langendorfer 1988). These data show that about 46 percent of the equipment surveyed had protective surfacing underneath. These data are misleading because the depth and condition of the surfacing material was not determined. The author of this book was one of the trainers for the survey, and participated in the public school survey and the later national surveys of public park playgrounds (Thompson & Bowers 1989) and preschool playgrounds (Wortham & Frost 1990). Although depth and condition of surfacing were not reported in the surveys, the author and an associate surveyed playgrounds in 13 states, measuring the depth of loose protective surfacing (sand, pea gravel, wood chips), and *found none that met the normal criterion of 8 to 12 inches deep. Conservatively, over 90 percent of playgrounds do not have surfacing that meets this depth criterion underneath and around equipment.* This estimate has been confirmed in conversations with other professionals who participated in the three national surveys.

PLAYGROUND FATALITIES

Playground fatalities are rare, based upon available statistics, but *most fatalities are not included in the data gathered.* The most comprehensive data in the world are from the United States NEISS system. Between March, 1985, and February, 1987, 28 play equipment-related deaths were reported to CPSC. Data available for the 1970s and 1980s revealed that falls from heights were the leading cause of playground fatalities. The data for 1985–1987 show that asphyxiation/strangulation was the second leading cause. It is possible that the growing awareness of the need for resilient surfaces under and around equipment has contributed to this shift.

A leading cause of death in 1985–1987 was children accidentally hanging themselves in swing chains and ropes. The four strangulation deaths on slides were caused by clothing getting caught in the apparatus or strangulation by ropes children were playing with. The two children hit by swings died of skull fractures. Fourteen of the 23 locations identified were homes. In contrast, 23 of 26 fatalities reported by Rutherford (1979) for 1973–1977 were attributed to falls from heights. However, the Rutherford data were collected from public playgrounds which present a different set of risks or hazards. Supervision at schools is virtually constant but it is sporadic at home; school equipment is usually of higher quality than that of home playgrounds.

A report from CPSC (December 1989), made available in 1990, reviewed data on fatalities from NEISS, the commission's files of death certificates, consumer complaints, newspaper clippings, and other data sources for fatalities that occurred from 1973 through September 1989. Over this 16-year period CPSC received reports of 276 playground equipment-related deaths. The data show that 86 of the 276 deaths involved falls, but falls were underreported because CPSC stopped collecting death certificates reporting accidental falls (except for one or two states) in 1973.

Among the 276 children fatally injured, over one-half were under 6 years of age, about two-thirds were under age 9, and about 90 percent were under age 12. Even though fatalities from falls were underreported, they accounted for 86 of the 276 deaths that were reported (it is believed that falls are the leading cause of death in playgrounds). Strangulation, primarily as a result of entanglement, was involved in 131 of the 276 deaths. Clothing was involved in at least 25 cases (mitten cords, jackets, ponchos, jacket hoods caught in protruding hardware). Ropes were frequently involved. Strangulation by entrapment typically involved the neck being caught in components between components between five and eight inches apart. Tipovers or failure of equipment (usually due to failure to anchor into the ground) were involved in 37 fatalities. Broken swing chains and deterioration of wood below ground level were involved in a few cases. Impact with moving equipment (swings) resulted in 16 fatalities. All but two of the victims were 6 years of age or younger. Other fatalities resulted from choking on protective caps, running into support poles, hitting a tree while swinging and hitting equipment in an unknown manner.

In November, 1987, a representative of the CPSC at a conference on playground safety in Brussels, Belgium, reported that the CPSC had initiated a multifaceted program to reduce the number and severity of injuries (Nichols 1987). Major aspects of this program include: updating injury data; defining hazard patterns for children–toddlers to age 12; identifying children's development patterns, age characteristics, and play behaviors with equipment types; revising existing handbooks and developing one for preschool playgrounds; and developing information programs and handbooks.

The responsibility for safety on playgrounds is a shared one involving manufacturers, designers, installers, and supervisors. Well-designed equipment is now available and bad equipment will probably always be available so intelligent choices must be made. Supervision and maintenance are local responsibilities and, increasingly, skillful assistance can be found. Proper use of play environments begins with the education of adults who are in charge of playground activity. New guidelines (CPSC) and standards (ASTM) are being developed and should be consulted by all playground developers.

PREVENTING PLAYGROUND INJURIES

In the following sections we will examine safety problems relevant to the most common playground equipment. Safety guidelines and standards (effective in 1990) from the United States Consumer Product Safety Commission (CPSC, 1981a; 1981b) and other countries will be compared and suggestions for practice will be identified.

Climbing Equipment

Climbing equipment (monkey bars, horizontal ladders, and so on) can be constructed from wood or metal. Wood, splinters and all, has certain advantages over bare metal. It is not as hot to bare skin (southern climates) and it is softer. The problem of splinters can be reduced, almost eliminated, by selecting high quality hardwoods and refinishing frequently with a high grade exterior and/or enamel. The relatively new powder coated metals (steel and aluminum) resist heat build-up and offer a satisfactory alternative to bare or painted metal. Monkey bars, like all other common equipment, are available in various sizes. One of the most obvious, yet often overlooked, preventive measures in accident prevention is matching the size of equipment to the physical size and abilities of children who will use that equipment.

Exposed, protruding bolts were common on almost all commercial metal equipment until recently. Some efforts have been made to install smooth protective caps over bolts, but these are generally poorly secured and falls have resulted from the caps pulling loose in the grasp of children. Another and more promising approach is to countersink or indent protruding bolts. Sharp, jagged edges and protruding ends of pipes often trap children's clothing or cause cuts and bruises. But the most serious criticism of monkey bars is the existence of a steel bar jungle waiting to catch the child who falls from the top. If you do not presently have a jungle gym, invest your money more wisely in fall free climbers; that is, climbers so designed that children would fall directly to the resilient surface in the fall zone.

The CPSC guidelines (1981) stipulate that support members and climbing bars of climbing equipment not be too wide nor too tall to match children's arm or leg reaching abilities and that rungs or components intended to be gripped by the hands should be designed to be easily grasped (approximately 1 ⅝ inches in diameter for five-year-olds). The Seattle guidelines (1986) suggest that the distance between rungs on the horizontal ladders not exceed 14". Climbers should not lure children to an easy climb to heights without providing a safe way to descend.

It is recommended that walkways or similar walking areas over 30 inches tall have protective barriers at least 38 inches in height. Increasingly, protective railings are being installed vertically rather than horizontally to discourage climbing and to reduce the possibility of entrapment. Access routes on climbers and to decks typically include ladder rungs, ladder-type steps, and stairways. These should be installed for safety in climbing—ladders with rungs at 75–90°; ladder-type steps at 50–75° and stairways at 35° angles or less.

Swings

Swings and swinging apparatus are involved by various surveys in about 25 percent of the injuries on playgrounds. Being hit by a swing seat is perhaps the most common hazard. Despite the ease of eliminating this problem by replacing wooden and heavy seats with canvas or rubber belts or lightweight material, an analysis of company catalogs (Butwinick 1974) showed that swing seats are constructed from rubber, canvas, polyethylene, wood, aluminum, and other metals and they weigh from 2 to 56 pounds. Three situations account for most of the swing seat-related accidents. The child falls from the swing onto a hard surface, the child falls from the swing and is hit on the head by the return sweep of the seat or the child runs or walks into the path of a moving swing. These accidents are particularly frequent for younger children who have not yet developed sufficient cause–effect thinking required to anticipate hazardous events. The swing is out of sight in the other direction so the temporarily unoccupied space may be considered safe by the prelogical thinker. An effective way to reduce risk is to construct a vertical tire barrier or low fence between the swings and the other play areas. A survey of accidents in an urban and a suburban system (Butwinick 1974) found that 22 percent of the equipment injuries in the urban system that used wooden seats occurred on swings, but in the suburban system which used only canvas belt-type seats, only 9 percent occurred on swings.

Swings are typically set too close together, often as close as 12 to 17 inches, making it difficult to swing without collisions. The author suggests 24 inches between swings and 36 inches between swings and support posts (Figure 9.1). Seat heights range from just above the ground to three or more feet high, rarely being fitted to the sizes of the children.

Combination swing-slide sets are common in backyards. They are usually quite flimsy, made of the cheapest material with every possible space loaded with exercise apparatus—slide, swings, glider, chinning bars, etc. Such equipment is often overloaded. It may be poorly installed, often secured to the ground by driving a heavy wire through a hole in the bottom of each leg into the ground. Constant motion may loosen this in a short time. Further, using improper tools to erect the set may result in its being placed into use in a loose, movable state, thus increasing the risk of structural collapse. The S-hooks on this equipment often pinch fingers and hands or entrap clothing and the small, flimsy chains do not provide a proper grip for holding on. Within a relatively short time the swivels supporting swing chains at the cross-bar tend to wear out, allowing the seat (and child) to fall to the ground. It is particularly important that all moving equipment or moving parts be inspected regularly for wear.

The CPSC (1981) recommends a minimum clearance of 18 inches between the outside edges of adjacent swings and 18 inches between the swings and frames or supporting structures. The guidelines of various countries stipulate the following:

	Distance Between Seats	Distance Between Seat And Frame
U.S.	18 in.	18 in.
Canada	900 mm (36")	600 mm (24")
Germany	600 mm (24")	600 mm (24")
Australia	600 mm (24" Preschool)	400 mm (16" Preschool)
	900 mm (36" Public)	600 mm (24" Public)
Britain	At least 1 ½ times the seat length	At least 1 ½ times the seat length

This author believes that the tolerances, 24" between swings and 24" between swings and support structures, are the more desirable of the group. Extra space can be secured by positioning swing supports at an angle with the supports leaning toward one another.

Seattle recommends that swing seats shall be slash proof, reinforced rubber sling-type. Australia and England specify impact absorbing, light in weight swing seats with relatively large impact areas on leading edges and corners. The CPSC specifies that swing seats be constructed of lightweight material such as plastic, canvas, or rubber and that all edges be smoothly rounded or finished. Tire swings are popular because they permit multiple occupancy and may provide less potential for harmful impact. These guidelines seem acceptable for most common applications. Although not specifically excluded by CPSC standards, the regulations of several countries preclude the sale and use of many animal-type swings seats with protruding elements. These are so dangerous that all of them should be removed from playgrounds. The 1991 CPSC Guidelines will probably prohibit such swings.

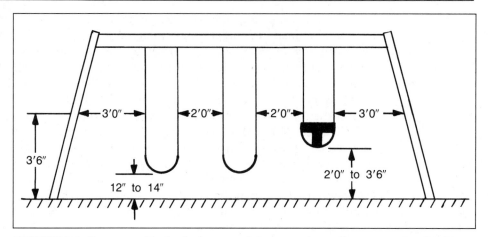

FIGURE 9.1 *European standards for space between swings allow a margin of safety.*

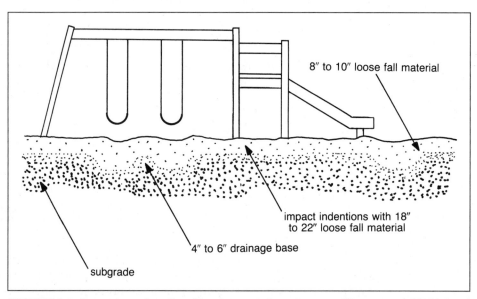

FIGURE 9.2 *Removing sub-soil to allow for extra-deep, loose, resilient material in high-impact areas is a growing safety practice.*

In order to make swings appropriate to various age or needs groups, special features must be considered: infant swing seats need safety straps; special swing seats, exerglides, wheelchair swings, etc. may be needed for special children; swing beam heights must be sized to age groups (the higher the swing beam, the higher the swinging potential); and, of course, a resilient surface must be maintained in all fall zones. Dimensions vary with the potential swing height. Because of the pitting effect in loose surface materials, extra depth—up to two feet—should be provided directly under swings. (Figure 9.2)

Tire swings featuring 360° pivotal swivel assemblies swing in every direction, unlike the to and fro action of common strap swings. Consequently, space between the extended arc of the swing and the support beams must be extended for safe swinging action. It is anticipated that the 1991 CPSC Guidelines will specify 30" to 36" of clearance between extended swing arc and support post.

Slides

The usual school playground-type slide is tall (up to 16 feet high) and narrow (less than 2 feet wide), with almost no protection from falling off the side (most slide accidents occur here). There may be no safety platform for the critical "transition zone" from the ladder to the slide so the younger child, growing in coordination, performs a delicate balancing act as she attempts to swing her legs and torso from the read (ladder) to the front (slide). At this point the slightest push can mean a fall to the ground or equipment below. A number of newer types of slides are now available that incorporate alternate access and exit routes; wide, enclosed areas in critical height zones; and platforms for movement from ladder to slide. These are available in varying heights, shapes (flat, wave, tunnel, roller, spiral), and sizes.

Because of the hazards from extreme heat (burns) and cold (sticking tongues), steel slides are rapidly being replaced by plastic slides. With *careful* selection, very durable plastic equipment can be secured. It is hoped that slides with excessive heights (9–15 feet) will soon be removed from manufacturers' inventories. Consumers should avoid these.

FIGURE 9.3 The side rails of slides should be high enough to prevent children from falling over the sides (photo and design by James Jolley).

The CPSC acknowledges four types of slides—straight, spiral, wave, and tubular (enclosed). Some are narrow and others are wide enough for two or more children to slide at once. They recommend a slope not exceeding 30°, but in actual application speed varies according to type of material used and length of slide as well as slope, and the age of children using the slide should be taken into account. The German standard specifies a maximum slope of 40° or in many areas not in excess of 50°. The CPSC recommends that the sides of slides be at least 2½ inches in height for the entire length of the sliding surface. The Australian standard specifies 4 inches for slide sides, the British 4.4 inches, and the German 6 inches. These dimensions appear to provide for safer use of slides than does the American dimension of 2.5 inches. The Australians prescribe minimum side heights of 19 mm (7½ inches) for preschool slides. Protective barriers should be installed at the top to help prevent falls over the sides. A platform deck "at least ten inches wide" at the top entry to the slide helps the child make the transition from the ladder to the slide. However, such a small deck area is insufficient for this purpose. Modern, multifunction structures (superstructures) typically employ decks four feet square to provide entry and exit surfaces to slides and other exercise options.

The CPSC recommends that exit surfaces of slides be at least 16 inches long and parallel to the ground and the exit itself should be 9 to 15 inches above the ground. The Seattle guidelines realistically propose 7″ to 12″ for preschool children and 7″ to 15″ for school-age children. Slide exits should be free of obstructions and the resilient surface immediately at the exit area should be extra deep—up to two feet—as extra protection from wear and pitting. Metal slide beds and bare metal decks should be oriented toward the north and *shaded* to prevent heat build-up from the sun. An increasing number of manufacturers are offering polyethylene slides that do not reach the high temperatures of metal ones. Slides designed into hillsides with proper design and installation can be even safer than regular slides due to the reduction of heights in a vertical fall.

Merry-Go-Rounds

Many people question whether merry-go-rounds should be used at all. They have a reputation for being hazardous and for having limited play function. Available accident data do not support the contention that they are among the most hazardous playground fixtures, but they are more limited in play function than some other types of equipment. The injury rate on merry-go-rounds could be reduced by wise selection, proper installation, proper surfacing in the fall zone, and some degree of supervision. Many existing merry-go-rounds are indeed demons. Many have open spaces in the platform large enough for children to fall through, weak axles that bend, foundations that give way to the extent that arms and legs can be trapped underneath, and protruding bolts that can increase the severity of injury. Most hazardous of all are types that have shearing actions in the undercarriage, allowing limbs to be severely broken, crushed, or amputated.

Butwinick's (1974) survey of an urban school system of 80,000 elementary school pupils over a 10-month period noted 21 accidents associated with merry-go-rounds. Five of these were caused by the equipment being too close to the ground, allowing feet to be caught underneath. Still other merry-go-rounds have exposed moving parts at the spindle-axle connection that invite intrusion. This can and does cut off fingers. The manufacture of some is so shoddy that railings break off after limited use, exposing jagged edges and eliminating the protection of hand-holds.

Merry-go-rounds are valuable for vestibular stimulation (sense of balance), motor activity, and dramatic play. The acceptable types have solid, circular bases with strong, rigid hand-holds and are free of shearing mechanisms underneath the circular base.

The CPSC recommends that the base of merry-go-rounds be of circular shape with handrails that do not protrude beyond the base. The rotating base should be solid to ensure that no part of the body can pass through an opening and contact a stationary object beneath the apparatus. This is particularly critical for many older merry-go-rounds have openings which allow children to stand or run inside, placing them at extremely high risk for serious injury. Poorly designed and badly worn merry-go-rounds frequently have exposed gear boxes or axles that can crush or amputate fingers. Such outmoded devices should be removed from the playground. Most new models have a solid base. The user must also be aware that children can and do crawl under merry-go-rounds and *the under-carriage should be free of shearing and crushing mechanisms*. Documentation on dozens of serious injuries from such mechanisms is now available. Because of the excessive wear, lack of maintenance, and pitting effect of resilient impact surfaces around merry-go-rounds, extra depth—up to two feet—should be used for loose surface material. Compact, secured (manufactured) impact material should be used whenever possible.

Many people have serious reservations about placing rotating equipment on playgrounds. The Seattle guidelines suggest speed-governing devices for rotary motion equipment to prevent dizziness and spatial disorientation. In applications where supervision is available, this may not be necessary. The Australian standard (Kompan, 1984) states:

> Because rotating apparatus presents physical and psychological hazards owing to the fact that once in motion children have no control over its movement, such equipment is not recommended for use in playgrounds unless the design overcomes these operational problems: p.29.

The present author believes that this statement merely sidesteps the issue. With serious attention to design, installation, maintenance, and supervision, reasonably safe yet challenging rotating equipment can be provided for children's play. Future revisions of national standards should deal with these needs. The American and the Canadian standards are good beginnings.

Seesaws

The seesaw is functionally narrow as a vehicle for play. Limited dramatic play is involved, no constructive play is involved, the child's thinking is minimally enhanced, little impact on the equipment is made—nothing is created. The same is true for a wide range of spring mounted equipment, consisting of a spring base with a plastic animal body for the child to sit on. They stand relatively idle on well-equipped playgrounds for older children where interesting choices are available. If used they are best placed on playgrounds for toddlers and preschoolers.

The consumer/user should examine the axle of the seesaw to ensure that the mechanisms cannot crush fingers or other body parts. A rubber bumper (a section of an automobile tire may be used) may be secured in the ground at each end or attached to the underneath side at each end to protect against crushing actions.

The CPSC concludes that the injuries involving seesaws arise from falls, being hit by a moving seesaw, and, in some cases, being punctured by splinters from worn, poorly maintained, or damaged wooden seesaws. They do not elaborate or provide any dimensional requirements for rocking apparatus. The Australians specify that neither end of the simple seesaw be more than one meter (39 inches) above ground level when the upper surface is in a horizontal position, and should have a maximum angle of 30° at the extremity of movement. Motion should be restrained toward the extremities of movement so that the effects of a sudden stop are minimized. Car tires can be embedded in the ground to absorb the impact (no steel radial tires). No part of the seat should move more than 1.8 meters above the ground and each seat should have a grip handle. *The suspension mechanism (where axle meets seesaw) should be enclosed to prevent access.*

Creative Play Materials

Creative materials are everywhere, in the cast-off junk of homes, schools, and industries, in the natural terrain of underdeveloped woodlands, and even in the five and dime stores of every shopping center. They need not be expensive and they need not be unduly hazardous.

FIGURE 9.4 *New see-saw designs prevent the crushing actions of many older versions (design by Kompan).*

FIGURE 9.5 *Creative play materials are everywhere. They need not be expensive or hazardous (IPA Conference, Tokyo, 1990).*

Given the paucity of creative materials on playgrounds, survey accounts of injuries while using them are obviously skewed, yet it is of interest to note their frequency. In Vernon's (1976) study, 68 percent of the teachers *never* allowed their children to engage in water play, 50 percent never provided for sand play, 25 percent never provided for dramatic play, and 50 percent never provided for construction play. Vernon found that 93 percent of all playground accidents were related to climbing apparatus, swings, slides, seesaws, and merry-go-rounds while all other categories, including play with creative materials, accounted for only 7 percent of injuries. National statistics by the United States Department of Health, Education and Welfare (1972) support these findings. In playground equipment injuries requiring medical treatment for the entire nation, climbing apparatus, seesaws, slides, and swings account for 88 percent (not including merry-go-rounds) of all injuries while all other equipment accounts for only 12 percent. More recent data (Nichols 1987) echoes these findings, showing that in 81 percent of total playground injuries, climbing apparatus, swings, and slides are implicated.

GENERAL HAZARD ANALYSIS

The overview on safety standards/guidelines presented herein is not intended to be exhaustive; the reader should refer to standards of countries and agencies (see Appendix B) for sources. Playground standards must be revised regularly to reflect growing knowledge. In addition to dealing with specific types of equipment and surfacing, standards generally contain recommendations on design and manufacture (strength, durability, hardware, function, load factors, etc.), installation (stability, dimensions, testing, zoning, manufacturer's instructions, etc.), maintenance (vandalism, wear, entrapment, broken parts, worn-out elements, lubrication, etc.), and to a lesser degree, supervision.

While design and manufacturing processes can be reasonably controlled by the imposition of mandatory standards, installation, maintenance, and supervision are normally controlled by local individuals, groups, or agencies and not subject to normal, acceptable forms of control or regulation. Further, a great deal of the playground equipment at preschools and public schools is hand-made, frequently resulting from organized community efforts using non-skilled personnel and scrap materials. From play value perspectives these playgrounds can be extremely valuable, but for ensuring a reasonable degree of safety, public education is critically important. Those responsible for any aspect of playground development or use should be trained in both play and playground safety. Some of the typical hazards to be considered are discussed in this section.

Entrapment

With the proliferation during the past decade of both manufactured and home-made playground equipment, the growing possibility of death or serious injury from entrapment, particularly the head, has emerged. The CPSC warns that accessible components of moving apparatus and climbing or sliding structures should not be of a configuration that can entrap any part of a user's body. Further, *no component or group of components should form an angle or opening that can trap a user's head*. The CPSC notes that exercise rings with diameters of 5 to 10 inches could present such an entrapment hazard and should be removed.

The Seattle standard states, "to guard against strangulation, equipment openings must be less than 5″ or more than 10″ inside diameter." The Canadian guidelines propose these same dimensions. However, these tolerances are not appropriate for some toddlers whose heads will pass through a 4 ½ inch opening. The present author proposes that a 3½ inch lower dimension replace the 5-inch dimension. It is likely that the revised CPSC Guidelines (1991) and the ASTM (1992) Standards will stipulate that 3½″ to 9″ openings as entrapment hazards. The issue of entrapment is complicated. Inverted angles are more likely to entrap a head than upright angles; horizontal openings more likely to entrap than vertical openings; openings where children could lose their footing more apt to entrap and injure than openings where footing can be maintained and the weight of the body supported by the legs rather than the head and neck. Further, openings in equipment (particularly wood) that originally would not entrap could change in configuration due to bending, warping or loose installation. Regular inspection and proper maintenance is essential.

Heights

Perhaps no other issue of playground safety is so widely disputed as heights allowable for climbing. It is acknowledged that most injuries and fatalities on playgrounds result from falls onto hard surfaces, but height is always implicated for the farther the child falls, the faster he falls and, potentially, the more damaging the result. The addition of shock-absorbing surfacing helps to protect children in falls, but the best surfacing loses its protective qualities under equipment exceeding a certain height. Consequently, climbing equipment must not encourage or allow climbing heights that exceed the cushioning properties of the surface below.

The CPSC guidelines stipulate that elevated surfaces over 30 inches have protective barriers but does not restrict climbing heights. The German standard restricts fall heights to 3 meters (9 feet, 9 inches) or 13 feet if ascent of the upper structural elements is more complicated. In practice, this suggests maximum deck heights of 9 feet, 9 inches or 13 feet, allowing for guard rails properly installed (vertically) to discourage climbing. The British standard limits heights of agility equipment to 2.5 meters (8 feet, 2 inches) regardless of its connection to other equipment. The Australian standard specifies this same maximum fall height. Given the injury data for falls, the great variation in protection offered by protective surfaces, and the virtually universal disregard for playground maintenance, the fall height *limit* of 8 feet seems more reasonable than greater heights for older children (school age). For pre-primary school age, heights should be more severely limited. In general, potential fall heights from equipment should not exceed by more than a few inches the reaching height of child users when standing erect on the protective surface underneath the equipment. In addition to reduction of likelihood of injury, this specification would also allow decks of sufficient height for children to stand erect underneath and use the under-deck areas for dramatic play. These recommended standards would hopefully void the sale and use of several popular types of equipment currently being sold in catalogs of some American manufacturers.

Pinch and Crush Points

The life- or limb-threatening pinch or crush points are most frequently found on the undercarriage of heavy, rotating, merry-go-round–type apparatus on the axle assemblies and at the end (ground contact areas) of seesaws, glider swings, and pulleys on cable rides. The CPSC (1981b, p. 8) guidelines state, "There shall be no accessible pinch, crush or shear points caused by components moving relative to each other or to a fixed component when the equipment is moved through its anticipated use cycle." The German, British, Australian, and Canadian standards contain similar guidelines.

A common excuse for manufacturing and using equipment with pinch and crush points is that the crush area (e.g., undercarriage of rotating equipment) would not be accessible if "used as intended." Such claims reflect profound ignorance of child behavior. In their normal play children will use any play equipment in a wide range of ways not "intended." If a potential hazard is present, they will be at risk. Consequently, designers must expect wide variation in play and plan for unusual and bizarre activity.

Protrusions and Sharp Areas

The CPSC (1981a, p.7) recommends that there be no protrusions or sharp areas that are likely to cut, puncture, or catch clothing. Common unacceptable protrusions include accessible bolt ends and exposed ends of tubing (hand-holds, railings). Protrusions on upper portions of equipment may catch clothing and result in suspension and strangulation. Test methods are spelled out by the CPSC. The edges of metal slide beds may work loose and allow fingers to cap over the edges, creating a sharp cutting effect as the child slides down, which results in serious cuts and occasional amputation of fingers.

The German standard prohibits splinters, protruding nails, and open ends of wire ropes. Projecting threads of bolts are to be durably covered. In addition, "There shall be no protruding elements or parts of equipment onto which a child could fall from a height of more than 500 mm" (20 inches). The British standard requires that exposed edges of materials be rounded to a radius of no less than 6 mm (.24 inch) or they should have curled edges or rounded capping. The Australian and Canadian standards prescribe that the edges of wood materials be chambered or rounded. The Canadian standard requires that all bolts and screws be countersunk or dome head and bolt ends shall be countersunk or covered with smooth caps. Caps and covers shall not be removable without the use of tools.

Suspended Hazards

The CPSC prohibits suspended cables, wires, ropes, or similar components within 45° of the horizontal and less than 7 feet above the ground surface. This guideline is not intended to eliminate items such as guard rails, cargo nets, or climbing grids. The recently introduced cable and chain balance equipment designed for children to walk on one cable suspended near the ground while holding onto a higher cable is not mentioned in the guidelines. Since children have been injured as a result of running into the cables, some means of protecting children is needed, *possibly* the installation of barriers to prevent running into the cables.

The Canadian and the Seattle guidelines state that there shall be no suspended elements less than 25 mm (1 inch) that could be contacted by a user in motion. The Seattle guidelines state that all suspended elements shall be highly visible to users. Visibility and size of component are obviously important in preventing injurious contact with suspended elements.

Slip-Resistant Surfaces

The subject of slip-resistant surfaces receives one sentence in the CPSC guidelines. Components intended primarily for the feet should have a slip-resistant surface. Seattle provides details: Concrete should have a broom finish; asphalt should have a "Durastone" overlay; log-end rounds or timber ends should not be used for play-area walking surfaces or stair steps because they hold moisture and promote slippery moss growth. The Australian standard specifies several alternatives to slick surfaces; narrow-width slats, cleats, perforated or embossed metal, ribbed or grooved metal or plastics, and timber free from smooth, painted, or polished surfaces.

Protective Railings

The CPSC prescribes protective barriers at least 38 inches high (school age children) around elevated walking surfaces above 30 inches high. These should surround the surface "except for necessary entrance and exit openings." The British prescribe protective rails at least 1 m (39 inches) high for platforms, access steps, and ladders rising more than 500 mm (20 inches) above ground level or adjacent surface. The CPSC does not attend to the subject but Britain, Australia, and Seattle require that space between horizontal railings be filled to discourage their use as steps for climbing. Vertical railings, of proper width to prevent entrapment, do not require such infilling. The Australian standard prescribes protective railings for heights above 500 mm (20 inches) and 1,200 mm (48 inches) for public equipment. The 48-inch standard is highly questionable because of apparent excessive height. The revised CPSC Guidelines (1991) will likely specify different dimensions for preschool and school-age children.

Consumer Information

Neither the CPSC nor the Australians require vendor's certificates specifying that the equipment being sold is in conformance with guidelines or standards. German equipment may be marked with the DIN test and control sign to prove conformity to German (DIN) standard, provided the product has passed the proper test. The British advise consumers to seek assurances from vendors that the British standard has been followed. All of the countries named here recommend that detailed instructions for assembly be included with the product. The CPSC, Germans, and British recommend that siting instructions—use zones, fall-zone surfaces, relationship to other structures, etc.—be provided with the product.

Toxic Materials and Poisonous Plants

Toxic materials may be introduced into playgrounds before the playground is built. For example, there are recorded instances (Freedburg 1983) of playgrounds being built under freeways, on top of landfills, and on sites of abandoned industrial plants. In addition, children are sometimes exposed to pesticides sprayed indiscriminately in play areas and to toxic wood preservatives in playground equipment. Unfortunately, the major national standards deal only with the toxicity of applied finishes. All prohibit coatings or impregnations on play equipment that are toxic. The CPSC recommends that manufacturers ensure that users of play equipment cannot ingest, inhale, or absorb through body surfaces any hazardous substances used in the treatment process.

Freedburg (1983) points out that children are presently caught in a regulatory gap. No federal agency protects children against toxic wood preservatives. Hopefully, the CPSC will address the need to protect children from toxic material on playgrounds as they revise the existing guidelines. A report prepared for the California State Department of Health Services by Consultants in Epidemiology and Occupational Health (C.E.O.H.), Inc. (1984) confirms that arsenic can be transferred from the surface of wood playground equipment treated with preservatives containing arsenic and that the arsenic can be washed off the hands. A concern is that ingestion of the arsenic might increase the risk of skin cancer. A 1983 document from the California State Department of Health Services estimated that the individual lifetime risk for persons using such playground equipment is "on the order of a few cases (of skin cancer) per hundred thousand persons." "Few" is construed to mean about two to three cases. Following a series of calculations the conclusion was reached that the comparative risk is "probably less than the increased lifetime risk of skin cancer from staying out-of-doors on a single day in July" (C.E.O.H. 1984:16). Further, the maximal arsenic exposure for children from using playground equipment is "within the normal variation of arsenic exposure for children" (p.12).

The Koppers Company, Inc. (1978) prepared an extensive review on the safety and durability of Wolmanized(R) wood products that are pressure treated with a compound containing "natural arsenic." Wolmanized material is probably the most common wood used by non-manufacturers (handy-men, carpenters, community playground builders, etc.). The Koppers Company report concludes, "Within the context of criteria applicable to Wolman CCA wood preservative and Wolmanized pressure-treated wood, safe means risk-free, non-injurious and non-hazardous" (p. 12). The present author found no reference to playground equipment in the report. Hopefully, the CPSC will address this and other concerns about children's exposure to toxic materials in their forthcoming revision of play equipment guidelines.

An Executive Summary, "Estimate of Risk of Skin Cancer from Dislodgeable Arsenic on Pressure Treated Wood Playground Equipment," conducted by the Directorate for Health Sciences for the U.S. Consumer Product Safety Commission (1990) was released in August, 1990. Seven playground equipment samples from major U.S. manufacturers and one comparison sample of unfinished pressure-treated wood from a retail store were tested.

The estimated risk of skin cancer for five out of the seven samples from manufacturers were judged to be a "negligible risk," with the dislodgeable arsenic below the detection level of < 1 in a million. The two remaining samples had detectable levels of 3–4 in a million which was described as a "small risk that should be reduced further if it can be practically accomplished." The estimated risk for the comparison sample was 8–9 in a million, suggesting that ". . . a possible hazard might be created when playground equipment is built with unfinished pressure treated wood from retail sources (U.S. Consumer Product Safety Commission 1990:3)."

Despite reports that the risk of using playground equipment treated with arsenic or other toxic materials is minimal, the consumer should heed the advice of the Federal Environmental Protection Agency (EPA) (*Parents Magazine*, May, 1985). The agency recommends that work involving wood preservatives or pre-treated material (such as Wolmanized lumber) be left to professionals who work with gloves, respirators, and clothes that can be discarded. Infants and toddlers crawling or playing on decks (or playground equipment) treated with wood preservatives (e.g., cresote, inorganic arsenic compounds, and pentachloro-phenol) "may be especially susceptible to ill effects since their tolerance to toxins is lower than that of adults" (p. 10). *The EPA recommends that decks containing these substances be sealed with at least two coats of shellac or other sealant.* The author recommends covering wood decks with an outdoor carpet. The extra cost of wood that does not require treatment with toxic materials (for example, redwood) may be a wise investment for areas where infants and toddlers play.

Many plants common to playgrounds are poisonous and should be removed from prospective playgrounds. When selecting new plants an expert plant nursery operator or other qualified person in the local area should be consulted to ensure that none are poisonous. A complete listing will not be attempted here since plant species vary widely across geographical areas. A few examples include certain varieties of the following: hollies, laurels, jasmine, rhododendron, and oleander.

Electrical Hazards

Although none of the national standards/guidelines refer to electrical hazards on playgrounds, they are all too common. Perhaps the most common is the existence of exposed air conditioners and electrical switch boxes on preschool playgrounds, particularly preschools at former family residences. All such electrical equipment should be fenced and non-accessible to children. Care should also be taken to ensure that electrical boxes, commonly located in yards of residences, containing connections for underground electrical utilities be securely locked. Boxes with missing locks invite young children to attempt to play inside the boxes, and result in serious injuries and fatalities.

Other hazards include electrocution or serious shock and burns resulting from children climbing guy wires, support poles via service ladders, and transmission towers. Television cable companies may lease space on existing electrical poles and sometimes install additional guy wires, leading to increased ease of climbing. Children climb to the vicinity of the electrical transmission lines and are severely shocked by high voltage lines. Older children with some knowledge of electricity are sometimes victims. Believing that they must touch the wires in order to be shocked they avoid direct contact but are shocked by the arcing phenomenon, more likely in humid areas. Several such cases as these have occurred in Texas during recent months. As this material was being written a young child was electrocuted after climbing on top of an air conditioner. A second was very seriously burned while playing inside a neighborhood electrical utility box (both in Austin, Texas). Adults must not only shield electrical apparatus from children but must also alert them to the potential hazards of playing on or in close proximity to such apparatus.

Signs

Recently, signs have appeared on playgrounds in increasing frequency. The CPSC merely states that responsible parties should "Consider color coding equipment for different age groups and posting explanatory signs in prominent locations." They do not specify what the signs should say or what specific purpose they should serve. The Seattle guidelines recommend placing interpretative signs for parents and teachers at the entry to all playgrounds. These signs would indicate:

- special features of the area
- suggestions for adult/child interaction
- age group or developmental skills served
- degree of difficulty

PLAE Inc. (1986) and Bruya (1988) expand the functions of signs to include: (1) information, (2) directions, (3) identification, (4) regulation, and (5) signs as curriculum. Wallach (1988) points to the use of signs for minimizing exposure to liability. She suggests signs that help children use equipment properly and that warn against major misuses of the equipment. The sign as a control device should fulfill a need, command attention, convey a clear meaning, command respect, and give adequate time for response (p. 26). An instrumental sign for the use of equipment and area should be placed at the entrance to the playground or near the equipment if no entrance is obvious.

PLAYGROUND SURFACING

Among all the variables contributing to playground hazards, ground cover is number one. And, ironically, ground cover is among the easiest variables to manipulate or change. Beginning with the design of a new school, park, or home site, particularly school sites, the prevailing line of reasoning can best be described as "bulldozer mentality." From design through construction to finished plant, everyone seems bent on destroying every blade of grass, every tree, every natural feature of the terrain in a seemingly insatiable urge to scrape everything into a sterile, smooth, moonlike surface, devoid of all life.

As soon as the natural terrain is destroyed the "concrete mentality" takes over. Someone remembers that a school is being built and that children attend schools. So vast areas are covered with asphalt and/or concrete and marked off into ball courts. Virtually no maintenance will be required and children can do what they are supposed to do—build strong healthy bodies and provide good material for the high school athletic teams. At most (not all) schools for young children, conscience prevails and commercial equipment is purchased and installed. Again the most trouble-free surface is concrete and asphalt, so the equipment is either installed on an out-of-the-way chunk of the existing slab or separate, smaller slabs are poured under and around each piece of equipment. However, there are options. When the budget is extremely limited or when hard surfaces must be reserved for "sports," playthings for younger children are simply stuck into postholes in the ground and secured by concrete.

Children and the rains arrive, cutting ditches, washing and wearing away top soil, exposing rocks and concrete foundations around the equipment and adjacent sidewalks, and destroying half-hearted efforts at seeding (rarely sodding) the remaining clay and rock cover. The hot sun beats down in summer and the teachers and children retreat to the shade of the building or into a nearby park, escaping the searing hot metal of slides and monkey bars and the reflected heat rays of concrete, asphalt, and barren ground.

Eventually the PTA comes to the rescue, a beautification project is initiated, trees are planted, a small plot is set aside for gardening, and several truckloads of top soil are hauled back in to cover the most eroded areas and to provide new concerns for the custodian when it turns to mud.

Throughout this entire saga, replayed over and over again in American schools, few seem to question the *method*. Play, perhaps the most important avenue for learning in early childhood, is given only marginal attention in the design and construction of school plants. The exceptions, of course, are two of the several important forms of play—namely exercise and games with rules. And even in planning for these forms, the errors are shameful—given minimal understanding of play development and playground construction.

It is both simple and smart to retain the natural, wooded terrain in areas surrounding proposed schools. It is quite another matter to replace it once it has been destroyed.

Similarly, it is simple and smart to provide a resilient surface under all climbing and moving equipment on the playground. In April 1973 a seven-year-old girl was tragically killed on a public school playground in Ogden, Utah, when she fell from climbing bars onto the hard surface below. Consequently, two months later the Ogden School District purchased 10,560 square feet of one-inch thick rubber matting at a cost of $17,000 (cost in 1978 was $31,680 for material alone and the cost in 1990 would exceed $100,000) for installation under potentially hazardous equipment.

CPSC guidelines call for the provision of certain types of resilient surfaces under and around climbing and moving equipment, but the most appropriate types from both economic and safety perspectives have yet to be determined. Engineering consultants of La Mirada, California, conducted a study, "Dynamic Impact Tests on Three Types of Protective Cushioning Mats, Vinyl, Rubber and UNIMAT," and determined that their ranges of satisfactory protection for falls from heights were, respectively, 4 feet, 5 feet, and 11 feet. Limited as this seems, the protection afforded can save lives and reduce serious injuries.

In 1951, the Los Angeles school system had the last of 11 playground deaths reported in a 20-year period with the fall of a 6-year-old boy from a swing onto an asphalt surface. In 1955, the school system installed rubber surfacing under its playground equipment. No further deaths were reported during the entire next decade and the incidence of fractures and concussions was reduced from 1.25 per school in 1951 to 0.47 in 1965 (Butwinick, 1974).

The high cost of commercial matting and the merits of such materials as compared to such inexpensive materials as sand and tanbark presently tip the scales in favor of the more inexpensive route for most applications. A commonly overlooked factor in the installation of commercial matting is that it requires an expensive, smooth, hard base such as asphalt or concrete for the more expensive mat. Through the use of community volunteers it is possible to develop a complete creative playground, using inexpensive materials, at less cost than that required for surfacing alone (base and resilient matting) on the all-commercial playground.

The CPSC warns that the majority of public playground injuries (60–70%) occur when children fall from equipment and strike the underlying surface and that 90% of the serious injuries result from falls to surfaces underneath equipment. Hard surfacing materials such as concrete and asphalt do not provide injury protection from accidental falls and are not recommended for use under playground equipment. At the time the CPSC guidelines were published (1981a; 1981b) the recommended method for testing surfaces was dropping an instrumented headform in guided free fall and measuring the linear acceleration response during impact. The surface should not exceed 200 g from the estimated fall height.

A number of specialists have questioned the appropriateness of this testing method and the American Society for Testing and Materials established a committee in 1987 to study the issue of safety surfaces for playground equipment and make recommendations for practice. A report is expected in 1991.

Major problems in identifying surfacing materials are the influence of environment on the surface, the variation in cushioning properties among surfaces, the availability of surfacing material, the potential for vandalism, problems of maintenance and cost. CPSC details some of the environmental problems.

Loose Materials

Organic (e.g., bark nuggets, mulch, shredded wood, cocoa shell, mulch).

- The trapped air necessary for protective cushioning is affected by rain and humidity.
- These materials decompose over time.
- They will freeze.
- Wet materials may allow for micro-organism growth.
- Wind blows these materials.
- They can be thrown into children's eyes.
- They may harbor insects.
- They may combine with dirt or other materials and lose their cushioning properties.
- They require constant maintenance.

Inorganic materials (e.g., sand, pea gravel)

- These materials may be blown or thrown into children's eyes.
- They are displaced by children's playing.
- They can harbor insects, broken glass, etc.
- They can combine with dirt or other material and lose their cushioning properties.
- When wet, sand becomes compacted.
- These materials may freeze (especially sand)
- Pea gravel is difficult to walk on.

FIGURE 9.6 Sand is an acceptable surfacing material that also has excellent play qualities.

- These materials require continuous maintenance.
- Wheel chairs will not roll on these materials.
- When installed adjacent to hard surfaces (wheeled vehicle tracks, etc.), they create slippery areas on the hard surface.

In the opinion of the present author, loose materials should never be used over concrete or asphalt because of the "pitting" effect, leaving hard surfaces insufficiently protected. Impact tests on sand, pea gravel, and shredded wood products have met with varying degrees of success, depending upon grade of material (e.g., fine or coarse) but when the material is kept in a non-compacted condition and retained at a designated depth of 8"–12" the impact-absorbing capability is generally judged acceptable in most applications. This excludes, of course, falls from excessively tall equipment. Laboratory test data submitted to the National Recreation and Park Association (1976a) resulted in the following conclusions:

Extremely Hazardous	Conditionally Acceptable	Acceptable
concrete	gym mats (2 in.)	sand (8–10 in.)
asphalt	double thick gym mats	
packed earth	rubber mats (1 ⅛ in.)	
	double thick rubber mats	
	pea gravel	
	wood chips	

In addition to providing "acceptable" cushioning properties when properly maintained at the proper depth, sand is also a relatively cheap and extremely good play material. These factors make it the material of choice in most low-budget applications. Pea gravel (very fine) provides "conditionally acceptable cushioning properties" but infants and toddlers may stick it in their ears or noses and it is not a good play material.

In its February, 1979 report, *Impact Attenuation Performance of Surfaces Under Playground Equipment*, the National Bureau of Standards National Recreation and Park Association (1976a) concluded that pea gravel failed the 200-g drop test for heights under 4 feet. Since this finding contradicts tests by the Franklin Institute and published data by playground equipment and surfacing companies, questions must be raised about the quality and size of material tested. It is commonly recognized that sand is available in a wide variety of types from fine to coarse, and that foreign materials such as clay and silt can cause hardening when mixed with sand. Similarly, "pea gravel" is a designation given material ranging in size from about 1/16 inch to about ½ inch in diameter. Even crushed rock, opposed to washed natural gravel, may be so designated.

In March, 1990 (Ramsey & Preston 1990), the Mechanical Engineering Division, Directorate for Engineering Sciences, U.S. Consumer Product Safety Commission released the most comprehensive test results of playground surfacing materials available at that time. Seven commonly used loose-fill materials, four unitary materials (manufactured mats), and two paving materials were subjected

TABLE 9.5   SUMMARY OF TEST RESULTS OF LOOSE-FILL MATERIALS: MAXIMUM DROP HEIGHT IN FEET FOR WHICH PEAK G DID NOT EXCEED 200

| Material | Ambient Conditions | | | Varying Material Conditions 9 Inch Depth | | | |
	6 Inch Depth	9 Inch Depth	12 Inch Depth	Compressed	30 deg F	120 deg F	Damp
Wood Mulch	10	>12	>12	>12	>12	N/A**	>12
Double Shredded Bark Mulch	8	11	>12	10	7	11	N/A
Uniform Wood Chip	6	10	>12	8	N/A	N/A	N/A
Fine Sand	6	7	>9	5	8	N/A	N/A
Coarse Sand	5	5	6	4	6	8	<4
Medium Gravel	7	>12	10	8	N/A	N/A	N/A
Large Gravel	5	8	6	8	7	N/A	N/A

to impact attenuation tests to establish the height from which a child, falling onto these surfacing materials, would not be expected to sustain a serious head injury. Such injuries are believed to occur when the acceleration sustained by the head during impact exciting 200 G's (200 x Acceleration of Gravity). Summaries of results are presented in Tables 9.5 and 9.6. The "medium gravel" tested passed through a ⅜ inch siene and the "large gravel" passed through a ½ inch siene.

Safety, economic factors, and play value should be addressed when comparing surfacing material. Both sand and pea gravel are relatively inexpensive but pea gravel is virtually useless as play material. Sand, on the other hand, is an excellent play material but is commonly criticized for the exaggerated possibility of harboring disease germs and parasites. A major claimed advantage for wood mulch is that wheelchairs can roll on it.

Soils

In general, soils produce lower peak acceleration than asphalt but not as low as most of the loose surfacing materials. Under conditions of outdoor play, most soils become firmly compacted under and around playground equipment and do not provide acceptable fall-zone surfacing.

Manufactured Materials (e.g., rubber mats, synthetic turf)

- These materials must be used on level, compact surfaces; e.g., asphalt, packed aggregate base.
- They are subject to vandalism.

- They may be inflammable.
- Their performance depends upon the base foundation.
- They may be constructed with toxic materials.

In addition to these drawbacks noted by CPSC, compact, manufactured surfaces are also very expensive, typically ranging from $8.00 to $14.00 per square foot installed (1990 prices) plus the cost of the solid base foundation (e.g., concrete or asphalt).

The compact materials are particularly desirable for cushioning roof-top (concrete) playgrounds commonly found at children's hospitals and in crowded, inner-city areas. They lack, however, the highly beneficial benefit of sand as a play medium.

During the 1980s a number of manufacturers produced artificial (manufactured) material for playground surfacing. A list of companies and locations are in Appendix C.

The Fibar System advertisements state, "A kid falling from a playground climber goes faster than the speed limit in a school zone." (When a 4-foot child falls from a height of 5-feet, he may hit the ground at 16 m.p.h.) The Fibar System uses a stone base layer which acts as a drainage system, covered by a water permeable geotextile fabric which keeps wood fiber on the surface. The top layer is 12 inches of wood fiber. The manufacturers state that no toxic materials are used and that the material does not harbor living organisms or collect dust when properly maintained. A major advantage claimed over sand and pea gravel is accessibility over the surface by wheelchairs.

The solid, compact manufactured safety surfaces include *Tuffturf*, *Breakfall*, *Child Safe*, *Safeplay*, *Security Blanket*, *Elastocrete*, and *Superturf*. The manufacturers claim that *Tuffturf* meets or exceeds the CPSC 200-g impact test up to seven feet, eight inches; it is non-toxic; it prevents puddling of water; it accommodates wheelchairs; and comes with a 10-year warranty.

The *Breakfall* advertisement claims that Breakfall is "America's safest playground surface," and that it meets the "CPSC 10-foot drop test." Beveled pieces of shock pad allow a smooth transition with adjacent areas. It is designed to be

TABLE 9.6   SUMMARY OF TEST RESULTS OF UNITARY MATERIALS: MAXIMUM DROP HEIGHT FOR WHICH PEAK G DID NOT EXCEED 200

Material		Ambient	30 deg F	120 deg F
Manufactured Mats	A	<5 Feet	<5 Feet	<5 Feet
	B	4 Feet	<4 Feet	<4 Feet
	C	>12 Feet	7 Feet	>12 Feet
	D	10 Feet	9 Feet	7 Feet
Pavements	Concrete	<1 Inch		
	Asphalt	1 Inch		

FIGURE 9.7 Making the playground safe
for children is only one side of the safety
picture; making the children safe for playgrounds is also important.

installed over a recessed concrete slab. *Child Safe* surfacing is installed in two
layers: a base binder of soft rubber particles and polyurethane binders and a
colored top layer of rubber particles and polyurethane binders poured in place
to provide a seamless installation with beveled edges for access. *Safeplay*, also
referred to as Cam-turf and Superturf, has a tufted surface linked to polyethylene
foam, "resistant to water, rot, mold, mildew and bacteria." It can be installed
over concrete, asphalt, or prepared rock, sand, gravel, or shell. The manufacturers report that this material exceeded the CPSC impact test requirements in
drops up to 12 feet. It has been installed at numerous Burger King, Wendy's,
and McDonald's playgrounds.

Security Blanket is composed of a synthetic turf bound to a resilient rubber/
urethane pad, factory produced to be laid in sections on site. Similar to Safeplay
it can be installed over a number of stabilized surfaces. Edging is accomplished
by installation of a curb. The advertisements claim it is easy to clean, hygienic,
fast drying, resistant to insects and rot, and meets government safety requirements. *Elastocrete* is manufactured in rubber slabs and pavers of various sizes
and shapes. They are fastened to solid surfaces such as asphalt or concrete using
adhesive and expansion anchor bolts. The advertisements claim they are water
permeable. Test results by Romaflex Inc. in 1985 state that Elastocrete meets the
200-g CPSC impact test requirements of up to six feet. Given the controversy
evolving around the appropriateness of the CPSC standard and heights on most
playgrounds, this represents a questionable degree of cushioning. The company

should be contacted for information about more recent results and possible modifications in the surfacing material *Superturf*.

Recently, a loose, non-compacted manufactured surface of chopped tires or chopped rubber material has been marketed. Cushion Turf, one of the companies involved, suggests a three- to four- inch sub-base of sand or pea gravel overloaded by four to six inches of Cushion Turf retained by treated wood landscaping timbers or other curb material. The chopped rubber is shipped in bags and can be stored for future maintenance. The overall cost of this material is roughly one-fourth the installed cost of compact manufactured surfaces. Cushion Turf reports that chopped tires meet CPSC guidelines for falls up to 13 feet.

SUPERVISION, MAINTENANCE, AND LIABILITY

In the relatively small number of injuries not included in categories of the previous chapter, most result from errors of maintenance rather than from errors in equipment design. For example, most documented sandbox injuries are caused by objects (such as broken glass) in the sand. Broken tricycle parts, other wheeled vehicle parts, protruding slivers of wood in stacking materials, and misuse of equipment are also cited in accident reports.

Misuse of equipment is related to the natural tendencies of children to extend themselves, to be daring, to show off, to engage in rough housing. Butwinick's (1974) survey found that 21 percent of accidents are caused by such factors as fighting, pushing , inattention, blind running, and foreseeable misuse. All of these factors are at least indirectly tied to the nature of supervision available for the playground. The U.S. Consumer Product Safety Commission (1975) noted that in-depth investigations of 54 playground injuries and deaths showed that an adult was present in only 4 cases. In 38 cases the victim was with 1 or more children and in 12 cases the child was alone when the injury occurred. It would appear that the presence of adults is a very relevant factor in the safety of children on playgrounds.

Supervision

How far should adult supervision go? Where is the dividing line between free, creative, meaningful play and overstructured routine? The author believes that risk taking is an essential ingredient of creative play, absolutely essential for growth of self-assurance and personal power to do and control. Risk taking, daring to do and be, can and should take place in a rich context of alternatives after the obviously taboo ones are omitted. The way in which the taboo alternatives are reduced or eliminated is quite important. A simple rule, "We will not chase a ball into the street," might be appropriate enough for a 12-year-old but completely inadequate for a group of 4-year-olds playing on an unfenced playground adjacent to a busy street. The removal of this particular alternative, running into the street, is ensured by constructing a fence. Four-year-olds do not live by rules alone, but they are learning to adjust to a system of social and cultural codes.

All too frequently adults expect rules to make up for poorly designed equipment, improper installation, poor maintenance, improperly sized equipment and, sterile equipment. Consider the "Student Behavior Guidelines" developed by a group of preprimary/primary teachers (four- to eight-year-olds) to be applied on their playground. Reflect on the apparent condition of the playground and the scope of equipment. In these guidelines both the rule and the punishment option(s), coded by number, are noted.

1. No fighting, pinching, and hitting.
   Example—Discipline Option 6: If a child fights at recess, he may lose the privilege of going outside.
2. No throwing rocks or other dangerous items.
   Example—Discipline Option 9: If sticks or rocks are thrown toward other children, spanking may be immediately administered.
3. The misuse, abuse, and/or destruction of outside play equipment will not be allowed.
   Example—Discipline Option 6: If riding toys are run into the fence, the student will not be allowed to use them.
4. Students may climb only on playground equipment.
   Discipline Options 3–8.
5. *Swings*—Only one child on a swing. Child must sit down. Child will swing in a straight line.
6. *Slide*—Child must use ladder to climb up. Only one child on slide and one on ladder. Child must sit down facing forward. No dirt, rocks, etc. may be placed on slide.
7. *Dome* (not present on playground)—Children are not to hang by their knees. Children are not to play inside dome. As soon as the child drops to the ground he must climb out. Children are not allowed to pull on those who are hanging.
8. *Walking bridge* (not present on playground)—Children may walk on the top while holding on. Only one child on the bridge at a time. Form one line while waiting to use the bridge.
9. *Vehicles* (not present on playground)—Bus: Four children may ride and two may push. Boat: Two children may ride and two may push. Wagons: One child may ride and one may pull. Tricycles: One child may ride at a time.
   Discipline Options 1–11 for rules 5–9.

Thus rigid rules and patterns of discipline are unsuccessfully substituted for the creation and maintenance of a developmentally appropriate, relatively safe playground. Imagine the sterility of child play resulting from such impossible rules—a group of little robot-zombies standing in line to engage in a brief mechanical activity, with total absence of physical contact, fearful to extend themselves lest the wrath of discipline rules one through nine be exacted. What complete and callous disrespect such rules betray for the powers of children to assist in responsible decision making and acting when treated with respect and skill by adults.

Children play wherever they must—in well-designed city parks or on crowded streets, in backyards or on deserted lots, on schoolyards or on roof-tops, in abandoned houses or in natural woodland. Many such places are potentially hazardous, especially for young children, for they involve heights, broken glass, deep water, busy traffic, and deep holes. Most American children play outside the supervision of their parents at some time during the day. They need planned, supervised playgrounds.

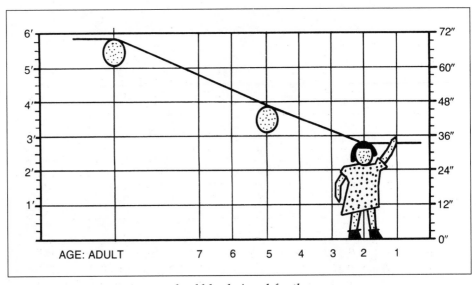

FIGURE 9.8 *Play equipment should be designed for the age-group users.*

Most of the activity on good playgrounds is free, unregulated play; children doing what comes naturally. Nonetheless, adult supervision is essential. The qualities of a good free-play supervisor are a result of training and biology/ intuition. He or she must be warm, friendly, energetic, love children, and preferably have a broad experiential base in such areas as nature, mechanics, carpentry, gardening, and so on. The person must be able to get involved, talk, question, and listen without being obtrusive. He or she must share and plan with the children. The type of person who will not do is the one who is concerned primarily with such matters as evaluating all the four-year-olds on gross motor skills, running races under the watchful eye of the stop watch, or choosing up sides for a competitive event. The shy, retiring, "don't get dirty" type will not do either. Children deserve more than an adult who sits under a shade tree directing his or her charges to abide by this or that rule.

Supervisors do intervene on occasion. Bullying or deliberate abuse of others is not allowed. Children do not venture into prohibited areas (streets, etc.). Direct intervention is rarely necessary for adults who understand the value of taking time to evaluate and plan with children. In addition, good playgrounds are sufficiently challenging to occupy the attention of children who would be more likely to create disturbances on poorly equipped areas.

Making the playground safe for children is only one side of the safety picture. Making the children safe for the playground is an equally important factor. Safety consciousness and safety ability are developed in children. These traits develop from repeated risk-taking experiences on a playscape carefully designed for gradually increasing complexity of movement. Children learn to exercise good judgement in risk taking by having many opportunities to risk at their present level of ability. The playground is so designed that younger or new children will have many experiences with easy-to-master equipment before they try their wings on the more difficult. Interestingly, when a wide range of equip-

FIGURE 9.9 *City park systems are increasing their use of manufactured surface materials. ("Child Safe" surfacing of rubber particles and polyurethane binders)*

ment and materials is available, most children are remarkably able to make wise choices. Others, especially when exposed to peer pressure, may need sensitive assistance by an adult.

One of the most compelling observations in my years of work with play groups is the apparently remarkable judgment and physical dexterity of children who enjoy regular, extensive periods on creative playgrounds. Newcomers to such groups, having no equivalent experiences, require careful supervision to prevent serious injury. Some do not seem to know how to play, having missed opportunities for play and involvement with adults. Children need adults who participate in their play, who provide the role models and the encouragement essential to creative activity on the playground.

Maintenance

Provisions for the safety of children at play begin with the rules laid down by a community reflecting its concerns for the young. No major housing facility should be allowed that fails to incorporate into its design facilities for play and standards for maintenance and supervision. This includes schools, child-care centers, apartment complexes, housing developments, and public parks. Communities need minimum standards and regulations for playgrounds that are equivalent in quality to their rules for property zoning, construction, health, and other vital human services.

Safety on the playground is a complex matter. No set of standards can prevent all accidents. There will be bruises, cuts, abrasions, and occasional fractures. Risk taking is an essential part of the growth process. We argue for playgrounds that are exciting, pose challenges, and allow creativity but that do not introduce features that are blatantly foreign to safety sense; for example, broken glass, hard surfaces under climbing and moving equipment, broken equipment, unnecessary, unprotected heights, poorly designed equipment, direct access to traffic, deep pits, deep water, or inadequate supervision.

The major tasks of playground personnel in respect to safety are: (1) selecting and/or developing criteria for selection and installation of equipment; (2) involving community people (including children) in the development of the playground. (our experience shows that involvement promotes pride in creation and results in better care of the play area by the community); (3) providing appropriate supervision; and (4) providing regular maintenance. Responsibilities for maintenance will vary from group to group. On school grounds the regular custodian usually takes care of minor cleanup and repair, with major repairs being requisitioned through the central maintenance office in large schools. Many schools have no apparent provisions for care of playgrounds (many have little or no equipment). City parks personnel usually care for public parks. Special citizens committees may personally care for, or hire staff to care for, joint venture playgrounds found in some major residential subdivisions. Whatever the context, careful attention must be given to playground maintenance.

Some of the common maintenance tasks are as follows:

1. Maintain resilient ground cover (sand) around major pieces of equipment.
2. Provide a resilient surface such as sand or tanbark under and around all climbing equipment and fixed equipment that moves (e.g., merry-go-rounds).
3. Pad metal legs of large equipment, and other surfaces that may cause injury on impact.
4. Remove, replace, or repair all broken or worn-out equipment.
5. Declare off limits to younger children all equipment designed for older children or equipment that is temporarily unsafe.
6. Smooth all jagged or rough edges.
7. Inspect all moving parts (e.g., swing swivels) of equipment regularly.
8. Plan with children to remove glass, loose rocks, cans, and other trash.
9. Develop buddy systems and provide constant supervision whenever pools or other deep water are used.
10. Enclose slides with platforms or attach slides to hills and mounds to prevent falls from the top.
11. Plan with children to rake sand areas regularly to extract foreign material such as glass and rocks.
12. Clean and paint or apply appropriate sealer to equipment regularly to prevent deterioration (avoid toxic exposure).
13. Clean out drains, add fill dirt, and dig trenches to drain standing water.
14. Work with other adults or professionals to develop optimum schedules for using the playground.
15. Discuss essential safety rules with children so that they understand the limits of their play. Reasonably controlled conditions are the middle ground between over-supervision and complete freedom in children's play.
16. Plan with children and concerned adults for the continuing development of the playground. The best playgrounds are never finished.

The CPSC specifies that a regular inspection and maintenance schedule is essential to ensure safety. "Suggested Public Playground Leader's Checklist" is in Appendix E. The Germans, Australians, and British also indicate that all equipment requires regular inspection and maintenance and recommend that manufacturers include maintenance instructions with playground apparatus. The Germans require the provision of detailed instructions, diagrams, and figures as necessary. Inspection, maintenance, and repair should be carried out by suitable (expert) personnel. If a piece of equipment is temporarily removed for repair or replacement, the anchoring elements remaining in the ground should be made safe.

There is no mutually agreed upon schedule for inspection and maintenance. The CPSC states that "inspections should be conducted on a frequent, regularly scheduled basis." A common sense approach would be to conduct an exhaustive inspection each month and a normal inspection each week, or more frequently when use is extensive or vandalism is common. Training should be provided for all involved adults (playleaders, teachers) on all aspects of safety to help ensure that they are *constantly* alert to potential hazards involving both equipment and child behavior. Obviously, inspection must be followed immediately by needed repairs. Records should be maintained for all inspections, maintenance, repairs, and injuries.

The Maintenance Checklist is a composite of maintenance items recommended by national agencies and observed by the author as having injury potential. No list, including this one, is likely to cover all potential hazards. It is not the intent of such lists that play challenge or novelty be reduced. Quite the contrary; with proper design playgrounds can be much more challenging than traditional ones, while ensuring a greater *degree* of safety. No playground is hazard free or completely safe. A major intent is to reduce life-threatening, permanent, serious injuries, while greatly enhancing the play value of the environment.

International Perspectives

The extensive study of playground injury data from several industrialized countries by King and Ball (1989) gives the following conclusions relevant to injury presentation on playgrounds:

- A significant proportion of accidents are caused by poor equipment design, layout, installation, and maintenance.
- Failure to provide ability- and size-appropriate equipment results in an overproportion of injuries to young children.
- Falls from equipment appear to account for fewer accidents than currently believed (CPSC data (1989) refute this claim).
- Home play equipment accidents appear to be more common than currently believed.
- Improved safety awareness (training) reduces accident rates.
- There is a strong case for more supervision to reduce inappropriate (dangerous) behaviors on playgrounds. Both parents and supervisors should be concerned.
- There are limits to which safety can be incorporated into design.
- Cutting back on play facilities is false economy because it forces children to play in dangerous areas such as streets.

- Accidents are caused by an array of interdependent factors:
  —inappropriate design and layout of playgrounds
  —inappropriate design of equipment
  —incorrectly installed equipment
  —inadequate maintenance
  —lack of age- and ability-related equipment
  —lack of adult supervision
  —dangerous behavior of children
  —misuse of equipment
  —unsuitable clothing for play
- *If standards were fully implemented a considerable number of injuries and some fatalities would be prevented.*

Liability

In workshops and conferences for play scholars and playground designers, the informal conversation invariably turns to the subject of lawsuits. Those who serve as expert witnesses in playground-related injury litigation have depressing stories to tell about face-to-face meetings with crippled, deformed, maimed, paraplegic children and their parents—people who invariably "trusted the system" to provide safe play equipment. Every major group that designs, manufactures, installs, maintains, or supervises playgrounds has now been taken to court. The judgements range up to an all-time high of over $30 million awarded to a child who fell onto concrete. The defendants in playground-related injury lawsuits now include private schools, public schools, P.T.A. groups, cities, parks and recreation departments, fast food franchisers, school principals, teachers, school boards, equipment installers, designers, builders, and manufacturers. Several of these groups have been sued repeatedly. Some seem oblivious to the threat that bad materials and practices pose for children, but most are actively seeking to improve their materials and/or practice and make playgrounds safe for children.

The author of this book is not an attorney and does not offer legal advice. He has served as an expert witness in numerous lawsuits, participated in the development of national standards, conferred regularly with attorneys, manufacturers, and colleagues in the field of play and playgrounds, and offers the following practical information for consideration by those assuming responsibility for playgrounds.

If contemplating the development of a playground, the individual or group should review the literature to become as informed as possible. A playground specialist with a proven record of experience in design should be consulted. University faculty representing architecture, psychology, education, physical education, and child development may be contacted to secure names of qualified people. Increasingly, playground equipment manufactures are training their representatives about safety and play value but care must be taken to ensure that competent people are selected. A few companies provide customized, playground services. The purchaser should ask about the company's liability insurance, record of lawsuits, and training of representatives. References should be checked. The company or individual selected should agree to affirm (*in writing*), upon completion of the project, equipment and installation will conform to national guidelines or standards.

If the playground is already in service, a specialist should be retained to evaluate all elements for play value and safety. The written report should contain a list of strengths and weaknesses and recommend what modifications and repairs are needed and how to make them. After modifications and repairs the specialist should confirm in writing that the playground conforms to national guidelines or standards. Manufactured equipment should not be modified without the approval of the original manufacturer. Any unapproved modifications may void the warranty and may release the manufacturer from liability.

Do-it-yourself projects are especially risky from legal perspectives: liability for child injury may endure for an extensive period. State laws should be checked to determine the nature of liability in a given state. Texas, for example, passed legislation recently to release individuals in volunteer activity from liability under certain conditions but *organizations* such as parent-teacher associations may still be sued. Individuals may investigate their homeowner's umbrella liability insurance policies for possible coverage in playground related projects.

Generally, agencies controlling playgrounds may be responsible for accidents occurring even when the school, business, agency, etc. is not open for business. Most playgrounds are accessible to children. Even if a fence is present the gates may not be locked and warning signs are not yet common on playgrounds. The playground, even though difficult to access, may be considered an "attractive nuisance." That is, it is available; children commonly play there; children see other children playing there; younger children may not understand that the playground is not intended to be used; it is attractive. Children can *reasonably* be expected to play there. A key concept in playground injury cases seems to be reasonable behavior. Under a given set of conditions (injury situation), is it reasonable to expect that children would play there?

So what should the playground sponsor do?

1. Secure professional assistance.
2. Secure liability insurance.
3. Check all supplies, workers, consultants, etc. carefully. Require references. Check the references.
4. Develop a maintenance program. Keep written records of playground evaluation, repair, etc. (Written records can work against the sponsor if they reveal negligence.)
5. Train all personnel regularly on playground safety.
6. Develop playground safety training for children.
7. Provide appropriate supervision on playgrounds.
8. Document all of the above.

In September, 1990, California Senate Bill 2733 was signed into law by the Governor. This Bill requires that all public playgrounds in the State be brought into compliance with the Consumer Product Safety Commission guidelines by the year 2000. Other States are considering similar legislation.

CONCLUSION

National surveys of public school, public park, and preschool playgrounds during 1987–1990 documented the hazardous conditions in American playgrounds and confirmed personal fears. Playgrounds in the United States are unduly hazardous and should be the subject of considerable public examination and correction. Traditional equipment—swings, climbers, slides, seesaws—are frequently poorly designed, improperly installed, inadequately supervised, and receive very little maintenance.

National standards and guidelines, developed by several industrialized countries, are increasingly shaping decisions about equipment design and over time should dramatically improve equipment and surfacing safety. The United States Consumer Product Safety Commission and the American Society for Testing and Materials are spearheading efforts to develop/improve American safety standards for both playground equipment and playground surfacing.

The selection of well-designed play equipment is merely the first step in improving playground safety. The leading cause of injuries, falling from heights onto hard surfaces, can be improved by the provision of approved surfacing, and good supervision and maintenance can reduce hazards. The threat of lawsuits and liability may be reduced by systematic attention to the guidelines in this section. Finally, we must not lose sight of the fact that children—not lawsuits—should be our major concern. We can have safer playgrounds and, at the same time, improve the play value of children's playgrounds.

REFERENCES

Bruya, L.D. (1988). Sand areas, wading areas, and signs, trees and pathways. In *The American Playground: A National Survey*, eds. L.D. Bruya & S.J. Langendorfer. Arlington, VA: American Alliance of Leisure and Recreation.

Bruya, L.D., & Langendorfer, S.J. (1988). eds. *The American Playground: A National Survey*. Reston, VA: American Alliance for Health, Physical Education, Recreation, and Dance.

Butwinick, E. (1974). Petition requesting the issuance of a consumer product safety standard for public playground slides, swinging apparatus and climbing equipment. Washington, DC: United States Consumer Product Safety Commission.

Consultants in Epidemiology and Occupational Health, Inc. (1984). *Evaluation of Risk to Children Using Arsenic-Treated Playground Equipment*. Washington, DC: Consultants in Epidemiology and Occupational Health, Inc.

Dale M. et al. (May, 1969). "Are Schools Safe?" Analysis of 409 student accidents in elementary school. *Clinical Pediatrics*. 8, 294–96.

Franzen, I.G. (1958). What do we know about the ways in which children get hurt. *NSC Transactions*. Volume 27.

Freedburg, L. (1983). *America's Poisoned Playgrounds: Children and Toxic Chemicals*. Oakland, CA: Youth News and Youth Communicator.

Hogan, P. (1988). *The Playground Safety Checker*. Phoenixville, PA: Playground Press.

King, K., & Ball, D. (1989). *A Holistic Approach to Accident and Injury Prevention in Children's Playgrounds*. London: LCS, Great Guildford House.

Kompan, Inc. (1984). *Playgrounds and safety: Comparisons between various playground equipment standards—American, Australian, British, German*. Winsor Locks, CT: Kompan, Inc.

Koppers Company, Inc. (1978). *A Review of Forty Years of the Safe and Versatile Usage of Wolman CCA and Wolmanized Pressure Treated Wood Products*. Koppers Company, Inc.

McFarland, R.A. (August, 1969). Injury—A major environmental problem. Chicago: *Architectural Environment Health*. 19, 244–56.

National Recreation and Park Association. (1976a). Proposed safety standard for public playground equipment. Arlington, VA: National Recreation and Park Association.

————. (1976b). Background and rationale for proposed public playground equipment safety standards. Prepared for the Consumer Product Safety Commission. Arlington, VA: National Recreation and Park Association.

————. (1976c). Proposed safety standard for public playground equipment. Developed for the Consumer Product Safety Commission. Arlington, VA: National Recreation and Park Association.

Nichols, G.C. (1987). Playground related injuries in the U.S.A. *Playground Related Injuries and Their Prevention*.

Brussels, Belgium: European Consumer Product Safety Association.

Ontario Ministry of Community and Social Services. (1972). Case studies. *In Creative Play Resources Bank.* Toronto: Youth and Recreation Branch, Ontario Ministry of Community and Social Services.

Parents Magazine. (May, 1985). Beware: Wood preservatives can kill. p. 10.

PLAE, Inc. (1986). *Play for All.* Berkeley, CA: PLAE, Inc.

Ramsey, L.F., & Preston, J.D. (1990). Impact attenuation performance of playground surfacing material. Washington, DC: U.S. Consumer Product Safety Commission.

Thompson, D., & Bowers, L. (eds.) (1989). *Where Our Children Play: Community Park Playground Equipment.* Reston, VA: American Alliance for Health, Physical Education, Recreation, and Dance.

United States Consumer Product Safety Commission. and surfacing. Washington, DC: U.S. Consumer Product Safety Commission.

————. (December, 1989). Playground equipment-related injuries involving falls to the surface. Washington, DC: Directorate for Epidemiology: Division of Hazard Analysis.

————. (August, 1990). Executive summary: Estimate of risk of skin cancer from dislodgeable arsenic on pressure treated wood playground equipment. Washington, DC: U.S. Consumer Product Safety Commission.

(April, 1975). *Hazard Analysis: Playground Equipment.* Washington, DC: Bureau of Epidemiology.

————. (July/August, 1978). Special summer safety issue. *CPSC Memo.* Washington, DC: The Commission.

————. (1981a). A handbook for public playground safety, Volume I. General guidelines for new and existing playgrounds. Washington, DC: U.S. Consumer Product Safety Commission.

————. (1981b). A handbook for public playground safety, Volume II. Technical guidelines for equipment

> *"An inviting and comfortable child care setting entices young learners to pause, play, and stay awhile, and actively supports the development of attention, memory, and mastery."*[1]

10

Infant/Toddler Play Environments

Parents and other caretakers seem to understand, perhaps intuitively, that infants and toddlers need play objects or toys, and safe, stimulating play environments. They also know that adults, themselves, enrich the quality of play. Witness the mother engaging her infant, day after day, in such ritualized play as "patty-cake" and "peek-a-boo."

As home rearing of the very young is supplanted by center rearing we see a growing interest in creating quality play environments. These environments are reflecting increasingly more sophisticated information about how infants and toddlers develop through play and how the design of play objects and environments contributes to development. Consequently, the primary issues addressed here are: What is the developmental progression of object/exploratory play in infants and toddlers? What are the qualities of good play objects or toys? What are the characteristics of high-quality play environments? How can caretakers provide for both play value and safety for infants and toddlers?

INFANT–TODDLER DEVELOPMENT AND PLAY OBJECTS

Throughout history, objects have been instrumental in children's play. The types and varieties of objects used vary widely across cultures and socio-economic

---

[1]Olds, A.R. (1990) Psychological and physiological harmony in child care center design. *Children's Environments Quarterly* 6:9.

groups. In the main, they represent the culture itself—its work/play distinctions, its level of technology, its gender manifestations, its tools and trades. The striking contrast between the simple, natural play objects or toys of children in primitive cultures and the glitzy, high-tech toys of children in highly industrialized societies exemplifies the striking differences. But whether the play objects are sticks and stones or Barbie dolls, erector kits, and Ninja Turtles, the play processes may be much the same—children taking on pretend roles, constructing, and organizing games. The benefits or outcomes of play with such diverse objects are matters of speculation and subjects of research.

Developmental Progression in Object Play

The toy play of children follows a developmental progression from the early insensitivity of newborns to the elaborate space-age, computerized games of the teenager. Sutton-Smith's (1986) excellent book, *Toys as Culture*, will be a primary source for tracing this progression.

During the first few weeks infants seem to be primarily concerned with food and comfort but we are beginning to understand that they see and hear much more than we originally thought. This was demonstrated in a pioneering study (Rubin 1990) sponsored by the Robert Wood Johnson Foundation. In the study of almost 1,000 premature babies, adults played with one-third of the babies during an intensive program of home visits. The rest of the babies received only regular medical checkups. On the average, children in the play program who weighed 4.4 to 5.5 pounds at birth had an I.Q. score 13.2 points higher at age 3 than those not receiving the play involvement. In addition, mothers of the play treatment group reported fewer behavioral problems among their children. Such simple, common tasks as rolling a ball to a baby appeared to offer the needed stimulation.

Infants: 0–12 Months

The play and toys commonly directed at infants by adults, though often conducted as much for the benefit of adults as for babies, seem to be sufficient in the first few months of infancy. The baby arrives with certain built-in mechanisms for early playful activities—ability to focus eyes (unsteadily), grasp objects, react to sounds, attention, and movement to speech. The usual toys—plastic rings, mobiles, crib displays, and sound devices (radio, television)—along with the verbal and touching support of an adult appear to provide appropriate visual and tactile stimulation for early play and development. Since the infant is dependent upon adults, the adult is responsible for creating or providing environments that capture babies' attention, engage their interest, support their natural exploratory behaviors, provide reasonable safety, and change with advancing age and development.

During the first year, language development and toy play development proceed hand in hand, so the adult should also be concerned that play with toys is accompanied by talk. The interactive, responsive talk of parents is preferred, of course, to the nonsensical babbling of radio, television, and toy recordings.

With continuing physical and linguistic stimulation and emotional support, early toys can be very simple. The typical toys do have stimulus value but bombardment of infants with a wide range of play objects is probably done for

FIGURE 10.1 *The adult is responsible for creating environments that support natural exploratory behaviors.*

adults as much as for infants—". . . toys are but a part of the message that parents give themselves about their concern for children's achievement. They may need it, even if the babies don't" (Sutton-Smith 1986:99).

During Piaget's sensorimotor period, infants gradually refine independent movements of hands, eyes, ears, feet, and mouth into synthesized movements. With increased control, the infant's attention is increasingly focused from its own body parts to play objects. Sutton-Smith suggests that early toys should have qualities similar to the infant's earliest play objects (her own body parts)—be soft and resilient, adaptable to mouthing, have multiple parts (as with fingers and toes), taste interesting, be reactive and graspable with one hand. In addition to such qualities in toys, there is support for such items as stainless steel mirrors (Lewis & Brooks-Gunn 1979). The type or range of toys available to infants during the early months is less important than the mere progression of infant/ parent play, doing interesting things together (perhaps with toys) and having some interesting things to play with (which may be toys). (White 1975; Sutton-Smith 1986). Playing "funny-faces," "tickling," "peek-a-boo," and "coochie, coochie, coo" are equally interesting.

During the second half of the first year the infant makes rapid growth in toy use. Increased mobility (crawling) takes the child into a new world of objects

FIGURE 10.2 During the second half of the first year the infant makes rapid growth in toy use.

which he explores with a vengeance—throwing, banging, dropping, rolling, pulling, pushing, taking apart (perhaps, putting together). The child now needs a wider variety of toys—mobiles, mirrors, water, containers, nesting blocks, balls, rings, soft toys, rattles, stuffed animals, push–pull toys, blocks, picture books. The parent continues to assume continuous supervision and contact and encourages the child's play by providing interaction, physical contact, and safe, developmentally appropriate play things and play spaces.

Object Play: 12–36 Months

By the end of the first year infants are engaging in a wide range of activities commonly classified as play, but which on closer examination may be classified more broadly as play, work, mastery, or exploratory activity (Garvey 1977; Rubin, Fein, & Vandenberg 1983; Sutton-Smith 1986). Play, like language, emerges over time and is learned. The parent is the primary teacher, beginning with early "peek-a-boo"-type games and object/toy exploration. The dominant form of infant play is not solitary, as is commonly assumed, but social, between parent and child.

Much of the child's activity during the second year is exploratory as well as playful—discovering properties (what it is like) and functions (what it can do) of objects. Exploration becomes play when the child adapts the object to his own pleasurable activities (e.g., stacking objects to knock them over). The child also "tests himself" or engages in mastery activities that promote problem solving and the acquisition of skills. Exploration is the search, mastery is the solution, and play is the transformation. In constructive activity the child explores the qualities of blocks, experiments with their functions (stacking, etc.), constructs to form a product (house), and repeats and modifies the action for sheer pleasure and satisfaction.

The developmental progression of object play during this period was observed by Lowe (1975). The following is a summary at each age level.

12 Months. The child uses the eating utensils appropriately. She will "drink" from the cup or "feed" herself with a spoon, or she might place the cup on the saucer and the spoon in the cup. However, the other objects will be used in an inappropriate manner such as waving, banging, or mouthing.

15 Months. At this age the child is more likely to "stir" or "pick up" the imaginary food and to link this with the action of self-feeding. She may also extend this self-feeding behavior to other objects; for example, dip the log into the truck and put it in her mouth. The 15-month-old will push the little truck and trailer back and forth on the table.

18 Months. This is the peak age for self-related activity. The child will feed and comb herself and wipe her face. She now begins to direct more attention to the doll—made to stand, sit, or jump, but not yet as a rule fed or combed.

21 Months. This appears to be a transitional stage at which doll-related activities for the first time equal or slightly outweigh self-related behavior. She will now feed and brush the doll and put the doll on the bed with clear intentions of putting it down to sleep. The child will also place the logs and the little man in one of the vehicles.

24 Months. Doll-related behavior is now dominant. The child will feed the doll or place it in a meal situation. When putting the doll to bed, she will include the essential elements (doll, bed, blanket) in an integrated manner. More care may go into making the bed than at the previous stage.

30 Months. The child can now make meaningful use of all elements. The doll will not only by seated on the chair but also pushed to the table, usually with the eating utensils in front of it. She may also search for absent objects that she needs for her play or she may even create these objects herself; for example, fold a piece of cloth to make a pillow.

36 Months. There is now a marked decline in overt versus implied feeding of the doll; that is, the child is more likely to place the doll at the set table than actually feed it. She will now hook the trailer to the truck.

During the second year the child is still engaged in sensori-motor operations, primarily of the exploration type. Over 80 percent of her time is spent alone and about 20 percent with the mother (White 1975). Therefore, solitary activity is dominant and most of this is exploratory activity, eating, and passing time. Later in the second year, dramatic or pretend play is observed in growing frequency. Earlier objects were used as things to explore, but now the child is beginning to use them according to their function (cars are pushed, dolls are hugged). Pretend play, like language, emerges through exploration and imitation of adults but is elaborated through repeated actions on objects (Piaget).

During the third year, pretend (dramatic, symbolic) and constructive activity occupy increasing amounts of time, employ a growing range of play objects,

FIGURE 10.3 *During the second year, solitary play*
is more common than play with parents.

and increasingly involve play with peers. The range of play objects is expanded to include sand and water, jigsaw puzzles, doll houses, cars and trucks, music devices, stacking and nesting blocks, simple tools and dress up materials, crayons, and books. Larger equipment includes swings, slides, teeter-totters, and climbing frames.

Object Play: Three- to Six-year-olds

Many toddlers exhibit skills that are characteristic of older children, so it is essential to consider the object play of typical older preschoolers and precocious toddlers. The three- to six-year-old period is one of rapid development in object play. Choices of toys now include a wide range and can be classified by types. Wolfgang and Phelps (1983) identified three categories: fluid, structured, and symbolic. Fluid materials (clay, paints, etc.) can be easily transformed. Structured materials (blocks, puzzles, etc.) are used to create a product. Symbolic materials (dolls, dress-up clothes, etc.) are used in symbolic or pretend play.

Another, broader category system was developed by Yawkey and Lopez-Toro (1985). Instructional materials (puzzles, stacking toys, etc.) are skills-oriented materials for reading, number, and visual and perceptual discrimination. Constructional materials (paints, clay, tools, etc.) are those used in building a product. Toys (dolls, cars, etc.) are miniature replicas of real and fantasy objects. Real objects (mud, pots and pans, etc.) are natural objects.

Research in preschools sheds light on the uses and values of toys and play objects. As children increase in age their capacity to play with non-realistic toys increases (McGhee, Ethridge, & Benz 1984; Einsiedler 1985) and constructional play may be integrated with pretend play (Zernignon-Hakes 1984). In structured constructional play with blocks children shift from object manipulation to symbolic or pretend play using the same objects. Unstructured toys create greater diversity in fantasy themes (McGhee, Ethridge, & Benz 1984; Robinson & Jackson 1985; Einsiedler 1985). Further, play with low-structured objects is associated with more sophisticated language and social-cognitive development (Einsiedler 1985).

Although among preschoolers, play with low-realistic toys increases with age and they continue to play longer with high-realistic toys than with low-realistic ones, younger preschoolers role playing is more evident with realistic toys, (Einsiedler 1985). McGhee, Ethridge, and Benz (1984) suggest that the results might be different over time as the novelty of realistic toys wears off. With the present bombardment of children with high realistic toys—G.I. Joe, Rambo, Transformers, Ninja Turtles—there is little opportunity for many children to sample the delights of low-realistic toys or to experience satiation, for the available array and accompanying hoop-la are seemingly endless.

Novelty, Realism, and Complexity

The *novelty* of a toy is a primary reason for children to explore it. The introduction of a novel object stimulates the child to get to know its properties. Exploration ceases once these properties are known. At that point play begins. This transition from exploration to play is apparent by a gradual relaxation of mood, evidenced not only by changes in facial expression, but in greater diversity of activities with the object. In play, the emphasis changes from the question of "What does this object do?" to "What can I do with this object?" (Hutt 1966).

Realism of toys is a second primary factor in children's play. Pulaski's (1970) study of five- to seven-year-olds showed that less structured toys (construction and art materials, simple rag dolls) elicited a greater variety of fantasy themes than did highly structured toys (realistic dolls, detailed toy buildings, cars, fully furnished doll house). However, high-fantasy children were less influenced by the realism of the toys apparently because tendencies toward fantasy were already well developed.

A third factor affecting exploration, curiosity, and play behavior of children is *complexity* of toys. Four- to seven-year-old children were asked to do anything they liked with a series of objects varying in complexity (Switzky, Haywood, & Islett 1974). The older children were more curious than the younger children, spending more time exploring the high-complexity objects. But, in general, the time spent playing decreased for both the older and younger children.

Based on the research pertaining to the relationship between play and play objects, it is safe to say that the critical characteristics of a play object are its relative degree of complexity and novelty. When a novel object is encountered, it will first be explored and then played with. The intensity of play is related to the degree of the novelty. With regard to the complexity of a play object, the amount and quality (creativeness, inventiveness) of play decreases as complexity increases. Caplan and Caplan (1973:159–160), the originators of Creative Playthings, aptly point to the fact that "Detail and reality can be a hindrance to free, creative play for the very young child, because he can use the toy only for what it was originally intended."

PLAY SPACES FOR INFANTS/TODDLERS

Physical environments may be as important for young children's development as social-interpersonal environments (Diamond 1988; Wachs 1989). Physical environment is an essential ingredient in development for it acts as a stage or setting for social transactions (Wohlwill & Heft 1987). For example, both noise and crowding negatively influence cognitive, language, and motivational development of infants (Wachs & Gruen 1982), and too much noise and confusion (Klaus & Gray 1968) or too much crowding (Bronfenbrenner 1974) can negatively influence development. Over-stimulation of very young at-risk infants in hospital settings also has negative effects on their development (Frost 1975). In practical terms, some children need quiet, orderly environments, while others seem to thrive in high-stimulus settings. Consequently, the outdoor (and indoor) environment should offer a range of options to meet such diverse needs of children. As the reader will see, this applies not only to matters of noise level organization of the environment, but also to the availability and types of toys, play materials, equipment, and natural features such as hills, plants, shade, light, etc.

FIGURE 10.4 *With careful planning, large play structures can be installed indoors. (Photo courtesy of BigToys)*

A series of studies by Wachs (1989) indicate that such environmental factors as noise and crowding lead to reduction in positive caregiver behaviors (such as adults' vocalization involvement and responsivity) and increased negative behavior (such as interference with the child's activities). Consequently, both the social interactions and the environmental setting must be considered when studying children and creating play spaces. Sensitivity to amount of space, spatial arrangement, and size of play groups appear to have a profound effect on the quality of child-care environments. The standardization of play environments is no less outmoded and incorrect than the common position that curriculum for young children should be standardized—that is, the same for everyone. Children are not created equal and do not develop at the same rate or in the same way. Multiple needs require multiple options and result in multiple outcomes. This is consistent with contemporary knowledge in child development (see Bredekamp, 1987). Individualized programs are essential in the classroom and in the outdoor play environment.

The behaviors of infants are at first reflexive-grasping, sucking, etc., but rapidly become more complex. Within a few weeks of birth the infant is exploring the immediate surroundings, trying on everything for size by hitting, pulling, pushing, and reacting to the consequences with pleasure, surprise, or dismay. Play begins early as the child explores objects around her, imitates the actions of adults, repeats actions for sheer joy, and begins to refine actions—elaborating movements, extending motor schemes, and, as mobility increases, widening the world beyond immediate surroundings. Language emerges as vocalizations are linked to actions. Through imitating language, playing with language, and with the support of adults and simple toys, the infant normally develops at a remarkable pace.

Understanding the nature of development is essential to providing developmentally relevant play spaces. Initially the infant needs and can use only simple toys or objects—objects that can be easily grasped, moved about, and safely mouthed and sucked (toys are for sucking). Very early in life the child needs to spend time outdoors to experience and benefit from fresh air, sunshine, and the range of stimuli (wind, sounds, animals, noises, texture, plants) available there. The observer of infants at play can easily conclude that they are "starving for stimuli" or their curiosity and interest seem to be limitless. During this early period Piaget's essential requirement for development—"action upon objects"—is clearly evident, so the adult faces the seemingly endless task of providing a sequence of increasingly complex challenges, opportunities, and materials for play.

QUALITIES OF AN INFANT/TODDLER PLAY ENVIRONMENT

What sort of place is a playground for babies and toddlers? Several design principles illustrate the parameters. The play environment should: 1) allow a wide range of movement; 2) stimulate the senses; 3) offer novelty, variety, and challenge; and 4) be safe and comfortable.

Allow a Range of Movement

The playground is a place to be rolled by an adult in a baby carriage, so for the younger ones a wheeled vehicle path, meandering among the interesting features of the outdoors, is a key feature. Later this same pathway will be used to support the child's first efforts to ride a tricycle, and, yet later, to support motor activity and dramatic play. Babies need materials that are gentle for crawling, kind for falling, and cool for sitting, so old conveyor belts, which cost nothing, have qualities that are superior to concrete and asphalt. For greater mobility and ease of movements (conveyor belts get wrinkles) the newer, poured-in place, resilient, manufactured surface materials are preferred. The high cost of such material is a common deterrent.

The overall environment should support a wide range of motor activities/ movement, ranging from a relatively confined space for infants to expansive areas for more able toddlers. The author designed a special outdoor infant space at the U.S. Army Fort Huachaca Army base featuring a 12' × 12' × 18" high mound, covered with outdoor carpet and bounded by carpet-covered foam boundaries for pulling up by infants. When infants developed the skills to climb over this boundary, they were allowed to play in the toddler area containing an array of challenges.

Mobility opens up new worlds to the infant for it allows him to locate and investigate new objects, place himself in spatial perspective, test his abilities, and begin the process of gaining control over his environment. The environment should support the development of motor power by stimulating a wide range of movement, geared to the child's emerging abilities—sitting, crawling, standing, jumping, grasping, pulling, pushing, walking, running, balancing, turning. The means of mobility itself, for example, the wheeled vehicle track, should promote more than just moving from one place to another. With ingenious thought, hills, tunnels, curves, intersections, water crossings, car washes, covered trellises, texture paths, play houses, and, eventually, printed road signs stimulate the desired movement. With such richness in place, most infants/toddlers don't

FIGURE 10.5 "Cruising bars" allow infants to pull themselves up and try their wobbly legs (Nova University playscape; design by Larry Michalk).

need adults to prod, push, and tell, but merely to provide support, encouragement, and a reasonable degree of safety.

Infants are also assisted in movement by cruising bars attached to fences, sides of buildings, and play structures. These allow them to pull up and support themselves as they traverse on wobbly, undeveloped legs from one activity to another. Grass serves as a soft, texture-rich, cool surface for crawling about and acts as a partial cushion in falls from ground level. Ramps, tunnels, decks, and stairs made of wood or other hard material can be padded with outdoor carpet for comfort in crawling, and can reduce heat build-up in metal materials.

Stimulating the Senses

Very young children are sensory-oriented beings, taking in impressions through seeing, hearing, tasting, smelling, touching, and moving (kinesthetic sense). The indoor environment and outdoor environment that is linked by wide, glass sliding doors allows maximum stimulation for activities and materials can flow in and out and the sights and sounds of both together can heighten the total effect. Soft music originating near the exit can envelop a sizeable area; light and shadow effects created by sunlight filtering through a slatted patio cover can complement the light coming through windows and reveal contrasting designs and feeling states while improving comfort levels of children in hot climates. Light is second only to food in controlling body function (Wurtman 1982) and lights of different colors affect blood pressure, pulse and respiration rates, and brain activity (Gruson 1982). Spending time outdoors and exposure to light through windows are crucial to health and development (Olds 1989). In addition, light is essential in estimating times of day.

The child's sense of touch and the exercise of this sense is essential in developing perception of form and shape (Ayres 1973) and textured elements "may be critical developmentally, therapeutically, and aesthetically" (Olds 1989:10). Touching and textures are commonly considered in designing outdoor play environments for infants and toddlers. Surfaces should include a variety of natural textures—sand, water, grass, shrubs, leaves, bark, smooth rocks—and man-made textures—materials of wood, metal , plastic with rough and smooth surfaces, and texture panels mounted in play structures or on fences and walls. A typical texture panel can be constructed by securing blocks, segments, or examples of materials of different textures with screws to a smooth, lacquered back-board. Recently, a growing number of manufacturers have been creating and distributing various types of interchangeable sensory panels to attach to their play structures.

The ever-valuable loose parts and found materials from kitchens and workshops, examined carefully for safety, are essential items for every playground. And no playground is complete without one or more storage facilities in the playground to provide for security from loss, protection from the elements, and convenience in storing and removing loose materials.

Sensory settings are comfortable when they provide moderate levels of stimulation and at the same time provide variety in sensory stimulation (Olds 1989). Extreme levels of fluctuation in stimulation can be frightening and disorienting to young children but moderate, predictable levels help to maintain responsivity and alertness, a state that Fiske and Maddi (1961) call "difference within same-ness." Both natural and built environments can offer comfortable, consistent stimuli while maintaining moderate diversity. Consider the wind blowing through trees or through chimes, the water flowing in a brook or in a built water-play channel, the smell of flowers or the odor of cookies baking, the sunlight filtering through trees or through netting fashioned over a play area. The stimulation of choice is frequently that experienced in nature but in many areas where children play, notably crowded city spaces, one must resort to creating environments. Hopefully, the creator will look first to nature.

Novelty, Variety, and Challenge

Infants and toddlers are growing at a rapid rate and seeking and exploring new challenges as rapidly as they encounter them. Abundance of things to explore is needed to help ensure that growth continues. Abundance means that the child is introduced to new (novel) objects, sights, and sounds as she becomes comfortable with old ones, and that she is introduced to new challenges as old ones are mastered. Overabundance or too much novelty and challenges that are too difficult are to be avoided. Just as we seek a comfortable balance in auditory and visual stimuli, we also seek a comfortable balance in exposure to play objects and other physical stimuli and challenges.

Novelty is ensured by designing an interesting play environment with both simple and complex features. There are private, contained spaces (or space) for creeping babies or those that Miller (1989) calls "tummy babies" or those not yet crawling. There are expanded spaces for "crawling babies" that demonstrate their ability to negotiate the more complex terrain and features. There are pull-up and pull-along cruise bars for the "cruising babies," and there are low hills and low play structures with multiple-level decks and attached apparatus—slides, climbers, ramps, tunnels, stairs—for the "climbing babies." The babies are separated from the running, jumping, kicking, careening toddlers and older children until they achieve such abilities themselves. This gradually takes place during the latter part of the second year. "When you have an infant of three months lying on his back watching tree patterns together with a two and a half year old who is learning to pour sand, it can be a disastrous combination" (Ferguson 1979). A note of caution is needed here. It should not be assumed that parents should protect infants from all social interchange with older peers. The parent significantly affects the infant's development of self-competency but the infant's early peer relationships, especially with older peers, can foster the development of interaction and competence in ways the parent–infant interaction cannot (Vandell & Mueller 1980).

Toddlers test their skills to the limit, running headlong down low wide slides imbedded in hills, pushing their wheel vehicles to the top of low hills and careening down to an inevitable crash at the bottom, and appearing surprised, even after several trials, that they have crashed. They express wonder, joy, frustration, and amazement as readily as they try out new challenges. Theirs is a world of exploring and practicing. Novel materials and sensory challenges support their exploration and their seemingly endless practice routines. Water and sand are poured from container to container and back again—dump and fill, dump and fill. Blocks are stacked and knocked down and started again. Adults assist in movement and growth by ensuring that other routines and other places are available and from time to time sitting with children to casually and playfully model new routines.

The research on novelty in the infant–toddler environment can be compared to the research on noise and visual stimuli. The provision of balance seems to be relevant for both sets of factors. Novelty may increase exploratory play (Rheingold & Eckerman 1970) or unfamiliarity may increase anxiety and decrease exploratory play (Castell 1970; Parry 1972). Some infants, in unfamiliar settings tend to stay close to adults (Rheingold & Eckerman 1970; Castell 1970) and are reluctant to venture into unfamiliar territory. Experience and balanced or gradual introduction of novelty and challenge appear to be key factors in ensuring success. Children need time to play, encouragement to play, and spaces to play that have plentiful objects and areas to explore but which do not introduce too much novelty. As children explore successfully, they will usually accept and master new challenges that are introduced gradually. In play as in work, success breeds success. A large variety of loose parts in the storage facilities allows adults to make choices based on their observations of children. The play environment changes on a schedule determined by the skillful caretaker. The caretaker also introduces children to places and spaces outside the play yard to ensure contact with natural features and built environments not available in the more controlled play yard, which is limited in size and contents.

The variety of play objects and their attributes are influential in the play of both infants and toddlers. Having access to many toys influences positively the play of 6-month-old infants but older infants (12 months) are influenced more by variety (frequent changing) of toys (Wachs 1985). Objects that make sounds or react when touched or pulled (responsive toys) and toys that are easy to manipulate (plasticity) increase the exploratory play of infants (McCall 1974). Thus, availability, variety, novelty, responsivity, and plasticity of play objects all influence infant play in ways that should be taken into account when setting up play environments (indoors or outdoors).

As infants become toddlers their needs, play behaviors, and peer relations are changing rapidly. The sheer size and portability of play objects influences their play. Large non-portable toys maximize peer interactions; small, manipulative toys discourage interactions; and settings with no toys result in negative affect (DeStefano 1976; DeStefano & Mueller 1982). Large objects help to prevent toddlers from getting in one another's way. Small objects lead to more struggles for possession.

There appears to be a sequence in toddler's object play as related to peer play. Object play precedes peer play (Mueller & Lucas 1975), as commonly observed in parallel play with toddlers playing in close proximity, using a common set of materials but not interacting with one another. Objects serve as the "currency of exchange" (Garvey 1977). As toddlers show, take, give, and exchange play objects with their peers, social and peer relations begin to take form. However, a radically different pattern has been seen with 6-month-old infants. Vandell, Wilson, & Buchanan (1980) observed more social interaction when objects were not present. It seems that play objects may distract young infants from peer interactions.

Most toddlers by age two are growing into pretend play and by age two and a half years are pretending with imaginary objects (Elder & Pederson 1978). The attributes of play objects influence toddlers' play and should be considered in toy selection and availability. Initially, theme-specific toys (corresponding to the play role) or prototypical toys (looking like the real thing) aid the child's transformations from reality to pretend or "play-like." The lower the level of familiarity, the more difficulty the toddler has in transformations. A real kitchen pan is easier to adapt to cooking than is a plastic or wood block, and a doll or car would pose even greater transformation problems (Fein 1975). Substitution of unrealistic objects represents high-level thought processes that have been developing since birth. Even during infancy the child has been "in training" through innumerable interactions with the parent, and early manifestations of pretend play are seen in infancy as mother and child engage in such games as "patty-cake," and "peek-a-boo." The materials for pretend play should be varied to match the individual developmental levels of children, and adults must continue to support through personal interaction this emerging play form.

> Environments, like all aspects of life are potent purveyors of stimulation, information, and affect, and their effects are always felt and incorporated in some way. . . . It is not sufficient that a setting be adequate. It must instead, be beautiful. (Olds 1988:182)

Safety and Comfort in Infant–Toddler Environments

In general, the safety guidelines produced for public playgrounds and older children's playground equipment by the Consumer Product Safety Commission cover the range of concerns about safety in preschool play environments. However, infants and toddlers have special safety needs that are not addressed by CPSC, and that are unlikely to be addressed in the CPSC guidelines now being developed. A safety checklist for infant/toddler playgrounds is located in Appendix D.

Ground Cover

As infants develop mobility and begin to "toddle" about the playground they are at constant risk of falling. Having a well-designed playground will ensure against sudden, abrupt change of levels and excessive heights, but protective surfacing is needed under and around climbing equipment and moving equipment such as swings and rotating devices. The most common material is sand of sufficient depth to cushion falls. Four to six inches (maintained in place) is appropriate for falls of up to 24 inches, which is the maximum height for early toddler play structures. As toddlers gain skills they may be exposed to gradually increasing heights and deeper surfacing will be required. In areas where falls occur only from ground level, well maintained grass is desirable. Outdoor carpeting makes decks more comfortable for "creepers and crawlers" and reduces scratches and abrasions. Dressing in pants helps protect knees. Old conveyor belts, free of protruding metal, or manufactured surfacing material, are more comfortable and safer than concrete wheeled vehicle paths.

Pea gravel should be avoided in infant–toddler playgrounds because children place it in noses, ears, and mouth and throw it. In 1988, 81 children were admitted to U.S. emergency rooms to be treated for ingesting materials on the playground (CPSC 1990, Personal Correspondence). The items ingested were not identified but reason and experience point to pea gravel as a common item. A growing number of authorities warn against pea gravel.

Gravel areas should not be used as surfacing but rather removed or covered (Ard 1986:40).

> Pea gravel and small wood chips are not a good ground surface on an infant/toddler play yard (Miller 1989:24). . . . gravel areas present problems that need to be thought through (Greenman 1985:9).

Keesee (1990) found pea gravel to be hazardous and a very poor play material. Toddlers were frustrated when pea gravel would not stick together for piling or building. They threw it at one another, tried to eat it, and had difficulty riding tricycles when pea gravel was on the track.

Foreign Objects and Obstructions

The play yard should be checked daily, before children go out to play, for trash or other foreign objects that may have accumulated since the last play time. There should be no protruding components of equipment that children can fall onto from other, higher areas of the equipment. Any such falls should culminate in a thick bed of sand or to approved resilient material. The play yard should be inspected and the children observed at play to identify any obstruction in the normal play patterns that is hazardous. For example, equipment may be located too close to the end of a slide. Portable equipment should not be allowed to accumulate at the end of slides, in fall zones around decks or climbers, or in the areas around swings.

Broken, Pinching, Sharp, Loose Elements

Over time and with use, play materials and large equipment deteriorate and wear out. A careful weekly inspection, coupled with daily, on-going alertness is needed to detect broken, loose elements or sharp edges and pinching areas. As soon as such defects are identified, the offending play material should be removed from use, secured and inaccessible to children, and promptly repaired.

Entrapment and Entanglement

The leading causes of fatalities on playgrounds are entrapment, entanglement (strangulation, asphyxiation), and falls onto hard surfaces. The emerging standards (ASTM and CPSC) for preschool and school-age children will likely identify spaces between two adjacent structural members ranging from 3½ inches to 9 inches as head entrapment areas. Since the width of infant–toddler heads is smaller, the lower dimension is particularly critical. The caretaker should ensure for herself that there are no spaces in equipment that could entrap a child's head, for head dimensions vary widely from child to child and very skinny bodies can fall through openings, allowing the child to become suspended by the head.

Loose items of clothing, cords, ropes, jewelry, frayed material, and other loose materials that could potentially loop around the child's head should not be allowed on the playground. Special caution should be observed as children play on slides. Items of clothing such as hoods on coats or cords connecting mittens may catch on protruding elements of the equipment and suspend the child by the neck as she slides down. Open S-hooks are particularly hazardous. In the opinion of the author, other, closed-type fasteners should replace S-hooks which are rarely closed properly.

Crush Points and Shearing Actions

Moving and rotating equipment tends to wear out faster than stationary equipment, especially at points (swivels, axles) where metal moves against metal. With wear, the open spaces are enlarged and fingers can be inserted and mangled or amputated. Regular maintenance (inspection, lubrication, repair) is essential. Poorly designed equipment can also crush and mangle body parts. Merry-go-round–type (rotating) devices should have round, solid bases (sitting areas) that allow no intrusion of body parts (fingers, legs, entire body) inside the space traversed by the rotating mechanism. Open base merry-go-rounds, pedal-a-round devices (tricycles attached to a central axle), and swinging gates (gates attached to a central axle) violate these guidelines.

The fulcrums or axles of see-saws are also common sources of pinching-crushing actions. They should be inspected to ensure that fingers or hands cannot be inserted into the mechanism. The bottom ends of see-saws should be padded or rubber bumpers (e.g., tires) should be positioned vertically in the ground to absorb the crushing action that occurs when the end of the see-saw hits the ground. Some manufacturers have designed reasonably safe see-saws. These include some of the spring mounted designs.

Swing Seats

Swing seats should be constructed of resilient, light-weight materials, and for infants and less-able toddlers, they should have strap-in seats that prevent falling out. There are desirable swings that fail to meet these criteria. Porch- or patio-type swings are typically made of wood and they are heavy. They should be supervised carefully to ensure that they are not pushed into children. Barrel swings, hung horizontally by two chains, also perform therapeutic and motor functions and can be suspended in a manner to reduce the swinging motion. Angling the point of connection of the chain swivel to the overhead support beam well outside of the vertical line of attachment to the barrel reduces the motion. Under no circumstances should swing seats with protruding elements (e.g., bolts, acorn nuts, animal noses and legs, ends of support bars) be installed in the play yard.

Electrical Hazards

All air conditioners and electrical boxes, transformers, and outlets should be fenced or otherwise made inaccessible to children. As this is being written, the Austin, Texas, newspapers carry an incident wherein a child climbed on top of an air conditioner and was electrocuted. Occasionally, proper electrical grounds are not connected or water, which drains from the system, leads to short circuits. Children should also be protected from access to electrical connection boxes in neighborhoods with underground utilities. All such boxes should be locked and unlocked ones should be reported immediately to the local electric company. Children should not be allowed to play on, or close to them. Guy wires for electrical poles should not be installed in playgrounds.

Toxic Materials and Choking Hazards

Play materials for infants and toddlers should not have parts that can lead to choking. All play materials, paint, shrubs, plants, trees, water, surfacing material, and equipment parts should be checked for possible presence of toxic materials. There is current disagreement about the potential effects of young children playing on pressure-treated lumber. One can avoid this controversy altogether by using untreated redwood, although use of redwood raises special environmental issues.

"The infant/toddler landscape has to be safe to eat" (Greenman 1985:5). Plant nursery workers are probably not familiar with the pattern and consequences of children "sucking on shrubs" so the local poison control center should be consulted.

The issue of cats contaminating sand appears to be exaggerated, but in some areas sandboxes need to be covered or other precautionary steps taken. There is no single definitive solution to the problem.

Safety Barriers

Infants and toddlers must receive special protection against traffic, fall hazards (ditches, drop-offs), and pools of water. State regulatory agencies typically require fences (with securable gates) four feet high around playgrounds at child care centers. Numerous national groups/standards including the National Swimming Pool Institute Standards, the U.S. Consumer Product Safety Commission Guidelines, the American Public Health Association Regulations, the National Building Code, and the National Recreation and Park Association Guidelines, call for fences (minimum height ranging from 4' to 6') around swimming pools with self-closing and self-latching gates. The author believes that all pool fences should be at least 6' high with gates that must be locked when the pool is not supervised by an adult. The fence should not be easy to climb.

Maintenance and Supervision

The reader should refer to Chapter 9 for extensive information, but in general, good, regular maintenance is even more essential for infants and toddlers than for older children, for they lack the cognitive skills to predict or engage in cause/effect thinking and their relatively underdeveloped motor skills restrict their abilities to master challenges in a safe manner.

Supervision is more direct and personal with infants and toddlers. They flit from activity to activity at a rapid and unpredictable rate and they are more prone to take risks than are older children. The adult–child ratio in the outdoors should equal that required by state regulatory agencies (about one adult to three or four infants or to six to eight toddlers). Supervision is an issue in many child injury law suits.

SPECIAL ESSAY
by Sue and Marshall Wortham, Matrix Design

We frequently design playgrounds for preschool and school-age children, but our special interest is researching and developing play environments for infants and toddlers. We divide these youngest age groups into nonmobile infants and very mobile toddlers.

For infants we consider play elements that will encourage the development of basic locomotor skills and sensory experiences. Since these little ones are within the sensorimotor period we include opportunities for seeing, hearing, smelling, and physically experiencing the out-of-door world. They can enjoy colors, sounds, plants, and flowers growing within their field of vision, and feel breezes and sunshine. The movement of shadows, fluttering of a windsock, and gentle tinkle of a windchime add to their enjoyment of expeditions outside. We design play equipment that will encourage exploration through crawling, standing, cruising, and walking. Babies within this age range we consider to be porch babies. They need to be able to sit in a loving lap and swing in a porch swing when they get tired of venturing about on their own.

Once the babies achieve somewhat stable ambulation, they become yard babies. These constantly in motion toddlers are ready to widen their field of exploration. For physical development they need small hills, equipment with tunnels, steps, and other physical features that will challenge them in their eager attempts to climb, run, jump, crawl through, sit on, and otherwise test their motor abilities. Wheeled toys of various types to push, pull or ride, plus a track or road to travel on, are a popular choice.

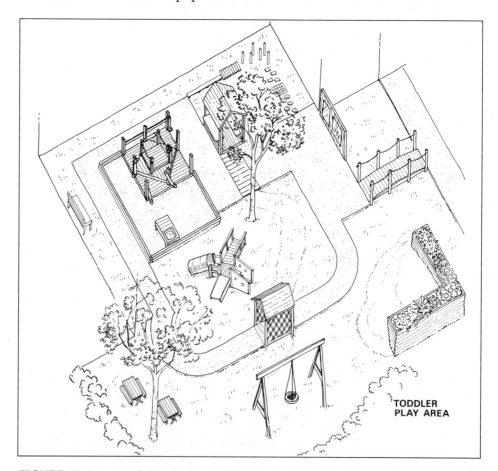

FIGURE 10.6 A sample layout for a toddler play area (Courtesy, Matrix Design Consortium; Sue and Marshal Wortham).

FIGURE 10.7 The "sensory-boat" for toddlers (Design by Sue and Marshal Wortham). Optimal location in sand play area.

The natural environment needs to include different textures to walk on, touch, pick up, and explore. Leaves, bugs, sticks, tree bark, flowers, vegetable plants, and sand and water are but a few of the artifacts of nature that will attract their attention.

These enthusiastic players also need opportunities for creative and dramatic play. Facilities for finger painting and experimenting with mud and clay are part of the outdoor activities that will foster exploration and expression. Dress-up accessories will encourage pretending and role play, while equipment and toys that involve more than one child facilitate social development.

These preoperational learners are extending their knowledge through sensory experiences. Besides the natural elements already in place, man-made materials such as music boards, wheels to turn, sand toys, and other elements that respond when acted upon widen their opportunities to explore the possibilities for making something happen.

When designing play spaces for toddlers, simple climbing equipment that is versatile is more useful than a complex piece of equipment that is a cut down version of structures for older children. Small spaces encourage confidence and exploration more than large, wide-open expanses. Changes in the natural topography such as a grassy berm are more appealing than randomly placed small versions of seesaws, merry-go-rounds, or other examples of scaled equipment. Low swings can be popular, but are not essential.

To enhance natural features at a toddler scale, we like to include small trees, shrubs, and flower pots and baskets hung or arranged so that they are easily seen. Shade structures with vines, animal cages, and water and sand play features provide rich experiences for learning and play.

A Toddler Playground, Stepping Stones School, Austin, Texas: Design by Isabel Keesee.

FIGURE 10.8 *A good play environment need not be expensive. This one was built for less than $500. Its special features are:*

FIGURE 10.9 *A grassy mound and polyethylene slide for motor play.*

FIGURE 10.10 *A texture wall for exploration.*

FIGURE 10.11 *A "deck and dish" for water play.*

FIGURE 10.12 *A sand play area.*

FIGURE 10.13 *A wheeled vehicle track for tricycles and, in the toddlers words, "for jogging."*

Most playgrounds for infants and toddlers that we visit underestimate the capacity of the smallest players to take advantage of outdoor play. While we are interested in improving the structures that we design for the under-threes, we are more interested in considering all of the natural and man-made components that promote development and play for this age group and how we can incorporate as many elements as feasible within the possibilities and constraints of each site that we design.

CONCLUSION

As child care shifts from home to center settings, growing attention is directed to creating safe, stimulating play environments for infants and toddlers. Young children, especially the very young, derive extraordinary developmental benefits from play, as revealed in studies of their interaction with objects, adults, and peers.

The object/toy play of children follows a developmental progression from simple "mouthing" objects of the infant to the Nintendo games of pre-teens. The early stimulus-seeking, exploratory play of infants, supported by familiar adults, aids cognitive, language, motor, and social development. Independent, sensorimotor movements become coordinated, synthesized movements. Exploration leads to adaptation and mastery. Pretend play enters the scene and transformations of objects to symbolic representations broaden thought, extend actions, and enhance development.

Play objects, initially simple and primitive, follow similar developmental progression. "Mouthing" and "rattling and banging" objects are expanded to include fluid materials, construction materials and symbolic materials. Realistic toys and non-realistic toys complement play. The caretaker helps children make developmentally relevant toy choices by considering such qualities as novelty, realism, complexity, function, safety, and durability.

Play spaces for infants and toddlers are as important as the play objects. Outdoor play environments should allow a wide range of movement; stimulate the senses; offer novelty, variety, and challenge; and be in harmony with nature. They should also be safe and comfortable. Safety involves such factors as design and maintenance of play materials, supervision, attention to boundaries, toxic materials, and ground cover.

REFERENCES

Ard, L.G. (1986), Outside with infants and toddlers. *Texas Child Care Quarterly* 10:39–45.

Ayers, A.J. (1973). *Sensory Integration and Learning Disorders.* Los Angeles: Western Psychological Services.

Bredekamp, S. (ed.) (1987). *Developmentally Appropriate Practice in Early Childhood Programs Serving Children from Birth through Age 8.* Washington, D.C.: National Association for the Education of Young Children.

Bronfenbrenner, U. (1974). *Is Early Intervention Effective?* HEW Publication #OHD, 76-30025. Washington, D.C.

Caplan, F., & Caplan, T. (1973). *The Power of Play.* New York: Anchor Press/Doubleday.

Castell, R. (1970). Effects of familiar and unfamiliar environments on proximity behavior of young children. *Journal of Experimental Child Psychology* 9:342–347.

DeStefano, C.T. (1976). Environmental determinants of peer social behavior and interaction in a toddler play group. Unpublished doctoral dissertation, Boston University.

DeStefano, C.T., & Mueller, E.C. (1982). Environmental determinants of peer social activity in 18-month-old males. *Infant Behavior and Development* 5:175–183.

Diamond, M. (1988). *Enriching Heredity: The Impact of the Environment Upon the Anatomy of the Brain.* New York: Free Press.

Einsiedler, W. (1985). Fantasy play of preschoolers as a function of toy structures. Paper presented at the international symposium of the Netherlands Organization for Postgraduate Education in the Social Sciences. Amsterdam, September 14–15.

Elder, J.L., & Pederson, D.R. (1978). Preschool children's use of objects in symbolic play. *Child Development* 49:500–504.

Fein, G. (1975). A transformational analysis of pretending. *Developmental Psychology* 11:291–296.

Ferguson, J. (1979). Creating growth producing environments for infants and toddlers. In *Supporting the growth of infants, toddlers, and parents*, (ed.) E. Jones. Pasadena, CA: Pacific Oaks College.

Fiske, D.W., & Maddi, S.R. (1961). *Functions of Varied Experience*. Homewood, IL: Dorsey.

Frost, J.L. (1975). At risk. *Childhood Education* 51:299–304.

Garvey, C. (1977). *Play: The Developing Child*. Cambridge, MA: Harvard University Press.

Greenman, J. (1985). Babies get out: Outdoor settings for infant-toddler play, *Beginnings* 2:7–10.

Gruson, L. (1982). Color has a powerful effect on behavior, researchers assert. *The New York Times*, October 19.

Hutt, G. (1966). Exploration and play in children. *Symposia of the Zoological Society of London* 18:61–81.

Keesee, I. (1990). A comparison of outdoor play environments for toddlers. Unpublished doctoral dissertation, University of Texas at Austin.

Klaus, R., & Gray, S. (1968). The early training project for disadvantaged children. *Monographs of the Society for Research in Child Development* 33, Serial no. 187.

Lewis, M., & Brooks-Gunn, J. (1979). *Social Cognition and the Acquisition of Self*. New York: Plenum Press.

Lowe, M. (1975). Trends in the developmental representational play in infants from one to three years—an observational study. *Journal of Child Psychology and Psychiatry* 16:33–47.

McCall, R. (1974). Exploratory manipulation and play in the human infant. *Monographs of the Society for Research in Child Development* 39, Serial no. 155.

McGhee, P.E., Ethridge, L., & Benz, N.A. (1984). The effect of level of toy structure on preschool children's pretend play. *The Journal of Genetic Psychology* 144:209–217.

Miller, K. (1989). Infants and toddlers outside. *Texas Child Care Quarterly* 13:20–29.

Mueller, E.C., & Lucas, T. (1975). A developmental analysis of peer interaction among toddlers. In *Peer Relations*, (eds.) M. Lewis & L. Rosenblum. New York: Wiley.

Olds, A.R. (1988). Designing for play: Beautiful spaces are playful places. *Children's Health Care* 16(3):218–222 Washington, D.C.: The Association for the Care of Children's Health.

————. (1989). Psychological and physiological harmony in child care center design. *Children's Environments Quarterly* 6:8–16.

Parry, M. (1972). Infant's responses to novelty in familiar and unfamiliar settings. *Child Development* 43:233–237.

Pulaski, M.S. (1970). Play as a function of toy structure and fantasy predisposition. *Child Development* 41:531–537.

Rheingold, H.L., & Eckerman, C. (1970). The infant separates himself from his mother. *Science* 168L:78–93.

Robinson, C.C., & Jackson, R. (1985). The effects of varying structure within a prototypical play object on the solitary pretend play of preschool children. Paper presented at the Association for Childhood Education International Study Conference. San Antonio, Texas, June 18–22.

Rubin, R. (1990). Extra care found to raise Preemies I.Q. *Dallas Morning News*, June 13.

Rubin, K.H., Fein, G.G., & Vandenberg, B. (1983). Play. In *Handbook of Child Psychology*, vol. 4: *Socialization, Personality, and Social Development* (4th ed.), (ed.) P.H. Mussen. New York: Wiley.

Sutton-Smith, B. (1986). *Toys as Culture*. New York: Gardner Press.

Switzky, H.N., Haywood, H.C., & Islett, R. (1974). Exploration, curiosity, and play in young children: Effects of stimulus complexity. *Developmental Psychology*, 19:321–329.

Vandell, D.L., & Mueller, E.C. (1980). Peer play and friendships during the first two years. In *Friendships and Social Relations in Children*, (eds.) H.C. Foot, A.J. Chapman, & J.R. SmithLondon: Wiley.

Vandell, D.L., Wilson, K.S., & Buchanan, R. (1980). Peer interaction in the first year of life: An examination of its structure, content, and sensitivity to toys. *Child Development* 51:481–488.

Wachs, T.D. (1985). Home stimulation and cognitive development. In *Play Interactions: The Role of Toys and Parental Involvement in Children's Development*, (eds). C.C. Brown & A.W. Gottfried. Skillman, N.J.: Johnson and Johnson.

————. (1989). The development of effective child care environments: Contributions from the study of early experience. *Children's Environments Quarterly* 6:4–7.

Wachs, T.D., & Gruen, G. (1982). *Early Experience and Human Development*. New York: Plenum.

White, B.L. (1975). *The First Three Years of Life*. New York: Prentice-Hall.

Wohlwill, J., and Heft, H. (eds.) (1987). The physical environment and child development. In *Handbook of Environmental Psychology*. D. Skokols, & I. Altman. New York: Wiley.

Wolfgang, C.H., & Phelps, P. (1983). Preschool play materials preference inventory. *Early Child Development and Care* 12:127–141.

Wurtman, R.J. (1982). The effects of light on the human body. *Scientific American* 1:68–77.

Yawkey, T.D., & Lopez-Toro, J.A. (1985). Examining descriptive and empirically based typologies of toys for handicapped and non-handicapped children. *Topics in Special Education* 5:47–58.

Zerningnon-Hakes, A. (1984). Materials mastery and symbolic mastery in construction play: Stages of development. *Early Child Development and Care* 17:37–48.

SUGGESTED READING FOR PRACTICAL IDEAS IN PLANNING INFANT–TODDLER PLAY ENVIRONMENTS

Ard, L.G. (1986). Outside with infants and toddlers. *Texas Child Care Quarterly* 10:39–45.

Bergen, D., Smith, K., & O'Neill, S. (1988). Designing play environments for infants and toddlers. In*Play as a Medium for Learning and Development*, (ed.) D. Berger. Portsmouth, N.H.: Heineman.

Ferguson, J. (1979). Creating growth producing environments for infants and toddlers. In *Supporting the Growth of Infants, Toddlers, and Parents*, (ed.) E. Jones. Pasadena, CA: Pacific Oaks College.

Frost, J.L., & J.Dempsey (1990). Playgrounds for infants, toddlers and preschoolers. In *A Guide to Parenting Education for School-Age Parents*, (ed.) B. Brizzolara. Austin: Texas Education Agency.

Greenman, J. (1985). Babies get out: Outdoor settings for infant-toddler play. *Beginnings* 2:7–10.

Miller, K. (1989). Infants and toddlers outside. *Texas Child Care Quarterly* 13:20–29.

Wortham, S.C. (1990). Infant-toddler playgrounds. In *Playgrounds for Young Children: American Survey and Perspectives*, (eds.) S.C. Wortham & J.L. Frost. Reston, VA: American Alliance for Health, Physical Education, Recreation, and Dance.

"My aim was clear and correct—to give children in towns the same chance for creative play as those in the country"[1]

11

Adventure Playgrounds

Adventure playgrounds were not the invention of an individual, but of the ingenuity of children everywhere who have always chosen the exciting never-never land of dump grounds, construction sites, and nature's areas for their play. Prior to World War II, before commercially built playgrounds became widespread, urban children spent much of their time playing in vacant lots and construction sites. The lots were used as garbage dumps by local residents and contained a wide assortment of refuse and junk including the kitchen sink. Children would spend hours constructing forts and clubhouses, and often the constructions would be aided by building materials and tools borrowed from a nearby construction site. Abandoned automobiles became airplanes and submarines, packing crates became castles and palaces. Often a lot would contain rival gangs whose members would delight in laying siege to their opponents' fort with garbage can lid shields and swords made from the slats of orange crates. Caves and tunnels would be dug, and potatoes would be roasted over bonfires. At dinner time parents would have to drag their children home.

In an attempt to keep children off the streets, well-intentioned adults began to build neighborhood playgrounds. Unfortunately, in designing the new playgrounds, the play interests of children were ignored. What had once been a

---

[1]Lady Allen of Hurtwood. (1968). (from the Preface). *Planning for Play.* Cambridge, MA.: MIT Press.

vacant lot filled with challenge, excitement, and a wealth of discarded materials became a sterile arena of concrete and steel. In her book *Planning for Play* (1968), the late Lady Allen of Hurtwood outlined the progression of playground development during the past 50 years (pp. 18–19).

I. *The prison period*. These playgrounds resemble prison exercise yards. They consist of a barren expanse of concrete or asphalt surrounded by a high fence. Lady Allen refers to these playgrounds as "an administrator's heaven and a child's hell."

II. *The ironmongery period*. During this period of playground construction, large metal climbing structures, slides, and other pieces of metal equipment were placed on the asphalt play areas. The common activity on this type of playground was climbing to the top of a metal structure and then falling or getting shoved to the pavement below. As noted in Chapter 3, this is the major cause of serious injury on playgrounds today. Unfortunately, these playgrounds of concrete and steel have lived up to the claims of their designers and have proven to be indestructible.

III. *The concrete pipe period*. Many playgrounds contain concrete sewer pipes of various sizes and dimensions. Playground builders intended for children to crawl through and on top of the pipes. Sometimes the pipes are covered with dirt to form a mound. What initially seemed like a good idea has proven to be extremely hazardous. One playground in Texas that made elaborate use of concrete pipes was closed shortly after opening due to the number of injuries that occurred.

IV. *The novelty period*. At the other end of the continuum are playgrounds that Lady Allen refers to as "over-elaborate, over-clever, too slick, the pride of the architects." These playgrounds often include play sculptures that are nice to look at, but are not very functional and usually hazardous. This type of playground is typically found in the midst of large public housing projects. The novelty of these static playgrounds soon wears off.

Children have ignored these traditional playgrounds in favor of the city streets and vacant lots. Architect Paul Friedberg sums up this phenomenon,

> Playgrounds that deny the child; that offer no chance of involvement, participation, or manipulation; that are devoid of choice, complexity, and interaction will be empty of children—a dead ground. The street will be a playground. (1970:27)

How, then, can a rich, stimulating environment be incorporated into a playground where children ranging from toddlers to teenagers can play safely? One answer lies in adventure playgrounds. In Scandinavia and England, educators and playground designers have long recognized the importance of allowing children the freedom to do their own thing. Adventure playgrounds provide children with the opportunity to mold and shape the play environment: to tear it down and to start over again. Here children can create the form and structure of their play rather than having it imposed by an unmanageable environment.

WHAT IS AN ADVENTURE PLAYGROUND?

The London Adventure Playground Association (LAPA) was established in 1962 to promote an understanding of the educational, social, and welfare values of adventure playgrounds and to assist in the development of new ones. The LAPA (Jago 1971) offers the following description of adventure playgrounds:

> An adventure playground can best be described as a place where children are free to do many things that they cannot easily do elsewhere in our crowded urban society. In an adventure playground, which can be any size from one third of an acre to two and a half acres, they can build houses, dens and climbing structures with waste materials, have bonfires, cook in the open, dig holes, garden, or just play with sand, water and clay. The atmosphere is permissive and free, and this is especially attractive to children whose lives are otherwise much limited and restricted by lack of space and opportunity.
>
> Each playground has two full-time leaders in charge who are friends to the children, and help them with what they are trying to do. There is a large hut on each playground and this is well equipped with materials for painting, dressing up and acting, modeling and other forms of indoor play. There is also a record player, table tennis and so on, so that in bad weather and in winter the adventure playground hut becomes a social center for many children who would have nowhere to play except the street.

History

Adventure playgrounds had their beginning in Denmark in 1943. C. Th. Sorensen, a landscape architect who had designed many playgrounds, observed that children seemed to enjoy playing with the scrap materials left on construction

FIGURE 11.1 *Safe use of fire and group cooking are basic elements in adventure playgrounds.*

sites more than on the finished playgrounds. The children also played with the scrap materials more creatively and for longer periods of time than with the equipment built for them. It was this observation that provided the inspiration for the first junk playground (later copied under the name adventure playground) which was built adjacent to a public housing project in Emdrup. John Bertelsen, a nursery school teacher and ex-seaman, was hired as a first play leader. Emdrup proved to be a great success. And though it is not now the vibrant place it once was, it served as a model for the adventure playgrounds that followed.

One of those inspired by Emdrup was Lady Allen of Hurtwood, an English landscape architect who organized adventure playgrounds in London in spaces left where buildings had been bombed out. Under the guidance of play leaders, children were encouraged to build their own constructions using rubble and other materials provided. Presently, there are a large number of adventure playgrounds scattered throughout London and other English cities. They are supported by neighborhood organizations and provide a wide range of activities for children.

THE ADVENTURE PLAYGROUND MOVEMENT

Sorensen's brain child was recreated in several areas of Denmark, notably Copenhagen, where a number of "byggelegepladsen," or "building playgrounds" as the Danes prefer to call them, are in operation. The best of these are the envy of "play people" everywhere, containing extensive areas for building, gardening, cooking, climbing, and caring for animals in both indoor and outdoor contexts. The Danish play leaders are committed to the notion that recreational areas should be designed for both children and adults in close proximity to their

FIGURE 11.2 Special playgrounds are installed on the roofs of department stores in Tokyo.

FIGURE 11.3 *The adventure playground movement is taking root in Japan.*

homes. In Copenhagen as early as 1939, a Building Act was passed requiring all building plans to include provisions for adequate playgrounds. In 1967, this provision was extended to all of Denmark.

The Swedish versions of the junk, building, or adventure playground are called, simply, play environments. The Swedes are reputed to have more playgrounds for children per capita than any other country in the world and direct observations do not leave one with much doubt about this. But, as in other European countries, only a small percentage of these are of a comprehensive nature. The best play environments in Sweden provide a wide array of activities for children and adults while the vast majority are of more limited design, typically a sand area with climbing structures, swings, slide, and a wheeled vehicle area.

In London, true adventure playgrounds are currently struggling to survive, but play environments of various types are continuing to receive support from organizations intent on promoting children's play. Other English cities, notably Birmingham, are keeping that adventure playground dream alive. In the main these are truly junk playgrounds, containing an unbelievable array of structures built from scrounged materials. A fence surrounds the area and the ever-present play building containing a play area, the play leader's space, and assorted tools and play materials.

The Japanese are expressing growing interest in outdoor play environments for children. Most of their playgrounds are small "vest pocket" types, scattered throughout cities, and featuring traditional swings, slides, and assorted climbers.

Little systematic attention is given to safety factors such as surfacing and heights. Special playgrounds are installed on the roofs of department stores in Tokyo. Here children play with an assortment of miniature vehicles and related props while parents shop. In recent years adventure-type playgrounds have sprung up. These are mainly in large city parks and include building areas, arts and crafts, animals, gardens and a wide array of play structures.

The adventure playground movement was slow to gain a footing in the United States. The American Adventure Playground Association (AAPA) was formed in April 1976 by a group of park and recreation professionals, educators, and commissioners in Southern California, with Bill Vance as the national chairman. Their major purpose was to promote the concept of adventure playgrounds in the United States through information services. In May 1977, the AAPA identified 16 adventure playgrounds in the United States. This, of course, did not include dozens of playgrounds built or being built by parent and community groups throughout the country (particularly in Pennsylvania, New York, California, Texas, and Georgia) using scrounged materials but lacking such features as full-time play leaders. Within a decade the AAPA had ceased to function but other groups were carrying on the tradition.

In 1979, a demonstration adventure playground was planned, built, and operated at Mountain Park in Houston, Texas. The playground, located on an eight-acre site in southwest Houston, was supported by the Mountain Park Foundation. The planners employed a set of design criteria (Sarahan & Hager 1980). A well-designed playground should:

- Provide opportunities for self-management.
- Provide materials which generate problem-solving challenges.
- Be designed for consistent and intensive use.
- Provide appropriate physical and social experiences.
- Conform to health and safety standards.
- Provide sufficient storage and maintenance facilities.
- Conform to the community's budget capacities.
- Preserve and accommodate community aesthetic values. (p. 35)

The organizers of Mountain Park set about to establish a rich collection of play areas within the adventure playground. These included a garden and nature center, storage areas, animal habitat, sand and water center, arts and craft area, picnic area, office area, and a courts and games area. A central concern was providing carefully selected and trained staff. Program leaders received three months of training; facilitators received a one-week orientation. The staff included educators with Master's degrees, artists, professional actors, special educators, environmental educators, and bilingual educators. The organizers concluded that, "There probably has never been a playground as professionally staffed as the Mountain Park adventure playground" (Sarahan & Hager 1980:100). Despite the impressive credentials of this group, ongoing training was required to meet the goals of the program.

An assessment of the program four months after initiation found that about 15,000 people had used Mountain Park, even though there was very little publicity. The most impressive opinions were those of the children:

"What I liked best about it was that everybody got to do what they wanted to do. There was something for everybody . . . we did not have to stand in line."

Brice Middleton

"My favorite part was the carpentry because I built an airplane a little longer than my arm and it weighed three pounds. My next favorite thing was playing with that big ball. I had the best time of (my) life, funnier than Astroworld."

Kyle Friedel

And sample comments from parents, teachers, and community leaders:

"Never have I taken a group of children anywhere that everyone so thoroughly enjoyed. Not once did a child say, "What can I do now?"

Ann Rasch, Teacher
J.R. Harris Elementary School

"Somebody should have thought of this years ago. Wonderful experience for urban children; fabulous experience for children of all ages."

Sharon Buner
Houston, Texas

"Thousands of children in our city lack the opportunity to discover what is possible for them to do, to know what reality permits and what it prohibits. Kids everywhere need to experiment, to build and tear down, to find out what works and what doesn't, to plan and discover, to predict and be surprised, to copy and try something new, to succeed and fail; and then try again. Jumping and running, hammering and sawing, climbing over and under, singing and performing, working in groups and going it alone, helping and receiving help, tasting disappointment and knowing joy, these are the tasks of childhood . . ."

James E. Clark, Director
Texas Treatment Center for Austin

The author has not heard more lucid expressions of the benefits of adventure playgrounds, nor more compelling arguments for their existence and growth. Despite the positive evaluations of those who enjoyed the playground, the Mountain Park experiment was short-lived. But the spirit survived and the group was reorganized as the Houston Adventure Playground Association, which established two new adventure playgrounds in 1986. The audience for these playgrounds (Mark Twain Elementary School and Freed Park) was after school, "latch-key" children. They are still operating in 1991.

Although it is acknowledged that evaluation of behavioral change attributable to participation in adventure playgrounds is complicated by numerous confounding variables, an evaluation of participants at Mark Twain Adventure Playground in Houston is of interest. A combination of surveys and standardized tests (Mauldin & Giles 1989) revealed the following:

- Parents and teachers were generally supportive of the program.
- The observed incidence of participants' aggressive behavior was reduced while opportunities for solving problems was increased.

- The staff was successful in creating an environment where children were accepted and free to express themselves creatively.
- Participants made significant gains in social responsibility and social problem solving (instruments used were the Children's Action Tendency Scale and the Social Problem Solving–The Open Middle Interview).
- Aggressive tendency on the CATS increased less from pretest to post-test for participants than non-participants.
- The number of physically and verbally aggressive solutions to conflict situations decreased significantly from pretest to post-test for participants (OMI).

These findings are particularly meaningful when one considers that the majority of participants were "latch-key" children, with special needs for adult contact and guidance and reduced opportunities for social skill and problem-solving development.

The Houston Adventure Playground Association (Photos courtesy of Flournoy Manzo).

The Houston Adventure Playground Association makes play opportunities available for after-school children.

FIGURE 11.4 & 11.5 Children learn to use tools.

FIGURE 11.6 They build their own houses . . .

FIGURE 11.7 create water canals . . .

FIGURE 11.8 and express themselves through art.

FIGURE 11.9 Skilled play leaders assist with techniques and help ensure safety.

AMERICAN AND INTERNATIONAL ASSOCIATIONS FOR THE CHILD'S RIGHT TO PLAY

The organization most responsible for promoting adventure playgrounds is the International Association for the Child's Right to Play (formerly International Playground Association [IPA]). The American Association for the Child's Right to Play is affiliated with the International Association. The IPA was founded in 1961 at a conference in Denmark established for that purpose. The first World President was C. Th. Sorensen. Stina Wretlind-Larsson (1979) writes that she and Max Siegumfeldt, Jens Sigsgaard, and Lady Allen of Hurtwood were instrumental in laying plans for the conference.

The second international gathering of the infant IPA was held in Zurich, Switzerland, in 1964, and membership was opened to playleaders as well as "professionals." During the next 3 years IPA grew by a modest 50 members, only a few from non-European countries (Abernethy & Otter 1979). The first American member of record was Mrs. Thomas B. Hess of Greenwich, Connecticut. The August, 1966 IPA *Newsletter* contained an address change for her. Pacific Oaks College and Children's School in Pasadena, California, was apparently the first American organization member, having joined in 1969. The Pacific Oaks play yards have remained (over two decades later) among the finest expressions of the adventure play concept in America.

By the early 1970s, membership was growing rapidly and national correspondents/representatives were installed in those countries with relatively large membership. The first American representative was Paul Hogan. The leaders in IPA began to feel that the name of the association was a handicap, suggesting the organization cared more about playgrounds than about children (Bengtsson 1979) so its name was changed to the International Association for the Child's Right to Play (IPA). This name was thought to reflect a much broader field of concern. Unfortunately, the new name has also proven to be a handicap, suggesting an activist, political emphasis and directing attention away from playgrounds. Let us hope that this broadening of concerns does not lead IPA along the path taken by the American Playground Association (Chapter 5), leading them farther and farther away from the original focus—playgrounds—until that emphasis is no longer of concern. By 1987, the IPA had grown to include members from 50 countries and the World Congress in Stockholm was attended by 25 Americans. Donna Seline followed Paul Hogan as U.S. Representative. In 1986, Joe Frost was elected U.S. Representative. A few months later the U.S. membership voted by-laws for formal organization as the American Association for the Child's Right to Play and a Board of Directors was formally established: Joe Frost, President and U.S. Representative; Sue Wortham, Treasurer; Marcia Guddemi, Newsletter Editor; Jay Beckwith, Harris Forusz, Roger Hart, Robin Moore, and Barbara Sampson, Board Members. Tom Jambor was elected U.S. President in 1988.

During this period of reorganization some major concerns were expressed in the themes of National (U.S.A.) conferences, with one devoted to safety, hosted by Harris Forusz at the University of Cincinnati in 1987, and another emphasizing playleadership, chaired by Robin Moore and hosted by Barbara Sampson, Executive Director of the American Association of Leisure and Recreation, in Washington, D.C., in 1988. International conferences of IPA are held every three years. The U.S. representation is strong at international conferences, having the largest group of participants from outside the host country at the 1987 conference in Stockholm and at the 1990 conference in Tokyo, where Robin Moore became the first American to be elected president of IPA. The 1993 international conference is scheduled for Sydney, Australia and the 1992 U.S.A. Conference is scheduled for Dallas, Texas.

PERSPECTIVES ON ADVENTURE PLAYGROUNDS

The best European playgrounds perhaps represent the "future today" in conceptualizing play environments. The concept of playground, limited in scope, will eventually be replaced by a more vital and comprehensive concept of outdoor environments for people of all ages, combining elements of nature, a wide array of play activities, and involving all family members in specially designed environments within their own immediate neighborhood.

The Play Leader

The key to a successful adventure playground is the play leader. The primary role of the leader is to facilitate a safe, happy play experience for each child while interfering as little as possible. Th. Sorensen warned against too much supervision and imposed structure for children. Writing in 1947 he stated,

> It is my opinion that children ought to be free by themselves to the greatest possible extent. A certain supervision and guidance will of course be necessary, but I am firmly convinced that one ought to be exceedingly careful when interfering in the lives and activities of children. (Allen 1968:55).

The play leader must also be a jack-of-all-trades. At times he or she will be called upon to be a teacher, administrator, carpenter, gardener, veterinarian, social worker, best friend, and substitute parent. In addition to the daily operation of the playground, the leader can serve as a community resource person by putting families in touch with various social services that can have a positive influence on the lives of children.

There are no set professional or educational qualifications for play leaders; however, there are identifiable qualities that a play leader should possess:

- Must like children.
- Should be able to communicate effectively with children of all ages.
- Accepting of a wide range of individual differences.
- Support the work of children with a minimum of interference.
- Be able to thrive in a chaotic environment.
- Have a good sense of humor.

A single set of qualifications, however, will not be appropriate in all settings. For example, an outstanding play leader in an outstanding playground in Copenhagen is an ex-farmer, having special skills in caring for the animals (chickens, goats, pigs, horses) as well as outstanding sensitivity and intuitive skill in working with children. In a ghetto area adventure playground in London a play leader expressed the view that rapport and success might include "smoking, swearing and shoving a bit." This statement is better understood when one views firsthand the social problems generated by poverty. Play structures and play buildings are sometimes burned by "outside groups" and varying degrees of vandalism are a frequent problem. Such problems seem less serious when the alternatives to playgrounds and play leaders—streets, alleys, roof tops, and abnormal influences—are considered.

Interaction with the children is only one of several play leader roles. A substantial amount of time is spent in scrounging materials and in building, repairing, or altering play structures. In London, vehicles are provided for searching out and hauling scrap, abandoned, or gift materials to the play site. The demand for such materials is so great that it is difficult to obtain sufficient quantities for the playgrounds. (In many areas of the United States almost unlimited materials are available to capable scroungers at low cost or no cost.) In London the play leaders spend some time building, particularly while the children are in school. Although there are opportunities for children to check out tools and create for themselves, the bulk of the building activity appears to be assumed by the play leaders. The ratio of adult/child building activity seems to be in proportion to the skill and sensitivity of the play leaders in involving children and the overall quality of the playground. On the more advanced London playgrounds there appears to be a genuine effort by play leaders to provide rich play experiences for children.

In Stockholm the author observed a group of children assisting a sow in giving birth to pigs. In Copenhagen one group of children fed and brushed the horses, cleaned the stables, and later prepared the horses for riding. On another playground children constructed hutches for their rabbits. And on a third, children prepared outdoor fires in the area designed for that purpose and set about to cook their evening meal. All of this with the unobtrusive involvement of play leaders.

In England, Denmark, and Sweden play leadership training is available and a system exists that pays trainees for working in playgrounds. While we are not aware that any such programs exist in the United States, many community colleges and universities have training programs on both professional and paraprofessional levels in the areas of child development and early childhood education. This type of training would be helpful for play leaders working with preschool and primary school age children.

The initial capital expense of an adventure playground is much less than that of a commercially built playground, but annual operating expenses are greater. The major portion of the playground budget will be used to pay substantial salaries to leaders. Play leadership is a new concept in the United States, so the salary will have to be determined by looking at similar jobs in other settings.

Playground Safety and Liability

Although adventure playgrounds have experienced great success in Europe during the past 30 years, they have been slow to gain acceptance in the United States. This is due to a combination of factors including objection to their untidy appearance, ignorance concerning the nature of children's play, and fear of injury and liability.

Adventure Playgrounds

DENMARK

FIGURE 11.10 *The main building—recreation center.*

FIGURE 11.11 *Part of every child's education should include the care of animals.*

FIGURE 11.12 *The best adventure playgrounds provide a wide array of tools.*

FIGURE 11.13 *A special play area in Copenhagen introduces children to driving automobiles.*

SWEDEN

FIGURE 11.14 *The extensive play-parks system of Sweden features "farms within cities" (Stockholm).*

FIGURE 11.15 *Playleaders and parents conduct family activities in parks.*

FIGURE 11.16
Water play
areas are
popular with
Swedish
children.

FIGURE 11.17
Trolley rides
are specially
designed for
fun and safety.

ENGLAND

FIGURE 11.18 Play busses take play materials to
the children.

FIGURE 11.19 Building areas in London make
extensive use of scrap materials.

The safety record of adventure playgrounds is excellent. Lady Allen reports that during a 10-year period, with the exception of cuts, scrapes, bruises, nail punctures, and a few fractures, few serious injuries have been reported on British or Scandinavian adventure playgrounds nor have any lawsuits been filed against them by parents. The Milpitas adventure playground in California has been in operation since 1970 and has a similar safety record. However, public liability coverage is essential in case someone does get injured on the playground. The London Adventure Playground Association recommends that new playgrounds take out public liability coverage, employer's liability, burglary, and fire insurance. If the adventure playground is built on the grounds of a school or public park, it may be covered by existing insurance.

A review of European data by Pat Fierro, Recreation Supervisor for Huntington Beach, California, did not find a single recorded fatality at any adventure playground during 25 years of operation. In yet another United States context, the Houston, Texas, Mountain Park adventure playground sponsors recorded few injuries. Only .014 percent of the 15,000 people attending the park during its first 4 months of operation sustained injuries and these were mostly skinned knees, scrapes, and hammered thumbs.

There appears to be an important reason why serious injuries are so rare on European adventure playgrounds. The children have more extensive experiences in climbing, jumping, swinging, balancing, judging, perceiving, and in risk taking than do their American counterparts, who typically have only 20 to 30 minutes of playground activity each day on fixed, uninteresting equipment. The author was amazed by the dexterity and skill of London children engaged in a game of tag after dark on an adventure playground consisting of rope tree swings over steep terrain, aerial walkways, and multilevel climbing structures, all involving potential risk for serious injury because of unprotected heights and assorted debris littering the ground. During the 1990 IPA conference in Tokyo, the author observed Japanese children, three- to five-years-old, engaging successfully in unusually challenging climbing activities involving ropes, ladders, and climbing platforms at heights forbidden in American playgrounds for preschool age children. The Japanese philosophy places responsibility for accident and injury with the user while encouraging challenge and mastery with adult (parent and playleader) supervision. The role of the adult is to assist in preparation of the environment and to provide encouragement and support.

Characteristics of the Play Environment

The area of the play environment should range from a minimum of one-third acre to about four acres; anything larger would be difficult to supervise properly. Adventure playgrounds vary greatly in size and function. The range includes a small city lot with nothing more than a pile of scrap lumber and a portable cart containing tools, to elaborate playgrounds with a permanent recreation building and areas for gardening, animal care, and ball play, as well as a construction area. If a permanent site cannot be secured, a trailer with chemical toilets would serve nicely as a playground office.

Figures 11.20 and 11.21 depict a sample adventure playground.[2] (No two adventure playgrounds are alike.) It covers approximately two acres and includes a permanent recreation center. The playground is staffed by two full-time play leaders as well as parent volunteers. The playground offers activities for children ranging from preschoolers to adolescents, and the recreation center is used by a wide range of community groups for meetings. The following is a description of important elements:

Fencing

The entire playground is usually enclosed by a fence. The main objection to adventure playgrounds is their untidy appearance. Therefore, the fence is constructed so that the playground cannot be seen from street level. Portholes, however, may be placed at intervals so that curious passers-by can view the children's activities. An enclosed playground also gives children a sense of being

---

[2]Appreciation is extended to Andrew P. Cohen for drawing the designs.

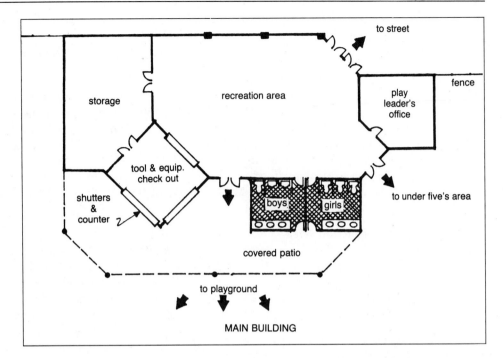

FIGURE 11.20 *Sample adventure playground site.*

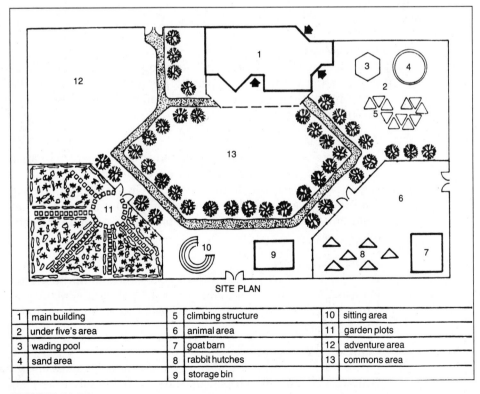

FIGURE 11.21

1	main building	5	climbing structure	10	sitting area
2	under five's area	6	animal area	11	garden plots
3	wading pool	7	goat barn	12	adventure area
4	sand area	8	rabbit hutches	13	commons area
		9	storage bin		

in their own private world. The fence should contain a large gate to allow trucks to enter.

Main Building–Recreation Center

Ideally the main building should contain the play leader's office; lavatories with access from both indoors and outdoors; storage area for play equipment; indoor play area equipped with art supplies, ping pong table, record player, etc.; storage and check out area for construction and gardening tools (this area should have shutters and a counter that opens to the outside so that children do not have to come inside to get their tools). Many Scandinavian buildings contain provisions (feed, etc.) for the care of animals. In Denmark the children pay a small fee for their animal feed but they must assume the responsibility for care of their animal(s).

Construction Area

This is the area in which the children build their club houses, forts, and other constructions, dig in the ground, light fires, and cook. A varied terrain makes for a more interesting environment. Large boulders and tree trunks are found on many Scandinavian playgrounds. The play leaders must check that all constructions on the playground are safe, not just when they are erected, but all the time.

Storage Bin

It is advisable to construct simple, open bins for storing scrap materials that the children will use for construction. The bin may be divided into compartments so that the materials may be sorted by size, shape, and weight. The bin should be placed so that deliveries of building materials may be easily made.

Garden Area

A garden area can provide a rich learning experience for children. Since children enjoy caring for their own plants, part of the garden should be divided into small plots. Stepping stones are sometimes placed throughout the garden to avoid trampling plants.

Animal Area

Part of every child's education should include the care of animals. Many playgrounds in Sweden and Denmark have animal houses that contain individual cages for children who do not have room in small apartments to keep their pets. On some playgrounds dozens of rabbit hutches are built and maintained by the children. In addition, pens and stables are provided for goats, chickens, pigs, and horses.

Under Five's Area

A separate area for children five and under should be placed away from the mainstream of the playground. This area should contain provisions for sand and water play, a bike path for wheeled toys, large outdoor building blocks, and a playhouse.

Commons Area

This is a flat grassy area that can be used for ball games and games with rules. Scandinavian and British playgrounds are frequently found adjacent to playing grounds where soccer and other competitive games are played.

Fire Pits

Part of the adventure playground experience includes building fires. Therefore, an area for small fires should be provided as well as a large pit for lighting bonfires on special occasions. Grills should also be provided so that children can cook. Many European playgrounds have a large pot over an open fire for making stew. Children bring various ingredients from home to contribute to the pot.

CONCLUSION: MAKING A COMMITMENT

In applying Lady Allen's classification scheme for playgrounds to the United States it is obvious that we have yet to emerge from the iron age. In order for adventure playgrounds to flourish in this country, a commitment must be made to provide quality play experiences for children. This commitment includes the active involvement of community members and governmental agencies in planning for play. When new housing developments and schools are planned, funds should be allocated to support recreation programs and full-time play leaders.

Given the growing estrangement of American children from their parents, the increasing tendency of both parents to work, the growing trend of reliance upon television for entertainment and peers for friendship and advice, the need for more satisfactory alternatives to socialization and care is compelling. For several reasons, adventure playgrounds offer one of the most favorable learning climates available for children in our society.

First, a growing body of research reveals the developmental benefits of play. Play has therapeutic benefits in that it allows children to play out their needs, concerns—yes, even their fears and frustrations from urban living. It promotes many aspects of cognitive development including verbal judgement, reasoning, manipulative skills, discovery, and divergent production. It improves problem solving, and language development, and enhances creativity. Play is one of our most important processes for passing on our culture. Culture arises in play and is enhanced and becomes more differentiated and complex through the role play of young children.

Play is also a great socializing agent, particularly in the context of a variety of rich, creative materials and sensitive adult play leaders—adults who are warm, skillful, well-trained, and who assist children in their constructions and their imaginative activities without becoming conspicuous or didactic. These are primary marks of an effective play leader. Such adults can indeed help to compensate for the frustration of broken homes, the absence of parents, and the conflicts that arise in family life, school activities, and crowded urban environments. Sensitive, caring adults are not just desirable. They are absolutely essential for young children. All too often, busy teachers in the context of academia do not have the time or the endurance to provide the human relationships required by young children.

Adventure playgrounds are light years apart from traditional playgrounds staffed with outmoded, galvanized, fixed equipment that is frequently hazardous and ill-suited for the developmental needs of children. The typical playground is equipped only for exercise play and ignores imaginative play, construction play, and the rich interactions between children and between children and adults that the adventure playground provides.

The adventure playground is a place where children are free to do many of those things that urban society has taken from them. They can play in the sand, dig holes, cook, build climbing structures and houses with scrap materials, learn to use tools, and otherwise develop those social, cognitive, and motor skills that are restricted by lack of space, materials, and opportunities in urban society. Through adventure playgrounds the advantages of the country and farm—working with animals, gardening, becoming one with nature—can be brought to the city and crowded school environments. Every urban child can profit from substituting the rich opportunities that adventure playgrounds provide for after-school television viewing. History will judge harshly those adults who hold the distorted, narrow view that children's play should be restricted to concrete and steel jungles and that play environments should be merely neat and tidy and appealing to the adult eye.

Those who spend long hours observing and participating with children at play, the adventure playground is seen as an antidote to frustrations and anxieties imposed on modern society by overspecialization, overindustralization, and overstructuralization of environments for children.

Experience in Europe during the past 30 years has shown that, besides the obvious benefits to children, adventure playgrounds exert a positive influence on the larger community. They bring people together, create a sense of community, and serve as a catalyst for other projects. They add to the quality of life.

REFERENCES

Abernethy, D., & Otter, M. (1979). History of IPA: Part II. *IPA Newsletter* 7:3–4. Sheffield, England.

Allen, Lady of Hurtwood. (1968). *Planning for Play*. Cambridge, MA: M.I.T. Press.

Bengtsson, A. (1979). History of IPA: Part III. *IPA Newsletter* 7:6–8. Sheffield, England.

Friedberg, P.M. (1970). *Play and Interplay*. New York: Macmillan.

Jago, L. (1971). *Learning through Experience*. London: London Adventure Playground Association.

Mauldin, M.A., & Giles, J.R. (1989). *Adventure Playground Final Evaluation Report*. Houston, TX: Mauldin Consulting Services.

Sarahan, N., & Hager, R. (1980). *Where Do The Children Play? On Adventure Playgrounds*. Houston, TX: The Park People, Inc.

Wretlind-Larsson, S. (1979). History of IPA: Part I. *IPA Newsletter* 7:15–17. Sheffield, England.

SUGGESTED READINGS

Allen, Lady of Hurtwood. (1974). *Adventure Playgrounds for Handicapped Children*. London: James Galt.

Bengtsson, A. (1974). *Adventure Playgrounds*. New York: Praeger.

——. (1974). *The Child's Right to Play*. Sheffield: International Playground Association.

——. (1970). *Environmental Planning for Children's Play*. New York: Praeger.

International Playground Association (1972). *Play and Creativity: Planning the Environment and Training Leaders*. Report of the Fifth International Conference, Vienna, September 1972.

International Playground Association (1969). *Playgrounds: With or Without Leadership?* Report of the Fourth International Conference, Paris, July 1969.

Lamberg, J. (1974). *Adventure Playgrounds*. London: Jonathan Cape.

A Little About Lots: The Do-It-Yourself Book on Improving Vacant Lots and Neighborhoods. The Parks Council of New York City, 80 Central Park West, New York, NY 10023.

National Playing Fields Association. (1976). *What is an Adventure Playground?* London: The Association.

Passantino, E.D. (1975). Adventure playground for learning and socialization. *Phi Delta Kappan* 56:329–333.

Pederson, J. (1985). The adventure playgrounds of Denmark. In *When Children Play*. (eds.) J.L. Frost and S. Sunderlin. Wheaton, MD: Association for Childhood Education International.

Rudolph, N. (1974). *Workyards: Playgrounds Planned for Adventure*. New York: Teachers College Press.

Salzer, M. (1974). A better world for big-city children to play in. *Current Sweden* 34, 5 pp.

Shaw, L.G. (1982). *Adventure Play Environments for Disabled Children*. Gainesville, FL: College of Architecture, University of Florida.

Sigsgaard, J. (1965). The playground in modern Danish housing. Reprint from *Danish Foreign Office Journal* 54, 8 pp.

Utzinger, R.C. (1970). *Some European Nursery Schools and Playgrounds*. Ann Arbor: Architectural Research Laboratory of the University of Michigan.

Ward, C., & Blunden, G. (1974). *Safety on Adventure Playgrounds*. London: National Playing Fields Association.

"All children need a place to play. They need space, informality, freedom to run around and make a noise, to express themselves, to experiment and investigate. Mentally and physically handicapped children . . . need this freedom even more than others."[1]

12

Playgrounds For All Children

Educators use a variety of labels, designations, and terms when referring to children with special needs. Terms such as exceptional, disabled, impaired, handicapped, and special are often used interchangeably, but may have different connotations. *Exceptional* refers to children who deviate from the norm to the extent that they need special services for optimum development. *Disabled* refers to children with reduced capabilities in one or more areas of exceptionality: physical disabilities (e.g., health and orthopedic impairments), communication disabilities (e.g., speech and hearing impairments), and developmental and learning disabilities (e.g., mental retardation, cerebral palsy, hyperactivity, multiple handicaps). Table 12.1 outlines these categories and their social and personal consequences. *Impairment* is sometimes used as a synonym for disability and refers to incapacity or injury.

Handicapped refers to physical, mental, emotional, or communication deficiencies that impair learning. Special is often used as a synonym for exceptional or handicapped but in the broadest sense includes giftedness.

The arguments against labeling children are compelling, including the possibility of stigmatizing, discrimination, loss of self esteem, and consequent negative developmental effects. There are indeed specific disabilities that must be diagnosed and treated. It is one matter, however, to identify needs and prescribe

---

[1]Allen, M. (1975). *Adventure Playgrounds for Handicapped Children*, Foreword London: James Galt.

TABLE 12.1   CATEGORIES OF DISABILITIES AND THEIR CONSEQUENCES

Category	Specific Handicaps	Social and Personal Consequences

Physical	Crippled
	Birth defects
	Blind and partially
	  sighted
	Neurological disorders
	
	  Cerebral palsy
	
	  Epilepsy
	
	Health impaired
		The child has problems with:
		Mobility
		Experiencing the world through all of
		  his senses
		Mastering his physical and human
		  environments
		People who are too helpful or too
		  demanding
		People who do not understand his
		  difficulties in gaining mastery over
		  his world
		Isolation
		Diminished energy

Communication	Speech
	Deaf and hard of
	  hearing
	Language disorders
	  of childhood
	
	Severe language delay
	Multihandicapped
		The child has problems with:
		Learning or using verbal symbols to
		  think and communicate about his world
		Isolation
		Dealing with academic learning which
		  requires the use of verbal symbols

**Development
  and learning**
	Mental retardation
	Behavior disorders
	Specific learning
	  disabilities
		The child has problems with:
		Reduced interest in the world
		Difficulty in relating positively to children
		  and/or adults
		Developing internal controls
		Failure to live up to expectations
		Rejection and isolation

treatment and quite another to classify, label, and group children together in neat packages, isolated from the mainstream. Granted, legal requirements for special services require identification of disabilities and professionals must know what disabilities they are treating, but society has taken the position that handicapped children must be educated in the least restrictive setting. This stand has been translated into law.

The Education for All Handicapped Children Act (P.L. 94-142) enacted in 1975 mandates that:

- All handicapped children (ages 3–18) must receive a free public education. (Beginning at age 3 allows early identification and education).

- An individualized educational plan must be prepared for each handicapped child.
- Evaluation instruments must be racially and culturally non-discriminatory.
- Handicapped and non-handicapped children must be educated together to the maximum extent possible.
- The law applies to both public and private schools.

On July 26, 1990, President Bush signed into law The Americans with Disabilities Act (P.L. 101-336). The ADA Act helps to assure full equality for people with disabilities. It extends to them civil rights similar to those available on the basis of race, sex, color, religion, and national origin as guaranteed by the Civil Rights Act of 1964. The ADA addresses public accommodations, businesses, and services operated by private entities, and provides that:

> "No individual shall be discriminated against on the basis of disability in the full and equal enjoyment of the goods, services, facilities, privileges, advantages, and accommodations of any place of public accommodation." (P.L. 101-336 Title III)

From ethical and moral perspectives, the principles that underlie P.L. 94-142 and P.L. 101-336 should apply not only to formal classrooms and educational settings but also to children's play and play environments. Placing and educating children in the least restrictive settings is consistent with law and with the guiding principles of the International Association for Children's Right to Play. Since the passage of P.L. 94-142, major efforts to mainstream children in play environments have been initiated. Two of these are the New York City project, A Playground for all Children (U.S. Department of Housing & Urban Development 1978), and the Play for All project (Moore, Goltsman, & Iacofano 1987). Both of these projects, to be discussed later, established guidelines and procedures for integrating all children (special and regular) in outdoor play environments. The title of this chapter, "Playgrounds for All Children," indicates the authors intent to pursue this goal.

Depending upon the nature of their disability, children may experience difficulty in such skills as: extent of exploration; initiation of activities; response and approach to others; attention to people, materials, and tasks; acceptance of limits and routines; respect for rights of others; seeing self as able to do and achieve.

Adults who work with special children must understand that there are broad individual differences between children with similar handicaps. Standardized educational fare is no more appropriate for them than for other children. Adults must approach children with expectations for growth. Perhaps the single most important principle in working with special children is that they can learn and they want to learn. They are human beings with normal needs for love, praise, attention, success, pleasure, and self-esteem, but, because of the social and personal consequences of their condition, it is more difficult for them to acquire them.

As we have seen in Chapter 1, play is the vehicle by which children develop and demonstrate competency in dealing with their environment. If a handicapping condition results in play deprivation, the child's competence in interacting with people and objects will also be lacking.

PLAY AND MENTALLY RETARDED CHILDREN

Mentally retarded children typically lack the skills needed to engage in higher level cognitive and social play. When placed on the floor in close proximity to toys, severely retarded children may not move from the position in which they are placed, reach out to examine toys, or imitate the actions of others. Down's Syndrome and autistic children tend to elaborate the same idea repeatedly during play (Riguet & Taylor 1981). The problem is further complicated by the attitudes and actions of people and institutions who care for retarded people and institutions who care for retarded children. Most agree that retarded children have the same play needs as other children, but retarded children, especially those in school, may have fewer opportunities to play and few materials and playgrounds that are designed for their play. The conclusions of Benoit (1955) over three decades ago are still relevant today.

- Adults may underestimate the potential of retarded children to develop skills in play.
- There has been limited thinking and writing on the subject of play and retarded children.
- Much of the existing play equipment and materials is questionable for normal children and is unsuitable for the retarded.
- Mental retardation is frequently linked with special deficiencies that make play difficult.
- There is an attitude of hopelessness toward teaching play activities to retarded children.
- There is prevailing ignorance concerning the importance of play in the development of both normal and retarded children.
- There is overconcern with accident and injury.

Once positive attitudes concerning play and retarded children have been developed, parents and care-givers are faced with the task of teaching retarded children how to play. Whereas play, imitation, and exploration occur as a matter of course in normal children, play and other associated behaviors must be systematically planned for and taught to retarded children.

A number of people have studied the play behaviors of mentally retarded children. Some tentative generalizations are available.

The social play and interactive behaviors of mentally retarded children (Down's Syndrome) differ significantly from that of normal children (Beeghly, Perry, & Cicchetti 1989). In general, mentally retarded children develop similarly, although at a slower pace, in object and social play (Motti, Cicchetti, & Stroufe 1983; Cunningham, et al. 1985). Children with Down's Syndrome compared to normal children have deficits in exploratory strategies, object switching during object play (Kopp, Krakow, & Johnson 1983; Loveland 1987), and they are significantly delayed in complexity of symbolic play (Beeghly, Perry, & Cicchetti 1989). Overall, children with Down's Syndrome have similar correlational patterns among indices of play maturity, cognitive development, and social interaction as normal children (Cicchetti & Mans-Wagener 1987; Beighley, Perry, & Cicchetti 1989). These likenesses are particularly striking among younger children.

Social play can be increased by direct teaching, prompting, and rehearsing roles, followed by positive reinforcement (Paloutzian, et al. 1971; Strain 1975). Integrating handicapped children into play situations with nonhandicapped or higher-functioning peer models also increases their social play (Morris & Dolker 1974; Devoney, Guralnick, & Rubin 1974). Thus, it seems that tools already at our disposal, i.e., direct instruction, modeling, and reinforcement, can be valuable allies in promoting social play among mentally handicapped children. Further, the currently popular concept of mainstreaming or integrating handicapped and nonhandicapped children in the classroom should be extended to the outdoor play environment.

Accumulating evidence and experience refute two prominent beliefs about handicapped children: 1) Handicapped children don't play (or don't want to), and 2) Play is merely a good way for handicapped children to pass the time (McConkey 1985). Handicapped children may not live up to adults' expectations and failure becomes a self-fulfilling prophesy. They often fail to play because their prepared environment is not stimulating and does not take into account developmental abilities and disabilities or because the regimen of group care provides little or no opportunity for play.

The more tenable and productive view is that handicapped children do learn through play and when given opportunities, materials, and adult support, they do play. (Quinn & Rubin 1984; McConkey 1985). A growing number of indoor environments, including classrooms, are being modified beyond the mere provision of traditional toys. These include "soft play environments" consisting of rooms filled with large vinyl-covered foam or air-filled mattresses in varying shapes, colors, and sizes (McConkey 1985). Colored lights and soothing music can heighten children's interest in special toys. Toys that light up or emit sounds enhance the effects that children are able to produce when playing with the toy and, consequently, sustain their play (Thomas, Phemister, & Richardson 1981). With the development of increasingly intricate electronics, children (and adults) with extreme physical handicaps can activate toys, play equipment, tape recorders, television sets, and video-games by pushing a pad, blowing, or sucking, or by merely breaking a light beam.

Mentally retarded children should be thoroughly evaluated to determine the extent of any motor or sensory deficits and a review of their behaviors should be conducted. This includes analysis of imitation behaviors, tracking and searching skills, language competencies, and social interaction skill. Additional behaviors that have rarely been measured by researchers and clinicians include frequency of action on play materials and toys; diversity of play behaviors, i.e., frequency of novel responses; range of toys or materials acted on; frequency of interaction between peers and number of different peers interacted with; affective or aggressive behavior during play periods (Wehman 1975:242).

In working with severely retarded children who have limited skills, it may be more appropriate to work on a wide range of parallel activities at a low developmental level rather than attempting to achieve a high level of sophistication in one play skill, i.e., block design.

PLAY AND BLIND CHILDREN

When young children are deprived of sight, the quality of their interaction with the environment is greatly reduced. They have much difficulty orienting to space and time and in separating reality from nonreality. As a result the play behavior of young blind children is greatly reduced and attempts to engage them in play may be difficult. Many are content to be left alone or to engage in repetitive, stereotyped behaviors (Sandler 1963:344–345).

Blind children, as well as those with other handicapping conditions (e.g., deaf, cerebral palsy, language impaired), share a common helplessness in negotiating special challenges and tasks. Many unwilling adults encourage this helplessness by assuming that such children cannot learn and by failing to provide stimulating environments. Such attitudes and practices have probably led to the findings that play is far less frequently pursued and considerably less important in the blind child's life than in the life of the child with full vision (Rothschild 1960; Tait 1973).

Lack of interest and involvement in the play of blind children need not be an accepted condition of their lives. Blind children are less imaginative in their play than sighted children (Singer & Streiner 1966) but special attention to training in fantasy play and imaginative story-telling helps to improve this condition.

As we have seen in previous chapters, spontaneous play is essential in the intellectual and affective development of the child. Although blind children possess normal intellectual potential, the full potential of a blind child may not be reached due to a lack of spontaneous play and an impoverished fantasy life. Well-meaning professionals may attempt to meet the play needs of blind children by involving them in organized group games and activities. However, these activities cannot be substituted for creative play which develops independently and spontaneously. Parents and educators must become more aware of the importance of play for healthy development and teach blind children how to play so that their full potentialities may be realized.

The following are suggestions for enhancing the play of blind children:

Planning for Play

Before the free-play period begins, discuss with the children the various play options that are available to them: equipment, materials, toys, games, activities, playmates. Have the children discuss their favorite play activities and what they intend doing during the play period.

Sensory-rich Play Environment

Design the play environment to include a wide variety of sensory cues to alert and guide the blind child in play, especially through the use of the senses of touch, hearing, and spatial perception. Large play equipment should remain in predictable locations to prevent accidental collisions. Subtle differences in changes of texture and/or slope of the walkway or areas surrounding play equipment would help to orient the child (Morris 1974). The child could be trained to sense the slight change in temperature that occurs when walking through a shadow cast by an adjacent or overhead play structure. Tactile maps placed at strategic points would also help to orient the child as would cassette tape recorders with directions. The environment should have a rich variety of textures and materials including sand, gravel, dirt, mud, large rocks; various textures of wood, water, grass, hills; places to crawl into, and through; things to climb, swing, and slide on; plants and animals.

Rehearsal

The teacher should rehearse with the child the use of the various play materials and equipment. For example, the teacher could practice with the child climbing up a slide and sliding down, rolling down a grassy hill, climbing up and down a play structure, and so on.

Reinforcement

The teacher should be constantly ready to reinforce appropriate play behavior and accomplishments of the child. Reinforcement should be gradually faded out so that play can become intrinsically rewarding.

Mainstreaming

Blind children should be placed in an integrated setting with sighted children. Children are the ultimate teachers of other children.

Feedback and Evaluation

The teacher should evaluate each play period with the children. It is not important that they stick to their original plan. What is important is that the teacher help the children to reflect on what they did and to offer encouragement and praise.

PLAY AND CHILDREN WITH BEHAVIORAL DISABILITIES

Behavior disorders are "deviation from age-appropriate behavior which significantly interferes with (1) the child's own growth and development and/or (2) the lives of others" (Kirk 1972:389). Children with behavior disorders compose the largest percentage of exceptional children. Children with behavior disorders may be extremely withdrawn or may exhibit severe acting-out behavior. They are children of average intelligence who do not interact effectively with their environment or with other people.

The best indication of positive social interaction of young children is age-appropriate play with other children. Instead of playing appropriately with toys or other children, autistic children frequently engage in self-stimulatory behaviors. For example, instead of moving a toy truck appropriately along the ground, the child might turn the truck upside down and spin the wheels for long periods. Or, the child might ignore toys and other people and sit in a corner of the room and rhythmically rock back and forth.

The basic procedures in behavior modification are (1) identification and measurement of maladaptive behavior to be extinguished and new adaptive behaviors to be taught, (2) systematic reinforcement to teach adaptive behavior,

(3) gradual fading out of reinforcement to be replaced by intrinsic, naturally occurring rewards. The adult controls both the conditions under which the behavior occurs (physical and social setting) and provides appropriate consequences (ignoring, reward) immediately following a target behavior.

PLAY THERAPY

Play therapy is a set of techniques used to help children with emotional behavioral problems. It is founded on psychoanalytic theory which is concerned with the dynamics of personality and the unconscious feelings of an individual. It is based upon the fact that play is the child's natural medium of self-expression, and, just as in adult therapy where an individual "talks out" his difficulties, in play therapy the child is provided an opportunity to "play out" feelings and problems (Axline 1969:9).

There are at least six theoretical approaches to the therapeutic use of play (Schaefer & O'Connor 1983; Schaefer 1985). The *psychoanalytic approach* to play therapy emphasizes the use of the therapist's interpretation of a child's words and actions to help the child achieve insight into his unconscious conflicts. The therapist seldom directly intervenes or attempts to structure the child's play but rather reflects on the child's words and actions. "I can see that you are very angry Billy." The goal of the *release* or *cathartic approach* is to work through emotional conflicts by symbolically directing the child's aggression toward the source of conflict. For example, a child may beat on a Bobo doll or symbolically hurt a parent by attacking a doll resembling a parent figure. Axline (1969) stresses the importance of creating a *climate of trust* in which the therapist shows acceptance of the child and trust in the child's ability to "play out" her own problems. The *play group approach* adds the influence of group dynamics to the therapeutic process. The *limit-setting approach* places emphasis on setting clear and enforceable rules regarding a child's behavior in the playroom. For example, if the child is very destructive or physically aggressive toward the therapist or other children, she might be removed from the playroom and not be allowed to return until the next scheduled session. The final approach uses behavior modification to extinguish maladaptive behavior and to teach new appropriate ones. Although these techniques represent different theoretical orientations, they are by no means mutually exclusive and may be used in conjunction depending upon the needs of the child.

Based upon the initial interview with the parents and child and on the therapist's initial observations of the child, long-term goals will be established. They might include such things as a decrease in aggressive, acting-out behavior; an expression of greater self-esteem; a decrease in anger and corresponding positive feelings directed towards a family member. Typically the child spends an hour at a time in the playroom with the therapist. At times the therapist may be nonassertive and observe the child for long periods without communicating. At other times she may take a very active role. Therapy may also be conducted with small groups of children. Axline (1969) developed basic principles of play therapy that still guide other professionals:

- The therapist must develop a warm, friendly relationship with the child as soon as possible.

- The therapist accepts the child exactly as she is.
- The therapist is alert in recognizing the feeling the child is expressing and reflects them back to her in such a manner that he gains insight into her behavior.
- The therapist demonstrates a strong belief in the child's ability to solve her own problems and provides her an opportunity to do so.
- The therapist does not attempt to direct the child's actions or conversation in any manner (this would not be true in behaviorally oriented therapy).
- Therapy should be viewed as a gradual process and it should not be hurried.
- The therapist establishes only those limitations that are necessary to anchor the therapy to the world of reality and to make the child aware of her responsibility in the relationship.

Carter (1987) divides play therapy into two types, directive and nondirective. In directed play therapy the therapist designs the activity, chooses the medium, and makes the rules. In nondirective play therapy the child chooses the mediums, rules, the way playthings are used, and the time for play. The nondirective approach is becoming increasingly popular.

The therapist provides a play environment, structured or unstructured, that will support three stages in play therapy evolution: 1) the establishment of intimacy between therapist and child, 2) the development of the child's ability to express his feelings symbolically, and 3) the development of congruence or harmony between the child's behavior and his or her level of development (Wright et. al. 1981).

Play therapy is based on the assumption that everything said or done by the child in the playroom has meaning to the child. However, it is difficult to understand and interpret all of a child's play messages. The task becomes easier when appropriate play materials are provided. For example, a child may enact family scenes by using dolls that represent family members. However, in the absence of dolls, a child may symbolically represent herself and a parent using a big and a little block, causing the therapist to miss the message. The playroom should contain a wide range of materials that lend themselves to self-expression. For example, a child should be able to express anger by punching dolls, or destroying clay figures, as well as by composing poems, writing stories, and painting pictures that depict her anger. Axline (1969, p. 54) suggests the following list of toys and materials:

nursing bottles	large rag doll
doll family	puppets
house with furniture	puppet screen
toy soldiers and army	crayons
equipment	clay
toy animals	finger paints
play dough	sand
pictures of people, horses, and	water
other animals	toy guns, peg pounding set
empty berry baskets to smash	paper dolls

variety of art materials   little cars and airplanes

didee doll

playhouse materials: table, chairs, cot, doll bed, stove, tin dishes, pans, spoons, doll clothes, clothes line, clothes pins, clothes basket

Parents and Teachers as Therapists

Parents and teachers may gain insights into the feelings of children and help them to work through emotional problems by conducting play sessions in the home or school. A range of resources is available to guide play sessions (see Yawkey & Pellegrini 1984). Guerney (1976) established guidelines for parents to use in play therapy. The same guidelines may also apply to teachers with slight practical modifications for use in the school.

- Set aside a specific time and place. In the beginning, one-half hour per week is sufficient. Later the length of the sessions can be increased. The time of the session should not be changed from week to week nor should a session be cancelled. It is important that a strict schedule be adhered to so that progress will not be impeded.
- Find a location where there will be no distractions. If the phone rings, let it ring. Make arrangements so that the session will not be interrupted by other adults or children. Play therapy is messy at times so find a room where there will be least concern if things get spoiled or broken.
- Toys should be selected in order to help the child release his aggressions and to represent his feelings (see Ginott 1960; 1961; Axline 1969). The toys should be reserved for use in the play session only. The child may not take or use toys out of the session.
- In setting up the first session, it is not necessary to go into a long explanation with the child. You may simply say you want to spend more time with him. Place the emphasis on *you* wanting to be together, have fun, and improve your relationship, not that you want to help *him*.

The role of a parent and teacher in a play session is to establish an atmosphere of free play and acceptance for the child. You set the stage by establishing time parameters and the few basic rules, but at the same time make it clear that what the child says and does in the session are totally up to him. The adult must be willing to follow the lead of the child. Therefore, it is important that the parent or teacher engage in:

No criticism

No praise, approval, or encouragement

No questions, leads, or invitations

No suggestions, advice, or persuasion

No interruptions or interference

No information

No teaching, preaching, or moralizing

No initiating a new activity

While it is important for the adult not to interfere, it is equally important for the adult to be fully involved with the child by giving complete attention to everything the child says and does. If the adult is asked to join in an activity, he should do so while focusing attention on what the child wants the adult to do, following his direction, and reflecting on his feelings. Play therapy can be very rewarding for both adult and child. The child is able to play out his feelings and the adult can learn more about his own feelings toward the child. It can strengthen and improve the quality of the relationship outside the therapy session.

PLAY AND PHYSICALLY HANDICAPPED CHILDREN

Children with physical handicaps include those who are crippled, have congenital defects, neurological disorders such as cerebral palsy and epilepsy, or other health impairments. The American Standards Association (1961) lists the following categories of physical impairments:

1. *Nonambulatory disabilities* are those impairments that, regardless of cause, confine individuals to wheelchairs.
2. *Semiambulatory disabilities* are those impairments that cause individuals to walk with difficulty or insecurity; examples include individuals with cardiac and pulmonary ills, those who require the use of braces, crutches, or canes, as well as persons who are arthritics, amputees, or spastics.
3. *Incoordination disabilities* include faulty coordination or play due to brain, spinal, or peripheral nerve injuries.

A child with a physical handicap may be of normal or superior intelligence. He may, however, have problems mastering his physical environment, especially environments that are not designed to accommodate physically handicapped persons. He may have difficulty dealing with his human environment in that he may encounter people who are too helpful of too demanding, or people who do not understand his physical difficulties. He may also suffer from isolation in that he may be excluded from the play activities enjoyed by nonhandicapped children of his age because of man-made barriers, both physical and personal.

In order to facilitate the play of physically handicapped children, special care must be taken in the design of the play environment. Playgrounds for handicapped children should be super-enriched environments that provide many opportunities for cognitive learning (symbolizing, conceptualizing, problem solving) as well as opportunities for physical learning (vestibular, kinesthetic, proprioceptive, and sensory). The elements of the play environment should be similar to those of creative playgrounds (Chapter 6): opportunities for sand, mud, and water play; play structures that provide opportunities for exploration; fantasy and gross motor play; digging and gardening; animal care; carpentry; and a wealth of loose parts to stimulate creative play.

The primary consideration in designing a playground for physically handicapped children is one of accessibility. All areas of the playground, plus all play apparatus and structures, must be accessible to all children, even children in wheelchairs. The following are suggestions for meeting this goal:[2]

1. The layout of the playground should allow for continuous circulation. A paved path, at least 36 in. wide to accommodate wheelchairs, should wind throughout the entire playground in an intersecting closed loop design (see Figure 12.1a).

2. Paths should not exceed a slope of 5 percent (a rise of 1 ft. over a distance of 20 ft.). Best suited to wheelchair travel are walks with slopes of 3 to 4 percent.

3. Ramps one uses to gain access to buildings, play apparatus, hills, bridges, etc. should not exceed a slope of 8.33 percent (a rise of 1 ft. over a distance of 12 ft.). Best suited for wheelchair travel are ramps with slopes of 6 percent (a rise of 1 ft. over a distance of 16.6 ft.) (see Figure 12.1b).

4. Sand and water play areas should be raised at least 30 in. high on one end with a 36 in. deep by 30 in. wide indentation to allow children in wheelchairs to enjoy and play without removal from chair (see Figure 12.3). However, wheelchair-bound children should be encouraged to leave the chair to play in sand and water, play on slide, or roll down hills.

5. Handrails should be provided on all ramps and play structures (see Figure 12.4).

6. Stairs should be avoided. If stairs are present they should not be recessed (see Figure 12.5).

7. Slides must provide access to all types of handicaps (see Figure 12.6).
   A. No ladders and legs should be used on slides.
   B. Slides should be embedded in a grassy mound. Access to the top of the slide should be a ramp or series of ramps.
   C. Grab bars should be provided along ramps and tops and bottoms of slides to accommodate the semiambulant.

8. Conventional swings are adequate for most handicapped children. For severely handicapped children, special swings can be used.

9. Spray pools could be considered for those who cannot be submerged in water. Spray pools should consist of the following:
   A. A jet of water which rises to a height of at least 7 ft. and then falls to a paved basin that has sufficient drainage.
   B. Benches should be provided in the spray area for those with restricted mobility.
   C. A clear area for movement of children in wheelchairs should be provided.

10. Gates and doorways should swing both ways and should be a minimum of 2 ft. 8 in. wide (see Figures 12.3–12.5).

11. Drinking and toilet facilities should be made accessible to all children.

---

[2]Adapted from "A Playground for all Children: Design Competition, August 1976," New York City Department of Planning and U.S. Department of Housing and Urban Development. By permission.

Designs by Louis Bowers.

FIGURE 12.1 Play environments for special children should be super-enriched environments that allow for continuous circulation.

Scottish Rite Hospital for Crippled Children in Dallas, Texas.*

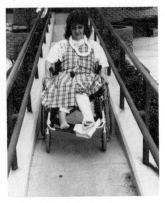

FIGURE 12.2 The primary consideration in designing a playground for physically disabled or crippled children is accessibility.

FIGURE 12.3 Sand and water play areas should be raised to accommodate children in wheelchairs.

FIGURE 12.4 Handrails should be provided on all ramps and play structures.

*Courtesy of Robert Walker, Administrator

Alternatives in Equipment Design.

FIGURE 12.5 *Maxidex, Inc. features linked play decks with wide access ramps. Height is reduced for ease of access.*

FIGURE 12.6 *The Maxidex play area for upper body exercise invites wheelchair access. Children are protected from falls by firm (for wheelchair travel) yet resilient (for safety) surface material.*

FIGURE 12.7 *This play area by Landscape Structures Inc. illustrates play equipment combinations that accommodate all children, disabled and non-disabled.*

FIGURE 12.8 *This BigToy play structure includes a large central deck where wheelchairs are parked while children are using the equipment.*

FIGURE 12.9 *Children's Playgrounds, Inc. custom designs and builds playgrounds for all children.*

DESIGNING PLAY ENVIRONMENTS FOR ALL CHILDREN

A major effort to develop a complete guide to the planning, design, and management of outdoor play environments for *all* children, including children with special needs, was initiated in 1984 by PLAE, Inc. (Play and Learning in Adaptable Environments). Play experience workshops were organized in 10 American cities (including one by the author in Austin, Texas), in which disabled adults and children reflected upon their play experiences and made recommendations on "designing for diversity" and making play environments safer and developmentally sound for all children. In 1986, professionals and specialists in fields related to children's play representing almost 200 agencies and institutions met at Stanford University to review and revise an initial draft of *Play for All Guidelines: Planning Design, and Management of Outdoor Play Settings for All Children* (Moore,

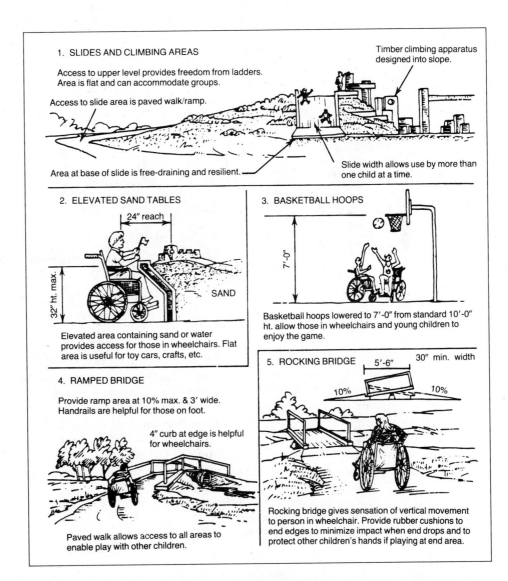

1. SLIDES AND CLIMBING AREAS

Access to upper level provides freedom from ladders. Area is flat and can accommodate groups.

Access to slide area is paved walk/ramp.

Area at base of slide is free-draining and resilient.

Timber climbing apparatus designed into slope.

Slide width allows use by more than one child at a time.

2. ELEVATED SAND TABLES

24" reach

32" ht. max.

SAND

Elevated area containing sand or water provides access for those in wheelchairs. Flat area is useful for toy cars, crafts, etc.

3. BASKETBALL HOOPS

7'-0"

Basketball hoops lowered to 7'-0" from standard 10'-0" ht. allow those in wheelchairs and young children to enjoy the game.

4. RAMPED BRIDGE

Provide ramp area at 10% max. & 3' wide. Handrails are helpful for those on foot.

4" curb at edge is helpful for wheelchairs.

Paved walk allows access to all areas to enable play with other children.

5. ROCKING BRIDGE   5'-6"   30" min. width

10%   10%

Rocking bridge gives sensation of vertical movement to person in wheelchair. Provide rubber cushions to end edges to minimize impact when end drops and to protect other children's hands if playing at end area.

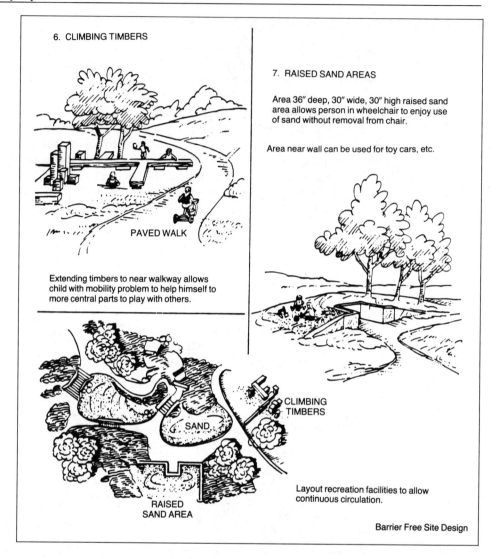

6. CLIMBING TIMBERS

7. RAISED SAND AREAS

Area 36″ deep, 30″ wide, 30″ high raised sand area allows person in wheelchair to enjoy use of sand without removal from chair.

Area near wall can be used for toy cars, etc.

PAVED WALK

Extending timbers to near walkway allows child with mobility problem to help himself to more central parts to play with others.

CLIMBING TIMBERS

SAND

RAISED SAND AREA

Layout recreation facilities to allow continuous circulation.

Barrier Free Site Design

Goltsman, & Iacofano 1987). The final document is a landmark publication for it combined the efforts of an extraordinary group of professionals in preparing the first comprehensive guide to outdoor play environments intended to accommodate the diverse needs of all children—special and normal.

The Play for All Guidelines support a common core of basic assumptions:

- children learn and develop through play.
- the quality and diversity of physical and social settings affect the quality and diversity of children's play.
- the quality and diversity of the social setting including play leadership directly affects play value.
- children with disabilities have a right to play opportunities.

- integration of disabled and able-bodied children is based on the concept of accessibility to the play environment *and* on the concept of positive, facilitative, attitude and awareness of the staff.
- the quality of play environments is threatened by liability costs and law-suits. Strategies and policies should be developed to protect the quality of children's play environments.

Louis Bowers, professor of Professional Physical Education at the University of South Florida has been researching and designing playgrounds for children with various physical and mental limitations and for able-bodied children since 1975. His playgrounds are designed to serve the physical, psychological, and social needs of all children. Experiences in touching, hearing, seeing, tasting,

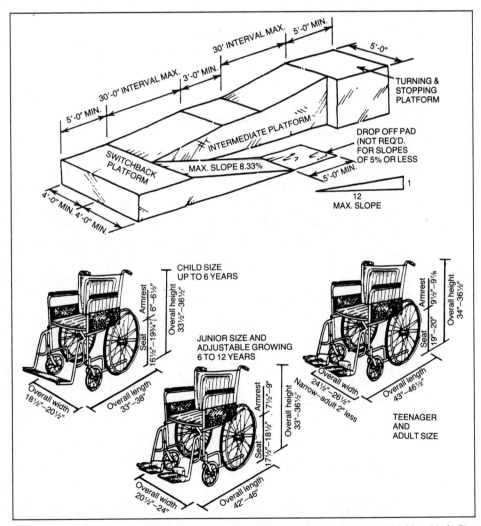

Adapted from "A Playground for all Children: Design Competition, August 1976," New York City Department of Planning and U.S. Department of Housing and Urban Development.

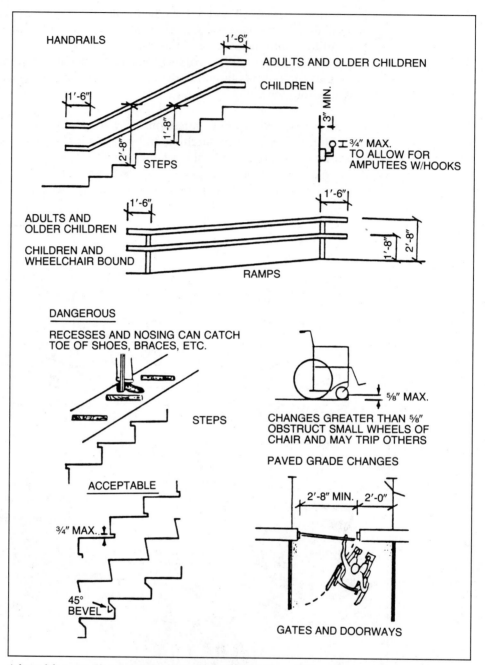

Adapted from "A Playground for all Children: Design Competition, August 1976," New York City Department of Planning and U.S. Department of Housing and Urban Development.

smelling, and/or feeling movement are essential in play (Bowers, 1983). Bowers advocates that a range of movement activities—rolling, crawling, climbing, walking, jumping, running, sliding—be built into an interconnected system of play. In addition, quiet activities should be included which stimulate the visual, auditory, tactile, and kinesthetic senses.

Bower's design principles (Bowers, 1979) include:

- play spaces should be accessible to all children and located in those areas of the community where children play.
- the distance between levels on play structures should be safe.
- play structures should incorporate a variety of inclines for children of varying ability levels.
- partially enclosed spaces should be provided which allow children to safely move and which serve as connecting links to other play areas.
- play equipment should be complex and stimulating, and a wide range of movable materials should be provided.
- interconnected play areas should provide easy movement through the entire play area.
- play equipment should be of sound design and materials should be non-toxic and durable.

Perhaps the most remarkable attitudinal outcome of the development of *Play for All Guidelines* is that high quality play environments for most children are high quality for *all* children—with fewer than predicted differences. Two major questions emerge: 1) What is a high quality play environment for most children, and 2) what adaptations are needed for *special* children? The answer to the first question is the subject matter for much of this book, but the answer to the second will be addressed here.

Providing for Special Needs

The special needs of handicapped children include: 1) special planning; 2) mobility, accessibility, and challenge; 3) play leaders with special skills; and 4) special attention to safety. Quotes in this section are from parents of handicapped children involved in the PLAE, Inc., Play for All Project.

Special Planning

A great deal of time and expense can be conserved by planning the playground for all children before any site preparation or construction has begun. Modifying existing playgrounds may require expensive alterations to existing slopes (e.g., wheeled vehicle tracks) and the addition of ramps to provide access to climbing/ sliding equipment. In many instances, the existing space will not allow ramp access to play apparatus because decks are too high or equipment is too close to fences and other permanent fixtures. Further, access by devices with wheels requires a surface, track, or ramp of sufficient density to support them. Sand, pea gravel, and other "loose" surfaces do not allow access by wheel chairs or other wheeled devices. In fact, sand and dirt will damage the moving mechanism (axles and bearings) of such equipment.

The people involved in planning should include play leaders, teachers, caretakers (depending on context—public park, public school, child-care center), administrators, special education personnel, playground specialists, parents, and the children themselves. The master plan should consider all the elements discussed in Chapter 6 plus the special planning/design elements discussed here. Throughout the planning process, care must be taken not to focus on disabilities to the extent that the playground lacks challenge and excitement.

> . . . it's important for a kid to be able to do as much as possible . . . you have to think
> about what abilities there are and try to design the playground toy or equipment
> around the ability. To hell with the disability. (parent)

Mobility, Accessibility, and Challenge

Careful design is even more important for handicapped children than for other
children. The specific types of handicaps of intended users of the playground
must be identified and provided for. Such provision begins with devising ways to
make children mobile. At the late Lady Allen of Hurtwood's adventure playgrounds in London, each child's handicap is assessed and transport vehicles are
designed or adapted to allow the children to propel themselves around the playground. Whatever the child's handicap, provisions are made (battery powered,
pedal powered with arms or feet, etc.) that allow independence of movement.

The play area must be transversed with tracks that accommodate wheel
chairs and adapted vehicles, giving proper attention to slope, width, type of
surface, and direct accessibility to play and structures. The material in these
tracks includes inexpensive conveyor belts, asphalt, and concrete, and, recently,
manufactured resilient material has been used in increasing frequency (see section on surfacing in Chapter 6). The major advantage of manufactured material
is its resiliency, which provides the extra margin of safety so essential for handicapped children. Consider the concerns and insights of parents of handicapped
children.

> . . . how do you roll a chair through the sand . . . I want the trail there but I'm afraid
> about what happens if you fall out . . . Why can't kids have that stuff like they put
> on high school running tracks? Is the stuff so expensive that there's no way that
> anybody in the world is really going to do it?

A critical issue is what do children see and do after they have access to
adapted vehicles for mobility and trails or tracks for access. The play structures
should include a broad array of graduated challenges which challenge the least
able and the most able. The level of challenge should be obvious to the child
and entry and exit areas should be available at various levels of challenge. None
of the challenges should impose unnecessary hazards. As manufacturers and
designers learn to meet the needs of handicapped children we will see a growing
array of options for all children. The key ingredients, flexibility and novelty, are
provided by materials that can be modified, moved, or changed from time to
time. A major barrier to the play of all children is equipment that is fixed in
concrete and designed to disallow any modifications. Again, consider the vision
of parents.

> I like kids to get in the mazes, to work on the arm strength . . . the things for hanging
> and crawling through . . . they have this big metal turtle, never seen a child on . . . she
> likes to climb things, push things, move things, slide, and, oh yes, swing.

Visionary designers and manufacturers are beginning to face the challenges
of accessibility, mobility, and challenge. Among those featured in this book,

Grounds for Play provides free standing super-structures; Landscape Structures, Iron Mountain Forge, and BigToys now offer access ramps, interchangeable panels, and exercise options; and Children's Playgrounds, Inc. provides complete custom design and installation service to accommodate all children. In 1990, Children's Playgrounds, Inc. published the first catalog supplement (known to the author) devoted exclusively to accessible structures. The catalog depicts imaginative, flexible, challenging structures for children of all ages and also provides educational assistance to the consumer. Consider this advice on pathways and circulation.

> When play events are limited, and there is a natural flow from one event to the next, the quality of children's play improves. No structure is fully accessible unless it is properly related to the sidewalks and pathways of the surrounding environment. Pathways should be a minimum of 4 feet wide for one wheelchair, 6 feet wide for two. Circulation must never dead end and should provide choices for: reversing direction; accessing facilities of lesser or greater degrees of challenge; accessing places to stop and to rest which offer shade and supplemental activities. (Children's Playgrounds, Inc. 1990:17).

To Ramp or Not to Ramp

Whether children in wheel chairs or other self-propelled adapted vehicles should be allowed access onto play structures was hotly debated at the 1984 PLAE conference at Stanford University. Two compelling events led the author to form a position on the issue. First, the handicapped people at the conference were asked their opinion on the issue. Without equivocation or reluctance they unanimously contended that children in wheel chairs should be provided safe access and be encouraged to use play structures to the limit of their abilities. Second, while attending a grand opening of an elementary school playground with ramp-accessible play structures, the author saw first-hand the extreme joy, delight, and effort of handicapped children six- to nine-years old enjoying their first-ever opportunity to join other children on a play structure. They rolled their wheel chairs over the ramp to a central holding area or parking zone on the structure, left their vehicles, pulled themselves through the challenges and dragged themselves with options provided back to their wheel chairs, rejecting the helping hands of over-anxious adults at every stage. The delight on children's faces and the tears on the faces of teachers made an indelible impression and erased any lingering personal doubts about the efficacy of access to play structures.

> We got a lot of good ideas from Jimmy, like the idea of using a knotted rope along with a ramp to allow a child to pull himself on his stomach (teacher)...ramps are better than stairs, stairs with rails are better than stairs without rails. (parent)

Access to play structures should not be an overriding emphasis in play environment design. Most playground activities can be accessible at ground level: water and sand play at elevated tables; overhead ladders and trapeze apparatus at reaching height (from wheel chairs); wheel-chair swings and other swings mounted over firm, protective surfaces; and nature areas, gardens, building areas, art areas, and animal areas—all can be reached by prepared paths or trails.

I would like to have my kids out there doing whatever they can do in as unstructured environment as is possible . . . My kid liked to be out in the park, wheeling around in his wheel chair, looking for birds . . . Once you get them there it's OK; it's just getting to it in the first place . . . I'd like to see a kid able to get into the park and get to something, because there are pathways and there aren't barriers. (parent)

Play Leaders with Special Skills

Play leaders are essential to the effective operation of playgrounds but they assume special roles and must have special skills in play environments that include handicapped children. The best examples of good play leadership are to be seen in the adventure playgrounds of Scandinavian countries. Lady Allen of Hurtwood was very successful in adapting their play leadership principles to her London adventure playgrounds for handicapped children.

The role of the play-leader is a vitally important one; his identity must be quickly recognized by visiting children. He or she must be an experienced, capable person, with a good working knowledge of different handicaps. He must be able to cope in emergency with fits, faints, asthmatic attacks, urine bags, calipers, prostheses, hearing aids, bumps and bruises. He is responsible for day to day organization of the playground; supervision and maintenance of equipment and structure; repairs and replacements; domestic supplies. He must be able to maintain good liaison with visiting staff, parents, voluntary workers and, on occasion, with visitors. He must be tactful, a stimulating leader of the playground team and a helpful supervision of trainee's programme. (Allen 1975:20)

The reader will recognize that Lady Allen's vision exceeded the usual expectations for "play supervisors." She not only created extraordinarily rich places for handicapped children to play but also helped play leaders develop a range of skills to match her expectations for the environment.

Although handicapped children require special care and attention, their parents and teachers find it difficult, at first, to expose them to such an apparently rough and ready atmosphere—so very different from the usual supervised "structured" play environment. It is precisley through such unstructured play, play that is freely chosen and enjoyed for its own sake, that the children learn new skills, gain self-confidence, take pride in their achievements, sort out fact from fancy, build up a picture of reality and extend their knowledge of the real world. It is amazing to see with what determination, excitement and courage they face and overcome risks and difficulties if given half a chance. (Allen 1975:3–4)

The skills of play leaders for handicapped and normal children are quite similar (see Chapter 13 for a full discussion of play leadership). Leaders for handicapped children must know more about the exact nature of their physical and mental capabilities and be prepared to provide psychological, physical, and emergency assistance (Shaw 1982:35). This includes first aid assistance related to disabilities. The leader must spend enough time with disabled children to develop personal relations and knowledge of their special needs.

Special Attention to Safety

All playgrounds including equipment should be properly designed and installed, and thoughtful provision should be made for maintenance and supervision.

The London Handicapped Adventure Playground Association*

The causal observer may notice little difference in Lady Allen's adventure playgrounds for handicapped children and typical adventure playgrounds. However, on closer observation the essential differences emerge. They include:

FIGURE 12.10 *Close supervision by well-trained playleaders.*

FIGURE 12.11 *Specially designed vehicles to ensure mobility of children despite their handicaps.*

FIGURE 12.12 *Trials throughout the playground to allow access to play opportunities.*

FIGURE 12.13 *Special design of water areas to allow riding vehicles to go into the water.*

FIGURE 12.14 *Raised fire pits to ensure easier access by all children.*

*Playgrounds established by the late Lady Allen of Hurtwood

Constant, informed attention to these factors will reduce the likelihood of injuries. Handicapped children require special attention to safety.

> Most disabled kids probably fall more, and if they do fall the results are usually worse, bones are brittle, I know Billy (fictitious) has had a number of broken bones already. (parent)

In a marvelous little book, the staff of London Handicapped Adventure Playground Association (1978) shared their experiences in operating reasonably safe playgrounds for children with almost every type of handicap. Most physically handicapped children are at first nervous or passive when introduced to challenging playgrounds. With reassurance and access to independent mobility, they soon leave their wheel chairs and join their more able-bodied friends in play.

Children with cerebral palsy, particularly those of preschool age, benefit from having the playground to themselves at first, for the actions of more lively children can trigger abnormal reflex patterns of movement. They will require extensive physical assistance in the beginning, but regular time spent at the playground results in relaxation and pleasure and improvement in physical and tactile skills.

Spina-bifida children, suffering some paralysis of the lower limbs, also need special mobile equipment. Problems of incontinence require help with urine bags. Protective, waterproof clothing allows them to play with water and helps to avoid injury. Protective head gear is needed for children with hydrocephalus (allied to spina-bifida), particularly for those with a tendency to petit mal. Careful supervision and special attention to surfacing under and around play structures is needed.

> For children with spina-bifida, the impact that for other children would be a minor fall can be serious. The bones are not as strong and they heal slowly too. (parent)

Blind or partially sighted and deaf or partially hearing children explore the playground fully on the very first visit. Once blind children are sure of their ground they play with great confidence and energy. Predictability is fundamental in ensuring their safety. Deaf children usually engage readily in role play and other social activities, but they require special care:

> ...you can't let them out of your sight, because they can't hear anything, traffic, a barking dog. It doesn't matter if it's an attack dog, she's going to walk right up to it. (parent)

Not unlike physically handicapped children, children with mental disabilities may be fearful and confused when first entering a playground. The play leader must welcome the children warmly and give continuing support. Over time, play assists in their language development. Autistic children engage in a wide range of sometimes unpredictable, "disorganized" behavior—running about wildly, jumping up and down, or simply sitting still. With opportunities and support for play, their concentration increases, and relationships with peers and playleaders improves. They should be carefully supervised to "prevent irresponsible or dangerous actions" (London Handicapped Adventure Playground Association, 1978).

Emotionally disturbed children appear to thrive in adventure playgrounds, representing one of the "great successes" of the London Handicapped Adventure Playground Association. The older children become interested in helping younger handicapped children. They enjoy building, keeping pets, painting, making bonfires, repairing mobile equipment, and helping the play leaders. They form secure relationships and learn to assume responsibilities for projects and pets.

Each type of handicap carries special needs and requires special attention to playground design, safety, and supervision. Some extraordinary concerns, not yet mentioned are:

-burns from metal-
. . . most playground equipment is all metal and it's always in the sun . . . with kids who have no sensation, they can burn themselves so awful and not even know it. Anyone who knows anything about handicapped children knows it takes a hell of a long time for some of that stuff to heal. (parent)

-fears-
. . . she has some fears and I think they're related to her lack of balance . . . we have dogs and cats in the neighborhood . . . she's mortally terrified of those things. (parent) When he was very small and couldn't get around hardly at all, he was terrified of everything . . . he's terrified of falling too. (parent)

-discrimination-
I'm really quite disappointed in what I think is a real lack of concern in the way people think about disabilities and design these things (play equipment). . . . The ramp was wonderful but instead of just labeling it "ramp" they have a big sign that says "handicapped." (parent)

CONCLUSION

In most every educational and public setting there are children with special needs—physically disabled, language disabled, and developmentally or learning disabled. With the passage of the Education for All Handicapped Children Act (P.L. 94-142) in 1975, nationwide efforts and resources were directed to reducing barriers to education of the disabled. This movement emphasized placing disabled children in the least restrictive educational setting. Recently, the focus has broadened from least restrictive classroom settings to outdoor play environments—to designing playgrounds not just for the non-handicapped majority, but for *all* children.

The design and use of playgrounds for all children requires attention to the special needs of the mentally retarded, the blind, those with behavior disorders, and other disabilities. Play therapy, with roots in the psychoanalytical tradition, is growing beyond the traditional confines of hospitals and special education centers to classrooms and homes. There are indications that as playgrounds are redesigned to meet a wider range of individual needs, play therapy will become a viable playground activity.

Good outdoor play environments for all children are, with relatively minor modifications, similar to the best playgrounds now used by non-handicapped children. The special modifications required are (1) special planning, (2) planning for mobility, (3) accessibility and challenge, (3) play leaders with special skills, and (4) special attention to safety.

Visionary designers and manufacturers are now designing special outdoor play environments and equipment for integration of all children in common playgrounds. Disabled children and their parents are among the best sources of information about their personal play needs.

REFERENCES

Allen, M. (1975). *Adventure Playgrounds for Handicapped Children*. London: James Galt.

The American Standards Association. (1961). *Specifications for Making Buildings and Facilities Accessible and Usable by the Physically Handicapped*. National Society for Crippled Children and Adults.

Axline, V. (1969). *Play Therapy*. New York: Ballantine.

Beeghly, M., Perry, B.W., & Cicchetti, D. (1989). Structural and affective dimensions of play development in young children with Down's syndrome. *International Journal of Behavioral Development* 12:257–277.

Benoit, E.P. (1955). The play problems of retarded children: A frank discussion with parents. *American Journal of Mental Deficiency* 1:41–55.

Bowers, L. (1979). Toward a science of playground designs. Journal of Physical Education, Recreation, and Dance 50:51–58.

Bowers, L. (1983). Tomorrow's Play. *Journal of Physical Education, Recreation, and Dance* 54:40–41.

Carter, S. (1987). Use of puppets to treat traumatic grief; A case study. *Elementary School Guidance and Counseling*, 21:300–306.

Children's Playgrounds, Inc. (1990). *Catalog Supplement: Accessible Structures*. Holliston, MA: Children's Playgrounds, Inc.

Cicchetti, D., & Mans-Wagener, L. (1987). Stages, sequences, and structures in the organization of cognitive development in Down's syndrome children. In *Research with Scales of Psychological Development in Infancy*, (eds.) I. Uzgiris, & J. McV. Hunt. Urbana, IL: University of Illinois Press.

Cunningham, C., Glenn, S., Wilkinson, P., & Sloper, P. (1985). Mental ability, symbolic play, and expressive language of young children with Down's syndrome. *Journal of Child Psychology and Psychiatry* 26:255–265.

Devoney, C., Guralnick, M., & Rubin, H. (1974). Integrating handicapped and nonhandicapped preschool children; Effects on social play. *Childhood Education* 50:360–364.

Ginott, H. (1961). *Group Psychotherapy with Children* New York: McGraw-Hill.

Ginott, H.G. (1960). A rationale for selecting toys in play therapy. *Journal of Counseling Psychology*, 24:243–246.

Guerney, L. (1976). Play therapy: A training manual for parents. In Schaefer, C. *The Therapeutic Use of Child's Play*. New York: Jason Aronson, Inc.

Kirk, S.A. (1972). *Educating Exceptional Children*. (2nd Ed.). Boston: Houghton Mifflin.

Kopp, C., Krakow, J., & Johnson, L. (1983). Strategy production by young Down's syndrome children. *American Journal of Mental Deficiency* 88:164–169.

London Handicapped Adventure Playground Association. (1978). *Adventure Playgrounds for Handicapped Children*. Unbridge, Middlesex, England: Bamber Press.

Loveland, K. (1987). Behavior of young children with Down's syndrome before the mirror: Exploration. *Child Development* 58:768–778.

McConkey, R. (1985). Changing beliefs about play and handicapped children. *Early Child Development and Care* 19:79–94.

Moore, R.C., Goltsman, S.M., & Iacofano, D.S., (eds.). (1987). *Play for All Guidelines: Planning, Design, and Management of Outdoor Play Settings for All Children*. Berkeley, CA: MIG Communications. (with contributions by Jay Beckwith and Lynda Scheneekloth and illustrations by Yoshiharu Asanoumi).

Morris, R.H. (1974). A play environment for blind children: Design and evaluation. *New Outlook for the Blind* 68:408–414.

Morris, R.J., & Dolker, M. (1974). Developing cooperative play in society withdrawn retarded children. *Mental Retardation* 13(6):7–9.

Motti, F., Cicchetti, D., & Stroufe, L.A. (1983). From infant affect expression to symbolic play: The coherence of development in Down's syndrome children. *Child Development* 54:1168–1175.

Paloutzian, R., Hasai, J., Streifel, J., & Edgar, L. (1971). Promotion of positive social interaction in severely retarded children. *American Journal of Mental Deficiency* 75(4):519–524.

Quinn, J.M., & Rubin, K.H. (1984). The play of handicapped children. In *Child's Play: Developmental and Applied*, (eds.) T.D. Yawkey and A.D. Pellegrini. New Jersey: Lawrence Erlbaum Associates.

Riguet, C.B., & Taylor, N.D. (1981). Symbolic play in autistic, Down's, and normal children of equivalent mental age. *Journal of Autism and Developmental Disorders* 11:439–448.

Rothschild, J. (1960). Play therapy with blind children. *New Outlook for the Blind*, 54:329–333.

Sandler, A.M. (1963). Aspects of passivity and ego development in the blind infant. *Psychoanalytic Study of the Child* 18:343–360.

Schaefer, E.E. (1985). Play therapy. *Early Child Development and Care* 19:95–108.

Schaefer, E.E & O'Connor, K.J. (1983). *Handbook of Play Therapy*. New York: Wiley.

Shaw, L. (1982). *Adventure Play Environments for Disabled Children*. Gainesville, FL: College of Architecture, University of Florida.

Singer, J.L. & Streiner, B.F. (1966). Imaginative content in the dreams and fantasy play of blind and sighted children. *Perceptual and Motor Skills* 22:475–481.

Strain, P. (1975). Increasing social play of severely retarded preschoolers with socio-dramatic activities. *Mental Retardation* 13(6):7–9.

Tait, P.E. (1974). Believing without seeing: Teaching the blind child in a "regular" kindergarten. *Childhood Education* 50:285–291.

Thomas, G.V., Phemister, M.R., & Richardson, A.M. (1981). Some conditions affecting manipulative play with objects in severely mentally handicapped children. *Child: Care, Health, and Development* 1:1–20.

U.S. Department of Housing and Urban Development. (1978). *A Playground for All Children*. Washington, D.C.: Superintendent of Documents.

Wehman, P. (1975). Establishing play behaviors in mentally retarded youth. *Rehabilitation Literature* 36(8): 238–246.

Wright, L., Everett, F., & Roisman, L. (1981). *Experimental Psychotherapy with Children*. Baltimore: Johns Hopkins University Press.

Yawkey, T.D., & Pellegrini, A.D. (eds.) (1984). *Child's Play and Play Therapy*. Lancaster, PA: Technomic Publishing Co.

"Play is activity that one is free to enter and free to leave."[1]

13

Play Leadership: The Role of Adults in Children's Play

The turn of the present century was a time of rapidly growing interest in playgrounds. Organized playgrounds in the form of outdoor gymnasia and sandgartens were spreading across the major northeast American cities. This activity and interest led to the organization of the Playground Association of America in 1907, and shortly thereafter to a growing number of publications on play. During this early period, the major emphasis was upon equipment but, with experience, play leaders began to understand the importance of adults—of play leadership—for helping to ensure play value and safety.

HISTORY OF PLAY LEADERSHIP

As organized playgrounds spread across the United States, it soon became apparent that..."without trained leadership the playground often becomes the gathering place of idlers, sometimes degenerating into a place where immorality is taught, vandalism occurs and damage is done to public property" (Lee 1926:116). In 1909, the Playground Association of America established guidelines for the training of play leaders and shortly thereafter the first training courses

---

[1]Mihaly Csikszentmihalyi (1975). *Beyond Boredom and Anxiety.* San Francisco: Jossey-Bass, p. 25.

323

for prospective play leaders were initiated. Such courses captured the attention of physical education leaders around the country and were introduced widely into schools of physical education. Curtis (1917) criticized this state of affairs . . . "the school that is merely a school of physical education is likely to attract people who care merely for the physical side" (p. 328). "It must be remembered, that the physical side is only one side of play, and that it is really no more physical than it is mental and social and moral" (p. 333). Despite good intentions, the play leadership training programs of the early 1900s appeared to be inadequate for the lofty goals envisioned for them. The play leader should be a . . . "person of refinement and personal worth . . . a social spirit . . . a good influence in the lives of children" (Curtis 1917:334). "The leader should have a good physique, enthusiasm, initiative, sound body, and an ability to endure physical and nervous strain and hard continuous work" (Lee 1926:119).

By 1925, playgrounds were well entrenched in public parks of the United States. Out of 748 cities reporting, 688 were conducting 5,121 playgrounds, employing 17,177 workers (Lee 1926:234) and the training and use of playleaders was continuing to grow. Unfortunately for the playground movement and for play leadership programs, the very character of the Playground Association of America was changed in 1911 when it became the Playground and Recreation Association of America. The change of emphasis from play to recreation and sports was accentuated when, in the mid-1930s, the Playground Association of America was reorganized as the National Recreation Association. The "play leader" was beginning to be viewed as the "recreation leader" (Jolley 1988). In 1936, play leaders and play leadership received major emphasis in a major publication of the National Recreation Association (*Playgrounds: Their Administration and Operation* by George D. Butler, 1936). By 1950, the term "play leader" was listed in the revised edition as a sub-category of types of workers under the recreation supervisor (Butler 1950), and the emphasis had shifted to sports organizers.

The merger of the National Recreation Association with other organizations in 1966 was merely an after-shock to play and play leadership, for their value and emphasis had long since been virtually abandoned in favor of recreation and sports. Although the National Recreation and Park Association currently holds out play morsels to the public in the form of an occasional article or conference workshop, their lack of concern and energy for children's play creates a major obstacle to the contemporary play and play leadership movement.

After almost a century of erratic emphasis, the ideals of play leadership proposed by American pioneers in play have all but become extinct in the public park system in the United States. Among industrialized countries, the Europeans, especially the Scandinavians, have been most successful in establishing play leadership training programs and in implementing play leadership in public playgrounds and parks. The literature emerging from their programs is a valuable aid to other countries interested in promoting play leadership, particularly in the context of adventure playgrounds (see Chapter 11, Adventure Playgrounds).

As described in Chapter 5, The Evolution of American Playgrounds, the play movement of the early 1900s followed two separate but related paths; the public park playground and eventual recreation emphasis, and the early childhood (day care, kindergarten) playground and its developmental emphasis. Public schools, a third major location for playgrounds, tended to be more influenced by the recreational than the developmental emphasis.

Drawing from Froebel, early kindergarten and preschool professionals viewed play as significant for the development of mind, character, and physical body. Early kindergartens and preschools were generally deficient in play materials and play leadership, but the best of the lot promoted specific roles for the teacher (Iowa Child Welfare Research Station 1934).

The adult was to expose children to various pieces of apparatus and play materials and then give them the opportunity to use them, under close supervision, in their own way. Although the general policy was "hands off," the adult was always there to protect children and direct them as necessary. Specific steps for adult intervention were established.

- Expose the child to materials.
- Wait until misuse before explaining correct uses.
- Support and reassure the child when using new equipment.
- Praise and commend when a difficult task is accomplished.
- For reluctant but capable children say, "Try it yourself," or "I'm sure you can."
- Give the slow, timid child time, then encourage by suggestion to use the materials or equipment.
- Follow the inclinations of the child. Say, "Wouldn't you like to slide too?" Redirect the child's attention away from material that he overuses. If this fails, remove the material or toy for a period of time.
- If a child throws small items ask him to pick them up before he plays with anything else.
- For continued offenses, the material or toy is removed from the child until he is willing to comply.
- Children should use large apparatus properly, e.g., take turns, no excessive crowding or pushing on the slide.

The early leaders in the nursery–kindergarten movement emphasized the importance of the adult role in shaping and promoting the development of the child through play (Palmer 1916). Unlike many present-day playground sponsors, they advocated matching size and complexity of play materials and apparatus to the age and developmental levels of children.

The issue of whether, and to what extent, adults should intervene in children's play is by no means closed. Across the professions concerned for children's play, the positions on this issue range from strictly "hands-off" to direct intervention and play tutoring.

Whether one decides to intervene in children's play, it should be clear that the extent of adult involvement or direction influences the very nature of the activity; that is, may determine whether play actually continues to exist. Huizinga (1950) eludicated the salient characteristics of play:

> First and foremost . . . play is a voluntary activity . . . It is never a task . . . Second, play is not 'ordinary' or 'real' life. It is rather a stepping out of 'real' life into a temporary

sphere of activity ... Third, play is distinct from 'ordinary' life both as to location and duration. It is 'played out' within certain limits of time and space. (p. 7–9).

The consequences of intervening in *play* per se are more potentially destructive than are the consequences of intervening in *games*. Play is unique, individual, and ephemeral, but games are systematic and can be repeated by others in other places (Avedon & Sutton-Smith 1971). Games have predictable outcomes while play is open-ended with no predictable outcome. Even the language used is different: play language is generic while game language is specific. Consequently, the prospective adult intervenor should consider the potential consequences before intervening in children's playful activities. If play is directed by others (adults) it may cease to become play. Adults may *dominate* play and destroy its "spirit"; that is, its freedom, spontaneity, and predisposition, its ephemeral existence, and consequently, its developmental benefits. Games on the other hand, are frequently passed on from generation to generation, rules are re-established, and players look to adults and older children for direction.

Research, philosophy, and experience offer perspectives that are useful in resolving the major issues: what does research say about adult intervention in children's play? Does intervention change play? Enhance development? Can children be "trained" to play? Should they be? Does training influence teacher behavior during play? These are a few of the questions to be examined in the following section.

FIGURE 13.1 First and foremost, play is a voluntary activity. It is never a task.

DOES INTERVENTION CHANGE PLAY AND ENHANCE DEVELOPMENT?

A number of researchers have investigated the effects of tutoring on low (Socio-economic Status) children's pretend play. Play tutoring improves the quality of children's play and results in improved creativity (Dansky 1980), problem solving (Rosen 1974), perspective taking (Smith & Syddall 1978), verbal intelligence (Saltz, Dixon, & Johnson 1977; Christie 1983), language development (Lovinger 1974), and ideational fluency (Christie 1983). It has also been confirmed that play tutoring results in more fantasy play and more complex play (Marshall and Hahn 1967; Feitelson 1972; Freyberg 1973).

In analyzing previous studies of the effects of play tutoring, Smith and Sydall (1978) questioned whether it was the tutor–child interactions or the play itself that led to gains in developmental indices. In their own study, they compared children in play-tutoring sessions with children in skills-tutoring sessions. The total number of contacts to specific children did not differ significantly between the two groups. The two groups showed equal improvement in general language and cognitive abilities. The play-tutored group increased their fantasy activity in free play and their performance on role-taking preference tests, more than the play-tutored group.

Smith and Sydall concluded that the advantages in language and cognitive skills ascribed to play tutoring in earlier studies may have been due to a lack of control for tutor contact in the non-play tutored or control groups. A critical issue thus arises: Is adult contact or play per se the key factor in play tutoring?

In a more recent study, Christie (1983) also found that both play tutoring and skills tutoring led to significant gains in mental age and ideational fluency scores and these gains still existed three months after the tutoring had ceased. As in the Smith and Sydall study, Christie's findings suggested that the play tutoring gains were caused primarily by adult contacts rather than by play. Both play tutoring and skills tutoring, then, are effective facilitators of cognitive growth.

A major implication drawn by the investigators in such studies is that early childhood educators should engage children in tutorial interactions during both play periods and academic work periods. But a note of caution is needed. What form of "play tutoring"? Should everyday practice for all children mirror the experimental short-term tutoring of low SES subjects in the studies? Across the series of studies cited above, several types of tutoring were employed. Smith and Sydall (1978) and Christie (1983) used similar methods. In play-tutoring sessions, the tutor attempted to engage the children in sociodramatic play by providing themes (grocery store, doctors, cooking) and suitable materials. Christie used Smilansky's (1968) strategies to encourage children to incorporate missing elements into their play. "Outside intervention" strategy involved making comments to encourage specific play behaviors, and "participation in the play strategy" involved the tutor actually taking on a role and modeling the desired behaviors. In both investigations, the skills tutoring was designed to engage children in activities that had a definite end product in mind (e.g., making puppets, lotto games).

Several points are relevant with regard to play tutoring and its effects. First, a series of studies support the view that play tutoring results in improvement of a range of cognitive abilities. Second, cognitive growth through play tutoring can be accomplished by several tutorial approaches, some of which do not fit the normal description of "tutoring." Tutoring is typically described as direct one-to-one, goal directed, academic instruction. Third, the play "tutoring" employed in the Smith and Sydall and Christie studies was relatively informal, process oriented, and guidance oriented rather than directive. In practice one should distinguish carefully between experimental language and language used in common classroom settings. Fourth, the issue of the relative benefits of tutoring per se versus adult–child interaction per se remains unresolved. Different kinds of tutoring were given to the play groups and the skills groups. In order to determine the effects of adult–child interaction, other experimental procedures (e.g., holding treatment constant, using control groups) must be employed. The most compelling conclusion from the studies is that tutoring (situation specific and including adult–child interaction) works. Fifth, it is generally recognized that some children do not engage in or engage very little in make-believe play. These children can be taught to engage in sociodramatic play (Smilansky 1968; Saltz, Dixon, & Johnson 1977; Dansky 1980).

PLAY LEADERSHIP IN PRACTICE

Having reviewed a sampling of the research on the effects of adult intervention on children's play, we now turn to practical applications of research, theory, and experience. The author does not believe that either research, theory, or experience are infallible guides to practice but will borrow from all three in proposing practical approaches. These approaches will be primarily applicable for preschool/school settings but also relevant for out-of-school contexts (homes, public play settings). They may be applied by teachers, parents, or designated public playground play leaders. The format for play leadership includes observing children at play, preparing for play and involvement in play. The author expresses appreciation to various sources that have influenced the following discussion (Smilansky 1968; Sutton-Smith & Sutton Smith 1974; Csikszentmihalyi 1975; Frost & Kissinger 1976; Singer 1977; Blalock & Hrncir 1980; Wade 1980; Griffing 1983; Dempsey 1985; Jones 1985; Fein & Rivkin 1986; Johnson, Christie, & Yawkey 1987; Yawkey 1990).

Preparing for Play: Time, Space, and Materials

In preparing for children's play, the adult considers time, space, and materials (Frost & Kissinger 1976; Griffing 1983; Johnson Christie, & Yawkey 1987). These are critical variables in determining the range and quality of play whether indoors or outdoors. The focus here is upon *free* play, or relatively unstructured, undirected play rather than structured, directed activities (teacher directed games, art, etc.), which resemble play. Most of the literature concerning time, space, and materials for play in child-care or school settings focuses upon indoor rather than outdoor environments. There are, indeed, many similar and complementary needs across these two play contexts. Child-care programs may integrate play indoors and outdoors, using both to support common themes over a period of time (e.g., role play following a field trip or reading a favorite story). Increasingly, designers of child-care facilities are considering the provision of indoor-outdoor linkages in building designs—sliding glass doors/walls to allow indoor-outdoor

FIGURE 13.2 *In planning for play the adult considers time, space, and materials.*

movement, covered porches or patios to link indoor-outdoor activities and to provide shelter and shade for outdoor play during hot periods or inclement weather. Whatever the context—indoors or outdoors—adults must prepare for the essential ingredients.

Time for Play

Given appropriate materials and freedom from intrusion by adults, children's dramatic play tends to gain intensity with time. For example, two or three, four- to six-year-old children initiate pirate play in an outdoor dramatic play prop (fishing boat). After a few minutes other children, hearing and seeing the excitement, join in. Roles are assumed or assigned: "You get the shark bait, I'll be the Captain!" As intensity builds, loose materials are added to the plot as plastic electrical spools are used for bait and, eventually, as more children join in, additional equipment is included in the play. As the boat becomes crowded and the rocking motion becomes too severe, two children declare, "Let's head for the fort, the pirates are coming!" They run to the nearby super-structure (fort) and prepare to defend it against the approaching pirates. Thus, many dramatic play sessions join intensity with *time*. As other children join the role play activity, more *space* is needed and more materials and equipment are integrated into the play. The play reached its height of intensity, child involvement, and materials inclusion about 20 minutes after it was initiated. In many child care/school settings the play would have stopped at this point because "free play time" was over. Several important implications emerge from this and similar observations.

The outdoor play roles of children are enhanced by *time* for development. They are also enhanced by a range of readily available materials and by the deliberate, careful planning and zoning of *space* and equipment to allow integration of equipment into play themes.

The amount of time needed for free play varies with ages of children and contexts of play. Thirty to 50-minute periods are needed for 4- and 5-year-old children (Johnson, Christie, & Yawkey 1987), but for kindergarten children in full-day programs one hour of free play is needed (Peters, Neisworth, & Yawkey 1985). Large blocks of play time are preferred over brief segments because play themes require time to develop and play should be relaxing and unforced.

The *minimum* times noted here should not be interpreted as maximum times. Many high-quality child-care centers focus on play and work/play activities throughout the day, for play is a primary vehicle for cognitive, social, and motor development. It is the vehicle that enables children to *progress or develop* " . . . along the development sequence from the sensorimotor intelligence of infancy to preoperational thought in the preschool years to the concrete operational thinking exhibited by primary children" (Bredekamp 1988:3). Therefore, " . . . child-initiated, child-directed, teacher-supported play is an essential component of developmentally appropriate practice."

What, then, should be the basic guide for allocating time for play? "Play begins, and then at a certain moment it is 'over'. It plays itself to an end" (Huizinga 1950:9). Play sets its own course and has its own meaning, and once it has been played, it is retained in memory and can be reenacted again and again. The consequences of fixed time intervals for play are separation from flow and conclusion and, consequently, from meaning and memory. Among the more significant features of play is "playing out" the theme or the game. The best play leaders are those who allow the play to gauge its own duration.

Space for Play

All play takes place on a playground, either material or symbolic (playgrounds of the mind). The space for play may be a table, stage, tennis court, housekeeping center, or formal outdoor playground. All are playgrounds. They may be " . . . forbidden spots, isolated, hedged round, hallowed . . . All are temporary worlds within the ordinary world, dedicated to the performance of an act apart" (Huizinga 1950:10.) Inside the play space, play is initiated and the rules apply. It is selected by the player and its boundaries reflect the theme which may condense or expand.

In the strict sense, space for play is not determined by fixed ratios of square feet per child but by child energy, imagination, and the nature of the play. In a practical sense, space for play reflects number of child players, age and developmental levels of children, type and range of play themes, materials and equipment, and time available for play.

In general terms, the preschool indoor environment should contain a minimum of about 50 square feet per active child and the outdoor environment a minimum of about 100 square feet per active child. Play environments for preschools and primary grades must contain a certain minimum total space in order to accommodate the classroom play and learning centers (e.g., housekeeping, manipulative, block area) and the outdoor play zones (e.g., exercise play, dramatic play, constructive play, organized games). These are minimum spaces and should be expanded to accommodate multiple classes and special play needs.

Some Effects of Space on Play

A number of researchers have explored the influence of differing space allotments and arrangements on children's behavior in indoor environments. Reducing play space while holding group size constant decreases running and increases physical contact (McGrew 1972), and increases imaginative play and onlooker behavior (Peck & Goldman 1978). Phyfe-Perkins (1980) suggested that the increased incidence of on-looker behavior may have resulted from the less socially-oriented children watching the dramatic play.

In an extensive study, Smith and Connolly (1980) examined the effects of various spatial densities—15, 25, 50 and 75 square feet per child (not including furniture). Reducing spatial density resulted in reduction of running, chasing, and rough-and-tumble play. When the spatial density was reduced to 15 square feet per child, aggression increased and group play decreased. Although the research is nonconclusive, the trend of findings suggests that changing spatial density does influence the behavior of children. In general, large open spaces may promote gross motor activity and aggressive behavior and reducing spatial density may reduce aggressive behavior and increases positive social interaction and dramatic play.

Investigation of outdoor play environments has focused on the type and arrangement of equipment rather than the amount of space or spatial density (number of children in a given space). The quality of outdoor play space influences children's behavior. Creative playgrounds or playgrounds with extensive varieties of equipment and portable play materials stimulate more dramatic and constructive play than do traditional playgrounds featuring isolated fixed equipment (see Chapter 6, Fundamentals of Playground Development).

Play Materials

Adults can solicit the desired types of outdoor play by providing the play props (materials and equipment) that encourage and support that play (Strickland 1979; Frost & Strickland 1985; Frost & Campbell 1985; Campbell & Frost 1985; Chiang 1985). If dramatic play is desired, dramatic play props are needed; if constructive play is preferred, tools and building materials are needed; if organized games are appropriate, flat grassy areas, hard surface areas, and game equipment are essential.

The type of indoor environment also signals to children what type of play should go on in the area. However, sterile or non-changing play areas may result in reduced involvement of children. The best indoor play areas, like those out-of-doors, are never finished but constantly evolving to introduce novelty and challenge as children develop and grow. Usage of play areas increases as contents change (Golden 1973; Griffing 1983). This weeks' housekeeping area may become next weeks' hospital or space ship. The range of play themes will vary by the range of environments and by the cognitive social enrichment provided by adults (books, field trips, etc.).

Whatever the setting, certain types of materials stimulate dramatic play while others result in different types of play. Low-structure items that have no pretend connotation, such as pipecleaners, metal cans, and construction paper, do not enhance pretend play (McLoyd 1983). Pretend roles *are* encouraged by large, moveable materials such as cardboard boxes, telephone spools, and hollow blocks. Manipulation and construction are encouraged by large numbers of small, nonthematic materials such as pieces of foam, unit blocks, and cardboard cylinders (Dodge & Frost 1986). When given options in outdoor environments, chil-

FIGURE 13.3 *Adults can encourage the desired types of outdoor play by providing the play materials and equipment that support that play.*

dren prefer materials that are moveable and action oriented and dramatic play is solicited in playgrounds with play houses, life-sized boats and cars, superstructures, and moveable play props (Frost & Campbell 1985; Campbell & Frost 1985; Frost & Strickland 1985).

Following his study of the equipment choices and play behavior of primary grade children in contrasting outdoor play environments, Strickland (1979) concluded:

> . . . playgrounds should provide a wide range (in type and amount) of play materials and equipment for children. . . . Limited numbers and kinds of equipment may not provide enough stimulation for children to be encouraged to participate in a wide variety of play experiences. The play materials should be multi-functional allowing for each piece of equipment to support a wide range of play behaviors. (pp. 116–117).

ADULT INTERVENTION IN PLAY

The previous discussion shows that there is disagreement about the extent to which adults should become involved in children's play. The extreme positions include "play tutoring" or directly teaching children how to play, on the one hand, to the view that the adult (teacher) "should sit in the shade and drink coffee" during free play or recess. Taking such positions into account, the author believes that children should indeed have extended periods of free play or recess without undue adult intervention. There should also be times when children, who are observed to experience reluctance or difficulty in play, should receive the support and encouragement of adults.

A number of writers have described adult roles for involvement in children's play. Peters, Neisworth, and Yawkey (1985) proposed three major strategies for indoor play: free discovery, promoted discovery, and directed discovery. These strategies were further developed by Yawkey (1990) and will be extended by the present author to outdoor environments.

In *free discovery*, children are free to explore, discover, and select among play material without adult direction. The typical play centers in preschool classrooms are indeed prepared by the teacher but the materials should be rich and varied. Although the writers did not discuss the outdoor environment, free discovery would function in the natural outdoor setting in much the same way.

In *prompted discovery*, the children play in a "prepared environment." The indoor play or learning centers are equipped or arranged to accommodate desired forms of play: tools and building materials (indoors or outdoors) for constructive play, water and containers for water play, art materials for art activities, etc. The adult actually encourages exploration aimed toward discovery of properties and concepts by:

- selecting and arranging the play materials.
- encouraging exploration.

FIGURE 13.4 In free discovery, children are free to explore without adult intervention.

- suggesting uses for objects.
- encouraging modeling by children.
- encouraging multiple uses for play materials.
- suggesting other uses for objects.
- using imaginative language in the play context.

In *directed discovery*, the adult lends direct assistance to children's play. The play environment (materials and arrangement) is influenced by the adult who also may enter directly into play. The intent of such involvement is to encourage creative uses of play materials leading to deeper understanding of their attributes and functions. Several levels of prompted discovery that may be considered are:

- suggesting other uses for play materials.
  "Perhaps the blocks will hold up the sides of your tunnel."
- questioning to extend uses for materials and to extend play themes.
  "Could you get a can of water from the hydrant to mix with your tortillas?"
  "Doctor, do you need to call your nurse on the telephone?"
- using verbal and physical prompts.
  "Show me how to roll the dough." "Can you use some more blocks?"
- modeling to encourage extended play.

FIGURE 13.5 *In prompted discovery, children play in a "prepared environment."*

Fallen and Umansky (1985) suggest adult modeling for children with special needs (children with handicaps or disabilities). Modeling is used with all children for teaching simple rhyming games and other repetitive activities.

Direct play teaching is used with handicapped children who do not play or who engage in very little play (Beers & Wehmann 1985). The present author believes that "direct play teaching" and "play tutoring" are contradictions of terms (play by its very nature is non-directed) and *does not recommend these approaches for normal children.* According to Beers and Wehman (pp. 430–431), for those children who cannot or do not engage in spontaneous play, direct teaching can benefit from:

- physical demonstrations and modelling followed by social reinforcers (hugs, praise, etc.).
- demonstration of the use of a toy or piece of equipment.
- task analysis and skills sequencing or breaking a play activity into small, discrete, manageable behaviors and teaching them a step at a time.
- commands, followed by guidance through successive steps and reinforcement.
  "Put your feet on the pedals." "Push, push." "That's great, Billy!"
- use of toys and play equipment as reinforcers, coupled with social rewards such as praise and attention.

The reader should note carefully, that Beers and Wehman (1985:431) do not advocate the use of concrete rewards (food, tally marks, coins) and even *among special needs children, only the severely handicapped need direct teaching strategies. For many special needs children, the provisions and arrangement of play materials and "occasional modeling" are sufficient.* Further, intrinsically motivated activities such as play can become work as a result of structuring and rewarding (Deci 1975; Condry 1977).

Play tutoring is similar to *direct play teaching* in that it involves direct, planned adult intervention and is intended to increase involvement of children in play. Play tutoring has been widely used in experimental studies and is generally found to be effective in extending play. It includes several steps (Johnson, Christie, & Yawkey 1987:32):

- the adult initiates a play episode.
- the adult assumes a role in the play.
- the adult assumes partial control over the play.
- the adult teaches new play behaviors.

Smilansky's (1968) well-known study illustrates two major dimensions of direct play intervention; inside intervention and outside intervention (p. 101).

Inside Intervention is the most direct form of play intervention. The adult joins the play, chooses a role, and enacts the role over a period of time. As an actor, the adult can direct children, and assist them in including missing components in their play. For example, if a child does not use make-believe in regard to objects, the adult, acting as a nurse may suggest, "Mrs. Jones, here is the medicine (handing her a block). You must give it to your baby. Call the hospital on the telephone (pointing to a boy)." The intervention is direct and forces the child to react. It includes modeling and opportunities for the adult to influence several children within a role play enactment. Both verbal and social interchanges are promoted through modeling, questioning and direct solicitation of child involvement.

Negative consequences of direct adult participation in children's play often result from intrusion by well-meaning but unskilled play leaders. Those who do not feel comfortable in playing with children should remain outside the play or allow the flow of the play to be directed by the children. The following are commonly observed results of awkward or unskilled involvement:

- adults may take leadership away from child play leaders.
- adults may use language or create roles that children do not understand.
- adult-directed roles or themes may be of no interest to children.
- adults may interfere with established (and working) role play.
- adults may influence children to follow their lead rather than initiating or creating for themselves.
- adults may make children dependent upon others for initiating play episodes.
- adults may cause the activity to become non-play.

Contrasted to inside intervention, in *outside intervention* the adult does not enter into the play and take on a role, but intervention is addressed to the play of the child. It uses questions ("How is your baby?), suggestions ("Let's take your baby to the hospital."), behavior clarification ("That worked for my baby."), influence in contact between players ("The other nurse can help you."), and directions ("Show the doctor where your baby hurts.") (Smilansky 1968:). Both outside and inside intervention are directed to the make-believe theme and the adult addresses the role person rather than the playing child. She encourages role playing, role transformations, and influences the flow of play.

The Adult as Play Leader

Aside from the very real requirement for a few special needs children to have direct, tutorial intervention, most play contexts and most children need a special type of adult to participate in their play. This special adult must be prepared to feel foolish in the beginning (Sutton-Smith & Sutton-Smith 1974). Taking on a role in children's play is a role-reversal for adults, but it is necessary to keep in touch with the meaning and feel of playfulness. The adult who remains aloof from play misses opportunities for engaging with and learning from children and, consequently, are deprived of one of the best sources of information for enriching their play and related activities.

Aside from direct and indirect interventions in play, the play leader provides related experiences which give children the substance for play roles. There are, perhaps, no better underpinnings for rich play than reading aloud to children and exposing them to many rich, first-hand experiences in the community. Daily read-aloud session and weekly or bi-weekly excursions are essential to play and learning.

The effective play leader is an observer, participator, and facilitator (Blalock & Hrncir 1980). As participator and facilitator the play leader is a resource person

FIGURE 13.6   *The adult who remains aloof from play misses opportunities to learn from children.*

who helps solve problems and offers suggestions for extending play (Kleiber & Barnett 1980). The play leader is concerned with maintaining the "flow of the activity" (Csikszentmihalyi 1975). During play the child's attention is narrowed and centered upon the present and there is no self-consciousness. Unless play becomes destructive, Csikszentmihalyi believes that, in the main, children should be allowed to play without interruption. Intervention can disrupt attention and flow of activity and thought. Instruction at appropriate points can help children to achieve "flow" in their activities. For example, concern that his tempera painting is becoming all gray may be alleviated by brief instruction on how to wash the brush before dipping into a new color.

The play leader must know when and how to phase in and out of children's play (Kleiber & Barnett 1980). Valuing play and understanding play are prerequisites, for children recognize when adults are forcing or "faking" their involvement. Playing with the child means that the adult is willing to become a follower and play partner. When the adult takes over the direction of play, pushing the original child leader aside, play breaks down or ceases to exist. Not all adults can easily become playmates for children.

Even in direct, inside intervention, adults should phase out of play when children are able to assume and assign roles, interact effectively with playmates, and maintain flow of play. Children should be free to create their own play roles and themes and to construct their own play environments. Adults are available when children *need* help, not available because children *rely* upon them. We want children to become self-initiating, responsible, self-reliant, "can-do" people.

There is great variation among adults, even teachers; some feel embarrassed and awkward about involving themselves in children's make believe play (Singer

FIGURE 13.7 *The effective play leader is sensitive to children's needs, helps them resolve their own problems, and extends their play options.*

1977). Both parents and teachers need to be educated about the values of play and the ways they can become involved to assist the development of children.

DOES PLAY TRAINING FOR TEACHERS MAKE A DIFFERENCE?

A number of investigators have prepared play training experiments to determine whether the behavior of teachers can be changed during their interactions with children at play. In general, the results show that teacher training programs of even a short duration influenced teacher behavior.

In a study of 56 child-care centers and 470 caregivers in Texas, Monroe (1983, 1985) found that the quality of center playgrounds rated significantly higher in centers with staff who participated in playground training of any kind or duration during the preceding year. The playground improvements included range of materials and equipment, safety, and overall design of the playground.

A play training program for teachers was developed by Wade (1980) and applied in an experiment with three- and four-year-old children and their teachers. The training program utilized five major components:

1. "What is Play?"
2. "Play and Child Development."
3. "Overview of Adult Guidance."
4. "Communicating with Children in Play."
5. "Techniques of Adult Guidance."

The training sessions were conducted for one and one-half hours each day for five days, through the use of small-group discussions, lecture, simulated games, training exercises, question and answer sessions, and demonstrations. "Content papers" for each topic were distributed in advance of the daily lessons. The entire training procedure, including procedures and content papers, is included in Wade (1980).

Children and teachers were observed in playground activities before and after the teacher training. Following training, significantly greater frequencies of children's play were found for the following types: parallel, group, constructive, dramatic, parallel-constructive, parallel-dramatic, group functional, group-constructive, and group-dramatic for all children (boys and girls), and rules games also increased for the boys. Solitary, functional, solitary-functional, solitary-dramatic, and group-games with rules decreased for all children.

Equally dramatic (and significant) changes were observed for teachers in the playground after the training program. Their verbal behavior changed. They engaged in more preparatory, dealing, questioning, extending, accepting, and praising categories with all children (boys and girls). Silence and teacher-talk categories decreased. Their non-verbal behaviors also changed, with significantly more behaviors from the smiling, positive contact, and positive nodding categories with all children. In sum, a brief five-hour training program for

FIGURE 13.8 Adults/playleaders can be friends as well as teachers.

teachers resulted in significant, positive, changes in the behavior of children and their teachers in playground activity.

Numerous other studies in preschools, using a variety of training procedures over varying periods of time, have shown equally compelling results. Training preschool teachers in encouraging sociodramatic and constructive play results in changes in adult-child interactions, and increases associative fluency of children in playground play (Dempsey 1985). Collier (1985) found that play training for teachers on observing children at play and techniques for facilitating their play results in improvement in children's verbal expression, verbal fluency, originality, and imagination test scores. The effects on teachers included increases in verbal interaction. Collier concluded that teachers, without extensive training, can effect significant changes in children's cognitive abilities through fostering their play. The effects of brief training on teachers appears to be long-term.

Common observation reveals that preschool caregiver's interactions with children during play time are minimal. Gowen (1987) approached this problem by developing a training program aimed at getting caregivers more involved with children. She aptly pointed out that play is by definition a self-directed activity. Consequently, the training for caregivers should use a nondidactic, facilitative approach emphasizing the child taking the lead and guiding development of the child's play behavior through interaction with the child's self-selected activities. The training program was straight-forward and simple, including assistance to caregivers on:

1. talking to children while they played (initially 50% of the time during play)
2. decreasing the amount of directive behavior
3. clarifying the distinction between directive and non-directive behavior
4. learning non-directive techniques
5. reducing verbal directives

The training sessions were effective in stimulating verbal interaction with the children during play time and meal time, and in maintaining a low proportion of caregiver directives. The caregivers level of education was predictive of success in distinguishing between directive and non-directive language but was not predictive of *use* of directive language until after intensive training was conducted.

This sampling of research discusses only preschool caretaker/teacher training effects on teacher and child behaviors. The influence of adult training is, of course, not limited to a particular class of adults or age group of children. The evidence for adult involvement in infant–toddler play (Nichols 1985; Steele & Hrncir 1985) and in primary school children (Rogers 1989; Perlmutter et al. 1989) is also compelling. Only a handful of play-training programs for adults (parents, caregivers, teachers, play leaders) currently exists in the United States. Whether we choose to extend, or not to extend, play leadership programs and, consequently, influence children's development through play, we should not subscribe to the careless assumption that adult involvement in children's play makes no difference.

CONCLUSION

Play leadership and adult intervention in children's play has been a topic of concern among professionals throughout the present century. Play leadership programs were established by recreation leaders in the early 1900s and child-care professionals made recommendations for supervising children's play at child-care centers.

A wide sampling of research shows that adult intervention changes children's play and is correlated with changes on various cognitive tasks. The changes are, in the main, considered to be positive.

The adult play leader considers time, space, and materials in preparing for play. These vary with age and developmental levels of children, indoor versus outdoor contexts, and the nature of anticipated and/or planned activities.

Adult intervention in play includes informal roles (free discovery, prompted discovery, and directed discovery), formal roles (direct play teaching, play tutoring, inside and outside intervention), and preparation for play activities (reading aloud, field trips).

Play training for teachers influences both teacher behavior and child behavior during play. Play training programs of even brief durations have significant effects. Common training programs emphasize understanding play, the value of play in child development, interaction with children during play, and learning non-directive techniques.

Insensitive, unskilled, excessive intervention in children's play by adults can interrupt the flow of play themes, block leadership roles of children, encourage dependency on adults, stifle self-confidence, and lead to the breakdown of play itself.

REFERENCES

Avedon, E.M. & Sutton-Smith, B. (1971). *The Study of Games*. New York: Wiley.

Beers, C.S., & Wehman, P. (1985). Play skill development. In *Young Children with Special Needs*, (eds.) N.H. Fallen and W. Umansky. Columbus, OH: Charles E. Merrill.

Blalock, J.B. & Hrncir, E.J. (1980). Using playleaders power. *Childhood Education*, 57:90–93.

Bredekamp, S. (ed.) (1988). *Developmentally Appropriate Practice in Early Childhood Programs Serving Children from Birth through Age 8*. Washington, D.C.: National Association for the Education of Young Children.

Butler, G.D. (1950). *Playgrounds: Their Administration and Operation*. New York: Barnes & Co.

Campbell, S. & Frost, J.L. (1985). The effects of playground type on the cognitive and social play behaviors of grade two children. In *When Children Play*. (eds.) J.L. Frost and S. Sunderlin. Wheaton, MD: Association for Childhood Education International.

Chiang, L. (1985). *Developmental Differences in Children's Use of Play Materials. Unpublished Doctoral Dissertation*. Austin: University of Texas.

Christie, J. (1983). The effects of play tutoring on young children's cognitive performance. *Journal of Educational Research*, 76:326–330.

Collier, R.G. (1985). The results of training preschool

teachers to foster children's play. In *When Children Play*, (eds.) J.L. Frost & S. Sunderlin. Wheaton, MD: Association for Childhood Education International.

Condry, J. (1977). Enemies of exploration: Self-initiated versus other-initiated learning. *Journal of Personality and Social Psychology*, 35:459–477.

Csikzentmihalyi, M. (1975). *Beyond Boredom and Anxiety*. San Fransisco: Jossey-Bass.

Curtis, H.S. (1917). *Education Through Play*. New York: Macmillan.

Dansky, J.L. (1980). Make-believe: A mediator of the relationship between play and associative fluency. *Child Development*, 51:576–579.

Deci, E. (1975). *Intrinsic Motivation*. New York: Plenum.

Dempsey, J.D. (1985). *The Effects of Training in Play on Cognitive Development in Preschool Children*. Unpublished doctoral dissertation. Austin: University of Texas.

Dodge, M.K., & Frost, J.L. (1986). Children's dramatic play: Influence of thematic and nonthematic settings. *Childhood Education*, 62:166–170.

Fallen, N.H. &nd Umansky, W. (1985). *Young Children with Special Needs*. Columbus, OH: Charles B. Merrill.

Fein, G., & Rivkin, M. (1986). *The Young Child at Play: Reviews of Research, Vol. 4*. Washington, DC: National Association for the Education of Young Children.

Feitelson, D. (1972). Developing imaginative play in preschool children as a possible approach to fostering creativity. *Early Child Development and Care*, 1:181–195.

Freyberg, J. (1973). Increasing the imaginative play of urban disadvantaged kindergarten children through systematic training. In J.L. Singer, *The Child's World of Make-Believe*. New York: Academic Press.

Frost, J.L., & Campbell, S.D. (1985). Equipment choices of primary-age children on conventional and creative playgrounds. In *When Children Play*, (eds.) J.L. Frost and S. Sunderlin. Wheaton, MD: Association for Childhood Education International.

Frost, J.L., & Kissinger, J.B. (1976). *The Young Child and the Educative Process*. New York: Holt, Rinehart, and Winston.

Frost, J.L., & Strickland, E. (1985). Equipment choices of young children during free play. In *When Children Play*, (eds.) J.L. Frost and S. Sunderlin. Wheaton, MD: Association for Childhood Education International.

Golden, L. (1973). *Occupational Awareness Through Dramatic Play*. Chapel Hill, NC: Frank Porter Graham Child Development Center.

Gowen, J.W. (1987). Facilitating play skills: Efficacy of a staff development program. *Early Childhood Research Quarterly*, 2:55–56.

Griffing, P. (1983). Encouraging dramatic play in early childhood. *Young Children*, 38:13–22.

Huizinga, J. (1950). *Homo Iudens*. Boston: Beacon.

Iowa Child Welfare Research Station. (1934). *Manual of Nursery School Practice*. Iowa City, IA: State University of Iowa.

Johnson, J.E., Christie, J.F., and Yawkey, T.D. (1987). *Play and Early Childhood Development*. Glenview, IL: Scott Foresman.

Jolley, J.A. (1987). *Playleadership: An American Historical Perspective*. Unpublished paper. Austin: University of Texas.

Jones, L. (1985). *Sociodramatic Play and Problem Solving in Young Children*. Unpublished doctoral dissertation. Austin: University of Texas.

Kleiber, D.A., and Barnett, L.A. (1980). Leisure in childhood. *Young Children*, 35:47–53.

Lee, J. (1926). *The Normal Course in Play*. New York: A.S. Barnes.

Lovinger, S.L. (1974). Socio-dramatic play and language development in preschool disadvantaged children. *Psychology in the Schools* 11:313–332.

Marshall, H., & Hahn, S.C. (1967). Experimental modification of dramatic play. *Journal of Personality and Social Psychology*, 5:119–122.

McGrew, W.C. (1972). *An Ethological Study of Chidren's Behaviors*. New York: Academic Press.

McLoyd, V. (1983). Effects of the structure of play objects on the pretend play of low-income preschool children. *Child Development*, 54:626–635.

Monroe, M.L. (1983). *Evaluation of Day Care Playgrounds in Texas*. Unpublished doctoral dissertation. Austin: University of Texas.

————. (1985). An evaluation of day care playgrounds in Texas. In *When Children Play*, (eds.) J.L. Frost and S. Sunderlin. Wheaton, MD: Association for Childhood Education International.

Nichols, F.H. (1985). Play and the preterm infant: Implications for parent education. In *When Children Play*, (eds.) J.L. Frost and S. Sunderlin. Wheaton, MD: Association for Childhood Education International.

Palmer, L.A. (1916). *Play Life in the First Eight Years*. Boston: Ginn.

Peck, J. & Goldman, R. (March, 1978). The behavior of kindergarten children under selected conditions of the physical and social environment. Paper presented at the meeting of the American Educational Research Association. Toronto, Canada.

Perlmutter, M., Kuo, F., Behrend, S.D., & Muller, A. (1989). Social influences on children's problem solving. *Developmental Psychology* 25:744–754.

Peters, D.L., Neisworth, J.T. & Yawkey, T.D. (1985). *Early Childhood Education: from Theory to Practice*. Monterey, CA: Brooks/Cole.

Phyfe-Perkins, E. (1980). Children's behavior in preschool settings—A review of research concerning the influence of the physical environment. In *Current Topics in Early Childhood Education* (ed.) L.G. Katz. (Vol 3, pp. 91–125) Norwood, NJ: Ablex.

Rogers, P.J. (1989). Teaching mathematics through play to primary school children. *Educational Studies* 15:37–51.

Rosen, C.E. (1974). The effects of sociodramatic play on problem-solving behavior among culturally disadvantaged preschool children. *Child Development* 45:920– 927.

Saltz, E., Dixon, D., & Johnson, J. (1977). Training disadvantaged children on various fantasy activities: Effects on cognitive functioning and impulse control. *Child Development* 48:367–380.

Singer, J.L. (1977). Imagination and make-believe play in early childhood: Some educational implications. *Journal of Mental Imagery* 1:127–144.

Smilansky, S. (1968). *The Effects of Sociodramatic Play on Disadvantaged Preschool Children*. New York: Wiley.

Smith, P.K. & Connolly, K.J. (1980). *The Ecology of Preschool Behavior*. Cambridge, England: Cambridge University Press.

Smith, P.K., & Syddall, S. (1978). Play and non-play tutoring in pre-school children: Is it play or tutoring which matters? *British Journal of Educational Psychology* 48:315–325.

Steele, C., & Hrncir, E. (1985). Adult suggestion: An enabler for pretend play in two-year-olds. In *When Children Play*, (eds.) J.L. Frost and S. Sunderlin. Wheaton, MD: Association for Childhood Education International.

Strickland, E. (1979). *Free Play Behaviors and Equipment Choices of Third Grade Children in Contrasting Play Environments*. Unpublished doctoral dissertation. Austin: University of Texas.

Sutton-Smith, B., & Sutton-Smith, S. (1974). *How to Play with Your Children (and When Not To)*. New York: Hawthorn.

Wade, C. (1980). *Effects of Teacher Training on Teachers and Children in Playground Settings*. Unpublished doctoral dissertation. Austin: University of Texas.

Yawkey, T.D. (1990). The role of adults in children's play. In *Playgrounds for Young Children: National Survey and Perspectives*. (eds.) S.C. Wortham and J.L. Frost. Reston, Virginia: American Alliance for Health, Physical Education, Recreation, and Dance.

APPENDIX A

Selected Manufacturers and Custom Designers/Builders

Big Toys
Northwest Design Products, Inc.
7717 New Market St.
Olympia, WA 98501
(206) 943-6374
1-800-426-9788

Children's Playgrounds, Inc.
55 Whitney St.
Holliston, MA 01746-6889
(508) 429-3870
1-800-333-2205

Grounds for Play
405 Dodson Lake Drive
Arlington, TX 76012
(817) 461-7529
1-800-552-7529

Iron Mountain Forge
One Iron Mountain Forge Drive
Farmington, MO 63640-0897
(314) 756-4591
1-800-325-8828

Kidstruction
P.O. Box 162048
Austin, TX 78716-2048
(512) 261-4404
1-800-245-8449

Kompan, Inc.
80 King Spring Road
P.O. Box 3536
Windsor Locks, CT 06096
(203) 623-4139

Landscape Structures/Mexico Forge
601 7th Street South
Delano, MN 55328
(612) 479-2546
1-800-328-0035

Learning Structures, Inc.
34 Columbia St.
Portsmouth, NH 03801
(603) 436-5911

Maxidex System
Wooden Environments, Inc.
1890 Evergreen Avenue
Speonk, NY 11972
(516) 325-1020
1-800-241-0854

Neverlands Play Designs
305 W. Milton
Austin, TX 78704
(512) 442-7613

Play Designs
P.O. Box 427
New Berlin, PA 17855
(717) 966-0444
1-800-327-7571

APPENDIX B

Sources: Standards/Guidelines for Playground Safety

American Society for Testing and Materials. *Standard for Public Playground Equipment* and *Standard for Playground Surfacing*. 1916 Race Street, Philadelphia, PA 19103. (expected in 1992).

Canadian Institute of Child Health. (1984). *Draft for Children's Play Spaces and Equipment*. (Draft 5, 1989). Canadian Institute of Child Health.

Deutsche Institut Fur Normung (D.I.N.). (1985). *Playground Equipment for Children: Concepts, Safety Requirements, Testing*. Berlin, West Germany: Deutsche Institut Fur Normung. Translation by British Standards Institution, Linford Wood, Milton Keynes , MK146LE. Tel: Milton Keynes (0908) 320033. Telex: 82577.

Kompan, Inc. (1984). *Playgrounds and Safety*: Comparisons between various playground equipment standards—American, Australian, British, German.

Seattle Department of Parks and Recreation. (1986). *Draft Design Guidelines for Play Areas*. Seattle, WA: 100 Dexter Avenue North, 98109.

U.S. Army Corps of Engineers. (1984). Planning and design of children's outdoor play environments—TM-803-11 (preliminary draft). Huntsville, AL: U.S. Corps of Engineers.

U.S. Consumer Product Safety Commission. (1981). *A Handbook for Public Playground Safety*, vol. I: General guidelines for new and existing playgrounds. Washington, DC: U.S. Consumer Product Safety Commission. Revised guidelines are scheduled for publication in late 1991.

———. (1981). *A Handbook for Public Playground Safety*, vol. II: Technical guidelines for equipment and surfacing. Washington, DC: U.S. Consumer Product Safety Commission.

APPENDIX C

Manufacturers and Suppliers of Artificial Playground Surfacing

Appleseed Design Services, Inc.
5 Post Oak Road, Suite 1820
Houston, TX 77027
(713) 622-1946

B.J.'s Park and Recreation
  Products
P. O. Box 15
Friendswood, TX 77546
(512) 625-2082

Breakfall
759 N. Milwaukee Street
Milwaukee, WI 53202
(414) 273-7828

Child Safe
Royal Athletic Industries, Ltd.
55 Lamar Street
W. Babylon, NY 11704
(516) 491-5577

Cushion-Turf
Iron Mountain Forge
P. O. Box 897
One Landrum Circle
Farmington, MO 63640-0897
1-800-325-8828
MO (314) 756-4591

Elastocrete
Romaflex Inc.
1815 Drew Road
Mississauga, Ontario, Canada
  L5S 1J5
(416) 677-1999

The Fibar System for Playgrounds
823 West Street
Harrison, NY 10528
1-800-FIBAR-21
NY (914) 835-1511

Safeplay
Superturf International, Inc.
15301 Dallas Parkway
Dallas, TX 75248
(214) 851-7033

Security Blanket
Sportec International, Inc.
1701 Greenville Ave., Suite 607
Richardson, TX 75081
(214) 907-0444

Superturf
P. O. Box 472492
2114 West Kingsley
Garland, TX 75047
(214) 278-9511

Tuffturf
Landscape Structures/Mexico Forge
601 Seventh Street South
Delano, MN 55328
1-800-328-0035
MN (612) 479-2546

APPENDIX D

Infant-Toddler Playground Maintenance Checklist*

Instructions: Check the playground thoroughly every week. Train all personnel to be alert constantly to playground hazards, and report and repair them promptly. Avoid the use of hazardous equipment until repaired.	Date Checked	Repair Needed	Date Repaired
1. Is there an 8-10 inch-deep ground cover (sand, or commercial material) under all swings, merry-go-rounds, slides, and climbing equipment? Is the resilient surface compacted or out of place? If concrete or asphalt is under equipment, is the manufactured impact attenuation product in place? Is pea gravel removed from the play area?			
2. Are there foreign objects or obstructions in the fall zones under and around fixed equipment?			
3. Are there obstructions to interfere with normal play activity?			
4. Are there climbing areas that would allow children to fall more than their reaching height when standing erect?			
5. Are concrete supports sticking above the ground? Are they secure?			
6. Are there sharp edges, broken parts, pinching actions, or loose bolts?			
7. Are there openings that could trap a child's head? Openings 3 to 9 inches wide should be avoided.			
8. Are there frayed cables, loose ropes, open S-hooks, or chains that could pinch or entangle?			

*Adapted from a checklist prepared for the Texas Department of Human Services by Joe L. Frost.

	Date Checked	Repair Needed	Date Repaired
9. Are timbers rotting, splitting, termite infested, or excessively worn? Probe under ground for rotting and termites.			
10. Are portable toys such as tricycles and wagons in good repair? Are small items that can choke children accessible to them?			
11. Are there protrusions that can catch clothing? Protrusions can include posts, bolts, and similar items.			
12. Are there crush points or shearing actions such as hinges and ends of seesaws and undercarriages of revolving equipment?			
13. Are swing seats excessively heavy? Do they have protruding parts such as animal noses or legs? Swing seats should be made of a soft, pliable material.			
14. Is the fence at least 4 feet high and in good repair? Can gates be securely fastened? Is there a separate area for infants?			
15. Are there electrical hazards on the playground such as accessible air conditioners, switch boxes, or power lines?			
16. Are there collections of contaminated water on the playground?			
17. Are there toxic materials on the playground? Are bare metal decks and slides that can inflict burns exposed to the sun?			
18. Do the grass, trees, and shrubs need care? Are they poisonous?			
19. Do children wear inappropriate clothing, such as capes, on climbing and moving equipment?			
20. Does the adult-to-child supervision ratio equal ratios required for indoor activity?			

Maintenance Checklist

Date Detected	Date Repaired	
		• Hard surfaces under and around equipment in fall zones
		• Resilient surface material pitted or scattered
		• Insufficient space between equipment
		• Equipment not sized for age of children
		• Entrapment areas
		• Excessive or unprotected heights
		• Shearing and crushing mechanisms
		• Cracking, bending, warping, rusting, breaking or missing components
		• Pinching actions, open S hooks, deformed rings, links, etc.
		• Loose or uncapped bolts, nuts, etc.
		• Worn bearings or axles
		• Worn swing hangers (swivels) or chains
		• Metal slides in direct path of sun
		• Slide beds loose, metal edges accessible to fingers
		• Heavy swing seats or seats with protruding elements
		• Exposed or damaged concrete footings
		• Equipment improperly anchored
		• Sharp edges and points
		• Exposed or projecting elements, caps missing
		• Railings of insufficient height
		• Railings invite climbing (horizontal instead of vertical)
		• Exposed metal in tires or swing seats
		• Suspended elements (e.g., ropes, cables) in movement areas
		• Deteriorated (splintered, cracked, rotting) wood
		• Broken or missing railings, steps, swing seats, rungs, deck components, etc.
		• Slippery footing areas on decks, steps, walkways
		• Trash (broken glass, foreign objects, etc.) in area
		• Vandalism (fire damage, broken or missing parts)
		• Obstacles (rocks, roots, trash, badly placed equipment) in movement area

Date Detected	Date Repaired	
		• Poor drainage (standing water) • Accessible electrical apparatus (air conditioners, switch boxes) climbable poles, guy wires, ladders accessing electrical lines • Fence not installed or in need of repair, gates not securable (younger children), extra protection for pools • Signs illegible and in poor repair • Moving parts not lubricated • Toxic materials • Foreign material or equipment parts in fall zone

APPENDIX F

Suggested Public Playground Leader's Checklist*

- Prepare written guidelines for playground operation, defining goals and procedures.
- Insist on first aid and accident training for playground leaders.
- Provide for constant supervision by establishing a written schedule.
- Instruct children and playground supervisors on how to use equipment. (Playground equipment safety should be taught in the classroom.)
- Conduct daily cleaning and check for broken glass and other litter.
- Do not permit children to use wet or damaged equipment.
- Do not permit too many children on the same piece of equipment at the same time; suggest that children take turns, or direct their attention toward other equipment or activities.
- Constantly observe play patterns to note possible hazards and suggest appropriate equipment or usage changes.
- Make periodic checkups, and request that worn or damaged pieces of equipment be replaced.
- Prepare written accident reports with special attention to surface conditions, type and extent of injury, age and sex of child, how the accident occurred, and weather conditions.

*Reprinted from CPSC *Handbook for Public Playground Safety:* (1981) Vol. I, p. 12.

Index